The Emergence
of Deviant Minorities

Social Problems and Social Change

The Emergence of Deviant Minorities

Social Problems and Social Change

Edited by

Robert W. Winslow
San Diego State College

*Selections from Commissions on Crime, Campus Unrest, Causes
and Prevention of Violence, Marijuana, Homosexuality and
Prostitution, and Obscenity and Pornography*

Paper edition by
Consensus Publishers, Inc.
San Ramon, California

Cloth edition by
Transaction Books
New Brunswick, New Jersey

THE EMERGENCE OF DEVIANT MINORITIES
Social Problems and Social Changes

Acquisition: *Joseph L. Dana*
Cover design: *Michael A. Rogondino*
Cover photograph: *Howard Harrison*

Library of Congress Catalog Card Number: 70-187917

International Standard Book Number: 0-87998-000-1 (paper)
International Standard Book Number: 0-87855-040-0 (cloth)

CONTENTS

PREFACE

In teaching sociology courses in the study of deviancy and ethnic minorities, I have been struck by basic similarities between these two fields and their relations to the study of social problems. Although these two areas each has its own literature, I find it increasingly difficult, especially in the light of the events of the last decade, to separate the two fields. It has long been maintained that ethnic minorities often resort to deviancy from societal norms as a means of achieving their aims; today it is the deviant groups that are adopting minority group rhetoric and goals and that are asking for first-class citizenship. Perhaps the success of ethnic minorities, particularly blacks, in winning gains in housing, education, employment, and civil rights is responsible for this trend.

Of course, not all deviants have staked a claim to minority status. My thesis applies primarily to "moral entrepreneurs," the people sometimes termed "victimless offenders." These include sex deviates such as homosexuals, prostitutes, and pornographers, whose "victims" are typically consenting adults. I also include drug offenders, but those who *use* illegal drugs rather than smugglers or sellers of drugs, because victimization for drug users per se is, at best, oneself. For somewhat the same reason I include the drunkenness offenders, who currently constitute one-third of the country's jail population. I also include most of those young people labeled "juvenile delinquents," the ones whose commitment of such victimless offenses as running away, truancy, incorrigibility, violation of curfew, has been their point of entrance into the juvenile justice system.

Following somewhat the same logic we may also include a "convicted minority" consisting of all people who have been convicted of crime or juvenile delinquency who have developed minority-like subcultures both in and outside of prison (or other institution). In sum, the people I have in mind are those whose morality or whose ways of life bring them into conflict with the law and values of society and who are coming out into the open to assert the validity—or at least the right to existence—of the value systems they subscribe to. These deviant minorities, like ethnic minorities, are no longer willing to submit to persecution and prosecution. Marijuana users are fighting for legalization of marijuana, pornographers are testing our censorship laws in the courts, and homosexuals are asserting that "gay is good."

Parallel with the "surfacing" of ethnic and deviant minorities has been a concern in government with investigating the claims of these minorities. It is the reports of these investigations that form the basis of this reader. Such reports are, in my opinion, the most thorough surveys presently available of the life styles, goals, problems, opinions, etc., of today's ethnic and deviant minorities. On the topic of race and ethnic (The Report of National Advisory Commission on Civil Disorders) relations, I have drawn selections from the Kerner Report (President's Commission on Law Enforcement and Administration of Justice) and the report of the President's Crime Commission. On youth, I have drawn from the Walker Report (*Rights in Conflict: The Walker Report to the National Commission on Causes and Prevention of Violence*). On juvenile delinquency, I have drawn from the President's Crime Commission (President's Commission on Law Enforcement and Administration of

Justice). On college radicalism, I have drawn from the report of the President's Commission on Campus Unrest. On homosexuality and prostitution, I have drawn from the Wolfenden Report (*Report of the Committee on Homosexual Offenses and Prostitution*). On marijuana, I have abstracted much of the LaGuardia Report. On drug abuse, and on the "convict minority" drunkenness, I have drawn again from the President's Crime Commission (President's Commission on Law Enforcement and Administration of Justice). Pornography is detailed from *The Report of The Commission on Obscenity and Pornography.* There are also excerpts from other sources but the bulk of the materials included here are from national commission reports. A brief discussion of these commissions and how they gathered their data is appropriate here.

The National Advisory Commission on Civil Disorders (the Kerner Commission) was appointed by President Lyndon Johnson in response to Executive Order 11365, July 27, 1967. Headed by Governor Otto Kerner of Illinois and Vice Chairman John V. Lindsay, Mayor of New York City, its composition was explicitly of moderate liberal character. Though moderate in its composition, the commission validated the claims of such spokesmen as Stokely Carmichael, Floyd McKissick, and Martin Luther King, Jr. Its principal methodology was expert testimony. During August through December of 1967, the commission heard over 130 witnesses, including federal, state, and local officials, experts from military and law enforcement agencies, spokesmen for universities and foundations, leaders of the black communities, and representatives of the business community. Commission members also personally visited eight cities where major disturbances had occurred, and staff members made field surveys in a total of 23 cities in which disorders occurred during the summer of 1967.

The report (*Rights in Conflict: The Walker Report to the National Commission on the Causes and Prevention of Violence*) was based upon a field survey of 3437 eyewitnesses and participants in the events surrounding the Democratic National Convention of 1968. The National Commission on Causes and Prevention of Violence was created by President Johnson in an Executive order 11412 dated June 6, 1968, and was extended in 1969 for an additional six months. The parent commission was directed by Milton S. Eisenhower, but Daniel Walker, a prominent Chicago attorney and civic leader, headed the study team on the events surrounding the Democratic National Convention. The provocative thoughts and conclusions of the Walker Report are formally ascribed to Daniel Walker.

The President's Commission on Law Enforcement and Administration of Justice (President's Crime Commission), appointed by President Johnson on July 23, 1965, through Executive Order 11236, was chaired by Nicholas deB. Katzenbach. In gathering its data, the Commission drew findings from over 300 surveys, polls, and research projects, some of which were origined by the commission and nationwide in scope.

The Committee on Homosexual Offenses and Prostitution, chaired by Sir John Wolfenden, C.B.E., was appointed by the British Parliament on August 24, 1954. The methodology included expert testimony and survey of official data on sexual offenses and offenders placed on probation.

The Mayor's Committee on Marijuana was appointed on September 13, 1938, following the passage of the Marijuana Tax Act of 1937. The New York Academy of Medicine, at the request of New York Mayor Fiorello H. LaGuardia, made a scientific and sociological study of the reported use of the drug in the city of New York. The sociological study was directed by Dr. Dudley D. Shoenfeld and was carried out by six police officers who were trained by Dr. Shoenfeld as social investigators. The method was participant observation. The clinical study consisted of two parts—the medical, including psychiatric, and the psychological. Doctor Karl M. Bowman directed the medical and psychiatric part of the study and Dr. David Wechsler the psychological part. The methodology was experimental research. Because of the tight controls imposed on the use of marijuana since 1938, no scientific study of the magnitude of *The LaGuardia Report* (report of Mayor LaGuardia's Committee on Marijuana) has been done since then, so despite its age it remains our single most authoritative source. There is a crying need for large-scale up-to-date research that combines experimental and survey techniques in this area.

The Commission on Obscenity and Pornography was appointed by President Johnson in accordance with Public Law 90-100, by which Congress established an advisory commission for the purpose of studying the causal relationship of obscene or pornographic materials to antisocial behavior and recommending ways of dealing with the problem. Expert testimony was the major method. Approximately 100 national organizations were invited to express their views on the subjects of obscenity and pornography, and open hearings were held in Los Angeles on May 4 and 5, 1970, and in Washington, D.C., on May 12 and 13, 1970. There were also national surveys, conducted by Response Analysis Corporation of Princeton, New Jersey and the Institute of Survey Research of Temple University, Philadelphia, Pennsylvania.

It can be seen from these descriptions that the composition of all these commissions was establishmentarian and moderate, and that their methodology was sober, objective, and scientific. The overall result—a thrust toward legal tolerance of deviant minorities is even more persuasive in view of the disinterestedness and the nonpartisanship of the commissions that sponsored the conclusions.

R. W. W.

one

INTRODUCTION: SOCIAL PROBLEMS AND DEVIANT MINORITIES— MINORITIES IN GENERAL

If the several social problems texts I have before me are representative, it would appear that one of the customary things to do in the first chapter is to unleash a barrage of definitions—of terms like social problems, deviant behavior, social pathology, and the like. Such a list satisfies the scientific canon that one define his terms at the outset, but in a book on social problems such a list produces at least two false impressions: (1) that the study of social problems is scientific and (2) that terms such as these can be satisfactorily defined with reference to things "out there," in the empirical world. The truth is that very few people in the field of social problems believe or contend that the field is scientific rather than normative, because the very act of selecting problems to be studied is based on normative assumptions. No matter how we define the term "social problems," as soon as we select a certain list of social phenomena to study as social *problems*, we implicitly state that those phenomena are undesirable, abnormal, sick, or bad—things we need to "do something about."

It is very difficult to define "deviance" or "social problems." Textbook authors usually talk about a mixed bag of things that seem to have no relationship to each other. Deviance includes both illegal acts and breaches of informal social norms that are not illegal acts. It includes victimless offenses and offenses with victims, socio-genic and psychogenic offenses, serious offenses and harmless ones. What textbooks term social problems often include forms of deviance: social conditions such as poverty, war, and famine; large- and small-scale phenomena—a wide spectrum of actions and conditions that have little in common except perhaps that "society" considers them to be social problems. The authors of these textbooks rarely present any proof that the general public or elected officials consider such items to be important problems; what we receive in most such books is the author's personal views of what's wrong in the world.

Many people (I make no claim that it is a majority) consider the following to be social problems: homosexuality, drug abuse, drunkenness in public places, and prostitution. We know that most of our elected officials, legislators, and judges consider these to be social problems, because they have passed or supported laws to deal with them. Probably most of the people in jail today are there be-cause they have been found guilty of indulging in one or more of these activities. These are all forms of deviance. Social problems may be a broader term that includes conditions such as poverty, minority group relations, war, famine, pollution, and population, none of which is considered deviance, except in the broadest sense. Most of this book is devoted to the social problems of deviance, but we shall also look at the more general problems of poverty and ethnic minority groups because of their close ties with problems of more immediate concern. I won't try to define the terms deviance and social problems, because it seems that almost anything has been labeled a deviance or a social problem without the need for recourse to any previous definition, except for something vague like "Deviance is an act where somebody is getting too much pleasure or having too much fun and not suffering enough because he doesn't think or act the way the majority does" or "Social problems are all the things or people who bother most of us, especially behavior that is different from our own."

If I had to I would define deviance as behavior not in accord with values necessary to the survival of man, behavior that endangers *other* men's lives, freedoms, and welfare. The problem with this definition is that it excludes most acts that legislators and government officials consider deviance. The drug abuser may endanger his own welfare, but not necessarily that of others, depending on how financially well off he is. The same is true of drunks, prostitutes, homosexuals, pornographers, most juvenile delinquents, peaceful demonstrators, chronic gamblers, and other "victimless offenders."

One term I shall try to define is *minority*, because I use this term in something of a new way, as applied to deviants. The definition I like best is Louis Wirth's: "We may define a minority as a group of people who, because of their physical or cultural characteristics, are singled out from the others in the society in which they live for differential and unequal treatment, and who therefore regard themselves as objects of collective discrimination."[1] This definition probably needs to be qualified somewhat, because now it is virtually synonymous with the term "social class." If we exclude people with fat fingers from work requiring digital dexterity, are such people then a *minority*? To my way of thinking, no, because the exclusion is based on reasonable grounds, on some condition relevant to the activity. If we were to exclude a person from such work because he had long (or short) hair, he would then be part of a minority because length of hair has nothing to do with digital dexterity.

Wirth's definition is too broad. It is not confined to racial and ethnic minorities (to be brief we'll simply call these "ethnic minorities"), but is broad enough to include *any group* subject to categorical discrimination, including the people officially termed deviants. The study of deviance is not the same as the study of minorities, but some groups called deviants are also minorities—hence the term *deviant minorities*. Not all deviants are minorities. In the way we use deviant minority here, only those deviants whose downgrading is based largely or exclusively on prejudice or stereotyping—i.e., on false information—are minorities.

To illustrate, I developed a list of 36 groups—racial, national, deviant, and fictitious. College students ($N = 39$) enrolled in a course in deviant behavior then rated these groups on a Bogardus Social Distance Scale (a scale developed originally by Emory Bogardus to measure tolerance toward racial and ethnic groups) by assigning one of the following answers to each of the 36 groups:

1. To close kinship by marriage
2. To my club as personal chums
3. To my street as neighbors
4. To employment in my occupation
5. To citizenship in my country
6. As visitors only to my country
7. Would exclude from my country

The median score was calculated for each group and the groups were rank-oriented from the group most tolerated (1) to the groups least tolerated (36).* It is evident from these data (Table 1-1) that deviants are generally held in lower regard than the ethnic minorities. (This of course reflects the relatively high tolerance of college students toward ethnic minorities, so these data are more illustrative than indicative of general public opinion.) The general rank-ordering of deviant groups here, however, is very similar to that in a similar study done by Simmons.[2]

Downgrading alone, however, doesn't make a group a minority. It can be validly contended that a person would not want deviants such as burglars, armed robbers, and forcible rapists on his street as neighbors or in his club or family because of the personal danger of injury or property loss or damage involved. This important refinement—whether the allegations made are relevant to the category —needs to be made before we label any group a minority. The question then is, "Which groups are downgraded because of stereotyped beliefs and irrational fears about the groups, and which are downgraded on the basis of reasonable fears?" There are several ways to get at this dimension of stereotyping. One way is to ask people why they downgrade various groups and then to analyze their open-ended responses for the presence of stereotyping based on what we know to be true of various groups. Simmons did this, and found several deviant groups—marijuana smokers, beatniks, adulterers, homosexuals, and political radicals—especially subject to stereotyping.[3]

Another method is to divide the respondents into two groups— those highly prone to stereotyping and those who are not. An unobtrusive way of doing this is to include nonexisting groups in our

---

* I am indebted to Steven Bell, a sociology student at San Diego State College, for these data computations.

4

TABLE 1-1   Average Social Distance Toward Various Groups

Groups	Median Social Distance
1. American Indians	1.11
2. Catholics	1.12
3. Armenians	1.18
4. Mexicans	1.23
5. Turks	1.28
6. Jews	1.29
7. Pireneans	1.35
8. Danireans	1.38
9. Japanese	1.39
10. Poor People	1.47
11. Student Radicals	1.5
12. Hindus	1.5
13. Blacks or Afros	1.6
14. Police	1.9
15. Chronic Marijuana Users	2.17
16. Ex-Cons	2.62
17. Juvenile Delinquents	2.62
18. Black Panthers	2.75
19. Wallonians	2.83
20. Prostitutes	2.88
21. Embezzlers	3.09
22. Homosexuals	3.1
23. White Collar Criminals	3.31
24. Alcoholics	3.37
25. Vagrants	3.7
26. Drug Addicts	3.8
27. Hell's Angels	4.25
28. Peeping Toms	4.52
29. Check Forgers	4.55
30. Professional Shoplifters	4.55
31. Burglars	4.64
32. Armed Robbers	4.967
33. Racketeers	5.0
34. Forcible Rapists	5.16
35. Murderers	5.25
36. Assassins	6.5

sample. If people downgrade these fictitious groups, they are responding stereotypically. Then if we compare the groups these people downgrade with those ranked by nonprejudiced people, we can isolate the groups—the scapegoat groups—especially downgraded by prejudiced people, and call these groups the deviant minority groups. Based on previous research by Eugene Hartley we included three fictional groups—Danireans, Pireneans, and Wallonians—in our sample.[4] Hartley found a high relationship between the ranking of these three groups and the existing groups, between .75 to .85 for multiple groups, which strongly suggests that if a person has stereotyped the fictitious groups, he has probably stereotyped the existing groups too. A similarly high relationship has been found between intolerance of deviant groups and intolerance of ethnic groups,[5] so if we separate the people who downgrade the fictitious groups, we shall also have separated the people who stereotype both the deviant and the ethnic minorities. Now we can compare these rankings with those of nonprejudiced people to see which groups the prejudiced raters are especially downgrading. To do this, I divided my student sample into two groups. The stereotyped thinkers were those who downgraded all three of the fictitious groups, while the nonprejudiced students were those who either gave the fictitious groups top rating (to close kinship by marriage) or indicated they did not know of such a group (*N*s of 19 and 20 respectively). The rank orderings of the two groups appear in Tables 1-2 and 1-3. If we take the difference between the medians for both groups, we get a measure of which groups are most prone to stereotype (Table 1-4). Oddly, in our sample it is not the ethnic minorities but the deviant minorities who are disproportionately the target of downgrading by prejudiced people. If we divide the deviant group in half, at the median, we find that almost without exception the groups of high difference are deviants of the type known as "victimless offenders" (Table 1-5). Simmons also describes these groups as groups subject to stereotyping. They include homosexuals, drug addicts, alcoholics, student radicals, Black Panthers, embezzlers, prostitutes, racketeers, chronic marijuana users, juvenile delinquents, ex-cons, and the police. As we can see by comparing Table 1-2 to Table 1-3, if we exclude the ratings of people who stereotype, these groups are not downgraded by nonprejudiced people. Were it not for prejudice, they would not be termed deviant. At least this is the way I read the data. And that is the theme of this book—that the so-called deviant minorities are

TABLE 1-2. Average Social Distance Toward Various Social
Groups Shown by Nonprejudiced People

Groups	Median Social Distance
1. Catholics	1.07
2. Jews	1.09
3. Turks	1.1
4. Mexicans	1.11
American Indians	1.11
5. Armenians	1.12
6. Japanese	1.14
Poor People	1.14
7. Police	1.2
8. Student Radicals	1.22
Hindus	1.22
9. Blacks or Afros	1.27
10. Ex-Cons	1.46
11. Black Panthers	1.63
12. Chronic Marijuana Users	1.78
13. Juvenile Delinquents	1.87
14. Homosexuals	2.33
15. Prostitutes	2.4
16. Alcoholics	2.5
17. Drug Addicts	3.0
18. Embezzlers	3.25
19. Vagrants	3.5
20. Check Forgers	4.0
21. Burglars	4.25
Peeping Toms	4.25
White Collar Criminals	4.25
22. Hell's Angels	4.38
23. Professional Shoplifters	4.58
24. Armed Robbers	4.81
25. Racketeers	4.84
26. Forcible Rapists	5.11
27. Murderers	5.18
28. Assassins	6.58

TABLE 1-3   Average Social Distance Toward Various Social
Groups Shown by Prejudiced People

Groups	Median Social Distance
1. American Indians	1.13
2. Armenians	1.26
3. Catholics	1.32
4. Mexicans	1.34
5. Blacks or Afros	1.59
6. Japanese	1.6
7. Poor People	1.66
8. Jews	1.8
9. Turks	1.87
10. Student Radicals	2.2
Hindus	2.2
11. Police	2.68
12. Ex-Cons	3.08
13. Homosexuals	3.28
14. Black Panthers	3.37
15. Alcoholics	3.43
16. Juvenile Delinquents	3.6
17. Chronic Marijuana Users	3.87
18. Vagrants	4.08
19. Prostitutes	4.2
20. White Collar Criminals	4.56
Embezzlers	4.56
21. Drug Addicts	4.66
22. Hell's Angels	4.68
23. Peeping Toms	4.84
24. Check Forgers	4.85
25. Murderers	5.0
26. Burglars	5.04
27. Professional Shoplifters	5.06
28. Armed Robbers	5.35
29. Assassins	5.67
30. Racketeers	5.75
31. Forcible Rapists	6.0

TABLE 1-4   Difference Between Social Distance Scores or
Prejudiced and Nonprejudiced People

Group	Difference Score
1. Chronic Marijuana Users	2.09
2. Prostitutes	1.80
3. Black Panthers	1.74
4. Juvenile Delinquents	1.73
5. Drug Addicts	1.66
6. Ex-Cons	1.62
7. Police	1.48
8. Embezzlers	1.31
9. Student Radicals	.98
10. Hindus	.98
11. Homosexuals	.95
12. Alcoholics	.93
13. Racketeers	.91
14. Forcible Rapists	.89
15. Check Forgers	.85
16. Burglars	.79
17. Turks	.77
18. Jews	.71
19. Peeping Toms	.59
20. Vagrants	.58
21. Armed Robbers	.54
22. Poor People	.52
23. Professional Shoplifters	.48
24. Japanese	.46
25. Blacks or Afros	.32
26. White Collar Criminals	.31
27. Hell's Angels	.30
28. Catholics	.25
29. Mexicans	.23
30. Armenians	.14
31. American Indians	.02
32. Murderers	−.18
33. Assassins	−.91

TABLE 1-5   Difference Between Social Distance Scores of
Prejudiced and Nonprejudiced People for Deviant Groups Only

Group	Difference Score
1. Chronic Marijuana Users	2.09
2. Prostitutes	1.80
3. Black Panthers	1.74
4. Juvenile Delinquents	1.73
5. Drug Addicts	1.66
6. Ex-Cons	1.62
7. Police	1.48
8. Embezzlers	1.31
9. Student Radicals	.98
10. Homosexuals	.95
11. Alcoholics	.93
12. Racketeers	.91
13. Forcible Rapists	.89
14. Check Forgers	.85
15. Burglars	.79
16. Peeping Toms	.59
17. Vagrants	.58
18. Armed Robbers	.54
19. Poor People	.52
20. Professional Shoplifters	.48
21. White Collar Criminals	.31
22. Hell's Angels	.30
23. Murderers	−.18
24. Assassins	−.91

regarded and treated as deviant only because of the operation of prejudice and stereotyping.

With the exception of "The Culture of Civility," all the readings in this book are drawn from government publications, each of which was prepared to examine some form of deviance. Almost all these reports state that much of what is believed about the deviant is untrue, i.e., stereotype. What makes these observations especially persuasive is that they come from government, and therefore authoritative sources. For example, *The Wolfenden Report, (Report of the Committee on Homosexual Offenses and Prostitution)* on homosexuality, debunks numerous myths about homosexuals: that homosexuality is a disease, that it is confined to or characteristic of members of certain professions, that homosexuals are partial to small boys, that there is a recognized "cure," and the like. *The LaGuardia Report* shatters numerous myths about marijuana: that it leads to use of heroin, that it activates violent antisocial tendencies, that it leads to insanity, and that it causes brain damage.

From these comprehensive reports comes a general image of the forms of deviance we have selected, forms that parallel the characteristics of the ethnic minorities. We find that the young, the poor, the homosexual, the alcoholic, and the drug offender tend to be subject to categorical discrimination in employment, education, housing, and the criminal justice system. Drunks are picked up by the police and railroaded through the lower criminal courts in complete disregard of due legal process. Drug addicts who go to hospitals for treatment under a "no bust" policy often find they are turned away because of discriminatory hospital practice. A homosexual who talks to a college class about homosexuality is subsequently dismissed from his job as a preschool teacher because three students who heard his talk turn him in to the school manager, who is afraid he would be dangerous to have around children. Young people of juvenile court age are continually denied due process— they have no right to bail, to trial by jury, or to appeal. Students are expelled from school because they are found possessing marijuana.

The responses of deviant minority members to these categorical discriminations are analogous to the behavior of ethnic minorities— "ghettoization." Drunks form their own subculture in certain relatively confined parts of the inner city known as "skid row," and there is a loose collectivization and cooperation in the formation of bottle groups. Drug users gather in well-known areas such as Haight-Ashbury in San Francisco, the East Village in New York, Sunset Strip in Los Angeles, Telegraph Avenue in Berkeley, the Strøget in Copenhagen, and the beach areas in many towns. Sex offenders—prosti-

11

tutes, homosexuals, transvestites—tend to congregate in the "tender-loin" areas of large cities. Juveniles tend to form their own separate and autonomous subcultures.

There is evidence of alienation among both deviant and ethnic minorities, particularly toward the police. The epithet "pig" for policeman is common to the vocabularies of the minority militant black or brown, the drug user, the juvenile delinquent, and the student radical. These varied groups perceive a common bond of alienation.

In this reader I have only included readings on the deviant and problem minorities—homosexuals, drug addicts, drunks, the youth, marijuana users, juvenile delinquents, prostitutes, the poor, and ethnic minorities. People in these categories comprise the vast majority of people in the criminal justice system today. From the points of view of numbers and current public concern, these minorities present important social problems, of concern to almost every-body. Other problems—burglary, murder, rape, robbery—though important in their seriousness, only affect the majority of people indirectly, through reports in the media. But in the matter of deviant minorities, the contrary is true: almost all of us have contact with members of these groups at least occasionally. Also, as shown in a chapter on "the convicted minority," a strong case can be made that more serious deviant careers almost invariably start with victimless offenses and progress to more serious ones perhaps due to factors relating to the prison experience.

The deviant minorities are also like minorities in at least one other important respect: they too are beginning to draw together and organize in order to defend themselves, demand certain rights, and generally combat the stereotypes directed toward them. This is the theme of an excellent article by Horowitz and Becker ("The Culture of Civility") which concludes this volume. Homosexuals have formed local, federated, and national homophile organizations such as The Mattachine Society, One, Inc., Gay Liberation Front, SIR, and the Daughters of Bilitis. They have begun to employ a rhetoric based upon that of the black power movement. LEMAR is an organization which has been formed in New York dedicated to the legalization of marijuana. Street organizations for drug users have sprung up in almost every metropolitan area. In some communities the young are now organizing into youth councils. Organizations for convicts like Seven Steps Foundation have arisen to help ex-cons overcome discrimination in employment and elsewhere. All these organizations are starting points in the emergence of deviant minorities, of groups asserting their right to exist in a pluralistic society and insisting upon toleration by the majority group.

In order to begin with some general perspective on minorities in general, Chapter 1, dealing with ethnic minorities, contains materials from three government reports—*The Kerner Report*, (National Advisory Commission on Civil Disorders), on race riots and their causes; *The Moynihan Report*, on the Negro family; and the report of the President's Commission on Law Enforcement and Administration of Justice, on crime among racial and ethnic minorities. We see here the themes of discrimination in employment, education, housing, and the criminal justice system. We see how ghettos develop, and the alienation and powerlessness that minority people feel, and why and how they perceive the police as symbols of white power. We see that many problems can be traced to a lack of group pride and solidarity and to disorganization of the family in particular. (This absence of family organization is also visible among juvenile delinquents, alcoholics, drug users, prostitutes, and homosexuals.) We also see, in the low crime and delinquency rates of the Oriental cultural enclaves, that family solidarity and group pride can reduce the magnitude of many of the problems accompanying minority group status. Perhaps if delinquents were to band together into organizations, their delinquency might become less violent. If drug addicts were also to organize, they might not need or want to engage in acts of violence or crime. If these things were to come to pass, perhaps the result would be the emergence of a more truly pluralistic society based on recognition and acceptance of divergent systems of belief and values.

Racism in American Society

The Kerner Report

SUMMARY OF REPORT

Introduction

The summer of 1967 again brought racial disorders to American cities, and with them shock, fear, and bewilderment to the nation.

The worst came during a two-week period in July, first in Newark and then in Detroit. Each set off a chain reaction in neighboring communities.

On July 28, 1967, the President of the United States established this Commission and directed us to answer three basic questions:

What happened?

Why did it happen?

What can be done to prevent it from happening again?

To respond to these questions, we have undertaken a broad range of studies and investigations. We have visited the riot cities; we have heard many witnesses; we have sought the counsel of experts across the country.

This is our basic conclusion: Our nation is moving toward two societies, one black, one white—separate and unequal.

Reaction to last summer's disorders has quickened the movement and deepened the division. Discrimination and segregation have long permeated much of American life; they now threaten the future of every American.

This deepening racial division is not inevitable. The movement apart can be reversed. Choice is still possible. Our principal task is to define that choice and to press for a national resolution.

To pursue our present course will involve the continuing polar-

From the National Advisory Commission on Civil Disorders, *Report of the National Advisory Commission on Civil Disorders* (Washington: U.S. Government Printing Office, 1968), pp. 1–7.

ization of the American community and, ultimately, the destruction of basic democratic values.

The alternative is not blind repression or capitulation to lawlessness. It is the realization of common opportunities for all within a single society.

This alternative will require a commitment to national action—compassionate, massive, and sustained, backed by the resources of the most powerful and the richest nation on this earth. From every American it will require new attitudes, new understanding, and, above all, new will.

The vital needs of the nation must be met; hard choices must be made, and, if necessary, new taxes enacted.

Violence cannot build a better society. Disruption and disorder nourish repression, not justice. They strike at the freedom of every citizen. The community cannot—it will not—tolerate coercion and mob rule.

Violence and destruction must be ended—in the streets of the ghetto and in the lives of people.

Segregation and poverty have created in the racial ghetto a destructive environment totally unknown to most white Americans.

What white Americans have never fully understood—but what the Negro can never forget—is that white society is deeply implicated in the ghetto. White institutions created it, white institutions maintain it, and white society condones it.

It is time now to turn with all the purpose at our command to the major unfinished business of this nation. It is time to adopt strategies for action that will produce quick and visible progress. It is time to make good the promises of American democracy to all citizens—urban and rural, white and black, Spanish-surname, American Indian, and every minority group.

Our recommendations embrace three basic principles:

To mount programs on a scale equal to the dimensions of the problems;

To aim these programs for high impact in the immediate future in order to close the gap between promise and performance;

To undertake new initiatives and experiments that can change the system of failure and frustration that now dominates the ghetto and weakens our society.

These programs will require unprecedented levels of funding and performance, but they neither probe deeper nor demand more than the problems which called them forth. There can be no higher priority for national action and no higher claim on the nation's conscience.

We issue this report now, four months before the date called for by the president. Much remains that can be learned. Continued study is essential.

As commissioners we have worked together with a sense of the greatest urgency and have sought to compose whatever differences exist among us. Some differences remain. But the gravity of the problem and the pressing need for action are too clear to allow further delay in the issuance of this report.

Part I—What Happened?

CHAPTER 1—PROFILES OF DISORDER

The report contains profiles of a selection of the disorders that took place during the summer of 1967. These profiles are designed to indicate how the disorders happened, who participated in them, and how local officials, police forces, and the National Guard responded. Illustrative excerpts follow:

Newark

. . . It was decided to attempt to channel the energies of the people into a nonviolent protest. While Lofton promised the crowd that a full investigation would be made of the Smith incident, the other Negro leaders began urging those on the scene to form a line of march toward the city hall.

Some persons joined the line of march. Others milled about in the narrow street. From the dark grounds of the housing project came a barrage of rocks. Some of them fell among the crowd. Others hit persons in the line of march. Many smashed the windows of the police station. The rock throwing, it was believed, was the work of youngsters; approximately 2500 children lived in the housing project.

Almost at the same time, an old car was set afire in a parking lot. The line of march began to disintegrate. The police, their heads protected by World War I-type helmets, sallied forth to disperse the crowd. A fire engine, arriving on the scene, was pelted with rocks. As police drove people away from the station, they scattered in all directions.

A few minutes later a nearby liquor store was broken into. Some persons, seeing a caravan of cabs appear at city hall to protest Smith's arrest, interpreted this as evidence that the disturbance had been organized, and generated rumors to that effect.

However, only a few stores were looted. Within a short period of time, the disorder appeared to have run its course.

❖   ❖   ❖

. . . On Saturday, July 15, [Director of Police Dominick] Spina received a report of snipers in a housing project. When he arrived he saw approximately 100 National Guardsmen and police officers crouching behind vehicles, hiding in corners and lying on the ground around the edge of the courtyard.

Since everything appeared quiet and it was broad daylight, Spina walked directly down the middle of the street. Nothing happened. As he came to the last building of the complex, he heard a shot. All around him the troopers jumped, believing themselves to be under sniper fire. A moment later a young Guardsman ran from behind a building.

The Director of Police went over and asked him if he had fired the shot. The soldier said yes, he had fired to scare a man away from a window; that his orders were to keep everyone away from windows.

Spina said he told the soldier: "Do you know what you just did? You have now created a state of hysteria. Every Guardsman up and down this street and every state policeman and every city policeman that is present thinks that somebody just fired a shot and that it is probably a sniper."

A short time later more "gunshots" were heard. Investigating, Spina came upon a Puerto Rican sitting on a wall. In reply to a question as to whether he knew "where the firing is coming from?" the man said:

"That's no firing. That's fireworks. If you look up to the fourth floor, you will see the people who are throwing down these cherry bombs."

By this time four truckloads of National Guardsmen had arrived and troopers and policemen were again crouched everywhere looking for a sniper. The Director of Police remained at the scene for three hours, and the only shot fired was the one by the Guardsman.

Nevertheless, at six o'clock that evening two columns of National Guardsmen and state troopers were directing mass fire at the Hayes Housing Project in response to what they believed were snipers. . . .

Detroit

. . . A spirit of carefree nihilism was taking hold. To riot and destroy appeared more and more to become ends in themselves. Late Sunday afternoon it appeared to one observer that the young people were "dancing amidst the flames."

A Negro plainclothes officer was standing at an intersection when a man threw a Molotov cocktail into a business establishment at the corner. In the heat of the afternoon, fanned by the 20 to 25 m.p.h. winds of both Sunday and Monday, the fire reached the home next door within minutes. As residents uselessly sprayed the flames with garden hoses, the fire jumped from roof to roof of adjacent two- and three-story buildings. Within the hour the entire block was in flames. The ninth house in the burning row belonged to the arsonist who had thrown the Molotov cocktail. . . .

✽   ✽   ✽

. . . Employed as a private guard, 55-year-old Julius L. Dorsey, a Negro, was standing in front of a market when accosted by two Negro men and a woman. They demanded he permit them to loot the market. He ignored their demands. They began to berate him. He asked a neighbor to call the police. As the argument grew more heated, Dorsey fired three shots from his pistol into the air.

The police radio reported: "Looters, they have rifles." A patrol car driven by a police officer and carrying three National Guardsmen arrived. As the looters fled, the law enforcement personnel opened fire. When the firing ceased, one person lay dead.

He was Julius L. Dorsey . . .

❀   ❀   ❀

. . . As the riot alternately waxed and waned, one area of the ghetto remained insulated. On the northeast side the residents of some 150 square blocks inhabited by 21,000 persons had, in 1966, banded together in the Positive Neighborhood Action Committee (PNAC). With professional help from the Institute of Urban Dynamics, they had organized block clubs and made plans for the improvement of the neighborhood. . . .

When the riot broke out, the residents, through the block clubs, were able to organize quickly. Youngsters, agreeing to stay in the neighborhood, participated in detouring traffic. While many persons reportedly sympathized with the idea of a rebellion against the "system," only two small fires were set—one in an empty building.

❀   ❀   ❀

. . . According to Lt. Gen. Throckmorton and Col. Bolling, the city, at this time, was saturated with fear. The National Guardsmen were afraid, the residents were afraid, and the police were afraid. Numerous persons, the majority of them Negroes, were being injured by gunshots of undetermined origin. The general and his staff felt that the major task of the troops was to reduce the fear and restore an air of normalcy.

In order to accomplish this, every effort was made to establish contact and rapport between the troops and the residents. The soldiers—20 percent of whom were Negro—began helping to clean up the streets, collect garbage, and trace persons who had disappeared in the confusion. Residents in the neighborhoods responded with soup and sandwiches for the troops. In areas where the National Guard tried to establish rapport with the citizens, there was a smaller response.

New Brunswick

. . . A short time later, elements of the crowd—an older and rougher one than the night before—appeared in front of the police station. The participants wanted to see the mayor.

Mayor [Patricia] Sheehan went out onto the steps of the station. Using a bullhorn, she talked to the people and asked that she be given an opportunity to correct conditions. The crowd was boisterous. Some persons challenged the mayor. But, finally, the opinion, "She's new! Give her a chance!" prevailed.

A demand was issued by people in the crowd that all persons arrested the previous night be released. Told that this already had been done, the people were suspicious. They asked to be allowed to inspect the jail cells.

It was agreed to permit representatives of the people to look in the cells to satisfy themselves that everyone had been released.

The crowd dispersed. The New Brunswick riot had failed to materialize.

CHAPTER 2—PATTERNS OF DISORDER

The "typical" riot did not take place. The disorders of 1967 were unusual, irregular, complex and unpredictable social processes. Like most human events, they did not unfold in an orderly sequence. However, an analysis of our survey information leads to some conclusions about the riot process.

In general:

The civil disorders of 1967 involved Negroes acting against local symbols of White American society, authority, and property in Negro neighborhoods—rather than against white persons.

Of 164 disorders reported during the first nine months of 1967, eight (5 percent) were major in terms of violence and damage; 33 (20 percent) were serious but not major; 123 (75 percent) were minor and undoubtedly would not have received national attention as "riots" had the nation not been sensitized by the more serious outbreaks.

In the 75 disorders studied by a Senate subcommittee, 83 deaths were reported. Eighty-two percent of the deaths and more than half the injuries occurred in Newark and Detroit. About 10 percent of the dead and 38 percent of the injured were public employees, primarily law officers and firemen. The overwhelming majority of the persons killed or injured in all the disorders were Negro civilians.

Initial damage estimates were greatly exaggerated. In Detroit, newspaper damage estimates at first ranged from $200 million to

$500 million; the highest recent estimate is $45 million. In Newark, early estimates ranged from $15 to $25 million. A month later damage was estimated at $10.2 million, over 80 percent in inventory losses.

In the 24 disorders in 23 cities which we surveyed:

The final incident before the outbreak of disorder, and the initial violence itself, generally took place in the evening or at night at a place in which it was normal for many people to be on the streets.

Violence usually occurred almost immediately following the occurrence of the final precipitating incident, and then escalated rapidly. With but few exceptions, violence subsided during the day, and flared rapidly again at night. The night-day cycles continued through the early period of the major disorders.

Disorder generally began with rock and bottle throwing and window breaking. Once store windows were broken, looting usually followed.

Disorder did not erupt as a result of a single "triggering" or "precipitating" incident. Instead, it was generated out of an increasingly disturbed social atmosphere, in which typically a series of tension-heightening incidents over a period of weeks or months became linked in the minds of many in the Negro community with a reservoir of underlying grievances. At some point in the mounting tension, a further incident—in itself often routine or trivial—became the breaking point and the tension spilled over into violence.

"Prior" incidents, which increased tensions and ultimately led to violence, were police actions in almost half the cases; police actions were "final" incidents before the outbreak of violence in 12 of the 24 surveyed disorders.

No particular control tactic was successful in every situation. The varied effectiveness of control techniques emphasizes the need for advance training, planning, adequate intelligence systems, and knowledge of the ghetto community.

Negotiations between Negroes—including your militants as well as older Negro leaders—and white officials concerning "terms of peace" occurred during virtually all the disorders surveyed. In many cases, these negotiations involved discussion of underlying grievances as well as the handling of the disorder by control authorities.

The typical rioter was a teenager or young adult, a lifelong resident of the city in which he rioted, a high school dropout; he was, nevertheless, somewhat better educated than his nonrioting Negro neighbor, and was usually underemployed or employed in a menial job. He was proud of his race, extremely hostile to both whites and middle-class Negroes, and, although informed about politics, highly distrustful of the political system.

A Detroit survey revealed that approximately 11 percent of the total residents of two riot areas admitted participation in the rioting, 20 to 25 percent identified themselves as "bystanders," over 16 percent identified themselves as "counter-rioters" who urged rioters to "cool it," and the remaining 48 to 53 percent said they were at home or elsewhere and did not participate. In a survey of Negro males between the ages of 15 and 35 residing in the disturbance area in Newark, about 45 percent identified themselves as rioters, and about 55 percent as "noninvolved."

Most rioters were young Negro males. Nearly 53 percent of arrestees were between 15 and 24 years of age; nearly 81 percent between 15 and 35.

In Detroit and Newark about 74 percent of the rioters were brought up in the North. In contrast, of the noninvolved, 36 percent in Detroit and 52 percent in Newark were brought up in the North.

What the rioters appeared to be seeking was fuller participation in the social order and the material benefits enjoyed by the majority of American citizens. Rather than rejecting the American system, they were anxious to obtain a place for themselves in it.

Numerous Negro counter-rioters walked the streets urging rioters to "cool it." The typical counter-rioter was better educated and had higher income than either the rioter or the noninvolved.

The proportion of Negroes in local government was substantially smaller than the Negro proportion of population. Only three of the 20 cities studied had more than one Negro legislator; none had ever had a Negro mayor or city manager. In only four cities did Negroes hold other important policy-making positions or serve as heads of municipal departments.

Although almost all cities had some sort of formal grievance mechanism for handling citizen complaints, this typically was regarded by Negroes as ineffective and was generally ignored.

Although specific grievances varied from city to city, at least 12 deeply held grievances can be identified and ranked into three levels of relative intensity:

First Level of Intensity

1. Police practices
2. Unemployment and underemployment
3. Inadequate housing

Second Level of Intensity

4. Inadequate education
5. Poor recreation facilities and programs
6. Ineffectiveness of the political structure and grievance mechanisms

Third Level of Intensity

7. Disrespectful white attitudes
8. Discriminatory administration of justice
9. Inadequacy of federal programs
10. Inadequacy of municipal services
11. Discriminatory consumer and credit practices
12. Inadequate welfare programs

The results of a three-city survey of various federal programs—manpower, education, housing, welfare, and community action—indicate that, despite substantial expenditures, the number of persons assisted constituted only a fraction of those in need.

The background of disorder is often as complex and difficult to analyze as the disorder itself. But we find that certain general conclusions can be drawn:

Social and economic conditions in the riot cities constituted a clear pattern of severe disadvantage for Negroes compared with whites, whether the Negroes lived in the area where the riot took place or outside it. Negroes had completed fewer years of education and fewer had attended high school. Negroes were twice as likely to be unemployed and three times as likely to be in unskilled and service jobs. Negroes averaged 70 percent of the income earned by whites and were more than twice as likely to be living in poverty. Although housing cost Negroes relatively more, they had worse housing—three times as likely to be overcrowded and substandard. When compared to white suburbs, the relative disadvantage is even more pronounced.

A study of the aftermath of disorders leads to disturbing conclusions. We find that, despite the institution of some post-riot programs:

> Little basic change in the conditions underlying the outbreak of disorder has taken place. Actions to ameliorate Negro grievances have been limited and sporadic; with but few exceptions, they have not significantly reduced tensions.
>
> In several cities, the principal official response has been to train and equip the police with more sophisticated weapons.
>
> In several cities, increasing polarization is evident, with continuing breakdown of inter-racial communication, and growth of white segregationist or black separatist groups.

CHAPTER 3—ORGANIZED ACTIVITY

The president directed the Commission to investigate "to what extent, if any, there has been planning or organization in any of the riots."

To carry out this part of the president's charge, the Commission established a special investigative staff supplementing the field teams that made the general examination of the riots in 23 cities. The unit examined data collected by federal agencies and congressional committees, including thousands of documents supplied by the Federal Bureau of Investigation, gathered and evaluated information from local and state law enforcement agencies and officials, and conducted its own field investigation in selected cities.

On the basis of all the information collected, the Commission concludes that:

The urban disorders of the summer of 1967 were not caused by, nor were they the consequence of, any organized plan or "conspiracy."

Specifically, the Commission has found no evidence that all or any of the disorders or the incidents that led to them were planned or directed by any organization or group, international, national or local.

Militant organizations, local and national, and individual agitators, who repeatedly forecast and called for violence, were active in the spring and summer of 1967. We believe that they sought to encourage violence, and that they helped to create an atmosphere that contributed to the outbreak of disorder.

We recognize that the continuation of disorders and the polarization of the races would provide fertile ground for organized exploitation in the future.

Investigations of organized activity are continuing at all levels of government, including committees of Congress. These investigations relate not only to the disorders of 1967 but also to the actions of groups and individuals, particularly in schools and colleges, during this last fall and winter. The Commission has cooperated in these investigations. They should continue.

Part II—Why Did It Happen?

CHAPTER 4—THE BASIC CAUSES

In addressing the question "Why did it happen?" we shift our focus from the local to the national scene, from the particular events of the summer of 1967 to the factors within the society at large that created a mood of violence among many urban Negroes.

These factors are complex and interacting; they vary significantly in their effect from city to city and from year to year; and the consequences of one disorder, generating new grievances and new demands, became the causes of the next. Thus was created the "thicket of tension, conflicting evidence and extreme opinions" cited by the President.

Despite these complexities, certain fundamental matters are clear. Of these, the most fundamental is the racial attitude and behavior of white Americans toward black Americans.

Race prejudice has shaped our history decisively; it now threatens to affect our future.

White racism is essentially responsible for the explosive mixture which has been accumulating in our cities since the end of World War II. Among the ingredients of this mixture are:

> *Pervasive discrimination and segregation* in employment, education and housing, which have resulted in the continuing exclusion of great numbers of Negroes from the benefits of economic progress.
>
> *Black in-migration and white exodus,* which have produced the massive and growing concentrations of impoverished Negroes in our major cities, creating a growing crisis of deteriorating facilities and services and unmet human needs.
>
> *The black ghettos* where segregation and poverty converge on the young to destroy opportunity and enforce failure. Crime, drug addiction, dependency on welfare, and bitterness and resentment against society in general and white society in particular are the result.

At the same time, most whites and some Negroes outside the ghetto have prospered to a degree unparalleled in the history of civilization. Through television and other media, this affluence has been flaunted before the eyes of the Negro poor and the jobless ghetto youth.

Yet these facts alone cannot be said to have caused the disorders. Recently, other powerful ingredients have begun to catalyze the mixture:

> *Frustrated hopes* are the residue of the unfulfilled expectations aroused by the great judicial and legislative victories of the Civil Rights Movement and the dramatic struggle for equal rights in the South.
>
> A *climate that tends toward approval and encouragement of violence* as a form of protest has been created by white terrorism directed against nonviolent protest; by the open defiance of law and federal authority by state and local officials resisting desegregation; and by some protest groups engaging in civil disobedience who turn their backs on nonviolence, go beyond the constitutionally protected rights of petition and free as-

sembly, and resort to violence to attempt to compel alteration of laws and policies with which they disagree.

The frustrations of powerlessness have led some Negroes to the conviction that there is no effective alternative to violence as a means of achieving redress of grievances, and of "moving the system." These frustrations are reflected in alienation and hostility toward the institutions of law and government and the white society which controls them, and in the reach toward racial consciousness and solidarity reflected in the slogan "Black Power."

A new mood has spung up among Negroes, particularly among the young, in which self-esteem and enhanced racial pride are replacing apathy and submission to "the system."

The police are not merely a "spark" factor. To some Negroes police have come to symbolize white power, white racism, and white repression. And the fact is that many police do reflect and express these white attitudes. The atmosphere of hostility and cynicism is reinforced by a widespread belief among Negroes in the existence of police brutality and in a "double standard" of justice and protection—one for Negroes and one for whites.

❊ ❊ ❊

To this point, we have attempted to identify the prime components of the "explosive mixture." In the chapters that follow we seek to analyze them in the perspective of history. Their meaning, however, is clear:

In the summer of 1967, we have seen in our cities a chain reaction of racial violence. If we are heedless, none of us shall escape the consequences.

CHAPTER 5—REJECTION AND PROTEST: AN HISTORICAL SKETCH

The causes of recent racial disorders are embedded in a tangle of issues and circumstances—social, economic, political and psychological—which arise out of the historic pattern of Negro-white relations in America.

In this chapter we trace the pattern, identify the recurrent themes of Negro protest, and, most importantly, provide a perspective on the protest activities of the present era.

We describe the Negro's experience in America and the development of slavery as an institution. We show his persistent striving for equality in the face of rigidly maintained social, economic and educational barriers, and repeated mob violence. We portray the ebb and flow of the doctrinal tides—accommodation, separatism, and self-help—and their relationship to the current theme of Black Power. We conclude:

> The Black Power advocates of today consciously feel that they are the most militant group in the Negro protest movement. Yet they have retreated from a direct confrontation with American society on the issue of integration and, by preaching separatism, unconsciously function as an accommodation to white racism. Much of their economic program, as well as their interest in Negro history, self-help, racial solidarity, and separation, is reminiscent of Booker T. Washington. The rhetoric is different, but the ideas are remarkably similar.

CHAPTER 6—THE FORMATION OF THE RACIAL GHETTOS[1]

Throughout the twentieth century the Negro population of the United States has been moving steadily from rural areas to urban and from South to North and West. In 1910, 91 percent of the nation's 9.8 million Negroes lived in the South and only 27 percent of American Negroes lived in cities of 2,500 persons or more. Between 1910 and 1966 the total Negro population more than doubled, reaching 21.5 million, and the number living in metropolitan areas rose more than five-fold (from 2.6 million to 14.8 million). The number outside the South rose eleven-fold (from 880,000 to 9.7 million).

Negro migration from the South has resulted from the expectation of thousands of new and highly paid jobs for unskilled workers in the North and the shift to mechanized farming in the South. However, the Negro migration is small when compared to earlier waves of European immigrants. Even between 1960 and 1966, there were 1.8 million immigrants from abroad compared to the 613,000 Negroes who arrived in the North and West from the South.

As a result of the growing number of Negroes in urban areas, natural increase has replaced migration as the primary source of Negro population increase in the cities. Nevertheless, Negro migration from the South will continue unless economic conditions there change dramatically.

Basic data concerning Negro urbanization trends indicate that:

Almost all Negro population growth (98 percent from 1950 to 1966) is occurring within metropolitan areas, primarily within central cities.[2]

The vast majority of white population growth (78 percent from 1960 to 1966) is occurring in suburban portions of metropolitan areas. Since 1960, white central-city population has declined by 1.3 million.

As a result, central cities are becoming more heavily Negro while the suburban fringes around them remain almost entirely white.

The twelve largest central cities now contain over two-thirds of the Negro population outside the South, and one-third of the Negro total in the United States.

Within the cities, Negroes have been excluded from white residential areas through discriminatory practices. Just as significant is the withdrawal of white families from, or their refusal to enter, neighborhoods where Negroes are moving or already residing. About 20 percent of the urban population of the United States changes residence every year. The refusal of whites to move into "changing" areas when vacancies occur means that most vacancies eventually are occupied by Negroes.

The result, according to a recent study, is that in 1960 the average segregation index for 207 of the largest United States cities was 86.2. In other words, to create an unsegregated population distribution, an average of over 86 percent of all Negroes would have to change their place of residence within the city.

CHAPTER 7—UNEMPLOYMENT, FAMILY STRUCTURE, AND SOCIAL
DISORGANIZATION

Although there have been gains in Negro income nationally, and a decline in the number of Negroes below the "poverty level," the condition of Negroes in the central city remains in a state of crisis. Between 2 and 2.5 million Negroes—16 to 20 percent of the total Negro population of all central cities—live in squalor and deprivation in ghetto neighborhoods.

Employment is a key problem. It not only controls the present for the Negro American but, in a most profound way, it is creating the future as well. Yet, despite continuing economic growth and declining national unemployment rates, the unemployment rate for Negroes in 1967 was more than double that for whites.

Equally important is the undesirable nature of many jobs open to Negroes and other minorities. Negro men are more than three times as likely as white men to be in low-paying, unskilled, or service jobs. This concentration of male Negro employment at the lowest end of the occupational scale is the single most important cause of poverty among Negroes.

In one study of low-income neighborhoods, the "subemployment rate," including both unemployment and underemployment, was about 33 percent, or 8.8 times greater than the overall unemployment rate for all United States workers.

Employment problems, aggravated by the constant arrival of new unemployed migrants, many of them from depressed rural areas, create persistent poverty in the ghetto. In 1966, about 11.9 percent of the nation's whites and 40.6 of its nonwhites were below the "poverty level" defined by the Social Security Administration (currently $3,335 per year for an urban family of four). Over 40 percent of the nonwhites below the poverty level live in the central cities.

Employment problems have drastic social impact in the ghetto. Men who are chronically unemployed or employed in the lowest status jobs are often unable or unwilling to remain with their families. The handicap imposed on children growing up without fathers in an atmosphere of poverty and deprivation is increased as mothers are forced to work to provide support.

The culture of poverty that results from unemployment and family breakup generates a system of ruthless, exploitative relationships within the ghetto. Prostitution, dope addiction, and crime create an environmental "jungle" characterized by personal insecurity and tension. Children growing up under such conditions are likely participants in civil disorders.

CHAPTER 8—CONDITIONS OF LIFE IN THE RACIAL GHETTO

A striking difference in environment from that of white, middle-class Americans profoundly influences the lives of residents of the ghetto.

Crime rates, consistently higher than in other areas, create a pronounced sense of insecurity. For example, in one city one low-income Negro district had 35 times as many serious crimes against persons as a high-income white district. Unless drastic steps are taken, the crime problems in poverty areas are likely to continue to multiply as the growing youth and rapid urbanization of the population outstrip police resources.

Poor health and sanitation conditions in the ghetto result in higher mortality rates, a higher incidence of major diseases, and lower availability and utilization of medical services. The infant mortality rate for nonwhite babies under the age of one month is 58 percent higher than for whites; for one to 12 months it is almost three times as high. The level of sanitation in the ghetto is far below that in high income areas. Garbage collection is often inadequate. Of an estimated 14,000 cases of rat bite in the United States in 1965, most were in ghetto neighborhoods.

Ghetto residents believe they are "exploited" by local merchants; and evidence substantiates some of these beliefs. A study conducted in one city by the Federal Trade Commission showed that distinctly higher prices were charged for goods sold in ghetto stores than in other areas.

Lack of knowledge regarding credit purchasing creates special pitfalls for the disadvantaged. In many states garnishment practices compound these difficulties by allowing creditors to deprive individuals of their wages without hearing or trial.

CHAPTER 9—COMPARING THE IMMIGRANT AND NEGRO EXPERIENCE

In this chapter, we address ourselves to a fundamental question that many white Americans are asking: Why have so many Negroes, unlike the European immigrants, been unable to escape from the ghetto and from poverty? We believe the following factors play a part:

The Maturing Economy: When the European immigrants arrived, they gained an economic foothold by providing the unskilled labor needed by industry. Unlike the immigrant, the Negro migrant found little opportunity in the city. The economy, by then matured, had little use for the unskilled labor he had to offer.

The Disability of Race: The structure of discrimination has stringently narrowed opportunities for the Negro and restricted his prospects. European immigrants suffered from discrimination, but never so pervasively.

Entry into the Political System: The immigrants usually settled in rapidly growing cities with powerful and expanding political machines, which traded economic advantages for political support. Ward-level grievance machinery, as well as personal representation, enabled the immigrant to make his voice heard and his power felt.

By the time the Negro arrived, these political machines were no longer so powerful or so well equipped to provide jobs or other favors, and in many cases were unwilling to share their influence with Negroes.

Cultural Factors: Coming from societies with a low standard of living and at a time when job aspirations were low, the immigrants sensed little deprivation in being forced to take the less desirable and poorer-paying jobs. Their large and cohesive families contributed to total income. Their vision of the future—one that led to a life outside of the ghetto—provided the incentive necessary to endure the present.

Although Negro men worked as hard as the immigrants, they were unable to support their families. The entrepreneurial opportunities had vanished. As a result of slavery and long periods of unemployment, the Negro family structure had become matriarchal; the males played a secondary and marginal family role—one which offered little compensation for their hard and unrewarding labor. Above all, segregation denied Negroes access to good jobs and the opportunity to leave the ghetto. For them, the future seemed to lead only to a dead end.

Today, whites tend to exaggerate how well and quickly they escaped from poverty. The fact is that immigrants who came from rural backgrounds, as many Negroes do, are only now, after three generations, finally beginning to move into the middle class.

By contrast, Negroes began concentrating in the city less than two generations ago, and under much less favorable conditions. Although some Negroes have escaped poverty, few have been able to escape the urban ghetto.

The Moynihan Report

The Negro Family

THE NEGRO FAMILY AND CRIME

That the Negro American has survived at all is extraordinary—a lesser people might simply have died out, as indeed others have. That the Negro community has not only survived, but in this political generation has entered national affairs as a moderate, humane, and constructive national force is the highest testament to the healing powers of the democratic ideal and the creative vitality of the Negro people.

But it may not be supposed that the Negro American community has not paid a fearful price for the incredible mistreatment to which it has been subjected over the past three centuries.

In essence, the Negro community has been forced into a matriarchal structure which, because it is so out of line with the rest of the American society, seriously retards the progress of the group as a whole, and imposes a crushing burden on the Negro male and, in consequence, on a great many Negro women as well.

There is, presumably, no special reason why a society in which males are dominant in family relationships is to be preferred to a matriarchal arrangement. However, it is clearly a disadvantage for a minority group to be operating on one principle, while the great majority of the population, and the one with the most advantages to begin with, is operating on another. This is the present situation of the Negro. Ours is a society which presumes male leadership in private and public affairs. The arrangements of society facilitate such leadership and reward it. A subculture, such as that of the Negro American, in which this is not the pattern, is placed at a distinct disadvantage.

Here an earlier word of caution should be repeated. There is much evidence that a considerable number of Negro families have managed to break out of the tangle of pathology and to establish

From *The Negro Family*, U.S. Department of Labor, Office of Planning and Research, (Washington: March 1965), pp. 29–40, 52–53.

themselves as stable, effective units, living according to patterns of American society in general. E. Franklin Frazier has suggested that the middle-class Negro American family is, if anything, more patriarchal and protective of its children than the general run of such families.[3] Given equal opportunities, the children of these families will perform as well or better than their white peers. They need no help from anyone, and ask none.

While this phenomenon is not easily measured, one index is that middle-class Negroes have even fewer children than middle-class whites, indicating a desire to conserve the advances they have made and to insure that their children do as well or better. Negro women who marry early to uneducated laborers have more children than white women in the same situation; Negro women who marry at the common age for the middle class to educated men doing technical or professional work have only four-fifths as many children as their white counterparts.

It might be estimated that as much as half of the Negro community falls into the middle class. However, the remaining half is in desperate and deteriorating circumstances. Moreover, because of housing segregation it is immensely difficult for the stable half to escape from the cultural influences of the unstable one. The children of middle-class Negroes often as not must grow up in or next to the slums, an experience almost unknown to white middle-class children. They are therefore constantly exposed to the pathology of the disturbed group and constantly in danger of being drawn into it. It is for this reason that the propositions put forth in this study may be thought of as having a more or less general application.

In a word, most Negro youth are in *danger* of being caught up in the tangle of pathology that affects their world, and probably a majority are so entrapped. Many of those who escape do so for one generation only: as things now are, their children may have to run the gauntlet all over again. That is not the least vicious aspect of the world that white America has made for the Negro.

Obviously, not every instance of social pathology afflicting the Negro community can be traced to the weakness of family structure. If, for example, organized crime in the Negro community were not largely controlled by whites, there would be more capital accumulation among Negroes, and therefore probably more Negro business enterprises. If it were not for the hostility and fear many whites exhibit towards Negroes, they in turn would be less afflicted by hos-

Children Born per Woman Age 35 to 44: Wives of Uneducated Laborers Who Married Young, Compared with Wives of Educated Professional Workers who Married After Age 21, White and Nonwhite, 1960[a]

	Children per Woman	
	White	Nonwhite
Wives married at age 14 to 21 to husbands who are laborers and did not go to high school	3.8	4.7
Wives married at age 22 or over to husbands who are professional or technical workers and have completed 1 year or more of college	2.4	1.9

[a] Wives married only once, with husbands present.

Source: 1960 Census, *Women by Number of Children ever Born,* PC (2) 3A, Tables 39 and 40, pp. 199–238.

tility and fear and so on. There is no one Negro community. There is no one Negro problem. There is no one solution. Nonetheless, at the center of the tangle of pathology is the weakness of the family structure. Once or twice removed, it will be found to be the principal source of most of the aberrant, inadequate, or anti-social behavior that did not establish, but now serves to perpetuate the cycle of poverty and deprivation.

It was by destroying the Negro family under slavery that white America broke the will of the Negro people. Although that will has reasserted itself in our time, it is a resurgence doomed to frustration unless the viability of the Negro family is restored.

MATRIARCHY

A fundamental fact of Negro American family life is the often reversed roles of husband and wife.

Robert O. Blood, Jr., and Donald M. Wolfe, in a study of Detroit families, note that "Negro husbands have unusually low power,"[4] and while this is characteristic of all low income families, the pattern pervades the Negro social structure: "the cumulative result of discrimination in jobs . . ., the segregated housing, and the poor schooling of Negro men."[5] In 44 percent of the Negro families studied, the wife was dominant, as against 20 percent of white wives. "Whereas the majority of white families are equalitarian, the largest percentage of Negro families are dominated by the wife."[6]

The matriarchal pattern of so many Negro families reinforces itself over the generations. This process begins with education. Although the gap appears to be closing at the moment, for a long while, Negro females were better educated than Negro males, and this remains true today for the Negro population as a whole.

Educational Attainment of the Civilian Noninstitutional Population 18 Years of Age and Over, March 1964

Color and Sex	Median School Years Completed
White:	
Male	12.1
Female	12.1
Nonwhite:	
Male	9.2
Female	10.0

Source: Bureau of Labor Statistics, unpublished data.

The difference in educational attainment between nonwhite men and women in the labor force is even greater; men lag 1.1 years behind women.

The disparity in educational attainment of male and female youth age 16 to 21 who were out of school in February 1963, is striking. Among the nonwhite males, 66.3 percent were not high school graduates, compared with 55.0 percent of the females. A similar difference existed at the college level, with 4.5 percent of the males having completed one to three years of college compared with 7.3 percent of the females.

The poorer performance of the male in school exists from the very beginning, and the magnitude of the difference was documented by the 1960 Census in statistics on the number of children who have fallen one or more grades below the typical grade for children of the same age. The boys have more frequently fallen behind at every age level. (White boys also lag behind white girls, but at a differential of one to six percentage points.)

Percent of Nonwhite Youth Enrolled in School Who are 1 or More Grades Below Mode for Age, by Sex, 1960

Age	Male	Female
7 to 9 years old	7.8	5.8
10 to 13 years old	25.0	17.1
14 and 15 years old	35.5	24.8
16 and 17 years old	39.4	27.2
18 and 19 years old	57.3	46.0

Source: 1960 Census, *School Enrollment,* PC(2) 5A, Table 3, p. 24.

In 1960, 39 percent of all white persons 25 years of age and over who had completed four or more years of college were women. Fifty-three percent of the nonwhites who had attained this level were women.

However, the gap is closing. By October 1963, there were slightly more Negro men in college than women. Among whites there were almost twice as many men as women enrolled.

There is much evidence that Negro females are better students than their male counterparts.

Daniel Thompson of Dillard University, in a private communication on January 9, 1965, writes:

As low as is the aspirational level among lower class Negro girls, it is considerably higher than among the boys. For example, I have examined the honor rolls in Negro high schools for about ten years. As a rule, from 75 to 90 percent of all Negro honor students are girls.

Dr. Thompson reports that 70 percent of all applications for the National Achievement Scholarship Program financed by the Ford

Foundation for outstanding Negro high school graduates are girls, despite special efforts by high school principals to submit the names of boys.

Fall Enrollment of Civilian Noninstitutional Population in College by Color and Sex—October 1963 (in Thousands)

Color and Sex	Population, age 14–34 October 1, 1963	Number Enrolled	Percent of Youth, Age 14–34
Nonwhite			
Male	2,884	149	5.2
Female	3,372	137	4.1
White			
Male	21,700	2,599	12.0
Female	20,613	1,451	7.0

Source: U.S. Bureau of the Census, *Current Population Reports*, Series P-20, No. 129 July 24, 1964, Tables 1, 5.

The finalists for this new program for outstanding Negro students were recently announced. Based on an inspection of the names, only about 43 percent of all the 639 finalists were male. (However, in the regular National Merit Scholarship program, males received 67 percent of the 1964 scholarship awards.)

Inevitably, these disparities have carried over to the area of employment and income.

In one out of four Negro families where the husband is present, is an earner, and someone else in the family works, the husband is not the principal earner. The comparable figure for whites is 18 percent.

More important, it is clear that Negro females have established a strong position for themselves in white collar and professional employment, precisely the areas of the economy which are growing most rapidly, and to which the highest prestige is accorded.

The President's Committee on Equal Employment Opportunity, making a preliminary report on employment in 1964 of over 16,000 companies with nearly 5 million employees, revealed this pattern with dramatic emphasis.

In this work force, Negro males outnumber Negro females

by a ratio of 4 to 1. Yet Negro males represent only 1.2 percent of all males in white collar occupations, while Negro females represent 3.1 percent of the total female white collar work force. Negro males represent 1.1 percent of all male professionals, whereas Negro females represent roughly 6 percent of all female professionals. Again, in technician occupations, Negro males represent 2.1 percent of all male technicians while Negro females represent roughly 10 percent of all female technicians. It would appear therefore that there are proportionately four times as many Negro females in significant white collar jobs than Negro males.

Although it is evident that office and clerical jobs account for approximately 50 percent of all Negro female white collar workers, it is significant that 6 out of every 100 Negro females are in professional jobs. This is substantially similar to the rate of all females in such jobs. Approximately 7 out of every 100 Negro females are in technician jobs. This exceeds the proportion of all females in technician jobs—approximately 5 out of every 100.

Negro females in skilled jobs are almost the same as that of all females in such jobs. Nine out of every 100 Negro males are in skilled occupations while 21 out of 100 of all males are in such jobs.[7]

This pattern is to be seen in the Federal government, where special efforts have been made recently to insure equal employment opportunity for Negroes. These efforts have been notably successful in Departments such as Labor, where some 19 percent of employees are now Negro. (A not disproportionate percentage, given the composition of the work force in the areas where the main Department offices are located.) However, it may well be that these efforts have redounded mostly to the benefit of Negro women, and may even have accentuated the comparative disadvantage of Negro men. Seventy percent of the Negro employees of the Department of Labor are women, as contrasted with only 42 percent of the white employees.

Among nonprofessional Labor Department employees—where the most employment opportunities exist for all groups—Negro women outnumber Negro men four to one, and average almost one grade higher in classification.

The testimony to the effects of the patterns in Negro family structure is widespread, and hardly to be doubted.

Whitney Young:

Historically, in the matriarchal Negro society, mothers made sure that if one of their children had a chance for higher education the daughter was the one to pursue it.[8]

The effect on family functioning and role performance of this historical experience [economic deprivation] is what you might predict. Both as a husband and as a father the Negro male is made to feel inadequate, not because he is unlovable or unaffectionate, lacks intelligence or even a gray flannel suit. But in a society that measures a man by the size of his pay check, he doesn't stand very tall in a comparison with his white counterpart. To this situation he may react with withdrawal, bitterness toward society, aggression both within the family and racial group, self-hatred, or crime. Or he may escape through a number of avenues that help him to lose himself in fantasy or to compensate for his low status through a variety of exploits.[9]

Thomas Pettigrew:

The Negro wife in this situation can easily become disgusted with her financially dependent husband, and her rejection of him further alienates the male from family life. Embittered by their experiences with men, many Negro mothers often act to perpetuate the mother-centered pattern by taking a greater interest in their daughters than their sons.[10]

Deton Brooks:

In a matriarchal structure, the women are transmitting the culture.[11]

Dorothy Height:

If the Negro woman has a major underlying concern, it is the status of the Negro man and his position in the community and his need for feeling himself an important person, free and able to make his contribution in the whole society, in order that he may strengthen his home.[12]

Duncan M. MacIntyre:

The Negro illegitimacy rate always has been high—about eight times the white rate in 1940 and somewhat higher today even though the white illegitimacy rate also is climbing. The Negro statistics are symptomatic of some old socioeconomic problems, not the least of which are underemployment among Negro men and compensating higher labor force propensity among Negro women. Both operate to enlarge the mother's role, undercutting the status of the male and making many Negro families essentially matriarchal. The Negro man's uncertain employment prospects, matriarchy, and the high cost of divorces combine to encourage desertion (the poor man's divorce), increases the number of couples not married, and thereby also increases the Negro illegitimacy rate. In the meantime, higher Negro birth rates are increasing the nonwhite population, while migration into cities like Detroit, New York, Philadelphia, and Washington, D.C. is making the public assistance rolls in such cities heavily, even predominantly, Negro.[13]

Robin M. Williams, Jr., in a study of Elmira, New York:

Only 57 percent of Negro adults reported themselves as married—spouse present, as compared with 78 percent of native white American gentiles, 91 percent of Italian-American, and 96 percent of Jewish informants. Of the 93 unmarried Negro youths interviewed, 22 percent did not have their mother living in the home with them, and 42 percent reported that their father was not living in their home. One-third of the youths did not know their father's present occupation, and two-thirds of a sample of 150 Negro adults did not know what the occupation of their father's father had been. Forty percent of the youth said that they had brothers and sisters living in other communities: another 40 percent reported relatives living in their home who were not parents, siblings, or grandparent.[14]

THE FAILURE OF YOUTH

Williams' account of Negro youth growing up with little knowledge of their fathers, less of their fathers' occupations, still less of family occupational traditions, is in sharp contrast to the experience of the white child. The white family, despite many variants, remains a powerful agency not only for transmitting property from one generation to the next, but also for transmitting no less valuable contracts with the world of education and work. In an earlier age, the Carpenters, Wainwrights, Weavers, Mercers, Farmers, Smiths acquired their names as well as their trades from their fathers and grandfathers. Children today still learn the patterns of work from their fathers even though they may no longer go into the same jobs.

White children without fathers at least perceive all about them the pattern of men working.

Negro children without fathers flounder—and fail.

Not always, to be sure. The Negro community produces its share, very possibly more than its share, of young people who have the something extra that carries them over the worst obstacles. But such persons are always a minority. The common run of young people in a group facing serious obstacles to success do not succeed.

A prime index of the disadvantage of Negro youth in the United States is their consistently poor performance on the mental tests that are a standard means of measuring ability and performance in the present generation.

There is absolutely no question of any genetic differential: Intelligence potential is distributed among Negro infants in the same proportion and pattern as among Icelanders or Chinese or any other group. American society, however, impairs the Negro potential. The statement of the HARYOU report that "there is no basic disagreement over the fact that central Harlem students are performing poorly in school"[15] may be taken as true of Negro slum children throughout the United States.

Eighth grade children in central Harlem have a median IQ of 87.7, which means that perhaps a third of the children are scoring at levels perilously near to those of retardation. IQ *declines* in the first decade of life, rising only slightly thereafter.

The effect of broken families on the performance of Negro youth has not been extensively measured, but studies that have been made show an unmistakable influence.

Martin Deutch and Bert Brown, investigating intelligence test differences between Negro and white first and fifth graders of different social classes, found that there is a direct relationship between social class and IQ. As the one rises so does the other: but more for whites than Negroes. This is surely a result of housing segregation, referred to earlier, which makes it difficult for middle-class Negro families to escape the slums.

The authors explain that "it is much more difficult for the Negro to attain identical middle- or upper-middle-class status with whites, and the social class gradations are less marked for Negroes because Negro life in a caste society is considerably more homogeneous than is life for the majority group."[16]

Therefore, the authors look for background variables other than social class which might explain the difference: "One of the most striking differences between the Negro and white groups is the consistently higher frequency of broken homes and resulting family disorganization in the Negro group.[17]

FATHER ABSENT FROM THE HOME

Lowest social class level		Middle social class level		Highest social class level	
Percent of White	Negro	Percent of White	Negro	Percent of White	Negro
15.4	43.9	10.3	27.9	0.0	13.7

(Adapted from authors' table.)

Further, they found that children from homes where fathers are present have significantly higher scores than children in homes without fathers.

	Mean Intelligence Scores
Father Present	97.83
Father Absent	90.79

The influence of the father's presence was then tested *within* the social classes and school grades for Negroes alone. They found that "a consistent trend within both grades at the lower SES [social class] level appears, and in no case is there a reversal of this trend: for males, females, and the combined group, the IQs of children with fathers in the home are always higher than those who have no father in the home.[18]

The authors say that broken homes "may also account for some of the differences between Negro and white intelligence scores."[19]

The scores of fifth graders with fathers absent were lower than

Mean Intelligence Scores of Negro Children by School, Grade, Social Class, and by Presence of Father

Social Class and School Grade	Father Present	Father Absent
Lowest social class level:		
Grade 1	95.2	87.8
Grade 5	92.7	85.7
Middle social class level:		
Grade 1	98.7	92.8
Grade 5	92.9	92.0

(Adapted from authors' table.)

Percent of Nonwhite Males Enrolled in School, by Age and Presence of Parents, 1960

Age	Both Parents Present	One Parent Present	Neither Parent Present
5 years	41.7	44.2	34.3
6 years	79.3	78.7	73.8
7 to 9 years	96.1	95.3	93.9
10 to 13 years	96.2	95.5	93.0
14 and 15 years	91.8	89.9	85.0
16 and 17 years	78.0	72.7	63.2
18 and 19 years	46.5	40.0	32.3

Source: 1960 Census, *School Enrollment,* PC (2) 5A, Table 3, p. 24.

the scores of first graders with fathers absent, and while the authors point out that it is cross sectional data and does not reveal the duration of the father's absence, "What we might be tapping is the cumulative effect of fatherless years."[20]

This difference in ability to perform has its counterparts in statistics on actual school performance. Nonwhite boys from families with both parents present are more likely to be going to school than boys with only one parent present, and enrollment rates are even lower when neither parent is present.

When the boys from broken homes are in school, they do not do as well as the boys from whole families. Grade retardation is higher when only one parent is present, and highest when neither parent is present.

The loneliness of the Negro youth in making fundamental decisions about education is shown in a 1959 study of Negro and white dropouts in Connecticut high schools.

Only 29 percent of the Negro male dropouts discussed their decision to drop out of school with their fathers, compared with 65 percent of the white males (38 percent of the Negro males were from broken homes). In fact, 26 percent of the Negro males did not discuss this major decision in their lives with anyone at all, compared with only 8 percent of white males.

A study of Negro apprenticeship by the New York State Commission Against Discrimination in 1960 concluded:

> Negro youth are seldom exposed to influences which can lead to apprenticeship. Negroes are not apt to have relatives, friends, or neighbors in skilled occupations. Nor are they likely to be in secondary schools where they receive encouragement and direction from alternate role models. Within the minority community, skilled Negro 'models' after whom the Negro youth might pattern himself are rare, while substitute sources which could provide the direction, encouragement, resources, and information needed to achieve skilled craft standing are non-existent.[21]

DELINQUENCY AND CRIME

The combined impact of poverty, failure, and isolation among Negro youth has had the predictable outcome in a disastrous delinquency and crime rate.

In typical pattern of discrimination, Negro children in all public and private orphanages are a smaller proportion of all children than their proportion of the population although their needs are clearly greater.

Percent of Nonwhite Males Enrolled in School Who are 1 or More Grades Below Mode for Age, by Age Group and Presence of Parents, 1960

Age Group	Both Parents Present	One Parent Present	Neither Parent Present
7–9 year	7.5	7.7	9.6
10–13 years	23.8	25.8	30.6
14–15 years	34.0	36.3	40.9
16–17 years	37.6	40.9	44.1
18–19 years	60.6	65.9	46.1

Source: 1960 Census, *School Enrollment,* PC(2) 5A, Tabe 3, p. 24.

On the other hand Negroes represent a third of all youth in training schools for juvenile delinquents.

Children in Homes for Dependent and Neglected Children, 1960

	Number	Percent
White	64,807	88.4
Negro	6,140	8.4
Other races	2,359	3.2
All races	73,306	100.0

Source: 1960 Census, *Inmates of Institutions,* PC (2) 3A, Table 31, p. 44.

It is probable that at present, a majority of the crimes against the person, such as rape, murder, and aggravated assault are committed by Negroes. There is, of course, no absolute evidence; inference can only be made from arrest and prison population statistics. The data that follow unquestionably are biased against Negroes, who are arraigned much more casually than are whites, but it may be doubted that the bias is great enough to affect the general proportions.

Again on the urban frontier the ratio is worse: three out of every five arrests for these crimes were of Negroes.

In Chicago in 1963, three-quarters of the persons arrested for such crimes were Negro; in Detroit, the same proportions held.

	Number of Arrests in 1963	
	White	Negro
Offenses charged total	31,988	38,549
Murder and nonnegligent		
manslaughter	2,288	2,948
Forcible rape	4,402	3,935
Aggravated assault	25,298	31,666

Source: Crime in the United States (Federal Bureau of Investigation, 1963) Table 25, p. 111.

In 1960, 37 percent of all persons in Federal and State prisons were Negro. In that year, 56 percent of the homicide and 57 percent of the assault offenders committed to State institutions were Negro.

	Number of City Arrests in 1963 [a]	
	White	Negro
Offenses charged total	24,805	35,520
Murder and nonnegligent		
manslaughter	1,662	2,593
Forcible rape	3,199	3,570
Aggravated assault	19,944	29,357

[a] In 2,892 cities with population over 2,500.

Source: Crime in the United States (Federal Bureau of Investigation, 1963) Table 31, p. 117.

The overwhelming number of offenses committed by Negroes are directed toward other Negroes: the cost of crime to the Negro community is a combination of that to the criminal and to the victim.

Some of the research on the effects of broken homes on delinquent behavior recently surveyed by Thomas F. Pettigrew in *A Profile of the Negro American* is summarized below, along with several other studies of the question.

Mary Diggs found that three-fourths—twice the expected ratio—

47

of Philadelphia's Negro delinquents who came before the law during 1948 did not live with both their natural parents.[22]

In predicting juvenile crime, Eleanor and Sheldon Glueck also found that a higher proportion of delinquent than nondelinquent boys came from broken homes. They identified five critical factors in the home environment that made a difference in whether boys would become delinquents: discipline of boy by father, supervision of boy by mother, affection of father for boy, affection of mother for boy, and cohesiveness of family.

In 1952, when the New York City Youth Board set out to test the validity of these five factors as predictors of delinquency, a problem quickly emerged. The Glueck sample consisted of white boys of mainly Irish, Italian, Lithuanian, and English descent. However, the Youth Board group was 44 percent Negro and 14 percent Puerto Rican, and the frequency of broken homes within these groups was out of proportion to the number of delinquents in the population.[23]

> In the majority of these cases, the father was usually never in the home at all, absent for the major proportion of the boy's life, or was present only on occasion.

(The final prediction table was reduced to three factors: supervision of boy by mother, discipline of boy by mother, and family cohesiveness within what family, in fact, existed, but was, nonetheless, 85 percent accurate in predicting delinquents and 96 percent accurate in predicting nondelinquents.)

Researchers who have focused upon the "good" boy in high delinquency neighborhoods noted that they typically come from exceptionally stable, intact families.[24]

Recent psychological research demonstrates the personality effects of being reared in a disorganized home without a father. One study showed that children from fatherless homes seek immediate gratification of their desires far more than children with fathers present.[25] Others revealed that children who hunger for immediate gratification are more prone to delinquency, along with other less social behavior.[26] Two psychologists, Pettigrew says, maintain that inability to delay gratification is a critical factor in immature, criminal, and neurotic behavior.[27]

Finally, Pettigrew discussed the evidence that a stable home is a crucial factor in counteracting the effects of racism upon Negro personality.

A warm, supportive home can effectively compensate for many of the restrictions the Negro child faces outside of the ghetto; consequently, the type of home life a Negro enjoys as a child may be far more crucial for governing the influence of segregation upon his personality than the form the segregation takes—legal or informal, Southern or Northern.[28]

A Yale University study of youth in the lowest socio-economic class in New Haven in 1950 whose behavior was followed through their eighteenth year revealed that among the delinquents in the group, 38 percent came from broken homes, compared with 24 percent of nondelinquents.[29]

Juvenile Delinquents—Philadelphia by Presence of Parents, 1949–1954

	White		
	All Court Cases	First Offenders	Recidivists
Number of Cases	20,691	13,220	4,612
Number not living with both parents	7,422	4,125	2,047
Percent not living with both parents	35.9	31.2	44.4

	Negro		
	All Court Cases	First Offenders	Recidivists
Number of Cases	22,695	11,442	6,641
Number not living with both parents	13,980	6,586	4,298
Percent not living with both parents	61.6	57.6	64.7

Source: Adapted from Table 1, p. 255, "Family Status and the Delinquent Child," Thomas P. Monahan, *Social Forces*, March 1957.

The President's Task Force on Manpower Conservation in 1963 found that of young men rejected for the draft for failure to pass the mental tests, 42 percent of those with a court record came from broken homes, compared with 30 percent of those without a court record. Half of all the nonwhite rejectees in the study with a court record came from broken homes.

An examination of the family background 44,448 delinquency cases in Philadelphia between 1949 and 1954 documents the frequency of broken homes among delinquents. Sixty-two percent of the Negro delinquents and 36 percent of white delinquents were not living with both parents. In 1950, 33 percent of nonwhite children and 17 percent of white children in Philadelphia were living in homes without both parents. Repeaters were even more likely to be from broken homes than first offenders.[30]

Crime and its Impact—
An Assessment

THE RELATIONSHIPS OF NATIONALITY WITH CRIME
AND DELINQUENCY BY CITY AREAS

The greatest contribution of data for public consideration of this problem was made through the series of studies in Chicago.[31] The use of ecological methods permitted them to go beyond the simple relationship between crime rates and nationality. It enabled them to demonstrate the operation of a relatively effective process of assimilation of these different nationality groups into the mainstream of American economic and social life. With this assimilation the high rates of crime and delinquency as well as a number of other social problems disappeared. It enabled them to focus public attention on the conditions of life, and on cultural and social change, rather than on inherent criminality as a function of national origin.

The problem of public stereotyping of certain nationality groups at that time as inherently criminal is not unlike the criminal stereotyping of the Negro and other minority groups today. These early studies did not attempt to refute the clearly demonstrable fact that the crime rates of certain nationality groups were disproportionately high. Instead, they amassed evidence to show that while this fact was attributable, in some measure, to the social and cultural traditions of these groups, mainly it was a consequence of the socially disorganized nature of the conditions under which they were forced to live. The overwhelming thrust of the evidence was that the high rates of crime were not a consequence of being German, Irish, Scandinavian, Polish, Italian, or Slavic, but a consequence of their life situation.

Three types of data were assembled for studying the relation of race, nationality, and nativity with crime and delinquency rates. These data related to

From The President's Commission on Law Enforcement and Administration of Justice, *The Task Force Report: Crime and Its Impact—An Assessment* (Washington: U.S. Government Printing Office, 1967), pp. 72–75.

(1) The succession of nationality groups in the high-rate areas over a period of years;

(2) Changes in the national and racial backgrounds of children appearing in the Juvenile Court; and

(3) Rates of delinquents for particular racial, nativity, or nationality groups in different types of areas at any given moment.[32]

Marked changes were noted in the composition of the population inhabiting the high delinquency and crime rate areas near the central district over a period of many years. The Germans, Irish, English-Scotch, and Scandinavians in Chicago were gradually replaced by the Italians, Polish, and persons from Slavic countries. Despite the change in population the rates remained high relative to other areas in the city. Nor were those families left behind by each nationality group the most delinquent. They actually produced fewer delinquents than their proportion in the population of the area would lead one to expect.[33]

As the older immigrant group moved out, their children appeared proportionately less often in the Juvenile Court, and the court intake reflected instead the disproportionate appearance of the new arrivals. Nor did the children of the disappearing nationality groups raise the court intake in their new areas either for foreign-born or native-born children.[34]

Comparison of the rates for whites and Negroes, native and foreign-born, and old and new immigrants, classified by the area rates for white delinquents, shows that all of these groups have rates that range from high to low. Each racial and nationality group shows a considerable range in rates. At the same time these different groups produce much the same rate when they live in the same areas.[35]

There is some difficulty in comparing the rates for different groups at any one time because of the concentration of the new groups in the high rate areas. Neverthless, when tracts are compared that are closely comparable in living conditions, very similar rates are revealed. In more recent comparisons of the rates for Negro and white delinquents in Chicago, considerable difficulty was encountered in identifying comparable areas for the two groups. Even in the same tracts the whites were found to occupy the better quarters and were,

52

of course, not subject to the same discrimination in access to employment and other opportunities.[36] In the last major sample in the Chicago studies, the 1934–40 Juvenile Court Series, application of a method of statistical standardization for partially equating the population distribution of white and Negro males yielded a standardized delinquency rate of 4.41 per 100 white youth age 10–17 and 14.55 per 100 Negro youth.[37] Despite this difference the study concludes,

> All of the materials in this study indicate that if situations could be found where Negro and white children had equal opportunities in all meaningful aspects of life, the widely observed differences in rates of delinquents would be greatly reduced and perhaps would disappear.[38]

This limitation in the ecological method, the difficulty of locating comparable living conditions for the comparison of the experience of different population groups, was explored in some detail in a study in Baltimore.[39] Two white and two Negro areas were selected so as to permit as full an equating as possible of the conditions of life and the demographic characteristics of the population between each pair of matched Negro and white areas. Because of the segregation each area was quite racially homogeneous. Furthermore, the paired areas had about the same size population, similar age and sex differences, predominantly lower occupational levels, the same low levels of education, comparable size households, generally low health status though somewhat lower in the Negro areas, and general comparability on such indices as condition of dwellings, homes with radios, refrigeration equipment, and presence of central heating unit. The chief differences were that the white populations, predominantly of foreign-born extraction, were a settled population of long residence in their areas, while the Negro populations had sizeable groups of new migrants. Home ownership was much greater among the whites, the Negroes being primarily renters. The Negroes also paid higher rents for comparable dwelling units. The whites were "one step up the occupation ladder above Negroes."[40]

The results showed considerably higher rates of felons convicted in 1940 in the Negro as compared to the matched white areas. The respectively paired Negro areas were 15.11 and 12.47.[41] The juvenile white rates for males were 2.36 and 2.21, while the rates for the delinquency rates, however, per 1000 population, age 6–17, for the years 1939–42 were much closer. The white rates were 14.4 and 22.0, while the Negro area rates were 26.7 and 28.4.[42]

The discrepancy in the crime rates might have been anticipated since, as we have already seen in other studies, the differences which did exist between the Negro and white areas are ones which show high associations with crime rates, such as the high percentage of home ownership in the white area, a stable white population and a mobile Negro population and somewhat higher occupational status in the white area, that is, more craftsmen, foremen, and kindred workers as contrasted with laborers and domestic service workers among the Negro population. What is surprising is the relatively close correspondence in delinquency rates despite these differences. Nevertheless, the study does indicate the grave difficulties in locating truly equated areas for such controlled comparisons.

The basic findings in the Chicago studies of the spatial distribution of nationally and racial delinquency rates have not gone unchallenged. The primary objection is that the concern with documenting the effects of the process of assimilation on the delinquency rates within each nationality group led to the neglect of significant differences in the crime and delinquency rates of nationality groups arising from different tolerances in their own cultural and historical tradition for various forms of deviance.[43] Reference has been made to the low rates of delinquency and crime in areas of Oriental settlement, to significant differences in the delinquency of children of Russian Jewish immigrants and Italian immigrants in New York City though they entered at much the same time, and to the high rates of arrest of Jewish boys for violating street peddling laws.[44] It seems to be generally conceded that these cultural differences can influence significantly the *actual* or *absolute* size of the delinquency rate.[45] However, the main propositions of the Chicago studies rest not so much on the actual size of the rates but the relationship between these rates. It is the *relative* difference between area rates for the same or different nationality groups depending on their length of residence in the city and the amount of movement toward the better integrated, more comfortable and settled areas toward the periphery of the city that supports the principal findings.[46]

THE CULTURAL ENCLAVE

One of the most significant findings of the ecological studies has been the identification of enclaves of culturally different insulated groups who have maintained low rates of crime and delinquency despite exposure to poverty, discrimination, exploitation, and disadvantageous conditions. Perhaps the most striking capacity to do this has been observed in areas of Oriental settlement in large cities. In Seattle a school district comprised of 90 percent Japanese boys showed a low delinquency rate of 5.7 despite the fact that the rate for the rest of the area was 27.7.[47] This district was located in a very deteriorated section of town with "the highest concentration of homicides, houses of prostitution, unidentified suicides, and cheap lodging-houses in Seattle.[48] Of the 710 boys who were sent to the Parental School (a boy's reform school) from 1919 to 1930 from Seattle, only three were Japanese, and the cases of these three indicated that they had lost "vital contact with the racial colony."[49]

This same type of situation was observed and studied in Vancouver. In an eight-year period (1928–36) a total of 4814 delinquents appeared in the Vancouver Juvenile Court.[50] Only 19 were Orientals. During this period the delinquency rate for the whites was 15.65 per 1000 and for the Orientals 1.0 per 1000.[51]

Further investigation revealed that the Oriental children in Vancouver resided in areas of high delinquency and they attended schools with bad delinquency records. Furthermore the status of the Oriental was low. He experienced discrimination and was often the subject of active hostility. The explanation seems to be that strenuous efforts were made to maintain family discipline and loyalty, to sustain a common concept and respect for their national origin, and to promote actively the pursuit and study of the Oriental religion, language, and culture.[52]

How long can this type of insularity maintain itself under the pressures for participation in modern life? There are historical examples to indicate that this is very difficult. A study of a Russian colony of immigrants in Los Angeles reported in 1930 that 5 percent of the children appeared before the juvenile court in the first 5 years of residence in a highly delinquent area. In the second 5 years of residence 46 percent were referred to the court, and in the next ten years 83 percent were referred to the court.[53] Similarly, in Honolulu it

55

was discovered that the Orientals who became involved in serious delinquency were most likely to be those who had previous associations with members of other groups.[54]

No one seriously suggests that it is easier to maintain control over the behavior of children in a high as compared to a low delinquency area but the fact is that many succeed. A recent study in New Haven suggests that the proper kind of family and school climate can provide a certain amount of insulation from highly delinquent surroundings and secure commitment to conventional goals.[55] The study included a sample of all youth born in Greater New Haven in 1942–44 whose supervising relative was on the Aid to Dependent Children rolls in 1950. Records were examined for the years between the sixth birthday and the nineteenth. Data came primarily from welfare, school, and police records. By 1962, a total of 34 percent had become known to the police or the juvenile court, compared to a delinquency rate of 18 percent for a control group of youth of the same age, sex, type of neighborhood, school performance, and lowest class level. However, the ADC group did show twice as many living in public housing, twice the number moving three or more times over an eleven-year period, three times as many Negroes, and over ten times more broken homes.[56]

The delinquency rates among the ADC group varied markedly by race, sex, and school performance, all the way from no delinquency cases among 75 white females who were successful in school to 71 percent arrested or referred to court among 38 Negro males who were failing in school.[57] Additional significant differences appear when family deviance and the nature of the neighborhood of residence are considered. A "deviant family" was defined as one in which "one or both parents are in prison or mental hospital, or the parent has had a series of marriages; separations, multiple illegitimacies, or 'cut and run' affairs."[58] Those from deviant families are more delinquent, 41 percent to 31 percent, but deviant families had twice as much effect on Negro as compared to white youth. School success seems to compensate to some extent for the effects of deviant families, since among the successful in school 33 percent from the deviant families were delinquent, and 27 percent of those from nondeviant families were delinquent. However, among those failing in school 71 percent from deviant families were delinquent as compared to 45 percent of those from nondeviant families.[59]

Consideration was also given to the effect of residing in a

deviant neighborhood, which was defined as of the lowest class standing in social and economic characteristics and having a high delinquency rate.[60] Negro youth were more than twice as likely as white youth to live in deviant neighborhoods. The effect of the deviant neighborhood is much greater on boys than on girls since 71 percent of the boys from deviant neighborhoods were delinquent compared to 47 percent of the boys from nondeviant neighborhoods, while the comparable percentages for girls were 14 and 16 percent.[61] Here again the effect of living in a deviant neighborhood is likely to be worse for those boys failing in school. Perhaps success in school insulates the boys to some extent from complete responsiveness to delinquent influences in the neighborhood or perhaps those least involved in neighborhood life are most likely to succeed in school. Among those boys failing in school who were from deviant neighborhoods, 82 percent were delinquent compared to 53 percent of the school failures from nondeviant neighborhoods, while the comparable percentages for the school successes were 44 and 37 percent.[62]

As this study points out, some factors are additive in their effects. If one is male, Negro, and a school failure, the chances of developing a delinquent record are greater than if any of these factors were different. Other factors seem to be interactive. They have a selective and sometimes a cushioning effect. School success may offset many of the effects of deviant neighborhoods or families. Also being from nondeviant neighborhoods or families is associated with lower delinquency rates despite failure in school.

two

YOUTH AS A MINORITY

Youth is a logical place to begin our analysis of deviant minorities, because it is probably the largest of all minority groups, certainly it is the earliest, and its members are subject to as much categorical discrimination as any other minority. Viewing young people as a minority may afford us insights into the phenomena of youthful deviance that no other perspective—such as anomie, status deprivation, cultural lag, social disorganization, and the like—can provide.

It is not really difficult to see youth as a group subject to categorical discrimination. Much of this is common knowledge. Eighteen-year-olds are old enough to be forced to fight and die for their country, but in most parts of the country they are not old enough to drink alcohol or, until very recently, to vote. Young people cannot make a civil contract to purchase goods, but they can sign waivers of their constitutional rights when they have been charged with a crime.

Young men below eighteen cannot marry without parental consent, but they can be charged with statutory rape for having sex with their girl friends. In court young people do not have such constitutional rights as the right to appeal, to bail, to pretrial release on their own recognizance, or to trial by jury. To show how far this attenuation of right extends, in California, all these rights are granted to every "person" by the California Constitution; but California courts have ruled that juveniles are not "persons."

Like other minorities, young people are more likely than the adult majority to be arrested, convicted, and incarcerated for extremely minor offenses, and in fact many delinquent careers are sparked by an early arrest for a relatively minor offense such as runaway, truancy, incorrigibility, or curfew—something that would not have been an offense for an adult. Young people in school are subject to a relatively repressive, coercive regime of external constraint and control that contrasts sharply with the relative freedom, responsibility, and independence that adults in our society have. This restrictive, externally controlled round of life for young people in schools has been sardonically characterized by Gerald Farber:

> Students are niggers. When you get that straight, our schools begin to make sense. . . . At Cal State L.A., where I teach, the students have separate and unequal dining facilities. . . . A student at Cal State is expected to know his place. He calls a faculty member "Sir" or "Doctor" or "Professor"—and he smiles and shuffles some as he stands outside the professor's office waiting for permission to enter. . . . What school amounts to, then, for white and black alike, is a twelve-year course in how to be slaves. . . . What makes this particularly grim is that the student has less chance than the black man to get out of his bag . . . because the student doesn't even know he's in it.[1]

The minority group perspective helps us to understand that many of the problems that develop in youth are an expression of that minority group status. The educational sequence from childhood to young adulthood can be seen as a process that develops youth into a deviant minority. As young people go through school, they become increasingly aware of their powerless position in society. In high school they have acquired many of the attributes of a minority group, however unselfconscious. The adolescent subculture in high school is highly independent of the adult world. Like other minority group subcultures, they develop a myth of their own eliteness and superiority, but the truth is that their microsocial system is a world of make believe, characterized by the materialistic values of adult society writ large. The themes of sophistication, sex, cars, and athletic prowess are direct manifestations of the adult value system. Hostility, at this stage, is not directed toward adults but rather toward other youth. Delinquency at the early high school stage is largely the product of competition among different groups for in-group status on the campus. At this stage they are not yet rebelling against the adult social system; rather they are acting out their version of the adult game, perhaps with an eye to their future status in society.

After graduation from high school, many young people are absorbed through employment or military service into adult society, which usually ends any delinquent impulses that may have occurred during adolescence because it ends the oppression that accompanies and characterizes minority status. The employee, respectable, well paid, is now a member of the majority. He can now do many of the things that before were illegal or that required parental consent: he can marry, vote, make contracts, drink, and do pretty much as he wishes. With this ascension to adult status, he generally loses contact with the adolescent social system and with it the impulse toward any expressive delinquency.

For other youngsters it is different. Some carry on their education, which usually only defers integration into adult society. Others join the disproportionate number of youth who are unemployed, or continue their education in a noncareer-oriented curriculum. These form the core of what has been termed "the youth culture," a subculture of young adults alienated against adult society and deliberately anti-adult in their values. This development in late high school and college marks the emergence of youth as a self-conscious deviant minority.

Youth culture participants are those young people who have become aware of the low place of youth in society either directly—through school expulsion, juvenile court sanction, or failure to obtain employment—or indirectly—through reading and reflection. The most visible result is the development of highly self-conscious political action groups on and off college campuses. These politicized deviant minority groups, through self-awareness, redirect the aggressive tendencies of young people away from themselves and toward the adult establishment. Such organizations as the Black Panthers, US, and the Nation of Islam in the black community and the Brown Berets in the Mexican-American community are politicized youth groups led by highly intelligent, self-aware, revolutionary leaders who, at least in their rhetoric, try to direct aggressions toward the Establishment rather than toward other youth groups (a principle that is occasionally violated). On college campuses, the development of political self-awareness and revolt against adult society are embodied in organizations such as SDS (Students for a Democratic Society), SNCC (Student Nonviolent Coordinating Committee), MDM (Movement for a Democratic Military), the Yippies (Youth International Party), Women's Liberation, Grass Roots Society, Friends of Black Panthers, and the like.

The readings in this chapter treat the emergence of youth's self-awareness from early high school through college years. The first excerpt, from the report of the President's Commission on Law Enforcement and Administration of Justice, portrays the adolescent social system of early high school and analyzes the problems that result from poverty and unemployment among youth. The second excerpt, from the U.S. Department of Labor *Manpower Report to the President, 1968*, documents the severity of unemployment in and after high school. The third reading, drawn from the report of the President's Commission on Campus Unrest, describes revolting college youth and concludes that they are a valid social movement, protesting the repression they are subject to in our society. Several theories discrediting the youth movement as "outside agitators," "hoodlums with no respect for law and order," and the like are debunked. The report concludes that the main causes of campus disorder are society's efforts to silence legitimate protests against "youthism"—the acts of police and teachers that attempt to prohibit young people from regulating their own conduct both in and outside of school. It describes the youth movement as a "counterculture" with totems and values—long hair, dirt, marijuana, and communal living—deliberately the opposite of those at work in adult society, and shows that there is a direct analogue between the tactics of violent youth groups and those of other militant minorities. The last part of the chapter, drawn from *The Walker Report*, shows how the police, the agents of adult society, deal with the expression of these countercultural values in a fashion appallingly similar to police reaction to the protests of black and brown minorities.

Adolescence as a Depressed Status

Juvenile Delinquency and Youth Crime

YOUTH IN THE COMMUNITY

The typical delinquent operates in the company of his peers, and delinquency thrives on group support. It has been estimated that between 60 and 90 percent of all delinquent acts are committed with companions.[2] That fact alone makes youth groups of central concern in consideration of delinquency prevention.

It is clear that youth groups are playing a more and more important part in the transition between childhood and adulthood. For young people today that transition is a long period of waiting, during which they are expected to be seriously preparing themselves for participation at some future date in a society that meanwhile provides no role for them and withholds both the toleration accorded children and the responsibilities of adults.[3] Some young people, however, lack the resources for becoming prepared; they see the goal but have not the means to reach it. Others are resentful and impatient with the failure of their stodgy elders to appreciate the contributions they feel ready to make. Many, slum dwellers and suburbanites both, feel victimized by the moral absolutes of the adult society—unexplained injunctions about right and wrong that seem to have little relevance in a complex world controlled by people employing multiple and shifting standards. Youth today accuse those ahead of them of phoniness and of failure to define how to live both honorably and successfully in a world that is changing too rapidly for anyone to comprehend.[4]

The very rapidity of that change is making it ever more difficult for young people to envision the type of work they might wish to commit themselves to, more difficult for them to find stable adult

From the President's Commission on Law Enforcement and Administration of Justice, *Task Force Report: Juvenile Delinquency and Youth Crime* (Washington: U.S. Government Printing Office, 1967), Chap. 2, pp. 47–52, 54–55.

models with whom to identify.[5] To fill the vacuum, they turn increasingly to their own age mates. But the models of dress and ideal and behavior that youth subcultures furnish may lead them into conflict with their parents' values and efforts to assert control. It has been suggested that, besides being more dependent on each other, youth today are also more independent of adults; parents and their young adolescents increasingly seem to live in different and at times antagonistic worlds. That antagonism sometimes explodes in antisocial acts.

Most of the youngsters who rebel at home and at school seek security and recognition among their fellows on the street. Together they form tightly knit groups in the decisions of which they are able to participate and the authority of which they accept as virtually absolute. Their attitudes, dress, tastes, ambitions, behavior, pastimes are those of the group.[6]

While the members are still young—before and during their early teens—such groups engage with apparent abandon and indifference in whatever seems like fun, delinquent and nondelinquent. Only some of what they do is seriously violent or destructive. Frequently, however, adults see even their minor misdeeds as malicious and defiant and label the actors troublemakers. The affixing of that label can be a momentous occurrence in a youngster's life. Thereafter he may be watched; he may be suspect; his every misstep may be seen as further evidence of his delinquent nature. He may be excluded more and more from legitimate activities and opportunities. Soon he may be designated and dealt with as a delinquent and will find it very difficult to move onto a law-abiding path even if he can overcome his own belligerent reaction and negative self-image and seeks to do so.[7]

Being labeled a troublemaker is a danger of growing up in suburbia as well as in the slums, but the suburbs are more likely to provide parental intervention and psychiatrists, pastors, family counselors to help the youth abandon his undesirable identity. It is much harder for the inner-city youth to find alternatives to a rebel role. Thus it is in the slums that youth gangs are most likely to drift from minor and haphazard into serious, repeated, purposeful delinquency.

It is in the slums, too, that young people are most likely to be exposed to the example of the successful career criminal as a person of prestige in the community.[8] To a population denied access to traditional positions of status and achievement, a successful criminal may be a highly visible model of power and affluence and a center of training and recruitment for criminal enterprise.

> *Johnny D. * * * was about the hippest cat on Eighth Avenue* * * *. *He was a man* * * * 21 * * *. *Johnny D. had been in jail since has was 17* * * *. *Johnny did everything. He used to sell all the horse [heroin] in the neighborhood* * * *. Everybody used to listen when he said something. It made sense to listen—he was doing some of everything, so he must have known what he was talking about* * * *. He sure seemed to know a lot of things. Johnny just about raised a lot of the cats around there* * * *
> Claude Brown, *Manchild in the Promised Land* (1965), pp. 104, 108–109.

Delinquent gangs are commonly blamed for much of the street crime that presently alarms the Nation. In fact, however, according to a detailed two-year study, recently completed, of the 700 members of 21 delinquent gangs, gang violence against persons is less frequent, less violent, and less uncontrolled than is generally believed. Only 17 percent of all the offenses recorded by observers included an element of violence, and about half of the violent offenses were committed against rival gang members. Much gang violence, in other words, appears to occur not against strangers but in attempts to achieve or preserve individual or gang status or territory.[9]

Many cities have sent youth workers into the streets to befriend gang boys and dissuade them from fighting. Street workers have often succeeded in their immediate objective of averting gang violence, but, with little more permanent to offer than bus trips and ball games, they have rarely managed to convert boys from total gang involvement to more socially acceptable pursuits.[10] Indeed, there are indications that street work has in some places had negative effects by creating a vacuum too likely to be filled by such destructive activities as using narcotics. Yet even the hard core delinquent whose gang is his life continues to share the conventional American belief that work and education are the right ways to get ahead in the world.[11]

DELINQUENCY AND THE SCHOOL

The complex relationship between the school and the child varies greatly from one school system to another. The process of education is dramatically different in the slum than in the middle-class suburb. The child and the problems he brings to school are different. The support for learning that he receives at home and in his neighborhood is different. The school systems themselves are very different. The slum school faces the greatest obstacles with the least resources, the least qualified personnel, the least adequate capability for effective education.

The school, unlike the family, is a public instrument for training young people. It is, therefore, more directly accessible to change through the development of new resources and policies. And since it is the principal public institution for the development of a basic commitment by young people to the goals and values of our society, it is imperative that it be provided with the resources to compete with illegitimate attractions for young people's allegiance. Anything less would be a serious failure to discharge our nation's responsibility to its youth.

The Commission recognizes that many in the field of education have identified the shortcomings of slum schools. The Commission recognizes too that in many places efforts are being made to improve various aspects of schools. But as a general matter our society has not yet been willing to devote resources sufficient for the radical changes necessary.

Recent research has related instances of delinquent conduct to the school-child relationship and to problems either created or complicated by schools themselves. First, in its own methods and practices, the school may simply be too passive to fulfill its obligations as one of the last social institutions with an opportunity to rescue the child from other forces, in himself and in his environment, which are pushing him toward delinquency. Second, there is considerable evidence that some schools may have an indirect effect on delinquency by the use of methods that create the conditions of failure for certain students. Mishandling by the school can lower the child's motivation to learn. It can aggravate his difficulty in accepting authority and generate or intensify hostility and alienation. It can sap the child's confidence, dampen his initiative, and lead him to negative definitions of himself as a failure or an "unacceptable" person.

Some schools, particularly in the poorest areas, are unable to deal with children who are neither ready nor able to learn. Asserting demands for performance that the child cannot meet, the frustrated teacher may become hostile and the child indifferent, apathetic, or hostile in turn. If the child is also rebelling at home, the effect is more immediate and the confrontation becomes intolerable to all. The too-usual result is that the child turns to other things that have nothing to do with academic learning, and the school finds a way to ignore him or push him out so the rest of its work can continue.

The following discussion attempts to identify ways in which some schools may be contributing directly or indirectly to the behavior problems of children and to assess the capacity of schools to prevent and manage such problems. In formulating its recommendations, the Commission has had the benefit of advice and assistance from the Office of Education in the Department of Health, Education, and Welfare.[12]

THE EDUCATIONALLY HANDICAPPED CHILD

Children enter the school system already shaped by their earlier experiences—many of them already handicapped in their potential for educational achievement.[13] The educational handicaps that seem most closely related to delinquency appear in the slum child.

He comes from a home in which books and other artifacts of intellectual accomplishment are rare. His parents, while they care about his education, are themselves too poorly schooled to give him the help and encouragement he needs. They have not had the time—even had they the knowledge—to teach him basic skills that are milestones painlessly passed by most middle-class youngsters: telling time, counting, saying the alphabet, learning colors, using crayons and paper and paint. He is unaccustomed to verbalizing concepts or ideas. Written communication may be rare in his experience.

It is sometimes assumed that the parents of children in slum neighborhoods do not value education. In fact, there is persuasive evidence of their commitment to an adequate education for their children.[14] Similarly, the youngsters themselves care a great deal about education. Indeed, there are indications that Negro and lower income students place a higher value on education than do white and higher income ones.[15]

But whether he and his parents value education or not, the tide of life soon begins to run against success in school for the child from the ghetto. Sordid surroundings, harsh or missing discipline, having to fight for what he wants, and taking over (far too soon) control of his own comings and goings—all adversely affect the odds against

67

him. To some extent, of course, these problems are also encountered in the middle-class school, but there they are usually less extreme, and there is a greater likelihood of useful assistance through counseling, guidance, special tutoring, or some other form of individual help.

THE SLUM SCHOOL

The manner in which the school system responds to the educational problems that the child brings with him is of extraordinary importance. It must be able to recognize these problems and to direct a battery of resources toward them.

Stimulated by the poverty program, recent and extensive studies have been made of the educational problems of children reared in slum communities. It has been clearly demonstrated that the educational system in the slums is less well equipped than its nonslum counterpart to deal with the built-in learning problems of the children who come to it. Schools in the slums have the most outdated and dilapidated buildings, the fewest texts and library books, the least experienced full-time teachers, the least qualified substitute teachers, the most overcrowded classrooms, and the least developed counseling and guidance services in the Nation.[16]

The inadequacies of facilities and teaching resources are aggravated by the slum school's increasing segregation, both racial and economic. Despite efforts to combat and prevent segregation, central cities are growing increasingly nonwhite and poor, suburban areas increasingly white and affluent. Educational achievement is generally lower among nonwhite lower income students, and so racial and economic segregation in the schools has the circular effect of exposing nonwhite lower income students to inferior examples of educational achievement. There is substantial evidence that the achievements and aspirations of students are strongly related to the educational backgrounds and performances of other students in their school,[17] and that nonwhite lower income students do better when placed in mixed or middle-class schools. Chief Justice Warren enunciated one destructive effect of racial segregation in Brown v. Board of Education of Topeka, the landmark school desegregation decision:

> To separate them from others of similar age and qualifications solely because of their race generates a feeling of inferiority as to their status in the community that may affect their hearts and

minds in a way unlikely ever to be undone. Social and economic separation compound the educational obstacles of racial segregation in many schools today.

The deficiencies of the slum school are further aggravated by a wide-spread belief that the intellectual capability of most slum children is too limited to allow much education. As a result standards are lowered to meet the level the child is assumed to occupy. Frequently the chance to stimulate latent curiosity and excitement about learning is irretrievably lost, and the self-fulfilling prophecy of apathy and failure comes true.[18]

It is increasingly apparent that grouping procedures often operate in this way. Children with educationally deprived backgrounds are often grouped on the basis of achievement of "ability" tests with built-in cultural biases.[19] The assumption is then made that these children lack ability, and standards are lowered accordingly. Thus, while grouping methods are designed to help tailor curriculum to individual needs and abilities, and while such methods could be valuable in channeling efforts to help educationally deprived children make up for lack of preparation, too frequently they are administered with a rigidity and oversimplification that intensify rather than ameliorate the slum child's learning problems.[20]

These problems are further reinforced by the lack of relationship between the instructional material usually provided by slum schools and the social, economic and political conditions of living in the slums.[21] To the youngster, the instruction seems light years away from the circumstances and facts of life that surround him every day. The following comments of a former delinquent are illuminating:

> It wasn't interesting to me, I liked the science books but I didn't dig the other stuff. Dick and Jane went up the hill to fetch a pail of water and all that crap. Mary had a little lamb. Spot jumped over the fence. See Spot jump over the fence. * * * I say, ain't this the cutest little story. And I took the book one day and shoved it straight back to the teacher and said I ain't going to read that stuff.
>
> When I took the test I think I was four point something so I was real low in English, but I mostly got all my English listening in the streets, from listening to people. I didn't pick up my

69

English mostly from school. (Can you read now?) I can read something that I am really interested in.

(Going back to junior high, what kind of things would you have liked to read, that would have made you interested?) Well, I could see Dick and Jane when I was in elementary school, but in junior high school I was ready to know about life, about how it really is out there. In elementary school it's painted like it is beautiful, everything is beautiful. (In a sing-song.) Get your education and you can go somewhere. I didn't want to hear that no more, because I had seen my brother go through the same thing. He quit school, he ain't making it. So I wanted to know, okay how can I get somewhere if I go to school. How is life in general? How is the government run? What's in the government right now that makes it hard for young people that graduate from high school to get somewhere? Why is it that people are fighting each other in the United States? Why is it that people can't communicate with each other? Society in general—what is it that society has said that we have to follow? How is the police structure set up? Why is the police hard on youth?

These are all the things I would have loved to learn in school. (Is that the way you think now or the way you thought then?) I used to want to know about the government. How it was structured. I wanted to learn how it was run—really. Back then I didn't know people were marching for their rights. I didn't know about that. (When did you find out?) In the streets.[22]

The slum child often feels a similar lack of relationship between school and his future in the adult world:

(What kind of school program were you doing? Vocational education?) Yeah, vocational training. (Did that prepare you for a job?) It was supposed to prepare me for a job but it didn't. (Did you try to get a job?) Yeah, I tried to get a job. The men said I wasn't qualified. (Did you think while you were in school that you would get a job?) That's right—that's why I stayed in school so I could get a job upon completion of high school because they put so much emphasis on getting a high school diploma.

"If you get a high school diploma, you can do this and you can do this, without it you can't do this." And I got one and I still can't do nothing. I can't get a job or nothing after I got one. [Ex-delinquent.][23]

There is evidence that many students become disillusioned earlier than this young man. Many students who are not taking college preparatory work seem to believe that regardless of their efforts or achievement, the system will not come through with anything but low status, low paying jobs after high school.[24] Present tasks and demands of the school therefore have little meaning or payoff. That problem, to be sure, lies not only in the schools' failure to prepare students adequately for the future, but also in the absence of adequate and equal employment opportunity. The U.S. Department of Labor[25] has shown that a Negro high school graduate has a greater chance of being unemployed than a white high school dropout—a subject dealt with in greater detail below.

Too often, as a result of the virtual absence of relation between it and the life he is living or will live, the school cannot hold the slum child's interest. It is boring, dull, and apparently useless, to be endured for a while and then abandoned as a bad deal.

FAILURE IN SCHOOL AND DELINQUENCY: THE DOWNWARD SPIRAL OF FAILURE

When the school system is not adequately equipped to meet the early learning problems a child brings to school with him, a cycle of deterioration and failure may be set in motion. As the youngster is "promoted" from grade to grade to keep him with his age mates but before he has really mastered his tasks, failure becomes cumulative. While he may have been only half a year behind the average in fourth grade, for example, recent evidence shows that the achievement gap may widen to three quarters of a year by sixth grade and to one-and-one-quarter years by eighth grade.[26]

The school failure, especially if he has developed a tough, indifferent façade, may give the impression that he does not care about his conspicuous failure to "make out" in school. In fact he probably cares a great deal, and even if the academic failure itself does not much matter to him, the loss of others' esteem does. He finds himself labeled a slow learner or a "goof-off." The school typically reacts to

71

his failure with measures that reinforce his rejection: by assigning him to a special class for slow students, by excluding him from participation in extracurricular activities, by overlooking him in assigning prestigious school tasks and responsibilities.[27]

The child, in self-defense, reacts against the school, perhaps openly rebelling against its demands.[28] He and others like him seek each other out. Unable to succeed in being educated, they cannot afford to admit that education is important. Unwilling to accept the school's humiliating evaluation of them, they begin to flaunt its standards and reject its long-range goals in favor of conduct more immediately gratifying.

That conduct may not at first be seriously delinquent, but it represents a push toward more destructive and criminal patterns of behavior. Moreover, it takes forms, such as repeated truancy, that end hope of improved academic achievement. It may lead to dropping out of school.

There is mounting evidence that delinquency and failure in school are correlated. For example, in comparison of a group of A and B students with a group of C and D ones (both working and middle class), the C and D ones were seven times more likely to be delinquent; boys from blue-collar backgrounds who failed in school have been found to be delinquent almost seven times more often than those who did not fail.[29]

It is of course difficult if not impossible to separate the part played by some schools from the innumerable other forces that may be related to the development of delinquent behavior. But both common sense and data such as these support the view that the high degree of correlation between delinquency and failure in school is more than accidental.

SCHOOL RESPONSE TO BEHAVIOR PROBLEMS

Student misbehavior is a real and urgent problem in many slum schools. Much youthful obstreperousness is best understood as a process of "testing" those in authority and demonstrating—partly for the benefit of peers—one's toughness and masculinity.[30] For many inner-city children, the teacher represents the first real challenge to their independence. While middle-class children, accustomed to the close supervision of parents or parent substitutes, defer almost automatically to the authority of the teacher, the slum child arrives at school in the habit of being his own master and is not about to surrender his autonomy upon demand.

The way in which the school responds to early signs of misbehavior may have a profound influence in either diverting the youngster from or propelling him along the path to a delinquent career. Not all teachers have trouble with "difficult" youngsters. Some, especially sensitive to what lies behind insolence and disobedience, adopt a firm but positive attitude that allows the task of learning to be carried on, if not always under placid conditions.

❋   ❋   ❋

Other teachers simply submit, ignoring as best they can commotions and disruptions of classroom routine—an alternative that avoids head-on conflict with autonomy-seeking youth but at the same time deprives them of instruction even when they choose to accept it.

❋   ❋   ❋

Many teachers, on the other hand, assume a right to unquestioning obedience. There results a sometimes ceaseless conflict between teacher and child. The child's assertions of autonomy are dealt with by the teacher, and eventually the school administration, as misbehavior, and sanctioned in a variety of ways. By labeling the youth a troublemaker and excluding him from legitimate activities and sources of achievement, the sanctions may reinforce his tendency to rebel and resist the school's authority. Nor is it easy for him to reform; grades lowered for misconduct, the stigma of assignment to a special class, and records of misbehavior passed on both formally and informally from teacher to teacher make his past difficult to live down. The conception he forms of himself as an outsider, a nonconformer, is of particular importance. With no other source of public recognition, such negative self-images become attractive to some young people,[31] and they begin to adapt their behavior to fit the labels applied to them. A process of defining and communicating a public character occurs, and some young people in a sense cooperate in actually becoming the delinquents they are said to be.

DELINQUENCY AND EMPLOYMENT

Growing up properly is difficult at best, but manageable with help at times of critical need. To become a fully functional adult male, one prerequisite is essential: a job. In our society a person's occupation determines more than anything else what life he will lead and how others will regard him. Of course other important factors—family, wealth, race, age—exert significant influence on his future. But for most young men, it is securing jobs consistent with their aspirations that is crucial, that provides a stake in the law-abiding world and a vestibule to an expanding series of opportunities: to marry, to raise a family, to participate in civic affairs, to advance economically and socially and intellectually.

Getting a good job is harder than it used to be for those without preparation. To be a Negro, an 18-year-old, a school dropout in the slums of a large city is to have many times more chance of being unemployed than has a white 18-year-old high school graduate living a few blocks away. Poorly educated, untrained youth from 16 to 21 years of age are becoming the Nation's most stubborn employment problem, especially in the large cities. Our current economy simply does not need the skills and personal attributes they have to offer.

YOUTH AND THE LABOR MARKET OF THE FUTURE[32]

Between 1960 and 1970 the available labor force is expected to rise by more than 1.5 million persons a year, an average annual increase nearly 50 percent greater than that which occurred during the first half of the 1960s and almost double that of the 1950s. Young workers, aged 14 to 24, will constitute nearly half (about 45 percent) of this increase.

One sign of greater difficulties ahead is the rising ratio of nonwhite workers joining the labor force—the workers who suffer most from lack of adequate education and training, shortage of unskilled jobs, and discriminatory barriers to employment. Between 1965 and 1970, the number of nonwhite youth reaching 18 will increase by 20 percent over the 1965 level. During the same period, the white population in the same age group will actually decrease, and will not regain the 1965 figure of 3.3 million until 1970. During the five-year period after that, the number of nonwhite 18-year-olds will again increase by 20 percent while the number of white 18-year-olds will increase by only 10 percent.

And young people compose the category of workers with the highest unemployment rate. In 1965 the average unemployment rates for youth between 16 and 24 decreased somewhat from the peak reached in 1963. But the unemployment rate of youth aged 16 to 21 was over 12.5 percent, two and one-half times that for all workers. The 1.1 million young people unemployed represented, therefore, one-third of the jobless workers in the country, and for them the familiar syndrome—minority group member, school dropout, unemployed—holds stubbornly true. Of the 26 million young people who will enter the labor force during the 1960s, an estimated 25 percent will not have completed high school. Only 45 percent will be high school graduates. Only 26 percent will have graduated from or even attended college.

EMPLOYMENT AND EMPLOYABILITY

Any young person meets a number of problems when he sets out to find a job. He must learn where and how to look, decide what to look for and, finally, make himself acceptable. If he is a school dropout or has a delinquency record, those problems are significantly more serious.

It is commonplace today to observe that educational preparation is increasingly required for getting and holding a steady job. One would expect, therefore, that dropping out of school and being unemployed might be related to each other. Undereducated youngsters are eligible only for unskilled jobs; it is hard for them to get information about the local job market; they lack prior work experience.[33] Most of them, consequently, do not in any real sense choose a job. Rather, they drift into one. And since such jobs rarely meet the aspirations that applicants bring with them, frustration typically results.

The search for a job may be even more discouraging when the young person has a delinquency record. There is evidence that many employers make improper use of records. A juvenile's adjudication record is required by the law of most jurisdictions to be private and confidential; in practice the confidentiality of these records is often violated. The employment application may require the applicant to state whether he was ever arrested or taken into custody, or employers may ask juvenile applicants to sign waivers permitting the court to release otherwise confidential information.

Many employers also inquire as to all arrests, whether or not a conviction resulted. About 75 percent of the employment agencies sampled in a recent study of employment practices in the New York City area stated that they ask applicants about arrest records and, as a matter of regular procedure, do not refer to any applicant with a record, regardless of whether the arrest was followed by conviction.[34] The standard U.S. Government employment application form (Form 57) has just recently been modified to ask for information concerning only those arrests that were followed by conviction, rather than all arrests as previously. The fact that the majority of slum males (estimates vary from 50 to 90 percent) have some sort of arrest record indicates the magnitude of this problem.

The delinquency label may preclude membership in labor unions or participation in apprenticeship training. Licensing requirements for some occupations, such as barbering and food service, may act as a bar to entry for those with a record of delinquent conduct.

THE EFFECT OF UNEMPLOYMENT

It does not take the slum youth long to discover the gap between what he had hoped for and thought he was entitled to as an American and what actually awaits him; and it is a bitter as well as an oft repeated experience. So he looks for some other way out.

The career decisions of these youths, and the reasons for them, are varied; many are not really decisions at all. Some find their way back to school or into a job training program. Some drift among low paying jobs. Those who have good connections with organized criminal enterprises may feel few restraints against following a career that, although illegitimate, is relatively safe and lucrative; they have seen many others thrive on the proceeds of vice, and it will not be hard for them to persuade themselves that the steady demand for illicit goods and services justifies providing them. Others try theft; some become good enough at it to make it their regular livelihood; others lack aptitude or connections and become failures in the illegal as well as the legal world—habitués of our jails and prisons. Finally, there are those who give up, retreat from conventional society, and search for a better world in the private fantasies they can command from drink and drugs.[35]

THE TRANSMISSION OF POVERTY FROM ONE GENERATION TO THE NEXT

Lack of educational preparation, an economy that does not need the young, availability of illicit "jobs," the effect of having an arrest record—all these decrease the slum youth's employment opportunities and increase his chances of becoming or continuing delinquent. Basic to the economics of delinquency is the transmission of poverty across the generations. Today, for the 18-year-old, employment is hard to find. What chance has a slum-dwelling six-year-old to break out of the cycle of poverty? Individual initiative may be important in determining an individual's destiny, but it is the economic and social forces shaping the way children are brought up, their preparation for adulthood by public institutions, their chances for self-improvement that perpetuate poverty.

The neighborhood in which the six-year-old has been growing up is disorganized and has a high rate of delinquency. His father may be struggling to support a large family on a low wage or, jobless, may have left or deserted his family. Chronic dependency of families is further reinforced by the failure of welfare laws to provide economic incentives for fathers to remain in the home.

The six-year-old now enters school. Although his parents value education, they realistically enough have little expectation that he will advance very far, and they have neither time nor skill to aid him. The slum school, as discussed above, is incapable of picking up the burden. He leaves school, or is pushed out at age 16, educationally unprepared, often already with an arrest record. He marries early or fathers illegitimate children. The cycle continues.

In earlier times, when muscle power was enough to earn a living, his slum-dwelling predecessors could with less difficulty break out of the cycle of poverty. A better job meant a chance to move into a better neighborhood. The better neighborhood was less crowded, had better schools, better social services. The poverty circle was broken, and, as shown by studies like McKay's, . . . delinquency rates were concomitantly reduced. The new American "immigrants" have much greater difficulty escaping the city's high-delinquency areas. They are confined there by the new economics of the job market and the old coin of racial prejudice. The ghettos expand, the citizen fears crime, the summer brings riots, and no less than the future of America's cities is threatened.

Underemployment of Youth

Manpower Report to the President, 1968

THE GAP FROM SCHOOL TO WORK

The essence of the problem is reflected in the paradox that emerges from the following two positions: The United States keeps larger proportions of its children in school longer than does any other nation, to insure their preparation for lifetime activity. Yet the unemployment rate among youth is far higher here than in any other industrial nation and had been rising sharply until the introduction of the Government's youth programs over the last four years.

Unemployment rates among youth, while highest for those in low-income minority group families, are substantially higher in all income groups than those considered desirable by any concept of acceptable unemployment rates that has been developed in our Nation. Thus, youth in the 14- to 19-year-old bracket from families with incomes of less than $3000 have unemployment rates of 17.4 percent, an extraordinarily high level. But even youth from families with incomes of $10,000 and over have unemployment rates of 7.7 percent—rates that are about double the national average and quadruple the rates of adults.

The differentials between youth and adult unemployment rates have persisted despite marked improvements in the overall employment situation. Examination of the character and dimensions of youth programs undertaken in the last four years, of the rise in youth unemployment rates before that, and of the demographic and economic factors at work suggests that the introduction of these special programs has been a key factor in keeping youth unemployment rates from rising even further in relation to adult rates.

The pattern of high unemployment rates among youth has become more pronounced in recent years. Though some differential be-

From U.S. Department of Labor, *Manpower Report of the President, 1968* (Washington, D.C.: U.S. Government Printing Office, 1968), pp. 111–14.

tween adult and youth rates has existed for decades, the gap has widened with the passage of time. . . .

While unemployment rates give some indication of why the school-to-work problem commands public attention, they are by no means the sole indicator of its dimensions. Unemployment rates do not reflect discouraged abstention from the job market, underemployment, or frustrating occupational misfits that may lead to quits and unemployment—problems on which there is, as yet, no adequate information. . . .

The youth for whom bridges to work are now most adequate are those with the intensive preparation provided by professional training at the college level or beyond. For them, careers are virtually assured and unemployment is at or very close to minimum levels. In fact, in many specialties there are numerous opportunities open for people with professional training. But sizable proportions of all other groups of youth—high school dropouts, high school graduates, and college dropouts—face serious uncertainties as they leave the academic world and begin the work for which school was to have prepared them.

The tremendous advantage college graduates have in entering the world of work can be seen from the unemployment rates for young adults. In March 1967, for example, 20- to 24-year-olds with a college degree had an unemployment rate of only 1.4 percent, compared with 5.3 percent for those with a high school diploma, and a completely unacceptable 10.5 percent for those who had completed only eight years of school.

Vocational preparation at the secondary and postsecondary levels has been progressively strengthened, however, under the impetus of the Vocational Education Act of 1963. This act has made possible extensive improvements in both the quantity and quality of vocational education offerings, which should mean better job preparation for many youth.

The problem of building bridges between school and work involves many fundamental elements in American life in addition to educational preparation. No one institution has or can have sole responsibility for helping youth to prepare for and make the transition from school to work without unreasonable and discouraging spells of unemployment. Some young people get help from teachers; some get help from school counselors, especially "if they are college material" and will therefore cross into the work world with greater ease at a later point. Many are placed by the Employment Service system. Others get help from social workers, police, neighborhood centers, youth programs, or individual employers to whom they apply. Personal contact (through acquaintances, friends, and relatives), which has always been a strong feature of the·job market in this country, is one of the most frequent ways of finding jobs. . . .

Recent studies suggest that we do not fully ·understand what the function of the parent is in preparing children for work, whether through education, training, or other means. Nor do we know what this parental activity contributes to the nation's economy. The importance of parental influence in determining the ultimate place of the child in society is suggested by various census data relating the education of parents to the education of their children. Where the father had graduated from high school, about 87 percent of sons aged 25 to 34 were also graduates. On the other hand, where the father did not graduate from high school, less than 60 percent of sons in this age group received high school diplomas. . . .

The need to supplement the activities of the parents through various parent-surrogate activities such as Head Start cannot be overestimated. Services that middle and upper income families provide their children as a matter of course are all too often missing in the low-income home. The availability of adequate substitutes may help break the intergenerational chains of poverty for many children from disadvantaged environments.

College and the Emergence of Youth as a Militant Minority

Report of the President's Commission on Campus Unrest

THE CAUSES OF STUDENT PROTEST

Our purpose in this chapter is to identify the causes of student protest and to ascertain what these causes reveal about its nature. Our subject is primarily the protest of white students, for although they have much in common with black, Chicano, and other minority student protest movements, these latter are nevertheless fundamentally different in their goals, their intentions, and their sources. In Chapter 3 we consider the special case of the black student movement.

We find that campus unrest has many causes, that several of these are not within the control of individuals or of government, and that some of these causes have worked their influence in obscure or indirect ways. Identifying them all is difficult, but they do exist and must be sought—not in order to justify or condemn, but rather because no rational response to campus unrest is possible until its nature and causes have been fully understood.

Race, the war, and the defects of the modern university have contributed to the development of campus unrest, have given it specific focus, and continue to lend it a special intensity. But they are neither the only nor even the most important causes of campus unrest.

Of far greater moment have been the advance of American society into the postindustrial era, the increasing affluence of American society, and the expansion and intergenerational evolution of

From the President's Commission on Campus Unrest, *Report of the President's Commission on Campus Unrest* (Washington: U.S. Government Printing Office, 1970), pp. 51–88.

liberal idealism. Together, these have prompted the formation of a new youth culture that defines itself through a passionate attachment to principle and an equally passionate opposition to the larger society. At the center of this culture is a romantic celebration of human life, of the unencumbered individual, of the senses, and of nature. It rejects what it sees to be the operational ideals of American society: materialism, competition, rationalism, technology, consumerism, and militarism. This emerging culture is the deeper cause of student protest against war, racial injustice, and the abuses of the multiversity.

During the past decade, this youth culture has developed rapidly. It has become ever more distinct and has acquired an almost religious fervor through a process of advancing personal commitment. This process has been spurred by the emergence within the larger society of opposition both to the youth culture itself and to its demonstrations of political protest. As such opposition became manifest—and occasionally violently manifest—participants in the youth culture felt challenged, and their commitment to that culture and to the political protest it prompts grew stronger and bolder. Over time, more and more students have moved in the direction of an ever deeper and more inclusive sense of opposition to the larger society. As their alienation became more profound, their willingness to use violence increased.

American student protest, like the student protest which is prevalent around the world, thus signifies a broad and intense reaction against—and a possible future change in—modern Western society and its organizing institutions. It thus appears to define a broad crisis of values with which the American people must now begin to cope.

Given that campus unrest reflects such broad historical forces and causes, it is perhaps not surprising that most Americans find student protest as puzzling as they obviously do.

Most Americans believe that protest comes only from groups which suffer injustice and economic privation: yet white student protestors come predominantly from affluent families, attend the better and the larger universities, and have ready access to the highest rewards and positions that American society can offer. Most Americans believe that protest arises only when the conditions at issue are getting sharply worse: yet the trend of American society, as most Americans see it, is one of progress, albeit sometimes slow, toward the reforms students seek—in personal income, in housing, in health, in equal opportunity, in civil liberties, and even in the national involvement with the war. And finally, most Americans believe that an authentic idealism expresses itself only in peaceful and humane ways: yet although students do manifest a high idealism, some student protest reveals in its tactical behavior a contrary tendency toward intolerance, disruption, criminality, destruction, and violence.

Thus, many Americans consider campus unrest to be an aberration from the moral order of American society. They treat it as a problem that derives from some moral failing on the part of some individual or group. The explanations of campus unrest that they adopt therefore tend to be single-cause explanations that clearly allocate blame and that specify remedies which are within the capacity of individuals, public opinion, or government to provide. Three such explanations enjoy particular popularity today.

One explanation attributes campus unrest to the machinations of outside agitators and subversive propagandists.

It is clear that in some cases of campus disruption, agitators and professional revolutionaries have been on the scene doing whatever they could do to make dangerous situations worse. It also is true that some of the most violent and destructive actions (such, perhaps, as the bombing in Madison, Wisconsin, this summer) are attributable to the influence, if not the actions, of small, trained, and highly mobile groups of revolutionaries. But it is equally clear that such agitators are not "the" cause of most large-scale campus protest and disorders. Agitators take advantage of preexisting tensions and seek to exacerbate them. But except for individual acts of terrorism, agitation and agitators cannot succeed if an atmosphere of tension, frustration, and dissent does not already pervade the campus. If agitation has contributed to campus unrest—and clearly, in various ways, it has—it has done so only because such an atmosphere has existed. What, then, created this atmosphere? The "agitator" theory cannot answer this question.

A second popular school of explanation holds that the atmosphere of dissent and frustration on campuses is the result of the pressing and unresolved issues which deeply concern many students. Clearly such issues do exist and do arouse deep feeling. Yet the conditions to which the issues have reference are in most cases not new ones. Why, then, have these issues recently emerged as objects of student protest and as sources of campus tension? And why has that protest become increasingly disruptive and violent? The "issues" theory does not answer these questions.

The third popular school of explanation argues that campus unrest is caused by an increasing disrespect for law and by a general erosion of all stabilizing institutions—a weakening of family (especially by "permissive" methods of child rearing), church, school, and patriotism. To some degree and in some areas, such an erosion of the stabilizing institutions in American society has indeed taken place. Yet we must ask: Why has this erosion taken place? The "breakdown of law" theory does not have an answer.

The basic difficulty with these explanations is that they begin by assuming that all campus unrest is a problem—a problem whose cause is a moral failure on the part of students or of society or of government, and which therefore has a specifiable solution. The search for causes is thus inseparable from the allocation of blame and the advocacy of some course of public action. As a result, causes which are not within human control or which do not lay the mantle of culpability upon specifiable individuals or groups tend to be ignored. Such "explanations" do not really explain. They only make campus unrest more bewildering—and more polarizing—than it need be.

In and of itself, campus unrest is not a "problem" and requires no "solution." The existence of dissenting opinion and voices is simply a social condition, a fact of modern life; the right of such opinion to exist is protected by our Constitution. Protest that is violent or disruptive is, of course, a very real problem, and solutions must be found to end such manifestations of it. But when student protest stays within legal bounds, as it typically does, it is not a problem for government to cope with. It is simply a pattern of opinion and expression.

Campus unrest, then, is not a single or uniform thing. Rather it is the aggregate result, or sum, of hundreds and thousands of individual beliefs and discontents, each of them as unique as the individuals who feel them. These individual feelings reflect in turn a series of choices each person makes about what he will believe, what he will say, and what he will do. In the most immediate and operational sense, then, it is these choices—these *commitments*, to use a word in common usage among students—which are the proximate cause of campus unrest and which are the forces at work behind any physical manifestation of dissent.

These acts of individual commitment to certain values and to certain ways of seeing and acting in the world do not occur in a vacuum. They take place within, and are powerfully affected by, the conditions under which students live. We will call these conditions the contributing causes of campus unrest. Five broad orders of such contributing causes have been suggested in testimony before the Commission.

They are:

The pressing problems of American society, particularly the war in Southeast Asia and the conditions of minority groups;

The changing status and attitudes of youth in America;

The distinctive character of the American university during the postwar period;

An escalating spiral of reaction to student protest from public opinion and an escalating spiral of violence; and

Broad evolutionary changes occurring in the culture and structure of modern Western society.

ISSUES AND OPINIONS

The best place to begin any search for the causes of student protest is to consider the reasons which student protestors themselves offer for their activities. There are many such reasons, and students are not reluctant to articulate them. These reasons—these positions on the major national issues of the day—must be taken seriously.

We must recognize, however, that students express a keen interest in a large number of issues. Even in the course of a single reenactment of the Berkeley scenario, the issues which are identified and discussed, and which in some degree are the reasons for student participation, can number in the tens or scores.

For example, a protest against university expansion into the neighboring community and against university complicity in the Vietnam War may lead to university discipline. Discipline or amnesty may then become the issue. On this issue there is a larger and more disruptive protest. The police are called. Police brutality now becomes the issue, and the demand is that the university intercede to get students released. The university says this is a matter for the civil courts. It is now attacked as inhuman and soulless and dominated by the material interests of its trustees, who need police and courts to protect those interests. At this point a building goes up in flames. What was the issue?

One must distinguish therefore between primary issues and secondary issues, which arise from protest actions or from the primary issues themselves. Three great primary issues have been involved in the rising tide of student protest during the past decade.

Both historically and in terms of the relative frequency with which it is the focus of protest, the first great issue is also the central social and political problem of American society: the position of racial minorities, and of black people in particular. It was over this issue that student protest began in 1960.

As the decade passed, the definition of this issue changed. At first, it was defined in the South as the problem of legally enforced or protected patterns of segregation. Later, the focus shifted to the problems of extralegal discrimination against blacks, in the North as well as in the South—a definition of the issue which later was summarized in the phrase "institutional racism." By the middle of the decade, the issue had shifted again and now was understood as a problem of recovering the black's self-respect and pride in his cultural heritage.

The targets of protest have shifted accordingly. At first, there was protest against local merchants for not serving blacks, against local businesses for not employing them, and against the university for tolerating discrimination in sororities and fraternities. Soon there were protests against discrimination in university admissions, and demands that more be done to recruit blacks and that more be done to assist them once admitted. Black students demanded, too, that the university begin to give assistance to local black communities, that it establish a curriculum in black studies, and that it recruit more black faculty to teach courses in these and other areas. As the target of protest moved from the society at large to the university, it also widened to represent the aspirations of other minority groups, often in a "Third World" coalition.

The second great issue has been the war in Southeast Asia. The war was almost from the beginning a relatively unpopular war, one which college youth on the whole now consider a mistake and which many of them also consider immoral and evil. It has continued now for more than five years, and it has pressed especially on youth. During the last decade, the war issue was less commonly the object of student protest than were questions of race, but as the years went by it became more and more prominent among student concerns.

This issue has also changed form and has become more inclusive over the years: it moved from protesting American intervention, to protesting the draft, to protesting government and corporate recruiting for jobs related to war, and, increasingly, to protesting university involvement in any aspect of the war, such as releasing information to draft boards, allowing recruiters on campus, conducting defense research, and permitting the presence of ROTC on campus.

A third major protest issue has been the university itself. Though at times this issue has been expressed in protests over curriculum and the nonretention of popular teachers, the overwhelming majority of university-related protests have dealt with school regulations affecting students, with the role of students in making those regulations, and more generally with the quality of student life, living facilities, and food services. The same impulse moves students to denounce what they feel to be the general regimentation of American life by large-scale organizations and their byproducts—impersonal bureaucracy and the anonymous IBM card. University regulation of political activities—the issue at Berkeley in 1964—has also been a prominent issue.

Since 1965 there has been steady liberalization in the rules affecting student living quarters, disciplining of students, rules affecting controversial speakers, and dress rules. Increasingly, universities and colleges have incorporated students into the rulemaking process. Yet the issue has lost none of its power.

What students objected to about discrimination against blacks and other racial minorities was simple and basic: the unfeeling and unjustifiable deprivation of individual rights, dignity, and self-respect. And the targets of protest were those institutions which routinely deprived blacks of their rights, or which supported and reinforced such deprivation. These two themes—support for the autonomy, personal dignity, individuality, and life of each person, and bitter opposition to institutions, policies, and rationales which seemed to deprive individuals of those things—could also be seen in the other two main issues of the 1960s: the war in Southeast Asia, and university regulation of student life. They may also be seen in the emerging student concern over ecology and environmental pollution.

These three issues—racism, war, and the denial of personal free-doms—unquestionably were and still are contributing causes of stu-dent protest. Students have reacted strongly to these issues, speak about them with eloquence and passion, and act on them with great energy.

Moreover, students feel that government, the university, and other American institutions have not responded to their analysis of what should be done, or at least not responded rapidly enough. This has led many students to turn their attacks on the decision-making process itself. Thus, we hear slogans such as "power to the people."

And yet, having noted that these issues were causes, we must go on to note two further pertinent facts about student protest over race and war. First, excepting black students, it is impossible to attribute student opposition on these issues to cynical or narrow self-interest alone, as do those Americans who believe that students are against the war because they are cowards, afraid to die for a cause. But in fact, few students have been called upon to risk their lives in the present war. It is true that male students have been subject to the draft. But only a small portion of college youth have actually been drafted and sent to fight in Vietnam, and it is reported that, as compared to the nation's previous wars, relatively few col-lege graduates have been killed in this war. It is *noncollege* youth who fight in Vietnam, and yet it is college youth who oppose the war—while noncollege youth tend to support it more than other segments of the population.

It is the same in the case of race. For black and other minority college youth, it hardly needs explanation why they should find the cruel injustice of American racism a compelling issue, or why they should protest over it. Why it became an issue leading to unrest among *white* college students is less obvious. They are not directly victims of it, and, as compared to other major institutions in the society, the university tends to be more open and more willing to reward achievement regardless of race or ethnicity.

Of course, students have a deep personal interest in these issues and believe that the outcome will make their own individual lives better or worse. Yet their beliefs and their protest clearly are founded on principle and ideology, not on self-interest. The war and the race issues did not arise primarily because they actually and materially affected the day-to-day lives of college youth—black students again excepted. The issues were defined in terms not of interest but of principle, and their emergence was based on what we must infer to have been a fundamental change in the attitudes and principles of American students.

This alteration of student principles cannot be said to have occurred because of racism or Vietnam. Racism was hardly something new to American society in 1960 or 1964—it had, of course, existed since the very beginning of the colonies, and in much more brutal and inhuman forms. Indeed, during the 1950s and 1960s, legally imposed segregation in the South was, at long last, beginning to wane, and the economic condition of the black American was slowly improving. As for Vietnam, even though America had not been engaged in a significant war for ten years when the major escalation in Vietnam occurred early in 1965, it could hardly be said that war was a new phenomenon in American society, or that most previous American warfare had been less brutal.

If, then, war and racism did not directly and significantly affect the daily lives and self-interest of the vast majority of American students; if war and racism were not new to American society; and if their horrors and injustices were, over time, marginally diminishing rather than increasing—the emergence on campus of these issues as objects of increasingly widespread student protest could only have been the result of some further cause, a change in some factor that intervened between the *conditions* (racism, war) in the country and their emergence as *issues* that led to student protest.

Clearly, whatever it is that transforms a condition into an issue lies in the eyes of the beholder—or, more precisely, in his opinions and perceptions. The emergence of these issues was causd by a change in opinions, perceptions, and values—that is, by a change in the culture of students. Students' basic ways of seeing the world became, during the 1960s, less and less tolerant of war, of racism, and of the things these entail. This shift in student culture is a basic—perhaps *the* basic—contributing cause of campus unrest.

THE NEW YOUTH CULTURE

In early Western societies, the young were traditionally submissive to adults. Largely because adults retained great authority, the only way for the young to achieve wealth, power, and prestige was through a cooperative apprenticeship of some sort to the adult world. Thus, the young learned the traditional adult ways of living, and in time they grew up to become adults of the same sort as their parents, living in the same sort of world.

Advancing industrialism decisively changed this cooperative relationship between the generations. It produced new forms and new sources of wealth, power, and prestige, and these weakened traditional adult controls over the young. It removed production from the home and made it increasingly specialized; as a result, the young were increasingly removed from adult work places and could not directly observe or participate in adult work. Moreover, industrialism hastened the separation of education from the home, in consequence of which the young were concentrated together in places of formal education that were isolated from most adults. Thus, the young spent an increasing amount of time together, apart from their parents' home and work, in activities that were different from those of adults.

This shared and distinct experience among the young led to shared interests and problems, which led, in turn, to the development of distinct subcultures. As those subcultures developed, they provided support for any youth movement that was distinct from—or even directed against—the adult world.

A distinguishing characteristic of young people is their penchant for pure idealism. Society teaches youth to adhere to the basic values of the adult social system—equality, honesty, democracy, or whatever—in absolute terms. Throughout most of American history, the idealism of youth has been formed—and constrained—by the institutions of adult society. But during the 1960s, in response to an accumulation of social changes, the traditional American youth culture developed rapidly in the direction of an oppositional stance toward the institutions and ways of the adult world.

This subculture took its bearings from the notion of the autonomous, self-determining individual whose goal was to live with "authenticity," or in harmony with his inner penchants and instincts. It also found its identity in a rejection of the work ethic, materialism, and conventional social norms and pieties. Indeed, it rejected all institutional disciplines externally imposed upon the individual, and this set it at odds with much in American society.

Its aim was to liberate human consciousness and to enhance the quality of experience; it sought to replace the materialism, the self-denial, and the striving for achievement that characterized the existing society with a new emphasis on the expressive, the creative, the imaginative. The tools of the workaday institutional world—hierarchy, discipline, rules, self-interest, self-defense, power—it considered mad and tyrannical. It proclaimed instead the liberation of the individual to feel, to experience, to express whatever his unique humanity prompted. And its perceptions of the world grew ever more distant from the perceptions of the existing culture: what most called "justice" or "peace" or "accomplishment," the new culture envisioned as "enslavement" or "hysteria" or "meaninglessness." As this divergence of values and of vision proceeded, the new youth culture became increasingly oppositional.

And yet in its commitment to liberty and equality, it was very much in the mainstream of American tradition; what it doubted was that America had managed to live up to its national ideals. Over time, these doubts grew, and the youth culture became increasingly imbued with a sense of alienation and of opposition to the larger society.

No one who lives in contemporary America can be unaware of the surface manifestations of this new youth culture. Dress is highly distinctive; emphasis is placed on heightened color and sound; the enjoyment of flowers and nature is given a high priority. The fullest ranges of sense and sensation are to be enjoyed each day through the cultivation of new experiences, through spiritualism, and through drugs. Life is sought to be made as simple, primitive, and "natural" as possible, as ritualized, for example, by nude bathing.

Social historians can find parallels to this culture in the past. One is reminded of Bacchic cults in ancient Greece, or of the *Wandervoegel*, the wandering bands of German youths in the nineteenth century, or of primitive Christianity. Confidence is placed in revelation rather than cognition, in sensation rather than analysis, in the personal rather than the institutional. Emphasis is placed on living to the fullest extent, on the sacredness of life itself, and on the common mystery of all living things. The age-old vision of natural man, untrammeled and unscarred by the fetters of institutions, is seen again. It is not necessary to describe such movements as religious, but it is useful to recognize that they have elements in common with the waves of religious fervor that periodically have captivated the minds of men.

It is not difficult to compose a picture of contemporary America as it looks through the eyes of one whose premises are essentially those just described. Human life is all; but women and children are being killed in Vietnam by American forces. All living things are sacred; but American industry and technology are polluting the air and the streams and killing the birds and the fish. The individual should stand as an individual; but American society is organized into vast structures of unions, corporations, multiversities, and government bureaucracies. Personal regard for each human being and for the absolute equality of every human soul is a categorical imperative; but American society continues to be characterized by racial injustice and discrimination. The senses and the instincts are to be trusted first; but American technology and its consequences are a monument to rationalism. Life should be lived in communion with others, and each day's sunrise and sunset enjoyed to the fullest; American society extols competition, the accumulation of goods, and the work ethic. Each man should be free to lead his own life in his own way; American organizations and statute books are filled with regulations governing dress, sex, consumption, and the accreditation of study and of work, and many of these are enforced by armed police.

No coherent political decalogue has yet emerged. Yet in this new youth culture's political discussion there are echoes of Marxism, of peasant communalism, of Thoreau, of Rousseau, of the evangelical fervor of the abolitionists, of Gandhi, and of native American populism.

The new culture adherent believes he sees an America that has failed to achieve its social targets; that no longer cares about achieving them; that is thoroughly hypocritical in pretending to have achieved them and in pretending to care; and that is exporting death and oppression abroad through its military and corporate operations. He wishes desperately to recall America to its great traditional goals of true freedom and justice for every man. As he sees it, he wants to remake America in its own image.

What of the shortcomings of other societies, especially the Soviet Union? Why does the new culture denounce only the United States? On this question, Drs. Heard and Cheek said in a memorandum to the President:

> The apparent insensitivity of students to Soviet actions and to evils in the Soviet system is at least partly explainable by considerations like these: *First*, they feel that by the wrongness of

our own policies, such as the war in Vietnam, we have lost our moral standing to condemn other countries. *Second,* there is an obsession with our own problems, a feeling that our own crises should occupy all our attention. *Third,* the fear of Communism is less than existed a decade ago.

Students perceive the Czech invasion as one more evil action by a powerful imperialist government, but they don't perceive it as a threat to the United States. Since the Sino-Soviet split, they see Communism as consisting of different and often competing national governments and styles. The Russians appear to repress their satellite countries, but students see that fact as parallel to American domination in *its* sphere of influence (the Dominican Republic, Guatemala, economic exploitation, etc.). They see the Russians as no better than [ourselves], maybe not as good, but feel more responsibility for our actions than for those of foreign powers.

The dedicated practitioners of this emerging culture typically have little regard for the past experience of others. Indeed, they often exhibit a positive antagonism to the study of history. Believing that there is today, or will be tomorrow, a wholly new world, they see no special relevance in the past. Distrusting older generations, they distrust the motives of their historically based advice no less than they distrust the history written by older generations. The antirationalist thread in the new culture resists the careful empirical approach of history and denounces it as fraudulent. Indeed, this antirationalism and the urge for blunt directness often lead those of the new youth culture to view complexity as a disguise, to be impatient with learning the facts, and to demand simplistic solutions in one sentence.

Understandably, the new culture enthusiast has at best a lukewarm interest in free speech, majority opinion, and the rest of the tenets of liberal democracy as they are institutionalized today. He cannot have much regard for these things if he believes that American liberal democracy, with the consent and approval of the vast majority of its citizens, is pursuing values and policies that he sees as fundamentally immoral and apocalyptically destructive. Again in parallel with historical religious movements, the new culture advocate tends to be self-righteous, sanctimonious, contemptuous of those who have not yet shared his vision, and intolerant of their ideals.

Profoundly opposed to any kind of authority structure from within or without the movement and urgently pressing for direct personal participation by each individual, members of this new youth culture have a difficult time making collective decisions. They reveal a distinct intolerance in their refusal to listen to those outside the new culture and in their willingness to force others to their own views. They even show an elitist streak in their premise that the rest of the society must be brought to the policy positions which they believe are right.

At the same time, they try very hard, and with extraordinary patience, to give each of their fellows an opportunity to be heard and to participate directly in decision-making. The new culture decisional style is founded on the endless mass meeting at which there is no chairman and no agenda, and from which the crowd or parts of the crowd melt away or move off into actions. Such crowds are, of course, subject to easy manipulation by skillful agitators and sometimes become mobs. But it must also be recognized that large, loose, floating crowds represent for participants in the new youth culture the normal, friendly, natural way for human beings to come together equally, to communicate, and to decide what to do. Seen from this perspective, the reader may well imagine the general student response at Kent State to the governor's order that the National Guard disperse all assemblies, peaceful or otherwise.

Practitioners of the new youth culture do not announce their program because, at this time at least, the movement is not primarily concerned with programs; it is concerned with how one ought to live and what one ought to consider important in one's daily life. The new youth culture is still in the process of forming its values, programs, and life style; at this point, therefore, it is primarily a *stance.*

A parallel to religious history is again instructive. For many (not all) student activists and protestors, it is not really very important whether the protest tactics employed will actually contribute to the political end allegedly sought. What is important is that a protest be made—that the individual protestor, for his own internal salvation, stand up, declare the purity of his own heart, and take his stand. No student protestor throwing a rock through a laboratory window believes that it will stop the Indochina war, weapons research, or the advance of the feared technology—yet he throws it in a mood of defiant exultation—almost exaltation. He has taken his moral stance.

An important theme of this new culture is its oppositional relationship to the larger society, as is suggested by the fact that one of its leading theorists has called it a "counterculture." If the rest of the society wears short hair, the member of this youth culture wears his hair long. If others are clean, he is dirty. If others drink alcohol and illegalize marijuana, he denounces alcohol and smokes pot. If others work in large organizations with massively complex technology, he works alone and makes sandals by hand. If others live separated, he lives in a commune. If others are for the police and the judges, he is for the accused and the prisoner. In such ways, he declares himself an alien in a larger society with which he feels himself to be fundamentally at odds.

He will also resist when the forces of the outside society seek to impose its tenets upon him. He is likely to see police as the repressive minions of the outside culture imposing its law on him and on other students by force or death if necessary. He will likely try to urge others to join him in changing the society about him in the conviction that he is seeking to save that society from bringing about its own destruction. He is likely to have apocalyptic visions of impending doom of the whole social structure and the world. He is likely to have lost hope that society can be brought to change through its own procedures. And if his psychological makeup is of a particular kind, he may conclude that the only outlet for his feelings is violence and terrorism.

In recent years, some substantial number of students in the United States and abroad have come to hold views along these lines. It is also true that a very large fraction of American college students, probably a majority, could not be said to be participants in any significant aspect of this culture posture except for its music. As for the rest of the students, they are distributed over the entire spectrum that ranges from no participation to full participation. A student may feel strongly about any one or more aspects of these views and wholly reject all the others. He may also subscribe wholeheartedly to many of the philosophic assertions implied while occupying any of hundreds of different possible positions on the questions of which tactics, procedures, and actions he considers to be morally justifiable. Generalizations here are more than usually false.

One student may adopt the outward appearance of the new culture and nothing else. Another may be a total devotee, except that he is a serious history scholar. Another student may agree completely on all the issues of war, race, pollution, and the like and participate in protests over those matters, while disagreeing with all aspects of the youth culture life style. A student may agree with the entire life style but be wholly uninterested in politics. Another new culture student who takes very seriously the elements of compassion and of reverence for life may prove to be the best bulwark against resorts to violence. A student who rejects the new youth culture altogether may nevertheless be in the vanguard of those who seek to protect that culture against the outside world. And so forth.

As we have observed elsewhere in this report, to conclude that a student who has a beard is a student who would burn a building, or even sit-in in a building, is wholly unwarranted.

But almost no college student today is unaffected by the new youth culture in some way. If he is not included, his roommate or sister or girlfriend is. If protest breaks out on his campus, he is confronted with a personal decision about his role in it. In the poetry, music, movies, and plays that students encounter, the themes of the new culture are recurrent. Even the student who finds older values more comfortable for himself will nevertheless protect and support vigorously the privilege of other students who prefer the new youth culture.

A vast majority of students are not complete adherents. But *no* significant group of students would join older generations in condemning those who are. And almost *all* students will condemn repressive efforts by the larger community to restrict or limit the life style, the art forms, and the nonviolent political manifestations of the new youth culture.

To most Americans, the development of the new youth culture is an unpleasant and often frightening phenomenon. And there is no doubt that the emergence of this student perspective has led to confrontations, injuries, and death. It is undeniable, too, that a tiny extreme fringe of fanatical devotees of the new culture have crossed the line over into outlawry and terrorism. There is a fearful and terrible irony here as, in the name of the law, the police and National Guard have killed students, and some students, under the new youth culture's banner of love and compassion, have turned to burning and bombing.

But the new youth culture itself is not a "problem" to which there is a "solution"; it is a mass social condition, a shift in basic cultural viewpoint. How long this emerging youth culture will last and what course its future development will take are open questions. But it does exist today, and it is the deeper cause of the emergence of the issues of race and war as objects of intense concern on the American campus.

The University Community

This change in the youth subculture derived from major changes in the social functions and internal composition of the American university.

The American university was traditionally a status-conferring institution for middle and upper-middle class families. As such, it was closely integrated with the family and work life of these social groupings, and its subcultures were appropriately cooperative.

The college experience provided an identity moratorium following childhood. Students spent the "best years of their lives" mostly enjoying themselves with good conversation, some study, football, dating, and drinking. The experience ended with a *rite de passage*, graduation, which was then followed by adulthood and entry into the serious world of work. The college was completely controlled by the serious adult world, but the student's experiences there were not seen by him or others as part of that world.

In the past few decades, the university has become increasingly integrated into the meritocratic work world. Grade pressures have grown steadily, and students have come to see the university as a direct extension of the adult world. Indeed, by the 1960s, this trend had moved down into the high schools and in some places even to the junior high schools, as formal education became the primary route to the best jobs in the postindustrial society.

The integration of higher education into the adult world of work was intimately associated with another historic change—the rapid expansion of higher education, and the dramatic increase in the proportion of high school graduates who entered college. In the early 1930s there were about a million and a quarter college students in the United States. In the fall of 1969, there were over seven million. By 1978, we may look forward to ten million, and there will be almost as many graduate students enrolled as there were undergraduates before World War II. The U.S. Office of Education now estimates that, nationally, 62 percent of all high school graduates will attend institutions of higher education.

As higher education expanded, it also lengthened. More and more students went on to enroll in graduate programs leading to advanced degrees; as they did, the vocational value of the under-graduate degree decreased. Students thus were under pressure to spend an ever longer period of time—well into their twenties and not infrequently into their early thirties—in schools which prepared them for the ever longer deferred work world.

More and more young Americans found themselves in an am-bivalent status for an ever longer time. Physically and psychologi-cally, they had long since become adult. As students in the merito-cratic system of higher education, they were already integrated into a part of the adult work world. Accordingly, they came to think of themselves as adults and to demand all the rights and privileges of adults. And yet, though in part they were treated as adults, they nevertheless remained financially dependent upon the adult world and were not yet full-fledged participants in adult work. Especially for older students, but increasingly for all students regardless of age, this condition created tensions and frustrations.

Against the background of this ambivalence, two further factors led the college student culture into an increasingly bitter sense of opposition to the larger society. One of these was affluence. Most college students during the past decade have grown up in the great-est affluence and freedom from the discipline of hard and unremitting work of any generation in man's history. Life, at least in its material aspects, has not been difficult for them, and they have thus found a great deal in the larger society, oriented as it is to work and produc-tion, that seems needless or strange.

That students increasingly rejected this larger society, and re-jected it passionately and in the name of moral principle, was the result of a second factor. The college students among whom the youth culture and campus unrest emerged were principally those from affluent families whose parents were liberals or radicals, and who attended the larger and more selective universities and colleges. They were part of the first generation of middle-class Americans to grow up in the post-Depression American welfare state under the tutelage of a parental generation that embodied the distinctive moral vision of modern liberalism. Insofar as these students learned the lessons that their parents and their experiences taught, they became, inevitably, more liberal than the older generation, which had grown up in a harsher time.

The parental generation's liberalism expressed itself most characteristically in the belief that their greatest personal fulfillment came not from work, income, power, or social status, but rather from the purely nonvocational pursuits of life—the activities of living well, and the rewards of identifying with right principles applicable to the society as a whole. They pictured work, money, discipline, and ambition to their children as having little intrinsic merit and as deserving correspondingly little praise. It was instead the high-minded virtues, such as compassion, learning, love, equality, democracy, and self-expression, which they considered worthy of respect and pursuit.

Not a few among this older generation believed that they managed to live strictly in accord with this hierarchy of values. Considering the decency and comfort of their lives, it is understandable that they could have entertained such hopes. But whether for reasons of modesty or because of aspirations for higher things for their children, they persistently passed over the fact that their own comfort was usually the fruit of hard work and self-discipline.

If the parents held views which did not justify or reflect their personal history of work and self-discipline, the children, brought up in conditions of affluence and freedom from worldy struggle, adopted those views not only as attitudes but also as habits of life. They began to live, in short, what their parents preached but did not entirely act upon. And as they brought their parents' high-minded ideals to bear upon American society in a thoroughgoing way, their vision of that society changed radically.

The parental values were strongly reinforced in the elite universities by the liberal values of faculty members. That faculty members began to have and to transmit such an outlook was the result of another development within the university community— the professionalization of the academy, by which professors became more mobile, more independent of the university administration, more oriented to research and publication, and, as a group, more ethnically diverse. As a result, the student subculture, particularly in the more selective schools, came to be far more liberal than the subcultures of students at other institutions or of the general population.

As higher education expanded, more and more students took

the values of liberal idealism as their code and habit of life. As they did, more and more students found themselves in increasing opposition to the larger society, which did not embody these values nearly so much.

The thoroughgoing idealistic liberalism of the student generation of the 1960s was the ideological beginning point of the student movement and of campus unrest as they exist today. It predisposed many students to oppose the Vietnam war, to react with fury over the use of police power to quell student disturbances, and to enlist themselves in wholehearted support of civil rights and the movement for black pride.

The student subculture reflected and, as it coalesced, magnified these changes of perception and value.

THE UNIVERSITY AS AN OBJECT OF PROTEST

As the midpoint of the 1960s was reached, campus unrest became more and more radical in character. Indictments of race discrimination and of the war grew more sweeping and soon encompassed the university, which itself became a major target of political protest. "University complicity" proved to be a powerful issue with which to mobilize students.

Yet despite the large volume of protest against the university, polls of student opinion do not in fact indicate widespread discontent with higher education. A winter 1968–69 poll revealed that only 4 percent of seniors and 9 percent of freshmen found higher education "basically unsound—needs major overhauling." Fifteen percent of freshmen and 19 percent of seniors said, "not too sound—needs many improvements." Fifty-six percent of seniors and 49 percent of freshmen found higher education "basically sound—needs some improvement." And 19 percent of seniors and 32 percent of freshmen voted for "basically sound—essentially good."

A survey in the spring of 1969 found that only 4 percent of college students noted strong assent, and 4 percent moderate assent, in response to the statement, "On the whole, college has been a deep disappointment to me." In response to the statement, "I don't feel I am learning very much in college," again 4 percent noted strong assent and 13 percent moderate assent. However, in response to the statement, "American universities have largely abdicated their responsibility to deal with vital moral issues," 9 percent indicated strong assent and 30 percent moderate assent.

These surveys suggest that most American students are not fundamentally discontented with their college and university education. But substantial numbers do seem to disapprove of their schools as *moral* institutions.

Those who feel that the universities have failed them in a larger moral sense are often the children of liberal, middle class families, well prepared to do college work, and with the highest expectations of their colleges. Why is it that the university has become the special target of so many of the very students who might be expected to find an institution devoted to the life of the mind particularly worthy of respect?

Partially, the answer may be found in the observation that Americans today have higher expectations of the university than they do of practically any other social institution. It is expected to provide models, methods, and meanings for contemporary life. It is an advisor to government and a vehicle for self-improvement and social mobility. Indeed, since science and critical method are enshrined in the university, it occupies a place in the public imagination that may be compared to that of the church in an earlier day.

It is precisely because of these high expectations that the university has forfeited some of its authority and legitimacy in the eyes of many "moderate" students. For radicals, perhaps, the university, as a part of the established society, may never have had much authority or legitimacy. But without the support of moderates, militant disruption could never have become a nationwide problem. The "moderate" campus majority makes common cause with the militants because student rebellion is not merely a crisis at the university. It is equally a crisis *of* the university itself—of its corporate identity, its purposes, and its justifications.

Despite the sophisticated style of many bright young people today, the freshman still looks forward to the great freedom and variety of college and anticipates the excitement of serious study and personal growth within a community of students and scholars. And if he does not expect it when he arrives, he learns to demand it once he has been there awhile.

According to the professed culture of the university, the principal values against which any activity or vocation are to be measured are justice, compassion, and truth. The rewards of such endeavors are pictured to be intellectual excitement, personal fulfillment, and a sense of having done something worthwhile. As the academy sees itself, these are the rewards of the scholarly life itself and the basis of the sense of community within the university. Thus, the student's expectations are raised even higher as he is integrated into university life and becomes acquainted with its distinctive values.

But it is usually not long before he realizes that college life bears little relation to his expectations, and that the university itself is often quite unlike what it pictures itself to be.

Far from being a "community of scholars," the large university today is much more like a vast and impersonal staging area for professional careers. Anxious to maintain their professional standing and not unresponsive to financial inducements, the professors appear to the freshman more like corporation executives than cloistered scholars. What these professors teach seems less the humane and civilizing liberal education the freshman anticipated than a body of impersonal knowledge amassed and accepted by an anonymous "profession." The student's role in this process of education is largely passive: he sits and listens, he sits and reads, and sometimes he sits and writes. It is an uninspiring experience for many students.

This is especially the case because the contemporary youth culture is so very different in its quality and intentions. For while that culture does value the life of the mind, it also places high value on the truth of feeling and on the cultivation of the whole person. This basic attitude is not easily reconciled with the idea at the heart of the modern university—that a scholar's proper work is the pursuit of probable truth, which is a goal that is thought to lie outside the preferences and tastes of the man who pursues it and to impose a stringent discipline upon him. Because this academic method is the very antithesis of the style of the youth culture, large numbers of students today are ill suited to university life and its academic pursuits.

Student reactions to higher education vary. Radicals increasingly express a desire to reorganize the university in order to have it act upon their own political convictions and programs. Others, less certain of their goals, seem to accept their personal disappointment or disinterest until an issue emerges on campus which symbolizes to them the university's "complicity" in social evils or its "hypocrisy" about its aims and practices.

The moral authority of the university was compromised as a result of its expansion and professionalization after World War II. For as it expanded, higher education in America changed. But these changes had primarily to do with physically accommodating the huge influx of students, with meeting the increasing variety of demands being made upon the university by government and business, and with satisfying the ever increasing appetite of the faculty for freedom, including the freedom to do things other than teaching. By the mid-1950s, universities were permitting faculty to accept research grants which, in some instances, were larger than the operating budget of their entire academic department.

As a result, new men of power walked the campus. Recognition for distinguished teaching and scholarship in the traditional manner, which rewarded knowledge pursued for its own sake, so that a medievalist might be as highly regarded as a chemist, became rarer. Certainly, knowledge for its own sake was still admirable, but scholars now could also hope to achieve wealth and power by proposing technological and political solutions to the problems of industry and government—and this cast doubt upon the university's claim that it was a center for disinterested research and teaching.

Are there any reforms which might solve the problems arising out of the university's loss of moral authority? The question has produced a serious debate in colleges and universities across the country, but no clear answer.

Some suggest the colleges and universities should relate themselves more fully to life around them and thus respond to the demand for "relevance." Others suggest they should withdraw further and thus free themselves from the taint of involvement with an impure society and government.

Some argue strongly that colleges and universities must make every effort to restore as soon as possible a meaningful core curriculum which would socialize youth into society and provide the basic education that any citizen should have. Others assert that it is impossible for any modern university to agree on what such a curriculum should be, and that even the modest efforts of colleges to provide a core curriculum should be abandoned as intellectually and culturally arbitrary.

Some have emphasized that the most serious educational failing of the university was to dilute its teaching function and to disorder its moral priorities by placing too great an emphasis on research and on establishing links to government and business. Others insist that the research emphasis and even consulting improve the university—and specifically improve the quality of teaching—by bringing it in closer touch with the frontiers of knowledge and with the practical needs that occasion research.

The Commission engages in no rhetorical evasion when it places against each interpretation largely contradictory interpretations of just what in the colleges and universities has led to the crisis and what should therefore be reformed. All these positions can be argued persuasively, and specific proposals for reform are as numerous as they are controversial.

Still, without attempting to endorse a particular point of view, we do think it can be said that some of the causes of student unrest are to be found in certain contemporary features of colleges and universities. It is impressive, for example, that unrest is most prominent in the larger universities, and that it is less common in those in which, by certain measures, greater attention is paid to students and to the needs of education, and where students and faculty seem to form single communities, either because of their size or the shared values of their members.

THE ESCALATION OF COMMITMENT AND REACTION

The emergence of the great issues of our time, the evolution of an oppositional college student subculture, and the changing nature of the university have all contributed to the development of campus unrest. Yet as we emphasized at the outset, these are no more than contributing causes. They explain—at least they suggest—the general direction in which opinion on campus was likely to move. Yet they do not suffice to explain why campus unrest developed at the time it did, or with the speed it did. Neither do they explain why tactics changed as they did.

We also pointed out at the outset that the direct functional cause of campus unrest has been the free existential act of commitment which each member of the student movement has made to a particular political vision, to the practice of expressing that vision publicly, and to particular acts of protest. To say this is to state more than a simple deductive truth, for the choice of an activist mode of expressing political opinion has important consequences for the development of that opinion itself.

Studies of activist youth reveal that in most cases students become activists through an extended process. They encounter others who are politically involved, assimilate their views, reassess their own thinking, engage in some political action, but make no conscious decision about what their politics will be, or how far they will go in pursuing activist modes of political expression. At some point, however, they discover that they have changed in some qualitative way, that they are no longer what they were, and that they now conceive of themselves as "radicals" or "activists."

This discovery often provokes or heightens in the activist a sharp sense of commitment to act in behalf of his vision of a just society. As he pursues such action, and especially as he does so in the face of opposition, his sense of commitment often grows. So, too, do the consciousness and decisiveness with which he chooses to commit himself to specific acts of protest.

These spiraling acts of will and choice lead the activist to reject the society which harbors the evils he commits himself to extirpate. For each act of commitment is a promise to make any sacrifice necessary to demonstrate against social evils and to promote justice. Over time, these acts of commitment amount to a conscious decision to alter one's ways of thinking and acting and to pursue some vision of a good society in an activist way. And thus, over time, they define the activist as one in an adversary relationship to the larger society.

Such acts of commitment may be compared, in their total effect, to sudden and intense religious conversions, through which an individual perceives anew the evil in the world and dedicates himself to the way of righteousness. For there is in the character of radical protest today an almost religious fervor, as there has been in other college movements in other nations in other times. The religious parallel suggests itself, too, for the way it illumines the problem of responding to campus unrest. For just as it has never worked to send guns—or lions—against religious converts, so too has it been unavailing to meet campus activism with force. Force only tests the mettle of the activist's commitment and thus ends not by weakening the movement but by strengthening it.

The idea of commitment is central to an understanding of campus unrest in part because it accurately describes why a demonstration happened when it did. In a very real sense, the answer is that it happened because, for whatever complex or even accidental reasons, somebody or some group decided, against the background of a general vision of the good society and of effective political action, to commit himself or itself to a particular act, in a particular place, at a particular time.

Thus, a radical commitment is as much a commitment to the act of protest itself as it is a commitment to certain positions on the issues and to a certain moral vision. Where issues are not compelling, there still may be protests. The upward spiral of protest reflects the intentions of the protestor as much as the circumstances and objects of his protest.

The notion of commitment helps to explain the escalation of tactics that occurred during the 1960s. For the radical commitment contains built-in dynamic processes which, in reaction to resistance, make opinions and tactical actions ever more radical.

Finally, students increasingly discovered that each issue was neither single nor simple. Once a student made the decision to be active, he became aware of the connectedness of all issues; and the more he saw, the more convinced he became that his stance was valid.

The University Environment

A university campus is an especially favorable place for those who wish to make such a commitment, for students and faculty can consider committing themselves in the almost certain knowledge that the act of commitment has no severe personal costs attached to it.

White students generally are freer than black students, non-students, and older people to act because they are subject to fewer competing commitments to family and job and because what job requirements they do have can be put aside at relatively little cost. This is also true of professors. But students especially may drop out of school, put off their studies for short or long periods, and delay taking examinations, without paying a great price.

The relative freedom of students to act without fear of immediate serious consequences is reinforced by the partial survival of the custom of treating students as adolescents who may be forgiven their errors. Students also benefit from the historic idea of university sanctuary, which would bar police and civil authority from enforcing law on campus except in extreme circumstances. Such norms, while never having the sanction of law in the United States as they have in other countries, have still had an influence.

Moreover, the erosion of the sense of community on many campuses has meant that fewer informal social controls are at work to deter students from engaging in new or unusual modes of behavior, even ones which may harm the university. There is less traditional school spirit, fewer personal relationships, more anonymity—and, therefore, fewer personal costs involved in the commitment to engage in radical action, or even in the decision to use the university as a means of furthering political ends.

Formal controls within the university—especially university disciplinary systems—have also grown weaker. At many universities today, students encounter little formal deterrence because university administrators and faculties have often failed to punish illegal acts. In part, this has been a result of their sympathy to student causes. It is certainly due as well to the feeling of outrage on the part of faculty members over the use of force against students by the police.

Just how sympathetic faculty members are to student unrest was suggested by a comprehensive survey conducted by the American Council on Education during 1967–68. It found that faculty members were involved in the planning of over half the student protests which occurred. (The vast majority of such protests were, of course, lawful and peaceful.) And in close to two thirds of them, faculty bodies passed resolutions approving of the protest.

The more general reason for the failure of the universities to preserve order and to discipline those who were disruptive or violent was that power in American universities is limited and diffuse. Their disciplinary and control measures were established on the assumption that the vast majority of faculty and students would be reasonable people who would support reasonable actions on common assumptions of what is reasonable, and that this majority would accept and support the specific goals of the university. These assumptions have become increasingly unrealistic.

Finally, the campus is a favorable environment for the growth of commitment and protest because the physical situation of the university makes it relatively easy to mobilize students with common sentiments and with a common predisposition to take direct political action. Their numbers serve to protect them from the isolation and criticism they would experience if they were dispersed throughout the larger society.

The increase in sheer numbers of students in the United States has magnified the significance of this fact. Only a small percentage of students on a campus of 20,000 or more are needed to create a very large demonstration. Thus, in 1965–66, although opinion polls indicated that the great majority of students still supported the Vietnam war and that antiwar sentiment was not more widespread among students than among the population as a whole, opposition on campus was able to have a disproportionate public impact because it was readily mobilized in protest demonstrations. Relatively small percentages of large student bodies have constituted the "masses" occupying administration buildings or bringing great universities to a halt.

Protest itself has become an activity accepted as proper and even honorable by the general student body. Students who are not participants in an act of protest will usually take no step to impede it—except sometimes in cases where violence is involved—and will seldom assist in imposing punishment upon their fellow students.

The Spiral of Commitment and Reaction

Within this unconstraining environment, then, many students freely committed themselves to the student movement. Those who did so were in turn subject to a number of evolutionary forces which tended to move their opinions and protest behavior toward the extreme.

To the extent that audience reaction was the proximate goal of student protest, the activists were at any given moment under a strong incentive to express themselves a little louder and a bit more forcefully than the last time—otherwise there was a possibility that people would become accustomed to acts of protest and begin to ignore them. Thus, the simple passing of time spurred the movement to go farther and farther afield of the tactics and perspectives of instrumentalist, reformist politics, and closer and closer to a thoroughgoing radical strategy.

A second dynamic at work in student activism arose out of frustration. In the struggle for desegregation in the South, activists had many successes. But a few years later, it had become only too clear that doing away with legalized segregation had not brought about genuine equality and integration. As the movement began carrying the fight for equality to the informal bases of discrimination, it met a growing political resistance. Social change of the magnitude in question takes a very long time even when all agree that there should be change. Yet patience has never been a charactristic of the young, and the deferment of gratification is something for which the student subculture has little sympathy.

In addition, there was growing frustration over the Vietnam war. With each instance of student protest, popular opposition to the war seemed to grow, and yet the war itself seemed no closer to an end.

Such frustrations were exasperating to energetic and impatient students. Their seeming failure—and it was only a seeming failure—to influence the course of events led them to adopt an ever more extreme view of the inadequacies of the American political system as a whole, and an ever more extreme way of expressing that view.

And there was a third dynamic operating within the movement. In any ideological group, the more extreme views and the more extremist members tend to wield disproportionate influence. For leaders are usually chosen because they embody and represent the values and qualities to which the group is dedicated. Thus, in activist groups, the leaders, who articulate members' views to the world at large and who interpret events to their followers, tend to be ideological purists.

Moreover, members of groups tend to talk in terms of what their group has uniquely in common, and that, for student activists, is their opposition to American society in its present form. Thus, as the group coalesces, as time passes, and as external hostility increases, that opposition becomes more important as a source of solidarity. As it becomes more important, views become more extreme.

As the student movement grew stronger, bolder, and more extreme, it began to encounter opposition—sometimes from within the university, but more often from outside it, especially in the form of the police or, less often, the National Guard. Often—usually as the result of some failure to control deadly weapons or the men carrying them—there was violence and injury, and on some occasions there was death. This developing opposition and its implementation by law

109

enforcement provided the fourth dynamic at work in the evolution of student opinion and tactics toward the extreme.

The encounters usually had the effect not of intimidating student protestors but rather of angering and emboldening them. They seemed to dramatize the participants' initial commitments and to reinforce their sense of the irreversibility of that commitment.

Most of the deaths have been accidents in the sense that they did not reflect the intention or policy of police and Guard units; and many—but not all—have been accidents in the sense that the policemen and guardsmen immediately involved acted in fear or passion, or through authentic inadvertence. But the operating rules and routines of many police and Guard units have made the probability of accidental death higher. Inadequate or nonexistent programs in attitude training, crowd-control work, and command and control have made it more likely that police or guardsmen would break discipline and, in fear or anger, behave defensively and brutally. Routinely carrying rifles and bayonets and ammunition also increased the chances of an accident.

Finally, rising tensions between student protestors and law enforcement officials also contributed to the likelihood of accident. For when students faced police, the confrontation was not only physical but also cultural and attitudinal. Hostilities and fears on both sides could become so great—especially when public rhetoric was growing hotter—that the probability of violence—with whatever weapons were at hand—became extremely high.

To recapitulate then: once the commitment was made, and once the protest organization was established, there were psychological and organizational mechanisms which would almost guarantee that it would persist. And more than persist: it was likely to become stronger. For the movement had its own culture, its solidarity, and its sense of being set apart from and against the outside society. It thus could easily interpret any event and any issue in ways that would contribute to the strengthening of the movement rather than to its weakening. Because the commitment was both for something and against something, either success or opposition was capable of intensifying it. Hostility and violent responses aided the movement, especially when, as often happened, they mobilized moderates. And each such event reinforced the intensifying and expanding student subculture, lent it greater solidarity, and led to a deeper alienation from American society. As the subculture coalesced in this way, student protest became less and less the result of specific issues or events, and more and more the expression of a generalized animus against the larger society.

EVOLUTIONARY CHANGES IN WESTERN SOCIETY

The final body of contributing causes of student unrest is the most difficult to formulate. These are certain broad, evolutionary changes occurring throughout the Western world, which has become a series of ever more complex and interconnected societies, organized in large-scale urban complexes, dependent on an increasingly sophisticated technology, dependent therefore upon education and especially upon the university, and increasingly susceptible to general immobilization or breakdown as a result of even tiny disturbances in any of its many subunits.

These long-range changes in society have created deep disaffection among youth, not only in the United States, but in most other Western countries as well. This wave of unrest has occurred while these societies are engaged in repairing many of the defects and evils for which social critics attacked them in the past. They are withdrawing or have withdrawn from their overseas colonies. They are engaged in extending the welfare features of their societies. They are giving increased attention to the problem of equality in income and in education. Thus, we do not deal with any simple revolt against the "evils of capitalism," as may be indicated by the fact that, in other countries as in this one, it is a revolt of middle-class rather than working-class youth.

What we face is a revolt among educated youth against certain features of liberal democratic capitalism—especially "the affluent society." There is growing opposition to the emphasis on material goods. Thus, French students proclaimed opposition to a "consumer" society, and American students, by their dress, their attitude toward material goods, and their direct statements, also express opposition to their society's emphasis on consumption. This opposition is not yet fully consistent, for critics of consumer society also see as one of its chief defects its failure to supply sufficient consumer goods to some strata of society. Nevertheless, the consumer goods criticism is real and strongly felt.

We may also point to a nascent—if still largely implicit—opposition to democracy which is beginning to receive serious formulation by some political theorists. The youth most active in the unrest now tend to feel that determination of political representation or policies by simple measures such as one man, one vote may be inadequate, and that the human qualities of the representatives and policies thus adopted must play a role in their acceptance. A rather elaborate critique of democracy from the left has been developed by one contemporary radical philosopher, Herbert Marcuse, and he and others have also attacked the virtue of tolerance in the present society.

A third aspect of what we might call Western, capitalist, liberal society to which many young people are now hostile is the emphasis on effort, disciplined work, and the mechanisms that encourage it and reward it. This is seen in the insistence that everyone should do "his own thing" and more that he should not suffer for it.

It would be an illusion to see this as being directed simply against some of the errors of this kind of society. This attack is directed as strongly—even *more* strongly—against those features of this kind of society that most of us consider virtues: its capacity to improve the material condition of people; its dependence on democracy and tolerance; its capacity to evoke work and effort and to reward work and effort.

Thus, the posibility cannot be overlooked that the true causes of the events we today characterize as "campus unrest" lie deep in the social and economic patterns that have been building in Western industrial society for a hundred years or more. It is at least remarkable that so many of the themes of the new international youth culture appear to revolve in one way or another about the human costs of technology and urban life, and how often they seem to echo a yearning to return to an ancient and simpler day.

End Note

Our theme in this chapter has been that the root causes for what we call campus unrest are exceedingly complex, are deeply planted in basic social and philosophic movements, and are not only nation-wide but also worldwide.

Given this view of the matter, how should the United States and American society deal with the problems of campus unrest, react to them, respond to them?

First, much good can be done through more understanding and better understanding. Substantive differences divide the proponents of the new culture from those of traditional American society. Superficial differences in style also separate them. But in addition to these differences, unnecessary tensions emerge from simple misunderstanding of one another. A large crowd of students may well appear threatening to others when it is in fact a normal gathering for communication. Language that affronts may have had no such intent. The university administrator who seeks to explain how and why a particular decision was made through a complex series of committee decisions is not by that fact giving a bureaucratic runaround to his inquirer. Understanding does not obliterate differences. But understanding can reduce incidents and clashes and the risks of greater distrust and violence.

Second, teachers, scholars, and parents may well find many of the adherents of the new culture to be inexperienced in affairs, impatient of explanations, uninformed about the world, rude and arrogant in their self-righteousness, and insufficiently alive to the importance of vital principles and ideals that are not central to the new youth culture. The only answer here is to seek to teach, to educate, and to inform. And in turn, the students will be found to have the capacity on some matters to educate and enlarge the perspective of the older generation.

Beyond that, it must be stressed again that much of what is commonly called "campus unrest" is not a problem. It is a condition. If a generation of American students are emerging to full adulthood affected in varying degrees by a different world view and a different set of values, accommodations to their perspectives can be made only over a long period of time and through the operation of the political process. In that case, we can only hope, and try to insure, that the American political system will continue to assist the peaceful coexistence or blending of different life styles.

       ❖   ❖   ❖

Reaction and Repression

The Walker Report

During the week of the Democratic National Convention, the Chicago police were the targets of mounting provocation by both word and act. It took the form of obscene epithets, and of rocks, sticks, bathroom tiles and even human feces hurled at police by demonstrators. Some of these acts had been planned; others were spontaneous or were themselves provoked by police action. Furthermore, the police had been put on edge by widely published threats of attempts to disrupt both the city and the Convention.

That was the nature of the provocation. The nature of the response was unrestrained and indiscriminate police violence on many occasions, particularly at night.

That violence was made all the more shocking by the fact that it was often inflicted upon persons who had broken no law, disobeyed no order, made no threat. These included peaceful demonstrators, onlookers, and large numbers of residents who were simply passing through, or happened to live in, the areas where confrontations were occurring.

Newsmen and photographers were singled out for assault, and their equipment deliberately damaged. Fundamental police training was ignored; and officers, when on the scene, were often unable to control their men. As one police officer put it: "What happened didn't have anything to do with police work."

The violence reached its culmination on Wednesday night.

A report prepared by an inspector from the Los Angeles Police Department, present as an official observer, while generally praising the police restraint he had observed in the parks during the week, said this about the events that night:

> There is no question but that many officers acted without restraint and exerted force beyond that necessary under the

From the National Commission on the Causes and Prevention of Violence, *Report of the National Commission on the Causes and Prevention of Violence* (Washington: U.S. Government Printing Office, 1968).

circumstances. The leadership at the point of conflict did little to prevent such conduct and the direct control of officers by first line supervisors was virtually nonexistent.

He is referring to the police-crowd confrontation in front of the Conrad Hilton Hotel. Most Americans know about it, having seen the 17-minute sequence played and replayed on their television screens.

But most Americans do not know that the confrontation was followed by even more brutal incidents in the Loop side streets. Or that it had been preceded by comparable instances of indiscriminate police attacks on the North Side a few nights earlier when demonstrators were cleared from Lincoln Park and pushed into the streets and alleys of Old Town.

How did it start? With the emergence long before convention week of three factors which figured significantly in the outbreak of violence. These were: threats to the city; the city's response; and the conditioning of Chicago police to expect that violence against demonstrators, as against rioters, would be condoned by city officials.

The threats to the city were varied. Provocative and inflammatory statements, made in connection with activities planned for convention week, were published and widely disseminated. There were also intelligence reports from informants.

Some of this information was absurd, like the reported plan to contaminate the city's water supply with LSD. But some were serious; and both were strengthened by the authorities' lack of any mechanism for distinguishing one from the other.

The second factor—the city's response—matched, in numbers and logistics at least, the demonstrators' threats.

The city, fearful that the "leaders" would not be able to control their followers, attempted to discourage an inundation of demonstrators by not granting permits for marches and rallies and by making it quite clear that the "law" would be enforced.

Government—federal, state and local—moved to defend itself from the threats, both imaginary and real. The preparations were detailed and far ranging: from stationing firemen at each alarm box within a six block radius of the Amphitheatre to staging U.S. Army armored personnel carriers in Soldier Field under Secret Service control. Six thousand Regular Army troops in full field gear, equipped with rifles, flame throwers, and bazookas were airlifted to Chicago on Monday, August 26. About 6000 Illinois National Guard troops had already been activated to assist the 12,000 member Chicago Police Force.

Of course, the Secret Service could never afford to ignore threats of assassination of Presidential candidates. Neither could the city, against the background of riots in 1967 and 1968, ignore the ever-present threat of ghetto riots, possibly sparked by large numbers of demonstrators, during convention week.

The third factor emerged in the city's position regarding the riots following the death of Dr. Martin Luther King and the April 27th peace march to the Civic Center in Chicago.

The police were generally credited with restraint in handling the first riots—but Mayor Daley rebuked the Superintendent of Police. While it was later modified, his widely disseminated "shoot to kill arsonists and shoot to maim looters" order undoubtedly had an effect.

The effect on police became apparent several weeks later, when they attacked demonstrators, bystanders and media representatives at a Civic Center peace march. There were published criticisms—but the city's response was to ignore the police violence.

* * *

That was the background. On August 18, 1968, the advance contingent of demonstrators arrived in Chicago and established their base, as planned, in Lincoln Park on the city's Near North Side. Throughout the week, they were joined by others—some from the Chicago area, some from states as far away as New York and California. On the weekend before the convention began, there were about 2000 demonstrators in Lincoln Park; the crowd grew to about 10,000 by Wednesday.

There were, of course, the hippies—the long hair and love beads, the calculated unwashedness, the flagrant banners, the open love-making and disdain for the constraints of conventional society. In dramatic effect, both visual and vocal, these dominated a crowd whose members actually differed widely in physical appearance, in motivation, in political affiliation, in philosophy. The crowd included Yippies come to "do their thing," youngsters working for a political candidate, professional people with dissenting political views, anarchists and determined revolutionaries, motorcycle gangs, black activists, young thugs, police and secret service undercover agents.

There were demonstrators waving the Viet Cong flag and the red flag of revolution and there were the simply curious who came to watch and, in many cases, became willing or unwilling participants.

To characterize the crowd, then, as entirely hippy-Yippie, entirely "New Left," entirely anarchist, or entirely youthful political dissenters is both wrong and dangerous. The stereotyping that did occur helps to explain the emotional reaction of both police and public during and after the violence that occurred.

Despite the presence of some revolutionaries, the vast majority of the demonstrators were intent on expressing by peaceful means their dissent either from society generally or from the administration's policies in Vietnam.

Most of those intending to join the major protest demonstrations scheduled during the convention week did not plan to enter the Amphitheatre and disrupt the proceedings of the Democratic convention, did not plan aggressive acts of physical provocation against the authorities, and did not plan to use rallies of demonstrators to stage an assault against any person, institution, or place of business. But while it is clear that most of the protestors in Chicago had no intention of initiating violence, this is not to say that they did not expect it to develop.

It was the clearing of the demonstrators from Lincoln Park that led directly to the violence: symbolically, it expressed the city's opposition to the protesters; literally, it forced the protesters into confrontation with police in Old Town and the adjacent residential neighborhoods.

The Old Town area near Lincoln Park was a scene of police ferocity exceeding that shown on television on Wednesday night. From Sunday night through Tuesday night, incidents of intense and indiscriminate violence occurred in the streets after police had swept the park clear of demonstrators.

Demonstrators attacked too. And they posed difficult problems for police as they persisted in marching through the streets, blocking traffic and intersections. But it was the police who forced them out of the park and into the neighborhood. And on the part of the police there was enough wild club swinging, enough cries of hatred, enough gratuitous beating to make the conclusion inescapable that individual policemen, and lots of them, committed violent acts far in excess of the requisite force for crowd dispersal or arrest. To read dispassionately the hundreds of statements describing at firsthand the events of Sunday and Monday nights is to become convinced of the presence of what can only be called a police riot.

* * *

Police violence was a fact of convention week. Were the policemen who committed it a minority? It appears certain that they were —but one which has imposed some of the consequences of its actions on the majority, and certainly on their commanders. There has been no public condemnation of these violators of sound police procedures and common decency by either their commanding officers or city officials. Nor (at the time this Report is being completed—almost three months after the convention) has any disciplinary action been taken against most of them. That some policemen lost control of themselves under exceedingly provocative circumstances can perhaps be understood; but not condoned. If no action is taken against them, the effect can only be to discourage the majority of policemen who acted responsibly, and further weaken the bond between police and community.

Although the crowds were finally dispelled on the nights of violence in Chicago, the problems they represent have not been. Surely this is not the last time that a violent dissenting group will clash head-on with those whose duty it is to enforce the law. And the next time the whole world will still be watching.

three

THE POOR AS A
MINORITY

The young are a minority in the sense that they have recognizable physical or cultural traits that set them apart from others and
operate as a basis for categorical discrimination. The poor may have
similarly visible traits—undernourished, diseased bodies, shabby
clothes, deteriorated housing—that police, teachers, welfare authorities, and other agents of society use for similar purposes of identification and discriminatory treatment. This discriminatory treatment
serves to maintain the cycle of poverty.

The first excerpt in this chapter, drawn from a United States
Department of Health, Education, and Welfare publication, discusses the problems of defining poverty within a shifting standard
of living and suggests that it is necessary to include the near-poverty
group in the definition of poverty. The second and third readings
suggest that the definition of unemployment should be changed to
refer not only to chronic unemployment but to include periods of un-

employment, i.e., unsteady work, and to contain some reference to quality of work and wages paid. These readings indicate that poverty will continue to be a problem in American society in years to come despite government antipoverty programs.

Health care is one area in which it is poignantly obvious that the poor are a minority. Senator Hubert Humphrey points out in the next essay that the poor not only suffer from disease-producing environmental conditions—poor nutrition, lack of medical care facilities, congested living, and the like—but that they are discriminated against in public health clinics when they go for care, through impersonal, inadequate treatment, without regard to human dignity.

The outcome of poverty conditions, according to the report of the President's Commission on Law Enforcement and Administration of Justice, is often a criminal career. But this is not the only, or even the most important conclusion to be drawn from this excerpt. The poor, especially the youthful poor and even more so the black and brown youthful poor, are members of a highly visible minority, with distinctive ways of dressing, talking, and walking. As a consequence they are more likely to be subjected to arrest and court processing because of "negative demeanor" in the eyes of the law. The poor also receive less in the way of community recreation and other facilities that help to prevent crime in other areas. Some theorists believe that the elimination of such discriminations would cause differences in crime between the poor and the middle class to disappear.

Poor and Near Poor: Projections for the 1970's

Delivery of Health Services for the Poor

The generally accepted federal government definition of poverty (Social Security Administration indexes) is a formula based on three times the minimum dollars required to feed a family of given size and location (rural-urban). Thirty million people in 1966 fall within the poor category. (By this definition, an urban family of four requires $3335 to be nonpoor). There is another version of this same formula defining a population called "low-income" which adds the "near-poor" and results in a universe of some 45 million persons. An urban family of four requires $4345 by this index.

Other definitions of poverty are based on minimum consumer expenditures; still others include non-economic criteria. These definitions result in different numbers of poor, slightly different populations, or both. A poverty definition based specifically on health needs embodies still another set of concepts. Neither the Social Security Administration Index nor any others specifically take medical care costs into account....

In developing the Social Security Administration Index, it was assumed that persons at or below the poverty line would have to rely on public or privately provided free care to meet their medical needs—that any outlay for other than the most rudimentary supplies could not be made except at the risk of cutting down on some necessity.

...The universe of need is determined by the number of individuals who fall within the Social Security Administration's low income definition (a combination of the "poor" and "near-poor" categories). In view of the general rise in standard of living and the spectacular rise in prices of medical services, the "near-poor" line is

From *Delivery of Health Services for the Poor*, U.S. Department of Health, Education and Welfare, Human Investment Program (December 1967), pp. 7–8.

a more realistic criterion of need for medical care and perhaps for an overall definition of poverty as well. . . .

Starting with the Census Bureau's *Current Population Survey,* the total "poor" poverty population (as distinct from the "near-poor") has been projected forward to 1972 by several sources. . . . Based on a preliminary figure of 32.9 million "poor" in 1965, it was estimated that there would be 28.5 million in 1972 (a drop of about 600,000 per year), and in 1973, 27.9 million "poor." With the poverty total for 1965 now revised down to 31.9 million, and the newly available tally for 1966 down to 29.7 million, it seems more reasonable to assume the number in 1973 would be no greater than 25–26 million if the present stringent definition remained in effect. With continued economic expansion and rising expectations this of course may not be plausible.

The number of total "poor" plus "near-poor" for 1959–1966 parallels the number of "poor," at a difference of about 15 million. In determining the universe of need for this analysis, the number of "poor" plus "near-poor" through 1973 is assumed to be on a parallel line to the projections of the "poor" population alone. The analysts who worked on various "poor" poverty population projections believe this to be a reliable assumption. It is felt that overall income distributions in this country will continue to be fairly constant over the next six or seven years, and the number of "near-poor" escaping poverty will be replenished in about the same numbers as those "poor" graduating to the "near-poor" category plus those coming into the world to live in poverty and those falling from non-poverty to poverty.

Limited data are available on what the "poor" portion of the low income population might look like in the early 1970s. For the total low income population, much depends on the state of the economy, the existence or nonexistence of antipoverty programs, and the effectiveness of present measures. Projections over this relatively short period of time, as far as detailed characteristics are concerned, are difficult and somewhat questionable. However, some generalizations can be made. It is likely that the poverty program emphasis will continue to be in the area of employment, the economy itself is likely to produce more jobs, with the result that a large percentage of the decrease in low income will be for men of working age and their families. But in the absence of new programs, the number of large families (with five or more children) in poverty will decline very slowly, if at all. Assuming no basic changes in attitudes toward nonwhites, the disproportionately higher number of nonwhite poor will continue. Similarly, the demonstration scale antipoverty educational programs are not expected to result in measurable reduction of poor youth by the early 1970s, but rather the numbers are expected to increase, if for no other reason than that of their projected increased proportion of the total population. The rural poor migration will probably continue, although at a slower pace than during the 1960s. Assuming an increase in Social Security benefits, the total number of elderly poor will certainly be reduced.

Casual and Chronic Unemployment

Manpower Report of the President, 1968

Over 11 million American workers were jobless and looking for work at some time during the prosperous year 1966. This was almost four times the average number (2.9 million) unemployed in any one week of the year. The total number out of work during 1967 was probably somewhat higher. Great progress in reducing unemployment has been made, however, since 1961, when the current economic upturn began. During that recession year, about 15 million workers had periods of unemployment.

The period without work was short (one to four weeks) for over 45 percent of the workers unemployed in 1966. Presumably, unemployment for many of them was due largely to voluntary job changes, some delay in finding work upon entry or reentry into the labor force, and the usual seasonal layoffs. Many secured jobs without outside help. And for those who sought or needed assistance through manpower programs, this help was limited in most cases to job placement services.

The 3.4 million workers with five to fourteen weeks of unemployment in 1966 may be regarded as an "in between" group. For many of these workers—as well as for those with still briefer periods without work—unemployment was a transitional experience, often cushioned to some extent by unemployment insurance and other benefits. But this group udoubtedly included many workers for whom unemployment of fourteen weeks, or even five weeks, had serious financial consequences.

Joblessness had hard and unequivocal implications, however, for the 2.7 million workers who were out of work for fifteen or more weeks in 1966—over a fourth of the year. More than 1 million of

From *Manpower Report of the President, 1968*, U.S. Department of Labor (Washington: U.S. Government Printing Office, 1968), pp. 18–20.

these workers—in cities, towns, and rural areas across the country—spent half or more of 1966 jobless and looking for work.

Any complacency as to the limited impact of extended unemployment among men in the central age groups, who are generally the most employable and have the heaviest family responsibilities, should be ended by these data. Close to 1.3 million men aged 25 to 44 had five or more weeks of unemployment during 1966, almost six times the number (226,000) shown by the monthly surveys. For men of this age group out of work 15 to 26 weeks, the differential between the two estimates was even greater (more than sevenfold—342,000, compared with 48,000). Clearly, the number of men of prime working age who are severely affected by joblessness is much higher than is indicated by the monthly unemployment data. And, to a lesser degree, the same is true for women.

With respect to the groups most affected by unemployment—the young, the poorly educated, the unskilled, older workers, and minority groups—the unemployment data based on experience during the year as a whole tell roughly the same comparative story as do the monthly estimates. However, the incidence of extended unemployment is shown to be greater in all groups than is suggested by the monthly figures for these groups. . . .

The widely noted 2-to-1 ratio in the extent of unemployment between nonwhite and white workers is borne out once more by these data. About 12 percent of all nonwhite workers had five weeks or more of unemployment in 1966, compared with 6 percent of all white workers. Most seriously affected were the nonwhites who were unskilled laborers—one out of every five was unemployed for five or more weeks during 1966.

The major achievements of the past five years in reducing unemployment—particularly long-term unemployment—must not be lost sight of, however. Despite very large additions to the work force between 1961 and 1966, the proportion of workers unemployed for five or more weeks of the year was cut nearly in half (from 11.6 to 6.4 percent). The general expansion in employment—aided by training and other programs focused on workers with persistent difficulty in finding jobs—brought an even sharper drop in the proportion of workers unemployed fifteen weeks or more (from 6.3 percent in 1961 to 2.8 percent in 1966). The improvement was sharpest in the proportion unemployed 27 weeks or more (which fell from 2.8 to 1 percent). Both white and nonwhite workers benefited from this reduction in extended unemployment.

The proportion of workers experiencing repeated spells of joblessness has also dropped significantly. Whereas in 1961, 6.2 percent of the work force had two or more periods of unemployment during the year, by 1966 the figure had fallen to 4 percent. And the proportion of workers reporting at least three spells of unemployment decreased nearly as much (from 3.3 to 2.3 percent).

Nevertheless, the proportion of workers with repeated spells of unemployment did not decline as much, in relative terms, as the overall proportion of workers with many weeks of joblessness. This statistical finding has both economic and policy significance. The improvement in economic conditions, reinforced by manpower programs, has been particularly effective in reducing the number of workers continuously unemployed for long periods; it has, for example, made it much easier for displaced workers to find new jobs. But apparently there has been less progress in reducing irregular or casual employment of unskilled workers or, as yet, in mitigating seasonal layoffs.

Most workers who experience extended unemployment are out of work two or more times during the year. Of the men out of work fifteen or more weeks in 1966, seven out of every ten were unemployed at least twice during the year. Of those with 27 weeks or more of unemployment, also seven out of ten had at least two spells of unemployment, and four out of every ten had three or more spells. These findings underline the need for enlarged efforts to enable the chronically unemployed to qualify for and obtain jobs that promise continuity of employment. There is also a need to explore ways of helping these workers to keep the jobs they get.

The Sub-Employed

Manpower Report of the President, 1968

The present measures of unemployment—limited, broadly, to persons who have no work at all and are actively seeking a job— are particularly inadequate for assessing the economic situation of disadvantaged workers in urban slums, and also rural areas. A broader, more useful concept for analysis of the problems of these groups—that of sub-employment—was introduced in 1967.

The concept of sub-employment broadens the traditional notions of attachment to the labor force and availability for work, and it introduces the issue of the quality of employment as represented by the level of wages. This is especially important for the development of manpower policy in poverty areas. The employed poor— with earnings below the poverty line even for full-time work—now represent a larger problem, at least in terms of numbers, than the unemployed. Yet they are a group which has so far received comparatively little attention.

Separate consideration of the different kinds of people included among the sub-employed is also essential. The sub-employed are a diverse group, with varied problems requiring different remedial approaches. No one policy will deal effectively with the employment problems of all the sub-employed, nor with all aspects of their problems.

Some of the sub-employed are unable to get or keep a job because of social-psychological characteristics or low motivation. But such difficulties must not be considered as characteristic of all the sub-employed. Nor can social-psychological barriers to employment be analyzed apart from the context of available opportunities.

Two obvious but crucial questions are: What are the reasons for the continuing high sub-employment among Negroes and other minority groups in large cities? What can be done to decrease it further? . . .

From *Manpower Report of the President, 1968*, U.S. Department of Labor (Washington: U.S. Government Printing Office, 1968), pp. 35, 83–84.

127

Sub-employment has declined sharply since 1961. The sub-employment rate, as presently measured, fell from 17 percent in 1961 to 10 percent in 1966.

Low earners were by far the larger of the two groups included in the index—6.7 million, as compared with 2.4 million with fifteen or more weeks of unemployment in 1966. And although the number of low earners declined substantially between 1961 and 1966 (by 16 percent), the improvement was not nearly as sharp as in the number with extensive unemployment (which decreased by more than 50 percent). Plainly, the problem of low earnings has been less responsive to the economic upturn than extended unemployment and, so far, has been less affected by manpower and antipoverty programs.

Slightly over half of the sub-employed were men despite the fact that their rate was considerably lower than that for women (9 percent, compared with 13 percent). Among both men and women, low earnings was a much more common problem than unemployment of fifteen or more weeks; the disparity was greater for women.

The economic disadvantage suffered by nonwhite men is sharply portrayed by the sub-employment data. Their sub-employment rate was 22 percent, compared with 8 percent for white men. Coupled with an unemployment rate almost three times as high as for white men was an equally disproportionate low-earnings rate. . . .

Health Services for the Poor: A Portrait of Failure

Three years ago Dr. George James observed that "poverty is the third leading cause of death in New York City." Dr. James was in a position to know—he was the city's health commissioner. His statement was intended to jolt the complacent, and it did.

The shock wave was strong because the statement was true. Poverty never appears on a death certificate. But it takes its toll: through failures in preventive medicine, fatal delays in seeking treatment, care that is inaccessible or inadequate, poor nutrition, congested living, and in many other ways that make disease more likely to happen, less likely to be checked, more likely to kill.

Throughout most of human history, and throughout much of the world today, poverty has been not the third, but the first, cause of death. It is the mark of an affluent society when heart disease and cancer claim more victims than the diseases directly associated with want and misery. . . .

Yet even for us, in our own time, affluence is only an outer shell. Beneath it are the hard facts of poverty's toll as a disabler and a killer.

In the United States today, nearly one out of every three persons in families with incomes under $2000 per year suffers from a chronic condition that limits his activity; for families with incomes above $7000, the figure is one in thirteen.

In the United States today, men in the age-range 45 to 64, the years of top productivity, average 50 days of disability per year among families with incomes under $2000; for the over $7000 income group, the figure is 14.3 disability days.

Those who are poor go to the hospital more often. They remain longer—an average of 10.2 days per hospital stay for the under $2000 group as contrasted with 7.2 days for the group above $7000. This is true despite the self-evident fact that they are less able to pay, less likely to have insurance which covers the bill.

From Hubert H. Humphrey, "The Future of Health Services for the Poor," *Public Health Reports* (U.S. Department of Health, Education, and Welfare, January 1968), pp. 1–5.

Another set of statistics tells a similar tragic story. The contrasting mortality and morbidity rates of our white and nonwhite populations confirm the inequality of health services.

A white baby born today can expect a life-span of 70.2 years, while a nonwhite baby has a life expectancy of 63.4 years—10 percent of a lifetime less. Four times as many nonwhite mothers die in childbirth. Twice as many nonwhite babies die in infancy.

When we turn the spotlight on specific diseases, we see further confirmation. Influenza and pneumonia take more than twice as high a toll among the nonwhite population. Tuberculosis—the great scourge of our grandparents' generation—is all but forgotten except among the poor and nonwhite. Venereal disease is now largely concentrated in the core of our great cities. Nearly all the remaining cases of diseases that need no longer occur at all—typhoid, diphtheria, poliomyelitis, and others—strike those who live in poverty.

Indeed, it would be possible to prepare a set of overlays of a map of the United States. One would indicate areas of high incidence of venereal disease, another of tuberculosis, another of high infant and maternal death rates, another of excessive disability rates from chronic disease. These overlays would cover almost identical territory. And that territory would coincide with another set showing where the poor are congregated—in inner cities and isolated rural areas. The shadow of poverty and the shadow of avoidable disease and early death are the same shadow. They beshroud the same land and the same people.

This fact is more than a national tragedy. It is a national reproach. It is more than unfortunate; it is unconscionable.

President Johnson has said:

Good health services are the right of every citizen, not the privilege of a few. No American should be denied the opportunity for good health care because he lives in a sparsely populated area or deep in the slums of a large city, because he is unemployed or under-privileged, because he is one of poverty's young or very old, because he lacks access to doctors, hospitals, or nursing homes, because he does not know where to find or how to use health services, or because his affliction extends beyond our present knowledge and our current discoveries.

He has also said, in a Special Message to the Congress, that we must aspire to "good health for every citizen, up to the limits of this country's capacity to provide it."

The President believes, and I believe, that this country's capacity is very high indeed. But cold statistical truths as enumerated show how very far below capacity we are performing for a great many of our citizens. . . .

What are the barriers that separate the poor from the health care that they need and that medical science is capable of providing them? What are the obstacles that we, as a society, must tear down?

First, there are barriers of accessibility. For a variety of reasons, good health care is difficult or impossible to obtain for many of our urban and rural poor.

One such barrier is based on actual shortages. As a nation we do not have enough physicians, enough dentists, enough nurses, enough supporting manpower, and enough hospital and nursing home beds to meet the needs of our people. These shortages affect everyone, regardless of socioeconomic status, to a greater or lesser extent.

For the poor the extent is greater, because of the barrier of maldistribution of the resources we have. In a study of the Watts area of Los Angeles, Dr. Milton Roemer found that 106 of the 251,000 people living in the district surveyed were physicians—a ratio about one-third that for Los Angeles County as a whole. Of these physicians only five were board-certified specialists. Two of the eight small hospitals in the district were approved by the Joint Commission on Accreditation; for most hospital services the people living in the district were dependent on Los Angeles County Hospital, ten miles and an hour's bus ride away.

Counterparts of these conditions can be found in almost every major city. For the rural poor, the distribution pattern is likely to be even more unfavorable.

Meanwhile, among nonwhites, the rate of recruitment and education of potential physicians and dentists is still dismally low. Students in low-income families are not entering medical and dental schools at anything like the rates necessary to do justice to their own professional interest or to the patients of all races whom they might serve after graduation.

Another barrier is cost of health service.

The price of medical and hospital care is rising faster than any other component of our economy. The advance of private health insurance over the past few years has benefited millions of Americans but few of the poor who are in most urgent need of help. The great legislative advances of Medicare and Medicaid are helping to lift the burden of cost from the shoulders of the aged and medically indigent, but we cannot delude ourselves that the cost barrier has been eliminated.

Finally, there is the problem of not knowing where to turn. Health services for the poor are fragmented and dispersed. Even those that exist are not easy to find. The individual who needs health care has to shop around for it. And, as Surgeon General William Stewart recently pointed out, "Among all the goods and services he purchases, health care is perhaps the most difficult for him to shop for intelligently. The Yellow Pages are of limited help and there is no Consumer's Guide. . . . The price tag is never displayed. . . . He usually has a very vague understanding of the kind of service he needs and a very inadequate basis for judging the quality of service he receives."

Elsewhere, Dr. Stewart has said, "Today the individual gets to the right place at the right time largely by happenstance. Many do not."

Thus, there are numerous barriers that place good health care beyond the convenient reach of the poor. And in addition to these barriers of accessibility, there are also barriers of acceptability.

For the care that our poor people receive leaves a great deal to be desired, even after they have run the obstacle course to obtain it. Dr. Kenneth Clement of Cleveland, in his keynote address at the recent centennial conference of the Howard University College of Medicine, described indigent medical care as seen through the eyes of those who receive it.

"It is delivered in ways that are depersonalized and lacking in continuity. There is no one health professional with whom the family can build a trusted relationship.

"It is fragmented care—if sick, go here; to be immunized, go there; if a specialty problem, go somewhere else.

"The care is rendered without care for the family as a unit. . . .

"It is often inaccessible. . . .

"The institutions are often distant from the poverty areas. . . . The inaccessibility is often increased by the failure of institutions to provide hours that do not require the patient to miss employment— and employment often without sick-time benefits."

Dr. Clement summed it up this way:

"The patient must often wait long hours at overcrowded clinics in public or voluntary hospitals, and is not infrequently told to return on some other day when those responsible for manning the clinics are not available. His desire for privacy is consistently ignored and his dignity in many ways degraded."

This is not a pleasant portrait of the health services received by one in almost every five Americans. It is a portrait of at least partial failure—by health departments, private medicine, hospitals, medical schools, voluntary agencies. There is plenty of failure to go around.

Slums and Slum Dwellers

Juvenile Delinquency and Youth Crime

The slums of virtually every American city harbor, in alarming amounts, not only physical deprivation and spiritual despair but also doubt and downright cynicism about the relevance of the outside world's institutions and the sincerity of efforts to close the gap. Far from ignoring or rejecting the goals and values espoused by more fortunate segments of society, the slum dweller wants the same material and intangible things for himself and his children as those more privileged. Indeed, the very similarity of his wishes sharpens the poignancy and frustration of felt discrepancies in opportunity for fulfillment. The slum dweller may not respect a law that he believes draws differences between his rights and another's, or a police force that applies laws so as to draw such differences; he does recognize the law's duty to deal with lawbreakers, and he respects the policeman who does so with businesslike skill and impartiality. Living as he does in a neighborhood likely to be among the city's highest in rates of crime, he worries about and wants police protection even more than people living in the same city's safer regions. He may not have much formal education himself, or many books in his house, and he may hesitate to visit teachers or attend school functions, but studies show that he too, like his college-graduate counterpart, is vitally interested in his children's education.[1] And while some inner-city residents, like some people everywhere, may not be eager to change their unemployment status, it is also true that many more of them toil day after day at the dullest and most backbreaking of society's tasks, traveling long distances for menial jobs without hope of advancement. Very likely his parents (or he himself) left home— the deep South, or Appalachia, or Mexico, or Puerto Rico—looking for a better life, only to be absorbed into the yet more binding dependency and isolation of the inner city.

From The President's Commission on Law Enforcement and Administration of Justice, *Task Force Report: Juvenile Delinquency and Youth Crime* (Washington: U.S. Government Printing Office, 1967), Chap. 2, pp. 43–45.

The children of these disillusioned colored pioneers inherited the total lot of their parents—the disappointments, the anger. to add to their misery, they had little hope of deliverance. For where does one run to when he's already in the promised land? Claude Brown, *Manchild in the Promised Land* (1965), p. 8.

A sketch[2] drawn from the limited information available shows that disproportionately the delinquent is a child of the slums, from a neighborhood that is low on the socioeconomic scale of the community and harsh in many ways for those who live there. He is 15 or 16 years old (younger than his counterpart of a few years ago), one of numerous children—perhaps representing several different fathers—who live with their mother in a home that the sociologists call female-centered. It may be broken; it may never have had a resident father; it may have a nominal male head who is often drunk or in jail or in and out of the house (welfare regulations prohibiting payment where there is a "man in the house" may militate against his continuous presence). He may never have known a grownup man well enough to identify with or imagine emulating him. From the adults and older children in charge of him he has had leniency, sternness, affection, perhaps indifference in erratic and unpredictable succession. All his life he has had considerable independence, and by now his mother has little control over his comings and goings, little way of knowing what he is up to until a policeman brings him home or a summons from court comes in the mail.

He may well have dropped out of school. He is probably unemployed, and has little to offer an employer. The offenses he and his friends commit are much more frequently thefts than crimes of personal violence, and they rarely commit them alone. Indeed, they rarely do anything alone, preferring to congregate and operate in a group, staking out their own "turf"—a special street corner or candy store or poolroom—and adopting their own flamboyant title and distinctive hair style or way of dressing or talking or walking, to signal their membership in the group and show that they are "tough" and not to be meddled with. Their clear belligerence toward authority does indeed earn them the fearful deference of both adult and child, as well as the watchful suspicion of the neighborhood policeman.[3] Although the common conception of the gang member is of a teenager, in fact the lower class juvenile begins his gang career much earlier and usually in search not of co-conspirators in crime but of companionship. But it is all too easy for them to drift into minor and then major violations of the law.[4]

That is not to suggest that his mother has not tried to guide him, or his father if he has one or an uncle or older brother. But their influence is diluted and undermined by the endless task of making ends meet in the face of debilitating poverty; by the constant presence of temptation—drugs, drinking, gambling, petty thievery, prostitution; by the visible contrast of relative affluence on the other side of town.[5]

THE PHYSICAL ENVIRONMENT

It is in the inner city that the most overcrowding, the most substandard housing, the lowest rentals are found. Farther out in the city, more families own their own homes; presumably more families are intact and stable enough to live in those homes and more fathers are employed and able to buy them. The inevitable influence of slum living conditions on juvenile behavor[6] need not be translated into sociological measurements to be obvious to the assaulted senses of the most casual visitor to the slum. Nor does the child who lives there fail to recognize—and reject—the squalor of his surroundings:

> Well, the neighborhood is pretty bad, you know. Trash around the street, stuff like that and the movies got trash all in the bathroom, dirty all over the floors. Places you go in for recreation they aren't clean like they should be, and some of the children that go to school wear clothes that aren't clean as they should be. Some of them, you know, don't take baths as often as they should. Well, my opinion is * * * it's not clean as it should be and if I had a chance, if my mother would move, I would rather move to a better neighborhood. [16-year-old boy.][7]

> It's sort of small. * * * It's something like a slum. Slum is a place where people hang out and jest messy, streets are messy, alleys are messes and a lot of dirty children hang around there. I would say it is a filthy place. [12-year-old boy.]

What the inner-city child calls home is often a set of rooms shared by a shifting group of relatives and acquaintances—furniture shabby and sparse, many children in one bed, plumbing failing, plaster falling, roaches in the corners and sometimes rats, hallways dark or dimly lighted, stairways littered, air dank and foul. Inadequate, unsanitary facilities complicate keeping clean. Disrepair discourages neatness. Insufficient heating, multiple use of bathrooms and kitchens, crowded sleeping arrangements spread and multiply respiratory infections and communicable diseases. Rickety, shadowy stairways and bad electrical connections take their accidental toll. Rat bites are not infrequent and sometimes, especially for infants, fatal. Care of one's own and respect for others' possessions can hardly be inculcated in such surroundings. More important, home has little holding power for the child—it is not physically pleasant or attractive; it is not a place to bring his friends; it is not even very much the reassuring gathering place of his own family. The loss of parental control and diminishing adult supervision that occur so early in the slum child's life must thus be laid at least partly at the door of his home.

The physical environment of the neighborhood is no better. In the alley are broken bottles and snoring winos—homeless, broken men, drunk every day on cheap wine. ("There are a whole lot of winos who hang around back in the alley there. Men who drink and lay around there dirty, smell bad. Cook stuff maybe. Chase you * * * and the yard ain't right. Bottles broke in the yard, plaster, bricks, baby carriages all broken up, whole lot of stuff in people's yards." [14-year-old describing his home.]) The buildings are massive sooty tenements or sagging row houses. ("I don't like the way those houses built. They curve * * * I don't like the way they look * * *. They make the street look bad." [13-year-old.])

On some stoops, apparently able-bodied men sit passing away the time. On others children scamper around a grandmother's knees; they have been on the streets since early morning, will still be there at dusk. The nearest playground may be blocks away across busy streets, a dusty grassless plot. ("There ain't no recreation around. There was a big recreation right across the street and they tore it down. * * * [T]hey just closed it up—instead of building a road they put up a parking lot. * * * There ain't enough playgrounds, and

137

if you go down to the railroad station, there is a big yard down there,
* * * cops come and chase us off. * * *" [14-year-old boy.]) Harlem,
for example, although it borders on and contains several major parks,

> is generally lacking in play space * * * [A]bout 10 percent of
> the area consists of parks and playgrounds, compared to over 16
> percent for New York City as a whole. The total acreage of 14
> parks and playgrounds is not only inadequate, but all the parks
> are esthetically and functionally inadequate as well. * * * For
> many of the children, then, the streets become play areas, and
> this, coupled with the heavy flow of traffic through the com-
> munity, results in a substantially higher rate of deaths due to
> motor vehicles among persons under 25 (6.9 per 100,000 com-
> pared to 4.2 per 100,000 for all of New York City). Youth in the
> Ghetto (Harlem Youth Opportunities Unlimited, Inc., 1964), pp.
> 100–101.

In addition to actual dangerousness, lack of recreation facilities
has been shown to be linked to negative attitudes toward the
neighborhood and those attitudes in turn to repeated acts of delinquency.[8]

Overcrowding alone is an obstacle to decent life in the slum.
In central Harlem, the population density is approximately 66,000
people for every square mile—a rate at which all the people in the
Nation's twelve largest cities would fit inside the city limits of New
York. Even apart from its effects on the soul, such packing has obvious implications for the crime rate. Some crime is a kind of collision;
when so many people are living and moving in so small a space, the
probability of collisions can only increase. Crowding has a harmful
effect on study habits, attitudes toward sex, parents' ability to meet
needs of individual children; clearly, crowding intensifies the fatigue
and irritability that contribute to erratic or irrational discipline.

Many of the people and activities that bring slum streets and
buildings to life are unsavory at best. Violence is commonplace:

> When I first started living around here it was really bad, but I
> have gotten used to it now. Been here 2 years. People getting
> shot and stuff. Lots of people getting hurt. People getting beat
> up * * *. Gee, there's a lot of violence around here. You see it
> all the time * * *. [14-year-old boy.]

Fighting and drunkenness are everyday matters:

> Sometime where I live at people be hitting each other, fighting
> next door. Then when they stop fighting then you can get some
> sleep * * *. [15-year-old boy.]

> Drinking, cussing, stabbing people, having policemen running
> all around mostly every day in the summertime. [14-year-old.]

Drug addiction and prostitution are familiar. The occupying-army
aspects of predominantly white store ownership and police patrol in
predominantly Negro neighborhoods have been many times re-
marked; the actual extent of the alienation thereby enforced and
symbolized is only now being generally conceded.[9]

four

THE GAY MINORITY

Homosexuality is generally portrayed in sociological and psychological literature as a kind of sickness or form of social maladjustment. The current view derives in part from the earlier theological view that homosexuality is sin, evil, something to be eradicated, and that homosexuals are unhappy people with defective, maternally dominant family backgrounds and with aberrant social relations. This view implies that they are sick, in need of cure, and we should figure out what is wrong with them so we can help them.

The minority group's perspective is radically different from this social maladjustment frame of reference. In this perspective, homosexuality is not an ailment or hereditary defect, but rather an alternative life style as valid as those of "straight society," and homosexuals are an oppressed minority group with striking similarities to other minority groups.

As with other minorities, much of what nonhomosexuals think of homosexuals is stereotyping: that all homosexual men are effeminate, that all homosexual women are masculine, that a homosexual can be recognized at a glance, that they are especially fond of sexual relations with children, that they are especially prone to violence, and that they are all unhappy. All of these stereotypical beliefs are disputed by empirical studies such as *The Wolfenden Report*, excerpts of which comprise this chapter. Like other minorities, homosexuals sometimes engage in protective clowning, sometimes try to pass as members of the majority ("straight") group, develop their own subcultural slang or argot, and are subject to categorical discrimination when their identity becomes known.

At first glance, of course, homosexuals seem much less like a minority group than blacks or browns because of the absence of observable differences that can be used for categorical discrimination. But the "closet queen"—the homosexual who tries to pass—may suffer the same identity crisis as the black with fair skin who tries to pass for white. Moreover, once a person becomes publicly labeled a homosexual, it is very difficult for him to remove the stigma (e.g., he may be required to register with the police as a "sexual psychopath").

The controversial conclusion of *The Wolfenden Report*—that homosexual acts between two consenting adults in privacy should be made legal—implies a clear recognition that homosexuals are a deviant minority rather than practitioners of evil, sin, or crime. The evidence adduced in this chapter all points to that conclusion. Removing the legal taint or stigma would allow many homosexuals to lead happier, more productive lives. In recent years homosexuals have established organizations such as Gay Liberation Front, One, Inc., Daughters of Bilitis, S.I.R., and the Mattachine Society for the explicit purpose of bringing homosexuals and homosexuality out into the open and ending legal and social repression of homosexuals as a minority. Homosexuals are beginning to emerge as a self-aware deviant minority.

The Nature of Homosexuality

The Wolfenden Report

18. It is important to make a clear distinction between "homosexual offenses" and "homosexuality." . . . For the latter, we are content to rely on the dictionary definition that homosexuality is a sexual propensity for persons of one's own sex. Homosexuality, then, is a state or condition, and as such does not, and cannot, come within the purview of the criminal law.

19. This definition of homosexuality involves the adoption of some criteria for its recognition. As in other psychological fields, an inference that the propensity exists may be derived from either subjective or objective data, that is, either from what is felt or from what is done by the persons concerned. Either method may lead to fallacious results. In the first place, introspection is neither exhaustive nor infallible; an individual may quite genuinely not be aware of either the existence or the strength of his motivations and propensities, and there is a natural reluctance to acknowledge, even to oneself, a preference which is socially condemned, or to admit to acts that are illegal and liable to a heavy penalty. Rationalization and self-deception can be carried to great lengths, and in certain circumstances lying is also to be expected. Secondly, some of those whose main sexual propensity is for persons of the opposite sex indulge, for a variety of reasons, in homosexual acts. It is known, for example, that some men who are placed in special circumstances that prohibit contact with the opposite sex (for instance, in prisoner-of-war camps or prisons) indulge in homosexual acts, though they revert to heterosexual behavior when opportunity affords; and it is clear from our evidence that some men who are not predominantly homosexual lend themselves to homosexual practices for financial or other gain. Conversely, many homosexual persons have heterosexual inter-

From Committee on Homosexual Offenses and Prostitution, *The Wolfenden Report* (London: Her Majesty's Printing Office, 1957), pp. 11–25 in 1962 edition.

course with or without homosexual fantasies. Furthermore, a homosexual tendency may not be manifested exclusively, or even at all, in sexual fields of behavior, as we explain in paragraph 23 below.

20. There is the further problem how widely the description "homosexual" should be applied. According to the psychoanalytic school, a homosexual component (sometimes conscious, often not) exists in everybody; and if this is correct, homosexuality in this sense is universal. Without going so far as to accept this view *in toto,* it is possible to realize that the issue of latent homosexuality, which we discuss more fully in paragraph 24 below, is relevant to any assessment of the frequency of occurrence of the condition of homosexuality. However, for the purposes of the main body of our report, and in connection with our recommendations, we are strictly speaking concerned only with those who, for whatever reason, commit homosexual offenses.

21. In spite of difficulties such as those we have mentioned in the preceding paragraphs, there is a general measure of agreement on two propositions: (i) that there exists in certain persons a homosexual propensity which varies quantitatively in different individuals and can also vary quantitatively in the same individual at different epochs of life; (ii) that this propensity can affect behavior in a number of ways, some of which are not obviously sexual; although exactly how much and in what ways may be matters for disagreement and dispute.

22. The first of these propositions means that homosexuality as a propensity is not an "all or none" condition, and this view has been abundantly confirmed by the evidence submitted to us. All gradations can exist from apparently exclusive homosexuality without any conscious capacity for arousal by heterosexual stimuli to apparently exclusive heterosexuality, though in the latter case there may be transient and minor homosexual inclinations, for instance in adolescence. According to the psychoanalytic school, all individuals pass through a homosexual phase. Be this as it may, we would agree that a transient homosexual phase in development is very common and should usually cause neither surprise nor concern.

It is interesting that the late Dr. Kinsey, in his study entitled *The Sexual Behavior of the Human Male,* formulated this homosexual-heterosexual continuum on a 7-point scale, with a rating of 6 for sexual arousal and activity with other males only, 3 for arousals and acts equally with either sex, 0 for exclusive heterosexuality, and intermediate ratings accordingly. The recognition of the existence of this continuum is, in our opinion, important for two reasons. First, it leads to the conclusion that homosexuals cannot reasonably be regarded as quite separate from the rest of mankind. Secondly, as will be discussed later, it has some relevance in connection with claims made for the success of various forms of treatment.

23. As regards the second proposition, we have already pointed out that a distinction should be drawn between the condition of homosexuality (which relates to the direction of sexual preference) and the acts or behavior resulting from this preference. It is possible to draw a further distinction between behavior which is overtly sexual and behavior, not overtly sexual, from which a latent homosexuality can be inferred.

It must not be thought that the existence of the homosexual propensity necessarily leads to homosexual behavior of an overtly sexual kind. Even where it does, this behavior does not necessarily amount to a homosexual offense; for instance, solitary masturbation with homosexual fantasies is probably the most common homosexual act, but many persons, though they are aware of the existence within themselves of the propensity, and though they may be conscious of sexual arousal in the presence of homosexual stimuli, successfully control their urges towards overtly homosexual acts with others, either because of their ethical standards or from fear of social or penal consequences, so that their homosexual condition never manifests itself in overtly sexual behavior. There are others who, though aware of the existence within themselves of the propensity, are helped by a happy family life, a satisfying vocation, or a well-balanced social life to live happily without any urge to indulge in homosexual acts. Our evidence suggests however that complete continence in the homosexual is relatively uncommon—as, indeed, it is in the heterosexual—and that even where the individual is by disposition continent, self-control may break down temporarily under the influence of factors like alcohol, emotional distress or mental or physical disorder or disease.

24. Moreover, it is clear that homosexuals differ one from another in the extent to which they are aware of the existence within themselves of the propensity. Some are, indeed, quite unaware of it, and where this is so the homosexuality is technically described as latent, its existence being inferred from the individual's behavior in spheres not obviously sexual. Although there is room for dispute as

to the extent and variety of behavior of this kind which may legitimately be included in the making of this inference, there is general agreement that the existence of a latent homosexuality is an inference validly to be drawn in certain cases. Sometimes, for example, a doctor can infer a homosexual component which accounts for the condition of a patient who has consulted him because of some symptom, discomfort or difficulty, though the patient himself is completely unaware of the existence within himself of any homosexual inclinations. There are other cases in which the existence of a latent homosexuality may be inferred from an individual's outlook or judgment; for instance, a persistent and indignant preoccupation with the subject of homosexuality has been taken to suggest in some cases the existence of repressed homosexuality. Thirdly, among those who work with notable success in occupations which call for service to others, there are some in whom a latent homosexuality provides the motivation for activities of the greatest value to society. Examples of this are to be found among teachers, clergy, nurses, and those who are interested in youth movements and the care of the aged.

25. We believe that there would be a wide measure of agreement on the general account of homosexuality and its manifestations that we have given above. On the other hand, the general position which we have tried to summarize permits the drawings of many different inferences, not all of them in our opinion justified. Especially is this so in connection with the concept of "disease." There is a tendency, noticeably increasing in strength over recent years, to label homosexuality as a "disease" or "illness." This may be no more than a particular manifestation of a general tendency discernible in modern society by which, as one leading sociologist puts it, "the concept of illness expands continually at the expense of the concept of moral failure."[1] There are two important practical consequences which are often thought to follow from regarding homosexuality as an illness. The first is that those in whom the condition exists are sick persons and should therefore be regarded as medical problems and consequently as primarily a medical responsibility. The second is that sickness implies irresponsibility, or at least diminished responsibility. Hence it becomes important in this connection to examine the criteria of "disease," and also to examine the claim that these consequences follow.

26. We are informed that there is no legal definition of "disease" or "disease of the mind"; that there is no precise medical definition

of disease which covers all its varieties; that health and ill health are relative terms which merge into each other, the "abnormal" being often a matter of degree or of what is accepted as the permissible range of normal variation; and that doctors are often called upon to deal not only with recognizable diseases, but also with problems of attitude and with anomalies of character and instinct.

The traditional view seems to be that for a condition to be recognized as a disease, three criteria must be satisfied, namely (i) the presence of abnormal symptoms, which are caused by (ii) a demonstrable pathological condition, in turn caused by (iii) some factor called "the cause," each link in this causal chain being understood as something necessarily antecedent to the next. An example would be the invasion of the body by diphtheria bacilli, leading to pathological changes, leading to the symptoms of diphtheria.

While we have found this traditional view a convenient basis for our consideration of the question whether or not homosexuality is a disease, it must be recognized that the three criteria, as formulated above, are oversimplified, and that each needs some modification. Moreover, there are conditions now recognized as diseases though they do not satisfy all three criteria. Our evidence suggests, however, that homosexuality does not satisfy any of them unless the terms in which they are defined are expanded beyond what could reasonably be regarded as legitimate.

27. In relation, first, to the presence of abnormal symptoms, it is nowadays recognized that many people behave in an unusual, extraordinary, or socially unacceptable way, but it seems to us that it would be rash to assume that unorthodox or aberrant behavior is necessarily symptomatic of disease if it is the only symptom that can be demonstrated. To make this assumption would be to underestimate the very wide range of "normal" human behavior, and abundant evidence is available that what is socially acceptable or ethically permissible has varied and still varies considerably in different cultures. From the medical standpoint, the existence of significant abnormality can seldom be diagnosed from the mere exhibition of unusual behavior, be this criminal or not, the diagnosis depending on the presence of associated symptoms. Further, a particular form of behavior, taken by itself, can seem to be within the range of the normal but may nevertheless be symptomatic of abnormality, the abnormality consisting in (i) the intensity and duration of the symptoms, (ii) their combination together, and (iii) the circumstances in

which they arise. Certain mental diseases, for example, can be diagnosed by the mere association of symptoms to form a recognized psychiatric syndrome, an example of this being schizophrenia, which has no known or generally accepted physical pathology. On the criterion of symptoms, however, homosexuality cannot legitimately be regarded as a disease, because in many cases it is the only symptom and is compatible with full mental health in other respects. In some cases, associated psychiatric abnormalities do occur, and it seems to us that if, as has been suggested, they occur with greater frequency in the homosexual, this may be because they are products of the strain and conflict brought about by the homosexual condition and not because they are causal factors. It has been suggested to us that associated psychiatric abnormalities are less prominent, or even absent, in countries where the homosexual is regarded with more tolerance.

28. As regards the second criterion, namely, the presence of a demonstrable pathological condition, some, though not all, cases of mental illness are accompanied by a demonstrable physical pathology. We have heard no convincing evidence that this has yet been demonstrated in relation to homosexuality. Biochemical and endocrine studies so far carried out in this field have, it appears, proved negative, and investigations of body build and the like have also so far proved inconclusive. We are aware that studies carried out on sets of twins suggest that certain genes lay down a potentiality which will lead to homosexuality in the person who possesses them, but even if this were established (and the results of these studies have not commanded universal acceptance), a genetic predisposition would not necessarily amount to a pathological condition, since it may be no more than a natural biological variation comparable with variations in stature, hair pigmentation, handedness and so on.

In the absence of a physical pathology, psychopathological theories have been constructed to explain the symptoms of various forms of abnormal behavior or mental illness. These theories range from rather primitive formulations like a repressed complex or a mental "abscess" to elaborate systems. They are theoretical constructions to explain observed facts, not the facts themselves, and similar theories have been constructed to explain "normal" behavior. These theoretical constructions differ from school to school. The alleged psychopathological causes adduced for homosexuality have, however, also been found to occur in others besides the homosexual.

29. As regards the third criterion, that is, the "cause," there is never a single cause for normal behavior, abnormal behavior or mental illness. The causes are always multiple. Even the invasion of the body by diphtheria bacilli does not of itself lead to the disease of diphtheria, as is shown by the existence of "carriers" of live diphtheria bacilli. To speak, as some do, of some single factor such as seduction in youth as the "cause" of homosexuality is unrealistic unless other factors are taken into account. Besides genetic predisposition, a number of such factors have been suggested, for instance, unbalanced family relationships, faulty sex education, or lack of opportunity for heterosexual contacts in youth. In the present state of our knowledge, none of these can be held to bear a specific causal relationship to any recognized psychopathology or physical pathology; and to assert a direct and specific causal relationship between these factors and the homosexual condition is to ignore the fact that they have all, including seduction, been observed to occur in persons who become entirely heterosexual in their disposition.

30. Besides the notion of homosexuality as a disease, there have been alternative hypotheses offered by others of our expert witnesses. Some have preferred to regard it as a state of arrested development. Some, particularly among the biologists, regard it as simply a natural deviation. Others, again, regard it as a universal potentiality which can develop in response to a variety of factors.

We do not consider ourselves qualified to pronounce on controversial and scientific problems of this kind, but we feel bound to say that the evidence put before us has not established to our satisfaction the proposition that homosexuality is a disease. Medical witnesses have, however, stressed the point, and it is an important one, that in some cases homosexual offenses do occur as symptoms in the course of recognized mental or physical illness, for example, senile dementia. We have the impression, too, that those whose homosexual offenses stem from some mental illness or defect behave in a way which increases their chances of being caught.

31. Even if it could be established that homosexuality were a disease, it is clear that many individuals, however their state is reached, present social rather than medical problems and must be dealt with by social, including penological, methods. This is especially relevant when the claim that homosexuality is an illness is taken to imply that its treatment should be a medical responsibility. Much more important than the academic question whether homo-

sexuality is a disease is the practical question whether a doctor should carry out any part or all of the treatment. Psychiatrists deal regularly with problems of personality which are not regarded as diseases, and conversely the treatment of cases of recognized psychiatric illness may not be strictly medical but may best be carried out by non-medical supervision or environmental change. Examples would be certain cases of senile dementia or chronic schizophrenia which can best be managed at home. In fact, the treatment of behavior disorders, even when medically supervised, is rarely confined to psychotherapy or to treatment of a strictly medical kind. This is not to deny that expert advice should be sought in very many homosexual cases. We shall have something more to say on these matters in connection with the treatment of offenders.

32. The claim that homosexuality is an illness carries the further implication that the sufferer cannot help it and therefore carries a diminished responsibility for his actions. Even if it were accepted that homosexuality could properly be described as a "disease," we should not accept this corollary. There are no *prima facie* grounds for supposing that because a particular person's sexual propensity happens to lie in the direction of persons of his or her own sex it is any less controllable than that of those whose propensity is for persons of the opposite sex. We are informed that patients in mental hospitals, with few exceptions, show clearly by their behavior that they can and do exercise a high degree of responsibility and self-control; for example, only a small minority need to be kept in locked wards. The existence of varying degrees of self-control is a matter of daily experience—the extent to which coughing can be controlled is an example—and the capacity for self-control can vary with the personality structure or with temporary physical or emotional conditions. The question which is important for us here is whether the individual suffers from a condition which causes diminished responsibility. This is a different question from the question whether he was responsible in the past for the causes or origins of his present condition. That is an interesting inquiry and may be of relevance in other connections; but our concern is with the behavior which flows from the individual's present condition and with the extent to which he is responsible for that behavior, whatever may have been the causes of the condition from which it springs. Just as expert opinion can give valuable assistance in deciding on the appropriate ways of deal-

ing with a convicted person, so can it help in assessing the additional factors that may affect his present responsibility.

33. Some psychiatrists have made the point that homosexual behavior in some cases may be "compulsive," that is, irresistible, but there seems to be no good reason to suppose that at least in the majority of cases homosexual acts are any more or any less resistible than heterosexual acts, and other evidence would be required to sustain such a view in any individual case. Even if immunity from penal sanctions on such grounds were claimed or granted, nevertheless preventive measures would have to be taken for the sake of society at large, in much the same way as it is necessary to withhold a driving license from a person who is subject to epileptic fits. This is particularly true of the offender who is a very bad risk for recurrence, but is not certifiable either as insane or as a mental defective.

34. When questions of treatment or disposal of offenders are being considered, the assessment of prognosis is very important, and expert advice may need to be sought on such questions as whether the factors that in the view of the doctors lead to diminished control, that is, diminished "responsibility," are capable of modification, or what environmental changes should be advocated or ordered to reduce the chances of a recurrence. Thus it is just as reasonable for a doctor to recommend that a paedophiliac should give up schoolmastering as it would be to recommend to another patient never to return to a hot climate.

35. Some writers on the subject, and some of our witnesses, have drawn a distinction between the "invert" and the "pervert." We have not found this distinction very useful. It suggests that it is possible to distinguish between two men who commit the same offense, the one as the result of his constitution, the other from a perverse and deliberate choice, with the further suggestion that the former is in some sense less culpable than the latter. To make this distinction as a matter of definition seems to prejudge a very difficult question.

Similarly, we have avoided the use of the terms "natural" and "unnatural" in relation to sexual behavior, for they depend for their force upon certain explicit theological or philosophical interpretations, and with these interpretations their use imports an approving or a condemnatory note into a discussion where dispassionate thought and statement should not be hindered by adherence to particular preconceptions.

36. Homosexuality is not, in spite of widely held belief to the contrary, peculiar to members of particular professions or social classes; nor, as is sometimes supposed, is it peculiar to the intelligentsia. Our evidence shows that it exists among all callings and at all levels of society; and that among homosexuals will be found not only those possessing a high degree of intelligence, but also the dullest oafs.

Some homosexuals, it is true, choose to follow occupations which afford opportunities for contact with those of their own sex, and it is not unnatural that those who feel themselves to be "misfits" in society should gravitate towards occupations offering an atmosphere of tolerance or understanding, with the result that some occupations may appear to attract more homosexuals than do others. Again, the arrest of a prominent national or local figure has greater news value than the arrest of (say) a laborer for a similar offense, and in consequence the Press naturally finds room for a report of the one where it might not find room for a report of the other. Factors such as these may well account to some extent for the prevalent misconceptions.

37. Our consideration of the problems we have had to face would have been made much easier if it had been possible to arrive at some reasonably firm estimate of the prevalence either of the condition of homosexuality or of the commission of homosexual acts. So far as we have been able to discover, there is no precise information about the number of men in Great Britain who either have a homosexual disposition or engage in homosexual behavior.

38. No inquiries have been made in this country comparable to those which the late Dr. Kinsey conducted in the United States of America. Dr. Kinsey concluded that in the United States, 4 percent of adult white males are exclusively homosexual throughout their lives after the onset of adolescence. He also found evidence to suggest that 10 percent of the white male population are more or less exclusively homosexual for at least three years between the ages of 16 and 65, and that 37 percent of the total male population have at least some overt homosexual experience, to the point of orgasm, between adolescence and old age. Dr. Kinsey's findings have aroused opposition and scepticism. But it was noteworthy that some of our medical witnesses expressed the view that something very like these figures would be established in this country if similar inquiries were made. The majority, while stating quite frankly that they did not

really know, indicated that their impression was that his figures would be on the high side for Great Britain.

＊   ＊   ＊

43. It is certainly true also . . . that the number of homosexual offenses known to the police has increased considerably. It does not, however, necessarily follow from these figures that there has been an increase either in homosexuality or in homosexual behavior; still less can these figures be regarded as an infallible measure of any increase which may have occurred during that period. Unlike some offenses (e.g., housebreaking) which, by their nature, tend to be reported to the police as they occur, many sexual offenses, particularly those taking place between consenting parties, become "known to the police" only when they are detected by the police or happen to be reported to them. Any figures relating to homosexual offenses known to the police will therefore be conditioned to a large extent both by the efficiency of the police methods of detecting and recording, and by the intensity of police activity. These factors vary from time to time and from place to place.

Clearly, the more efficient the police methods of detection, the higher the proportion of offenses detected. It was to be expected that the more intensive training given to police officers in recent years, particularly in methods of detection, would result in the discovery of a higher proportion of offenses; but this does not necessarily indicate that more offenses have occurred. We understand, too, that efforts have been made in recent years to improve the methods by which offenses known to the police are recorded, and these may have been reflected in higher figures without any necessary implication of a higher number of offenses. Lastly, the extent to which the police follow up suspicions of homosexual behavior varies considerably as between one police force and another according to the outlook of the senior officers; and sometimes even within a given police force the intensity of action varies from time to time along with the ups and downs of public indignation aroused, or public annoyance caused, by the behavior of the offenders.

In brief, therefore, it would be dangerous to argue from the police statistics alone either that there was an overall increase or that homosexual behavior was most prevalent in those areas where the number of cases recorded as known to the police was the highest.

44. Some of us have a definite impression, derived from what we have observed or read, and by inference from the tenor of evidence submitted to us, that there has been an increase in the amount of homosexual behavior. Others of us prefer, in the absence of conclusive evidence, not to commit themselves to expressing even a general impression.

45. Those who have the impression of a growth in homosexual practices find it supported by at least three wider considerations. First, in the general loosening of former moral standards, it would not be surprising to find that leniency towards sexual irregularities in general included also an increased tolerance of homosexual behavior and that greater tolerance had encouraged the practice. Secondly, the conditions of war time, with broken families and prolonged separation of the sexes, may well have occasioned homosexual behavior which in some cases has been carried over into peace time. Thirdly, it is likely that the emotional insecurity, community instability, and weakening of the family, inherent in the social changes of our civilization, have been factors contributing to an increase in homosexual behavior.

Most of us think it improbable that the increase in the number of offenses recorded as known to the police can be explained entirely by greater police activity, though we all think it very unlikely that homosexual behavior has increased proportionately to the dramatic rise in the number of offenses recorded as known to the police.

46. Our medical evidence seems to show three things: first, that in general practice male homosexuals form a very small fraction of the doctor's patients; secondly, that in psychiatric practice male homosexuality is a primary problem in a very small proportion of the cases seen; and thirdly, that only a very small percentage of homosexuals consult doctors about their condition. It is almost impossible to compare the incidence of homosexual behavior with the incidence of other forms of sexual irregularity, most of which are outside the purview of the criminal law and are therefore not recorded in criminal statistics; our impression is that of the total amount of irregular sexual conduct, homosexual behavior provides only a very small proportion. It cannot, however, be ignored. The male population of Great Britain over the age of fifteen numbers nearly 18 million, and even if the Swedish figures . . . , which are the lowest figures relating to incidence that have come to our notice, are

at all applicable to this country, the incidence of homosexuality and homosexual behavior must be large enough to present a serious problem.

47. Our conclusion is that homosexual behavior is practiced by a small minority of the population, and should be seen in proper perspective, neither ignored nor given a disproportionate amount of public attention. Especially are we concerned that the principles we have enunciated above on the function of the law should apply to those involved in homosexual behavior no more and no less than to other persons.

THE PRESENT LAW AND PRACTICE

(i) General Review

48. It is against the foregoing background that we have reviewed the existing provisions of the law in relation to homosexual behavior between male persons. We have found that with the great majority of these provisions we are in complete agreement. We believe that it is part of the function of the law to safeguard those who need protection by reason of their youth or some mental defect, and we do not wish to see any change in the law that would weaken this protection. Men who commit offenses against such persons should be treated as criminal offenders. Whatever may be the causes of their disposition or the proper treatment for it, the law must assume that the responsibility for the overt acts remains theirs, except where there are circumstances which it accepts as exempting from accountability. Offenses of this kind are particularly reprehensible when the men who commit them are in positions of special responsibility or trust. We have been made aware that where a man is involved in an offense with a boy or youth the invitation to the commission of the act sometimes comes from him rather than from the man. But we believe that even when this is so that fact does not serve to exculpate the man.

49. It is also part of the function of the law to preserve public order and decency. We therefore hold that when homosexual behavior between males takes place in public it should continue to be dealt with by the criminal law. Not all the elements in the apprehension of offenders, or in their trial, seem to us to be satisfactory, and

on these points we comment later. But so far as the law itself is concerned we should not wish to see any major change in relation to this type of offense.

50. Besides the two categories of offense we have just mentioned, namely, offenses committed by adults with juveniles and offenses committed in public places, there is a third class of offense to which we have had to give long and careful consideration. It is that of homosexual acts committed between adults in private.

❉   ❉   ❉

52. We have indicated . . . our opinion as to the province of the law and its sanctions, and how far it properly applies to the sexual behavior of the individual citizen. On the basis of the considerations there advanced we have reached the conclusion that legislation which covers acts in the third category we have mentioned goes beyond the proper sphere of the law's concern. We do not think that it is proper for the law to concern itself with what a man does in private unless it can be shown to be so contrary to the public good that the law ought to intervene in its function as the guardian of that public good.

53. In considering whether homosexual acts between consenting adults in private should cease to be criminal offenses we have examined the more serious arguments in favor of retaining them as such. We now set out these arguments and our reasons for disagreement with them. In favor of retaining the present law, it has been contended that homosexual behavior between adult males, in private no less than in public, is contrary to the public good on the grounds that—

  (i) it menaces the health of society;
 (ii) it has damaging effects on family life;
(iii) a man who indulges in these practices with another man may turn his attention to boys.

54. As regards the first of these arguments, it is held that conduct of this kind is a cause of the demoralization and decay of civilizations, and that therefore, unless we wish to see our nation degenerate and decay, such conduct must be stopped, by every possible means. We have found no evidence to support this view, and we cannot feel it right to frame the laws which should govern this

country in the present age by reference to hypothetical explanations of the history of other peoples in ages distant in time and different in circumstances from our own. In so far as the basis of this argument can be precisely formulated, it is often no more than the expression of revulsion against what is regarded as unnatural, sinful or disgusting. Many people feel this revulsion, for one or more of these reasons. But moral conviction or instinctive feeling, however strong, is not a valid basis for overriding the individual's privacy and for bringing within the ambit of the criminal law private sexual behavior of this kind. It is held also that if such men are employed in certain professions or certain branches of the public service their private habits may render them liable to threats of blackmail or to other pressures which may make them "bad security risks." If this is true, it is true also of some other categories of person: for example, drunkards, gamblers and those who become involved in compromising situations of a heterosexual kind; and while it may be a valid ground for excluding from certain forms of employment men who indulge in homosexual behavior, it does not, in our view, constitute a sufficient reason for making their private sexual behavior an offense in itself.

55. The second contention, that homosexual behavior between males has a damaging effect on family life, may well be true. Indeed, we have had evidence that it often is; cases in which homosexual behavior on the part of the husband has broken up a marriage are by no means rare, and there are also cases in which a man in whom the homosexual component is relatively weak nevertheless derives such satisfaction from homosexual outlets that he does not enter upon a marriage which might have been successfully and happily consummated. We deplore this damage to what we regard as the basic unit of society; but cases are also frequently encountered in which a marriage has been broken up by homosexual behavior on the part of the wife, and no doubt some women, too, derive sufficient satisfaction from homosexual outlets to prevent their marrying. We have had no reasons shown to us which would lead us to believe that homosexual behavior between males inflicts any greater damage on family life than adultery, fornication or lesbian behavior. These practices are all reprehensible from the point of view of harm to the family, but it is difficult to see why on this ground male homosexual behavior alone among them should be a criminal offense. This argument is not to be taken as saying that society should condone or approve male homosexual behavior. But where adultery, fornication and lesbian

behavior are not criminal offenses there seems to us to be no valid ground, on the basis of damage to the family, for so regarding homosexual behavior between men. Moreover, it has to be recognized that the mere existence of the condition of homosexuality in one of the partners can result in an unsatisfactory marriage, so that for a homosexual to marry simply for the sake of conformity with the accepted structure of society or in the hope of curing his condition may result in disaster.

56. We have given anxious consideration to the third argument, that an adult male who has sought as his partner another male may turn from such a relationship and seek as his partner a boy or succession of boys. We should certainly not wish to countenance any proposal which might tend to increase offenses against minors. Indeed, if we thought that any recommendation for a change in the law would increase the danger to minors we should not make it. But in this matter we have been much influenced by our expert witnesses. They are in no doubt that whatever may be the origins of the homosexual condition, there are two recognizably different categories among adult male homosexuals. There are those who seek as partners other adult males, and there are paedophiliacs, that is to say men who seek as partners boys who have not reached puberty.[2]

57. We are authoritatively informed that a man who has homosexual relations with an adult partner seldom turns to boys, and vice versa, though it is apparent from the police reports we have seen and from other evidence submitted to us that such cases do happen. A survey of 155 prisoners diagnosed as being homosexuals on reception into Brixton prison during the period 1st January, 1954, to 31st May, 1955, indicated that 107 (69 percent) were attracted to adults, 43 (27.7 percent) were attracted to boys, and 5 (3.3 percent) were attracted to both boys and adults. This last figure of 3.3 percent is strikingly confirmed by another investigation of 200 patients outside prison. But paedophiliacs, together with the comparatively few who are indiscriminate, will continue to be liable to the sanctions of criminal law, exactly as they are now. And the others would be very unlikely to change their practices and turn to boys simply because their present practices were made legal. It would be paradoxical if the making legal of an act at present illegal were to turn men towards another kind of act which is, and would remain, contrary to the law. Indeed, it has been put to us that to remove homosexual behavior between adult males from the listed crimes may serve to protect

minors; with the law as it is there may be some men who would prefer an adult partner but who at present turn their attention to boys because they consider that this course is less likely to lay them open to prosecution or to blackmail than if they sought other adults as their partners. If the law were changed in the way we suggest, it is at least possible that such men would prefer to seek relations with older persons which would not render them liable to prosecution. In this connection, information we have received from the police authorities in the Netherlands suggests that practicing homosexuals in that country are to some extent turning from those practices which are punishable under the criminal law to other practices which are not. Our evidence, in short, indicates that the fear that the legalization of homosexual acts between adults will lead to similar acts with boys has not enough substance to justify the treatment of adult homosexual behavior in private as a criminal offense, and suggests that it would be more likely that such a change in the law would protect boys rather than endanger them.

58. In addition, an argument of a more general character in favor of retaining the present law has been put to us by some of our witnesses. It is that to change the law in such a way that homosexual acts between consenting adults in private ceased to be criminal offenses must suggest to the average citizen a degree of toleration by the Legislature of homosexual behavior, and that such a change would "open the floodgates" and result in unbridled license. It is true that a change of this sort would amount to a limited degree of such toleration, but we do not share the fears of our witnesses, that the change would have the effect they expect. This expectation seems to us to exaggerate the effect of the law on human behavior. It may well be true that the present law deters from homosexual acts some who would otherwise commit them, and to that extent an increase in homosexual behavior can be expected. But it is no less true that if the amount of homosexual behavior has, in fact, increased in recent years, then the law has failed to act as an effective deterrent. It seems to us that the law itself probably makes little difference to the amount of homosexual behavior which actually occurs; whatever the law may be there will always be strong social forces opposed to homosexual behavior. It is highly improbable that the man to whom homosexual behavior is repugnant would find it any less repugnant because the law permitted it in certain circumstances; so that even if, as has been suggested to us, homosexuals tend to proselytize, there is no valid

reason for supposing that any considerable number of conversions would follow the change in the law.

59. [I]n only very few European countries does the criminal law now take cognizance of homosexual behavior between consenting parties in private. It is not possible to make any useful statistical comparison between the situation in countries where the law tolerates such behavior and that in countries where all male homosexual acts are punishable, if only because in the former the acts do not reflect themselves in criminal statistics. We have, however, caused inquiry to be made in Sweden, where homosexual acts between consenting adults in private ceased to be criminal offenses in consequence of an amendment of the law in 1944. We asked particularly whether the amendment of the law had had any discernible effect on the prevalence of homosexual practices, and on this point the authorities were able to say no more than that very little was known about the prevalence of such practices either before or after the change in the law. We think it reasonable to assume that if the change in the law had produced any appreciable increase in homosexual behavior or any large-scale proselytizing, these would have become apparent to the authorities.

60. We recognize that a proposal to change a law which has operated for many years so as to make legally permissible acts which were formerly unlawful, is open to criticisms which might not be made in relation to a proposal to omit, from a code of laws being formulated *de novo*, any provision making these acts illegal. To reverse a long-standing tradition is a serious matter and not to be suggested lightly. But the task entrusted to us, as we conceive it, is to state what we regard as just and equitable law. We therefore do not think it appropriate that consideration of this question should be unduly influenced by a regard for the present law, much of which derives from traditions whose origins are obscure.

61. Further, we feel bound to say this. We have outlined the arguments against a change in the law, and we recognize their weight. We believe, however, that they have been met by the counter-arguments we have already advanced. There remains one additional counter-argument which we believe to be decisive, namely, the importance which society and the law ought to give to individual freedom of choice and action in matters of private morality. Unless a deliberate attempt is to be made by society, acting through the agency of the law, to equate the sphere of crime with

that of sin, there must remain a realm of private morality and immorality which is, in brief and crude terms, not the law's business. To say this is not to condone or encourage private immorality. On the contrary, to emphasize the personal and private nature of moral or immoral conduct is to emphasize the personal and private responsibility of the individual for his own actions, and that is a responsibility which a mature agent can properly be expected to carry for himself without the threat of punishment from the law.

62. We accordingly recommend that homosexual behavior between consenting adults in private should no longer be a criminal offense.

five

THE DRUG MINORITY

A wealth of public misinformation about drugs and drug use has resulted in stereotyping of drug users. Our social distance scale (Introduction) showed both drug addicts and chronic marijuana users to be low on the Bogardus Social Distance Scale, and that this downgrading tends to be much higher among generally prejudiced people than among nonprejudiced people. If these results are generalizable, this means that drug abusers are the target of much prejudice, and thus a minority group. We also saw that national, racial, and ethnic minorities were accorded a much higher place than they had been in previous studies. Perhaps this means that there has been a transfer of the scapegoat mantle to the new targets of aggression—the drug subculture, student radicals, homosexuals, and other newly visible deviant minorities.

The two readings contained in this chapter serve principally to point out the fallacies in the numerous stereotypes of the drug user. The first reading is from *The LaGuardia Report*. This report, published in 1944 is the only thorough scientific study of marijuana available today. It exposes as fallacious such widely held beliefs as that marijuana is addicting, that it leads to harder drugs, that it causes insanity, that it promotes sexual license and crime, and that it reduces intellectual capacity. The overwhelming thrust of *The La-Guardia Report* was in the direction of legalizing marijuana, which would probably have done away with the marijuana user's status as a social minority, since much of the public attitude toward marijuana users has to do with their breaking the law.

The second excerpt, drawn from the report of the President's Commission on Law Enforcement and Administration of Justice, contains a broader discussion of drugs termed "narcotics" under the law. Critical of the law, the Commission validates the LaGuardia Commission observations on marijuana and observes that the law labels a ludicrous variety of substances, addicting and nonaddicting, stimulant and depressant, "narcotics," yet the law contains no definition of what a narcotic is, which means that a narcotic is whatever the legislators decide to say it is. The narcotics laws are quite harsh, and have often resulted from public panic. Their application seems to aggravate rather than to alleviate the drug problem.

The President's Commission points out the many foibles involved in drug legislation, but it fails to tackle the basic issue that we address in this text. It would help to view the drug user as a member of a minority group in school, employment, the eyes of the law, socially, and in nearly all other institutional areas of society. His low status is caused not by his actions; drug users of almost all types are capable of normal or near normal behavior. Marijuana is used casually by engineers, computer programmers, entertainers, and people of important position and high social status without any apparent interference in their efficiency. Even heroin addicts are known to maintain a normal level of efficiency and to live a long time so long as they have access to heroin. Their troubles usually begin only after it is discovered that they are drug users.

No doubt this perspective clashes with one that treats drug use as a sickness or as the result of abnormal social background or seductive and malevolent peer group ties. We present it here as an alternative for the reader to consider. Drug abusers usually resist "therapy" or "cure" precisely because they do not think of themselves as "sick," but rather as defenders of an alternative value system that they hold to be valid (even though the majority of society does not).

The Marijuana Problem in the City of New York

The LaGuardia Report

The Mayor's Committee on Marijuana decided to confine its investigations to a limited area. For a number of reasons the Borough of Manhattan seemed to be the most profitable section of the city in which to concentrate. In order to crystallize our particular project we deemed it advisable to direct our efforts to finding answers to the following questions:

1. To what extent is marijuana used?
2. What is the method of retail distribution?
3. What is the general attitude of the marijuana smoker toward society and toward the use of the drug?
4. What is the relationship between marijuana and eroticism?
5. What is the relationship between marijuana and crime?
6. What is the relationship between marijuana and juvenile delinquency?

In the course of our investigations, we have made extensive use of subjective data obtained from those who were actual smokers of marijuana and directly acquainted with its effects and those who were not smokers, but, because of residence, occupation or other interests, were acquainted with the general subject.

ORGANIZATION OF STAFF

In October 1939 Police Commissioner Lewis J. Valentine designated Deputy Chief Inspector Daniel Curtayne, Lieutenant Edward Cooper, Sergeant Bernard Boylan and Detective Joseph Loures of the Narcotic Squad of the Police Department of the City of New

From The Mayor's Committee on Marijuana, *The Marijuana Problem in the City of New York* (Lancaster, Pa.: Jaques Cattell Press, 1944), pp. 290–302, 308, 311–15, 331–34, 339, 385–88, and 394–403.

York to cooperate with the Mayor's Committee on Marijuana. These police officials submitted a list of intelligent young officers with a suitable background. From this list, six officers were selected: two policewomen, and four policemen, one of whom was a Negro. They were: Mr. James Coen, Mr. William Connolly, Mr. Benjamin Weissner, Mr. John Hughes, Miss Adelaide Knowles, and Miss Olive Cregan. These police officers were encouraged to read literature on the subject of marijuana and to familiarize themselves with some of the characteristics of the plant, as well as of marijuana cigarettes. They became expert in detecting the aroma of burning marijuana, and were thus able to recognize it and to identify its use in a social gathering.

Regular assignments were made by the director of the survey. At intervals each officer dictated a general report on his activities and findings to a stenographer engaged by the Committee. Frequent conferences were held in the office of the director of the survey, at which time individual reports were discussed in detail and evaluated. An attempt was made to give the "marijuana squad" a psychological approach to the performance of their duties.

At no time were these officers permitted to make known their activity to other members of the police force, or to make arrests. This arrangement was considered essential in order that they might maintain an effective role of investigator without being in any respect recognized as police officers. Although they were members of the police force and constantly in contact with violators of law, their immediate superiors cooperated to an extreme degree by allowing the "marijuana squad" to report directly to the director of the survey.

While on duty the squad actually "lived" in the environment in which marijuana smoking or peddling was suspected. They frequented poolrooms, bars and grills, dime-a-dance halls, other dance halls to which they took their own partners, theatres—backstage and in the audience—roller-skating rinks, subways, public toilets, parks, and docks. They consorted with the habitues of these places, chance acquaintances on the street, loiterers around schools, subways, and bus terminals. They posed as "suckers" from out of town and and as students in colleges and high schools.

We highly commend these officers individually for their exceptionally good performances. The aid given by Deputy Chief Inspector Daniel Curtayne, Lieutenant Edward Cooper, Sergeant Bernard

Boylan, and Detective Joseph Loures throughout deserves mention and appreciation. At times we must have been a source of annoyance to them, but our requests were always cheefully met and assistance heartily extended.

METHOD OF RETAIL DISTRIBUTION

In general, marijuana is used in the form of a cigarette. Occcasionally some individuals chew the "weed" and seem to get the same effect as do others through smoking. The common names for the cigarette are: muggles, reefers, Indian hemp, weed, tea, gage, and sticks. Cigarettes made of marijuana differ in size as do cigarettes made of tobacco: they are long, short, thick, or thin.

The price varies in accordance with the accepted opinion as to the potency of the marijuana used in the cigarettes, and this appears to be determined by the place of origin. The cheapest brand is known as "sass-fras," and retails for approximately three for 50 cents. It is made of the marijuana that is grown in the United States. Smokers do not consider such marijuana very potent. They have found that they must consume a greater number of cigarettes in order to obtain the desired effect colloquially termed as "high." This opinion, expressed by smokers in the Borough of Manhattan, is at variance with that of some authorities who believe that marijuana grown in the United States is as potent as the marijuana grown in other countries.

The "panatella" cigarette, occasionally referred to as "meserole," is considered to be more potent than the "sass-fras" and usually retails for approximately 25 cents each. The hemp from which the "panatella" is made comes from Central and South America.

"Gungeon" is considered by the marijuana smoker as the highest grade of marijuana. It retails for about one dollar per cigarette. The "kick" resulting from the use of this cigarette is reached more quickly than from the use of "sass-fras" or "panatella." It appears to be the consensus that the marijuana used to make the "gungeon" comes from Africa. The sale of this cigarette is restricted to a clientele whose economic status is of a higher level than the majority of marijuana smokers.

A confirmed marijuana user can readily distinguish the quality and potency of various brands, just as the habitual cigarette or cigar smoker is able to differentiate between the qualities of tobacco. Foreign-made cigarette paper is often used in order to convince the buyer that the "tea is right from the boat."

There are two channels for the distribution of marijuana cigarettes—the independent peddler and the "tea-pad." From general observations, conversations with "pad" owners, and discussions with peddlers, the investigators estimated that there were about 500 "tea-pads" in Harlem and at least 500 peddlers.

A "tea-pad" is a room or an apartment in which people gather to smoke marijuana. The majority of such places are located in the Harlem district. It is our impression that the landlord, the agent, the superintendent, or the janitor is aware of the purposes for which the premises are rented.

The "tea-pad" is furnished according to the clientele it expects to serve. Usually, each "tea-pad" has comfortable furniture, a radio, victrola, or, as in most instances, a rented nickelodeon. The lighting is more or less uniformly dim, with blue predominating. An incense is considered part of the furnishings. The walls are frequently decorated with pictures of nude subjects suggestive of perverted sexual practices. The furnishings, as described, are believed to be essential as a setting for those participating in smoking marijuana.

Most "tea-pads" have their trade restricted to the sale of marijuana. Some places did sell marijuana and whisky, and a few places also served as houses of prostitution. Only one "tea-pad" was found which served as a house of prostitution, and in which one could buy marijuana, whisky, and opium.

The marijuana smoker derives greater satisfaction if he is smoking in the presence of others. His attitude in the "tea-pad" is that of a relaxed individual, free from the anxieties and cares of the realities of life. The "tea-pad" takes on the atmosphere of a very congenial social club. The smoker readily engages in conversation with strangers, discussing freely his pleasant reactions to the drug and philosophizing on subjects pertaining to life in a manner which, at times, appears to be out of keeping with his intellectual level. A constant observation was the extreme willingness to share and puff on each other's cigarettes. A boisterous, rowdy atmosphere did not prevail and on the rare occasions when there appeared signs indicative of a belligerent attitude on the part of a smoker, he was ejected or forced to become more tolerant and quiescent. One of the most interesting setups of a "tea-pad," which was clearly not along orthodox lines from the business point of view, was a series of pup tents arranged on a roof-top in Harlem. Those present proceeded to smoke their cigarettes in the tents. When the desired effect of the drug had been obtained they all merged into the open and engaged in a discussion of their admiration of the stars and the beauties of nature.

Because of the possibility of spreading disease, note should be taken of what seems to be a custom known as "pick-up" smoking. It is an established practice whereby a marijuana cigarette is lit and after one or two inhalations is passed on to the next person. This procedure is repeated until all present have had an opportunity to take a puff or two on the cigarette.

Occasionally a "tea-pad" owner may have peddlers who sell their wares in other localities and at the same time serve as procurers for those who wish to smoke marijuana on the premises.

One also finds other methods of retail distribution. After proper introduction, one may be able to purchase the cigarette in certain places. This is not an easy procedure, but it can be accomplished. In some bar-and-grills, restaurants, and bars our investigators were able to establish contact with someone who, in turn, would introduce them to a peddler who apparently made regular rounds of these places in order to sell cigarettes. It appears that the owners of such places are not aware of this practice, and in many instances they would discharge any employee known to be directly or indirectly associated with the sale of marijuana.

On rare occasions public guides, if properly approached would refer one to a place where the "reefer" could be bought. There was no evidence that the guide received money when acting as go-between. Terminal porters, mainly Negroes, appeared to be more directly connected with the traffic of marijuana. They were more conversant with the subject and it was easier for them to establish contact between purchaser and peddler.

Marijuana smoking is very common in the theatres of Harlem according to the observations of the investigators. We have reason to believe that in some instances, perhaps few in number, employees actually sold cigarettes on the premises. In the Harlem dance halls smoking was frequently observed either in the lavatories or on the main floor. The patrons as well as the musicians were seen in the act of smoking. There was no evidence of sales being made by employees on the premises, or that there was any gain on the part of the owners or employees in permitting this practice. Whereas the smoking of marjuana was not encouraged, nothing was done to prohibit such practice.

There are specific sections in the Borough of Manhattan where the sale of marijuana cigarettes appears to be localized: (1) the Harlem district; (2) the Broadway area, a little east and west of Broadway and extending from 42nd Street to 59th Street. While it is true that one may buy the cigarette in other districts, it is not as easily obtainable as in the two localities mentioned.

THE MENTAL ATTITUDE OF THE MARIJUANA SMOKER TOWARD SOCIETY AND MARIJUANA

Most of the smokers of marijuana coming within the scope of our survey were unemployed, and of the others most had part-time employment.

Occasional, as well as confirmed, users were all aware of the laws pertaining to the illegal use of the drug. They did not indulge in its use with a spirit of braggadocio or as a challenge to law as has been reported by some investigators in other districts. They did not express remorse concerning their use of marijuana, nor did they blame this habit as a causative factor in the production of special difficulties in their personal lives. Except for musicians there appeared to be no attempt at secretiveness on the part of the habitual smoker. This attitude is in marked contrast to that usually taken by those addicted to morphine, cocaine, or heroin.

The consensus of marijuana users is that the drug is not harmful and that infrequent or constant use of marijuana does not result in physical or mental deterioration.

In describing the most common reaction to the drug they always stated that it made them feel "high." Elaboration of just what the smoker meant by "high" varied with the individual. However, there was common agreement that a feeling of adequacy and efficiency was induced by the use of marijuana and that current mental conflicts were allayed. Organic illness was not given as a cause for smoking "reefers."

A person may be a confirmed smoker for a prolonged period, and give up the drug voluntarily without experiencing any craving for it or exhibiting withdrawal symptoms. He may, at some time later on, go back to its use. Others may remain infrequent users of the cigarette, taking one or two a week, or only when the "social setting" calls for participation. From time to time we had one of our investigators associate with a marijuana user. The investigator would bring up the subject of smoking. This would invariably lead to the suggestion that they obtain some marijuana cigarettes. They would seek a "tea-pad," and if it was closed the smoker and our investigator would calmly resume their previous activity, such as the discussion of life in general or the playing of pool. There was apparently no signs indicative of frustration in the smoker at not being able to gratify the desire for the drug. We consider this point highly significant since it is so contrary to the experience of users of other narcotics. A similar situation occurring in one addicted to the use of morphine, cocaine, or heroin would result in a compulsive attitude on the part of the addict to obtain the drug. If unable to secure it, there would be obvious physical and mental manifestations of frustration. This may be considered presumptive evidence that there is no true addiction in the medical sense associated with the use of marijuana.

The confirmed marijuana smoker consumes perhaps from six to ten cigarettes per day. He appears to be quite conscious of the quantity he requires to reach the effect called "high." Once the desired effect is obtained he cannot be persuaded to consume more. He knows when he has had enough. The smoker determines for himself the point of being "high," and is ever-conscious of preventing himself from becoming "too high." This fear of being "too high" must be associated with some form of anxiety which causes the smoker, should he accidentally reach that point, immediately to institute measures so that he can "come down." It has been found that the use of such beverages as beer, or a sweet soda pop, is an effective measure. Smokers insist that "it does something to the stomach" and that it is always associated with "belching." A cold shower will also have the effect of bringing the person "down."

Smokers have repeatedly stated that the consumption of whisky while smoking negates the potency of the drug. They find it very difficult to get "high" while drinking whisky, and because of that smokers will not drink whisky while using the "weed." They do, however, consume large quantities of sweet wines. It is their contention that this mild alcoholic beverage aids the drug in producing the desired effect. Most marijuana smokers insist that the appetite is increased as the result of smoking.

We have been unable to confirm the opinion expressed by some investigators that marijuana smoking is the first step in the use of such drugs as cocaine, morphine, and heroin. The instances are extremely rare where the habit of marijuana smoking is associated with addiction to these other narcotics.

MARIJUANA AND EROTICISM

In the popular agitation against the use of marijuana, its erotic effects have been stressed repeatedly. As previously stated in this report, our investigators visited many "tea-pads" in the Borough of Manhattan. It is true that lewd pictures decorated the walls but they did not find that they were attracting attention or comment among the clientele. In fact one of the investigators who was concentrating his attention on the relation between marijuana and eroticism stated in his report that he found himself embarrassed in that he was the only one who examined the pictures on the wall.

Numerous conversations with smokers of marijuana revealed only occasional instances in which there was any relation between the drug and eroticism. At one time one of our investigators attended a very intimate social gathering in an apartment in Harlem, having succeeded in securing the position of doorman for the occasion. There was a great deal of drinking, and the dancing was of the most modern, abandoned, "jitter-bug" type. This form of dancing is highly suggestive and appears to be associated with erotic activity. The investigator made careful observation of those who were dancing, and found that there was no difference between the ones who were and the ones who were not smoking "reefers." Similar impressions were received after careful observations in public dance halls, places where they knew that some persons were under the influence of marijuana.

Visits to brothels which occasionally also served as "tea-pads" revealed that the use of marijuana was not linked to sexuality. These observations allow us to come to the conclusion that in the main marijuana was not used for direct sexual stimulation.

CRIME

One of the most important causes of the widespread publicity which marijuana smoking has received is the belief that this practice is directly responsible for the commission of crimes.

During our investigation many law enforcement officers, representing various federal, state, and local police bureaus, were interviewed and asked for a confidential expression of opinion on the general question of crime and marijuana. In most instances they unhesitatingly stated that there is no proof that major crimes are associated with the practice of smoking marijuana. They did state that many marijuana smokers are guilty of petty crimes, but that the criminal career usually existed prior to the time the individual smoked his first marijuana cigarette. These officers further stated that a criminal generally termed as a "real" or "professional" criminal will not associate with marijuana smokers. He considers such a person inferior and unreliable and will not allow him to participate in the commission of a major crime.

In the period beginning October 1939 and ending November 1940, the Police Department made 167 arrests for the possession and use of marijuana. Classified according to race they were: white, 33 men, 4 women; Latin American, 26 men, 2 women; Negro, 83 men, 6 women; Latin American (colored) 9 men, 1 woman; British East Indies 1; Filipino 1; Chinese 1.

Classified according to age, 12 percent were between the ages of 16 and 20, 58 percent between the ages of 21 and 30, 24 percent between the ages of 31 and 40, and 6 percent between the ages of 41 and 50.

During the period under discussion, the Police Department confiscated approximately 3000 pounds of marijuana.

The sale and use of marijuana is a problem engaging the vigilance of the New York Police Department. However, the number of officers available for such duty is limited. Officers specifically assigned to the Narcotics Division of the Police Department are acquainted with the problem, but the majority of the officers are fundamentally without authoritative knowledge regarding this subject.

The relation between marijuana smoking and the commission of crimes of violence in the city of New York is described by Dr. Walter Bromberg, psychiatrist-in-charge of the Psychiatric Clinic of the Court of General Sessions, in an article published in the *Journal of the American Medical Association:*

In the South of this country (New Orleans) the incidence of

marijuana addicts among major criminals is admittedly high. Sporadic reports from elsewhere in the country of murders and assaults due to marijuana appear in the press frequently. It is difficult to evaluate these statements, because of their uncritical nature. The bulletin prepared by the Foreign Policy Association lists ten cases "culled at random from the files of the U.S. Bureau of Narcotics" of murders and atrocious assault in which marijuana was directly responsible for the crime. Among the ten patients, the second, J. O., was described as having confessed how he murdered a friend and put his body in a trunk while under the influence of marijuana.

J. O. was examined in this clinic; although he was a psychopathic liar and possibly homosexual, there was no indication in the examination or history of the use of any drug. The investigation by the probation department failed to indicate use of the drug marijuana. The deceased, however, was addicted to heroin.

Our observations with respect to marijuana and crime were made in the Court of General Sessions over a period of five and a half years. The material in that court is limited as to residence to New York County, although it must be remembered that the offenders come from many sections of the country and are of many racial types. This is important, because the British investigators have noted in India that cannabis does not bring out the motor excitement or hysterical symptoms in Anglo-Saxon users that occur in natives. There are several other difficulties in collecting reliable material, one being the complete dependence on the history and statements of the prisoners without an opportunity for objective tests or other corroborative check, as in the case of other drugs, e.g., heroin or morphine. During routine interviews of some 17,000 offenders in six and a half years, several hundred have been found who had direct experience with marijuana. Their testimony checks with experimental results and clinical experiences with regard to the symptoms of intoxication, the absence of true addiction, and the negative connection with major crime. Especially is this noteworthy among sexual offenders and in cases of assault or murder. The extravagant claims of defense attorneys and the press that crime is caused by addiction to marijuana demands careful scrutiny, at least in this jurisdiction. . . .

Most of the narcotic cases in New York County are heard in the Court of Special Sessions, where misdemeanants are handled and where indictments on charges of the possession of drugs for use are returned. In the Court of Special Sessions in the same six-year period, of approximately 75,000 indictments for all crimes, 6000 resulted in convictions for the possession and use of drugs. Since neither the law, the district attorney nor the police department makes any distinction between the several kinds of narcotics in arraignments or indictments, there were no figures from which to estimate the number of users of marijuana as distinguished from the number of users of other drugs. A system of sampling the 6000 cases was therefore adopted in order to furnish an approximate estimate of the total number of marijuana users who came into conflict with the law.

In this sampling the records of 1500 offenders, or 25 percent of the 6000, were examined. Of these, 135 were charged in connection with marijuana. From this fact it was estimated that about 540 offenders, or 9 percent of all drug offenders coming to the Court of Special Sessions in six years, were users of marijuana. In analyzing this sample of 135 cases, it was found that 93 offenders had no previous record, the previous charges or charges of 8 concerned only drugs, 5 had records including drug charges and 29 had records not including drug charges. Among those with longer records, that is, from four to seven previous arrests, none showed progression from the use of drugs to other crimes.

As measured by the succession of arrests and convictions in the Court of General Sessions (the only method of estimation) it can be said that drugs generally do not initiate criminal careers. Similarly, in the Court of Special Sessions, only 8 percent of the offenders had previous charges of using drugs and 3.7 percent had previous charges of drugs and other petty crimes. In the vast majority of cases in this group of 135, then, the earlier use of marijuana apparently did not predispose to crime, even that of using other drugs. Whether the first offenders charged with the use of marijuana go on to major crime is a matter of speculation. The expectancy of major crimes following the use of cannabis in New York County is small, according to these experiences.[2]

MARIJUANA AND SCHOOL CHILDREN

One of the most serious accusations leveled against marijuana by special feature writers has been that it is widely used by the school children of this nation. These authors have claimed that it has so detrimental an effect on development that it is a major factor in juvenile delinquency. This phase of the marijuana problem was deemed serious enough to merit primary consideration in our study of the marijuana problem in New York City—specifically in the Borough of Manhattan. We decided to attack this aspect of the problem along the following lines:

1. To observe schools in order to see if pupils bought marijuana cigarettes from any peddlers operating in the neighborhood.

2. To investigate thoroughly complaints made by parents to school and police authorities relative to marijuana and its use by school children.

3. To interview principals, assistant principals, and teachers of many of the schools in New York City with reference to our project.

4. To gather relevant statistics from various city bureaus and private agencies.

Unknown to the school authorities, our investigators had under surveillance many of the schools in the Borough of Manhattan. They would observe a particular school for a number of consecutive days, watch loiterers and suspicious characters in the locality, and, under certain circumstances, follow some of the children. This procedure was repeated at varying intervals in different localities. From time to time the investigators would return to some of the schools which they previously had kept under surveillance. Attention was naturally concentrated upon those schools from which emanated the most numerous complaints and which were located in suspected neighborhoods. We must admit that it would have been possible for such sales to have taken place during the time that our investigators were not on duty, but we came to the conclusion that there was no organized traffic on the part of peddlers in selling marijuana cigarettes to the children of the schools we observed.

Certain of the school authorities deserve special commendation for their alertness in singling out suspicious characters loitering in the vicinity of their schools. While investigating one of the suspected schools, our investigators who were loitering in the neighborhood were suspected and treated as "suspicious characters" by the school authorities.

During the period of this survey the Police Department, while engaged in an entirely separate criminal investigation, received a lead indicating the sale of marijuana to children in a certain high school. As a result, one pupil was arrested and convicted for selling cigarettes to his classmates.

In the Harlem district we discovered a few places where school children gathered during and after school hours for the purpose of indulging in smoking ordinary cigarettes, drinking alcoholic beverages, and engaging in homosexual and heterosexual activities. One of our investigators, having gained entrance to such a place, ostentatiously displayed marijuana cigarettes which he had with him. The madam of the place promptly cautioned him against using the "weed" and insisted that at no time did she permit any person to smoke it on her premises.

A surprising number of school children smoking ordinary cigarettes were noted. A checkup revealed that these cigarettes were being illicitly sold by men on the street and in candy stores in the "loose" form. It is possible that this trade in ordinary cigarettes is occasionally misinterpreted as trade in "reefers."

* * *

From the foregoing study the following conclusions are drawn:

1. Marijuana is used extensively in the Borough of Manhattan but the problem is not as acute as it is reported to be in other sections of the United States.

2. The introduction of marijuana into this area is recent as compared to other localities.

3. The cost of marijuana is low and therefore within the purchasing power of most persons.

4. The distribution and use of marijuana is centered in Harlem.

5. The majority of marijuana smokers are Negroes and Latin-Americans.

6. The consensus among marijuana smokers is that the use of the drug creates a definite feeling of adequacy.

7. The practice of smoking marijuana does not lead to addiction in the medical sense of the word.

8. The sale and distribution of marijuana is not under the control of any single organized group.

9. The use of marijuana does not lead to morphine or heroin or cocaine addiction, and no effort is made to create a market for these narcotics by stimulating the practice of marijuana smoking.

10. Marijuana is not the determining factor in the commission of major crimes.

11. Marijuana smoking is not widespread among school children.

12. Juvenile delinquency is not associated with the practice of smoking marijuana.

13. The publicity concerning the catastrophic effects of marijuana smoking in New York City is unfounded.

THE CLINICAL STUDY

Plan and Scope

Interest in the effects of marijuana on the human subject follows two main lines: first, concerning what may be called pleasurable effects which account for its widespread use; and second, regarding undesirable effects, including those leading to criminal and other antisocial acts.

✶ ✶ ✶

The clinical study here described was designed to afford information not found in marijuana literature but necessary for any comprehensive view of marijuana action. For obtaining this information there were these requisites: an adequate number of subjects for the study, a clear understanding of the mental and physical make-up of each subject, a uniformity of environmental factors, accurately graded dosage of marijuana, and standardized methods of obtaining and recording marijuana effects. In addition to defining the usual and unusual effects of marijuana, as shown by subjective and objective symptoms and alterations in behavior and in physical reaction, the study was expected to answer questions which must arise in consideration of the problem as a whole. Of special importance are these: Do marijuana users show fundamental traits differentiating them from nonusers? Do users present evidence of psychological or physical damage directly attributable to the drug? What

178

are the pleasurable effects which account for the widespread usage of marijuana? To what extent does it lead to antisocial or dangerous behavior?

The sections covering the clinical study are under the following headings:

A. Medical Aspects
    1. Symptoms and Behavior
    2. Organic and Systemic Functions
B. Psychological Aspects
    1. Psychophysical and Other Functions
    2. Intellectual Functioning
    3. Emotional Reactions and General Personality Structure
    4. Family and Community Ideologies
C. Comparison Between Users and Nonusers from the Standpoint of Mental and Physical Deterioration
D. Addiction and Tolerance
E. Possible Therapeutic Applications

ORGANIZATION FOR THE STUDY

The clinical studies were carried out at the Welfare Hospital,[3] a New York City hospital for chronic diseases on Welfare Island. The quarters assigned to the study consisted of a ward of eight beds for the group to be studied at any one period, an adjoining ward of two beds for the study of individuals of the group, three additional rooms with equipment for special examinations, and a diet kitchen for the preparation of the subjects' meals.

Four female nurses were employed and the subjects in the larger ward were under constant supervision. In addition to routine records, each nurse reported the behavior on the subjects while she was on duty. Guards were assigned from the Department of Correction and the New York City Police Force for the subjects drawn from the Riker's and Hart Island penitentiaries and the House of Detention for Women.

The facilities of the Third Medical Division laboratory were used for general clinical laboratory examinations and for more detailed study of organ functioning. For measurement of psychological reactions, special apparatus was provided. A description of equipment used for each division of the study is given under its proper section.

SUBJECTS SELECTED FOR THE STUDY

For the purpose of establishing a uniform plan of procedure to be followed throughout the study, test group of five individuals who had had no previous experience with marijuana was selected. These were volunteers who were paid for their services. They were of a low socio-economic level, but classified as of better than average intelligence. Only one of the group came within the range of what is considered normal personality. They represented the type of person who would readily take to marijuana were the opportunity offered.

The main group, 72 subjects, was drawn from the inmates of the penitentiaries at Riker's and Hart Islands and the House of Detention for Women, all of which are under the supervision of the Department of Correction of New York City. There were two advantages in selecting subjects from this particular group: first, they could be kept under continuous observation throughout the period desired, and second, they constituted an excellent sample of the class in New York City from which the marijuana user comes. The subjects all volunteered for the study after having its purpose and the part they were to take in it fully explained to them.

Race, Sex and Age.   Of the group, 65 were males and 7 were females; 35 were white, 26 were Negroes, and 11 were Puerto Ricans. The ages ranged from 21 to 37 years except for one who was 45 and another who was 43. Of the women, 6 had been opium addicts for a number of years.

Previous Experience with Marijuana.   Forty-eight of the group, including six of the women, gave a history of marijuana smoking. The extent of the usage was variable; for some it was occasional, while others had indulged in the habit fairly steadily over a period of years. Of the 48 users, those who were sellers of marijuana were probably the most consistent smokers, as in carrying on the traffic they would endeavor to keep a stock on hand. But in any instance, the number of cigarettes smoked during any stated period would vary according to circumstance. Thus one user stated that he smoked from two to six marijuana cigarettes a day, another from 10 to 15 a day, another three or four a week, and another five or six a month. Those who smoked daily are here classified as steady users, those who smoked when opportunity was offered but not daily, as occasional users.

The users had all been deprived of marijuana from the time of their arrest, the shortest period being two weeks, the longest, one

TABLE 5–1

Previous experience with marijuana of 48 subjects

Years of Use	Number of Steady Users	Number of Occasional Users
1–5	13	4
6–10	16	4
over 10	9	2
Total	38	10

year and ten months. They all stated that the habit had often been interrupted voluntarily and the enforced discontinuation of it had caused no discomfort.

Health Record. The subjects were individually selected by Dr. Allentuck as suitable for the study. A physical and neurological examination at the hospital showed no evidence of disease. However, the Wassermann and Kline tests gave positive results for six subjects and the Kline test alone was positive for two and doubtful for two. These figures are consistent with those of the population from which the group was selected. Of the 12,000 inmates of the Riker's Island Penitentiary in 1940 and the 8000 in 1941, 10 percent reacted positively to serological tests.

Intelligence Record. Sixty subjects (40 users and 20 nonusers) to whom the Bellevue Adult Intelligence Test was given had an average IQ of 99.3, range 70 to 124. The average IQ of the user group was 96.7, range 70 to 124, while that for the nonuser group was 104.5, range 93 to 114. When analyzed according to racial distribution, the two groups were even better equated intellectually than the total results indicate. Of the 28 white subjects examined, the average IQ of the 13 users was 106.1, range 77 to 124, and that of the 15 nonusers was 106.3, range 96 to 114. The 19 Negro users had an average IQ of 92.6, range 70 to 112, and the five Negro nonusers averaged 98.8, range 93 to 101. Although in the colored group the nonusers averaged 6.2 points higher than the users, it must be taken into account that the number of Negro nonusers tested was small. The average IQ of the eight Puerto Rican users was 91.0, range 72 to 100; that is, they were very similar in mental ability to the Negro users. From the results obtained from the Bellevue Adult Intelligence Test, one may conclude that neither the users nor the nonusers were inferior in intelligence to the general population.

MARIJUANA USED

The marijuana that was used for oral administration was supplied by Dr. H. J. Wollner, Consulting Chemist of the United States Treasury Department. It was in the form of an alcohol fluid concentrate, the alcohol content ranging from 55 to 67.3 percent and the content of solids from 22.9 to 33.6 gm. per 100 cc. According to the bio-assay made by Dr. S. Loewe of the Department of Pharmacology of the Cornell University Medical School, the strength of the fluid concentrate was found to be from 71 to 90 percent of that of the U.S.P. fluid extract for cannabis marketed by Parke, Davis and Company. The fluid extract was not miscible with water and had a characteristic, disagreeable taste which made it easily recognized. For these reasons the concentrate was evaporated to a viscid consistency and made into pill form, with glycyrrhiza as the excipient. Each pill was equivalent to 1 cc. of the concentrate. For controls, glycyrrhiza pills without marijuana were used.

Several products prepared by Dr. Roger Adams in his investigation of the chemistry of marijuana were used. A comparison of their action with that of the concentrate will be found below.

In addition to the concentrate, marijuana cigarettes were used. These were obtained from supplies confiscated by the New York City Police. Each contained approximately from .4 to .8 gm. of marijuana. As the quality of the marijuana varied and the amount of active principles taken in with the smoke was unknown, there was no exactness in dosage. In general, however, it appeared that smoking two cigarettes were equivalent to taking one pill.

The minimal dose of the concentrate which produced clearcut effects was 2 cc. During the repeated observations on each member of the group larger doses were given, commonly up to around 8 cc. and in one instance up to 22 cc. For smoking, from one to as many as eleven cigarettes were used.

The Active Principles. Determination of relative potencies of drugs having similar action can be made on human beings to a limited extent only. The comparison is based on easily measurable effects on some organ or system on which the drug has a highly selective action, but the existing state of the system influences greatly the ensuing result. Marijuana effects come mainly from action on the central nervous system. The type and degree of response of this system to stimuli of various origins vary in different individuals and in the same individual at different times. When marijuana is given the pre-existing state cannot be classified but it has influence in determining the response, and the same dose of marijuana does not produce identical effects in different subjects or in one subject at different times. In general, however, when the dose given is definitely effective the responses are of a fairly uniform character.

For this reason the relative potency of the active principles supplied by Dr. Roger Adams could be determined only approximately. The principles used were the natural tetrahydrocannabinol, the synthetic isomer, and the synthetic hexylhydrocannabinol. These all brought on effects similar to those of the marijuana concentrate. The estimate of their relative potency is as follows: 1 cc. of the concentrate, representing the extraction from 1 gm. of marijuana, had as its equivalent 15 mg. of the natural tetrahydrocannabinol, 60 mg. of the synthetic hexylhydrocannabinol, and 120 mg. of the synthetic tetra compound. In explaining the differences in the estimated potencies, the rates of absorption must be taken into account since the action of marijuana depends on the amount of active principle absorbed and its concentration in the brain at a certain time.

The main conclusion is that the action of the marijuana concentrate is dependent on its tetrahydrocannabinol content and that the synthetic compounds retain the action of the natural principle.

PROCEDURE

The procedure for examining the main group of subjects was adopted in the light of the experience gained from the preliminary study.

The subjects were brought to the hospital in groups of from six to ten, and they stayed there from four to six weeks.

Each subject had his history taken and was given a physical, neurological, and psychiatric examination on the day of admission. Since it has been shown that pulse variation is the most constant index of marijuana action, the pulse rate was recorded every half hour during the day with the subjects at rest for five minutes before each reading.

During the following days, through careful observation by the director, the general make-up of the subject, his personality, the character of his responsiveness, and his behavior in new surroundings were determined both before and while he was under the influence of marijuana. Additional information came through the nurses' reports.

In addition, each subject was given a series of tests before and after the administration of marijuana in order that the changes brought about by the drug might be measured. Included among these tests were psychological tests for mental functioning and emotional reactions, psychomotor tests for both simple and complex psychophysical functions, tests to determine such abilities as musical aptitude and the perception of time and space, and laboratory examinations to test the functioning of the various organs and systems of the body.

MEDICAL ASPECTS, SYMPTOMS AND BEHAVIORS

Samuel Allentuck, M.D.

*   *   *

In the study of the actions of marijuana in respect to subjective and objective symptoms and behavior, the marijuana was given a number of times to each of the subjects in the form of the concentrate taken by stomach. The amount given ranged from 2 to 22 cc., in most cases from 2 to 5 cc. After marijuana was taken, the systematic action became evident in from one-half to one hour and the maximum effects were seen in from two to three hours. They passed off gradually, usually in from three to five hours, although in some instances they did not completely disappear until twelve or more hours.

Of the symptoms occurring, a feeling of lightness in the head with some dizziness, a sensation of floating in the air, dryness of the throat, hunger and thirst, unsteadiness, and heaviness in the extremities were the most frequent. Tremor and ataxia, dilation of the pupils, and sluggishness in responsiveness to light were observed in all subjects.

From observations on the behavior and responses of the subjects, it was found that a mixture of euphoria and apprehension was generally present. If the subjects were undisturbed there was a state of quiet and drowsiness, and unawareness of surroundings, with some difficulty in focusing and sustaining mental concentration. If they were in company, restlessness, talkativeness, laughter and joking were commonly seen. A feeling of apprehension, based on uncertainty regarding the possible effects of the drug and strengthened by any disagreeable sensations present, alternated with the euphoria. If the apprehension developed into a state of real anxiety, a spirit of antagonism was shown. However, any resistance to requests made to the subjects was passive and not physical and there was no aggressiveness or violent behavior observed. Erotic ideas or sensations when present took no active expression.

Six of the subjects developed toxic episodes characteristic of acute marijuana intoxication. The dosage varied from 4 to 8 cc. of the concentrate, and the episodes lasted from three to six hours, in one instance ten hours. The effects were mixtures of euphoric and anxiety states, laughter, elation, excitement, disorientation, and mental confusion.

The doses given were toxic to the individuals in question but not to others taking the same or larger ones. Once the drug had been taken the effects were beyond the subject's control. The actions described took unusual expression because for the particular subject at a particular time the dose was unusually effective. A corresponding toxicity did not occur from cigarettes for here the effects came on promptly and on the appearance of any untoward effects, the smoking was stopped.

In three of the subjects a definite psychotic state occurred, in two shortly after marijuana ingestion, in one after a two-week interval. Of the first two, one was an epileptic and the other had a history of heroin addiction and a prepsychotic personality. The third was considered a case of prison psychosis. The conclusion seems warranted that given the potential personality make-up and the right time and environment, marijuana may bring on a true psychotic state.

ORGANIC AND SYSTEMIC FUNCTIONS

Samuel Allentuck, M.D.

The functions of the body organs and systems were studied in the manner common to hospital practice according to the methods and with the equipment in use at Welfare Hospital. The study was designed to show not only the effects of varying doses of marijuana but also whether subjects who had long been users of the drug gave evidence of organic damage. The tests were made before the drug was administered, during its action, and often in the after period. The heart and circulation, blood composition, kidney, liver and gastro-intestinal function, and basal metabolism received special consideration.

SUMMARY

The most consistent effect of marijuana observed in this division of the study was an increase in pulse rate which began shortly after the taking of the drug, reached a peak in about two hours, and gradually disappeared. In a few instances a temporary sinus tachycardia or sinus bradycardia was noted, but except for these there were no abnormalities in rhythm. The increase in pulse rate was usually accompanied by a rise in blood pressure.

There was in general an increase in the blood sugar level and in the basal metabolic rate, quite marked in some subjects, but in the majority the levels reached did not exceed the high normal limits.

An increase in the frequency of urination was often observed. There was, however, no appreciable increase in the total amount of urine passed during the drug action.

Hunger and an increase in appetite, particularly for sweets, was noted in the majority of the subjects, and the taking of candy or sweetened drinks brought down a "too high" effect of the drug. Nausea and vomiting occurred in a number of instances, diarrhea only during psychotic episodes.

On the other hand, the blood showed no changes in cell count, hemoglobin percent, or the urea nitrogen, calcium, and phosphorus figures. The figures for the circulation rate and vital capacity and the results of the phenolsulfonphthalein test for kidney infection and the bromsulfalein test for liver function were not different from those of the control period. The electrocardiograms showed no abnormalities which could be attributed to a direct action on the heart. In the few observations on gastric motility and secretion no evidence of marijuana action on these functions was obtained.

The positive results observed, increase in pulse rate and blood pressure, increase in blood sugar and metabolic rate, urge to urinate, increased appetite, nausea and vomiting, and diarrhea, were not intensified by an increase in dosage, for they could occur in an equal degree after the administration of any of the effective doses within the range used. All the effects described are known to be expressions of forms of cerebral excitation, the impulses from this being transmitted through the autonomic system. The alterations in the functions of the organs studied come from the effects of the drug on the central nervous system and are proportional to these effects. A direct action on the organs themselves was not seen.

PSYCHOLOGICAL ASPECTS
PSYCHOPHYSICAL AND OTHER FUNCTIONS

Robert S. Morrow, Ph.D.

In this phase of the study an effort was made to determine the effect of marijuana on various psychomotor and some special mental abilities. Appraisal of these effects was made wherever possible through the use of standardized tests. A number of different tests were orginally tried under varying experimental conditions on the group of five volunteer subjects who had never before taken marijuana. Only those tests were retained which, in the course of this preliminary investigation, demonstrated the greatest potentialities.

SUMMARY AND CONCLUSIONS

1. The effect of marijuana on the psychomotor functions depends primarily on the complexity of the function tested. Simpler functions like speed of tapping and simple reaction time are affected only slightly by large doses (5 cc.) and negligibly, if at all, by smaller doses (2 cc.). On the other hand, the more complex functions like static equilibrium, hand steadiness, and complex reaction time may be affected adversely to a considerable degree by the administration of both large and small doses of marijuana.

2. The function most severely affected is body steadiness and hand steadiness. The ataxia is general in all directions rather than predominant in any particular axis.

3. The effects produced by larger doses (5 cc.) are systematically, though not necessarily proportionately, greater than those brought about by small doses.

4. The time required by the drug to exert its maximum effect varies somewhat with the function and size of dose, but, on the whole, time curves for both functions and dosages have similarity of

form. The effect of the drug begins from one to two hours after ingestion and reaches its peak at the fourth hour, after which it declines so that by the eighth hour most of it is dissipated.

5. When marijuana is taken in cigarette form the psychomotor effects are similar in character and trend to those observed after the ingestion of the drug but they occur much sooner and taper off more quickly.

6. The effects seem to be essentially the same for women as for men, except that women are sometimes affected maximally at the second or third hour after the drug is administered. In women the return to the normal condition is in some instances quicker and more abrupt than it is in the men.

7. Nonusers generally seem to be more affected by the drug when it is ingested than are users.

8. Auditory acuity is not affected by marijuana.

9. There is no evidence that musical ability, of nonmusicians at least, is improved by marijuana.

10. The ability to estimate short periods of time and short linear distances is not measurably affected by the ingestion of marijuana.

INTELLECTUAL FUNCTIONING

Florence Halpern, MA

In this phase of the study investigation was directed primarily toward establishing the effect of marijuana on the subject's intellectual functioning. An attempt was made to determine what changes in mental ability occur under different amounts of the drug, what direction these changes take, when they are first measurable, and how long they persist.

❖   ❖   ❖

CONCLUSIONS

1. Marijuana taken either in pill or in cigarette form has a transitory adverse effect on mental functioning.

2. The extent of intellectual impairment, the time of its onset, and its duration are all related to the amount of drug taken. Small doses cause only slight falling off in mental ability while larger doses result in greater impairment. The deleterious effect is measurable

earlier with large doses than with small ones, and the impairment continues for a greater length of time with large doses than with small ones.

3. The degree of intellectual impairment resulting from the presence of marijuana in the system varies with the function tested. The more complex functions are more severely affected than the simpler ones.

4. In general, nonusers experience greater intellectual impairment for longer periods of time than the users do. This suggests the possibility of an habituation factor.

5. The falling off in ability which occurs when an individual has taken marijuana is due to a loss in both speed and accuracy.

6. Indulgence in marijuana does not appear to result in mental deterioration.

EMOTIONAL REACTIONS AND GENERAL PERSONALITY STRUCTURE

Florence Halpern, MA

The purpose of this part of the study was twofold: to discover (1) what effect marijuana has on the emotional reactivity of the person taking it, and (2) what differences in emotional reaction and general personality structure exist between the marijuana user and nonuser.

SUMMARY AND DISCUSSION

. Under the influence of marijuana changes in personality as shown by alterations in test performance are slight. They are not statistically significant and indicate only tendencies or trends. Moreover, the drug effect is not always in proportion to the amount taken, nor are the changes consistently in one direction. In many instances the effect of small doses (2 cc.) or of marijuana cigarettes is the opposite of the effect of larger doses (5 cc.).[4]

The personality changes observed when the subject is under the influence of 2 cc. of marijuana or marijuana cigarettes demonstrate that the subject experiences some reduction in drive, less objectivity in evaluating situations, less aggression, more self-confidence, and a generally more favorable attitude toward himself. These reactions can be ascribed to two main causes, namely, an increased feeling of relaxation and disinhibition and increased self-confidence. As the drug relaxes the subject, the restraints which he normally imposes on himself are loosened and he talks more freely than he does in his undrugged state. Things which under ordinary circumstances he would not speak about are now given expression. Metaphysical problems which in the undrugged state he would be unwilling to discuss, sexual ideas he would ordinarily hesitate to mention, jokes without point, are all part of the oral stream released by the marijuana.

At the same time that he verbalizes more freely, there is a reduction in the individual's critical faculty. This is probably due both to the intellectual confusion produced by the drug and to the less exacting attitude his feeling of relaxation induces. He holds himself less rigidly to the standards of his undrugged phase and does not drive himself to achieve. He is satisfied with himself and willing to accept himself as he is. This self-satisfaction undoubtedly helps produce the feeling of self-confidence which allows the subject to come out more freely in fields which he formerly avoided. This increased confidence expresses itself primarily through oral rather than physical channels. Physically the subject reports pleasant sensations of "drifting" and "floating" and he allows himself to become enveloped in a pleasant lassitude.

After the administration of larger doses of marijuana (5 cc.) the pleasurable sensations appear to be outweighed by concomitant feelings of anxiety and, in some cases, of physical distress, such as nausea. Under these circumstances, for many subjects there is little increase in confidence but rather heightened insecurity which precludes outgoing reactions and tends to evoke generally negativistic attitudes to most stimuli.

It is important to note that neither the ingestion of marijuana nor the smoking of marijuana cigarettes affects the basic outlook of the individual except in a very few instances and to a very slight degree. In general the subjects who are withdrawn and introversive stay that way, those who are outgoing remain so, and so on. Where changes occur the shift is so slight as to be negligible. In other words reactions which are natively alien to the individual cannot be induced by the ingestion or smoking of the drug.

Although in most instances the effects of the drug are the same for the user and the nonuser, there are some differences both in kind and extent. Where the effects for the two groups are in the same direction they generally are more marked in the case of the nonuser. This is not unexpected in view of the nonuser's lack of habituation to the drug action. For the nonuser his present experience is a strange, even hazardous one, and the uncertainty and anxiety attendant upon this impairs the sense of well-being which the drug produces in the user. Thus the nonuser frequently feels less secure when he is "high" than he does normally and is less well adjusted than he is in ordinary circumstances.

When the productions of the undrugged marijuana user are studied, certain personality traits which serve to differentiate him from the nonuser and from the "average" individual can be discerned. As a group the marijuana users studied here were either inhibited emotionally or turned in on themselves, making little response to stimuli in the world about them. People with this type of personality generally have difficulty adjusting to others and are not at ease in social situations. This withdrawal from social contacts apparently finds little compensatory or sublimating activity elsewhere. These subjects did not have a desire or urge to occupy themselves creatively in a manner which might prove socially useful. They showed a tendency to drift along in passive fashion and gave a good portion of their attention to relatively unimportant matters. These men were poorly adjusted, lonely, and insecure. As indicated by their history they seldom achieved good heterosexual adjustment.

CONCLUSIONS

1. Under the influence of marijuana the basic personality structure of the individual does not change but some of the more superficial aspects of his behavior show alteration.

2. With the use of marijuana the individual experiences increased feelings of relaxation, disinhibition, and self-confidence.

3. The new feeling of self-confidence induced by the drug expresses itself primarily through oral rather than through physical activity. There is some indication of a diminution in physical activity.

4. The disinhibition which results from the use of marijuana releases what is latent in the individual's thoughts and emotions, but does not evoke responses which would be totally alien to him in his undrugged state.

5. Marijuana not only releases pleasant reactions but also feelings of anxiety.

6. Individuals with a limited capacity for effective experience and who have difficulty in making social contacts are more likely to resort to marijuana than those more capable of outgoing responses.

FAMILY AND COMMUNITY IDEOLOGIES

Adolph G. Woltmann, MA

At the outset of the study it seemed worth while to supplement the quantitative data by some qualitative procedures of the projective type which might throw light on the social reactions of the individuals who were being studied. One of the methods that has shown its possibilities, particularly in its use with children, is the play technique in which the individual is permitted to give free expression to some of his unconscious motivations in a way that is not immediately apparent to him. The limitation of this technique is the fact that it is highly interpretive, but it has the advantage of permitting observations of the subject's personality reactions in problem situations.

Such a study was accordingly carried out on 18 subjects in the early part of the investigation.

*　　*　　*

SUMMARY AND CONCLUSIONS

Eighteen subjects who participated in the marijuana study were subjected to the play situation with the idea of seeing whether the pattern of play or the ideas investigated were materially altered in consequence of the ingestion of the marijuana. Among the ideologies which were appraised were: (1) attitude toward family set-up; (2) attitude toward different occupations; (3) attitude toward income; (4) attitude toward situations ordinarily calling for aggression, namely an attempted burglary of his home and sexual infidelity on the part of his wife; (5) attitude toward authority.

In general the subject's attitude toward family and community ideologies as manifested in play did not change markedly as a result of the ingestion of marijuana. The subjects (in play) were not intolerant of infidelity or aggressive toward lawbreakers either before or after the ingestion of marijuana. On the whole the initial passive reactions already observed in other parts of the study were likewise observed in the play situation experiment. The only very definite change as a result of the ingestion of marijuana was in their attitude toward the drug itself. Without marijuana only four out of 14 subjects said they would tolerate the sale of marijuana while after ingestion eight of them were in favor of this.

Another significant manifestation in the play situation pertains to the construction of the community set-up. In general the community was less orderly and well organized when the subjects had had marijuana. It is probable that this poor organization may be ascribed to the generally indifferent attitude and lack of motor coordination already observed in the more controlled studies.

On the whole, the experiment with play technique gave less information as to the effect of marijuana on subjects than had been hoped for. This may have been due to the incompleteness of the method employed or possibly to the fact that this technique is designed to give data about the basic personality of the individual rather than such alterations in it as might be caused by pharmacological agents.

COMPARISON BETWEEN USERS AND NONUSERS FROM THE
STANDPOINT OF MENTAL AND PHYSICAL DETERIORATION

A careful testing of the motor and sensory functions of the nervous system was included in the general physical examination of each subject. Of motor functions, reflex activity and muscular response and coordination were determined; of sensory function, perception of touch, pain, and temperature stimuli; of specialized functions, taste, hearing, and vision. In the eye, the corneal and light reflexes were tested and a retinal examination was made. In this neurological examination no pathological conditions were found in any of the subjects.

In the psychiatric examination attention was paid to general intelligence and knowledge in relation to the subject's background, to relevancy of talk in conversation, to orientation as to time, place and situation, to memory of past and recent events, to ability in simple arithmetic, to judgment in reaching decisions, and to the presence of abnormal mental content shown by delusions, hallucinations, obsessions, and ideas of persecution. There was no evidence of disordered cerebral functioning in any of the group.

As would be expected, differences in grades of intelligence and in orderliness in thinking and reasoning were noticeable. The Bellevue Adult Intelligence Test was administered to a total of 60 male subjects, 40 marijuana users and 20 nonusers. The average IQ for the user group was 96.7, range 70 to 124, and for the nonuser group the average IQ was 104.5, range 93 to 114. Both groups may therefore be classified as of average intelligence.

When analyzed according to racial distribution the two groups were even better equated intellectually than the total results indicate. For the 28 white subjects examined (13 users and 15 nonusers) the average IQ for the users was 106.1, range 77 to 124, and for the nonusers the average IQ was 106.3, range 96 to 114. There were 24 Negro subjects, 19 users and 5 nonusers. The average IQ for the users was 92.6, range 70 to 112, while for the nonusers the average IQ was 98.8, range 93 to 101. Although the nonusers averaged 6.2 points higher than the users, it must be taken into account that the number of Negro nonusers tested was small. In any event, the disparity in results would not be considered significant. The average IQ of the 2 Puerto Rican users was 91.0, range 72 to 100.

Reports on mental deterioration due to toxic, organic, or psychotic factors as given in the literature reveal that in such cases the individual scores on the Bellevue Adult Intelligence Test show marked irregularity, depending upon the functions involved in the deteriorative process. As a group, the marijuana users tested in this study showed very even functioning, and what little irregularity occurred can be explained on the basis of language and racial factors.

The physical and psychiatric examinations were of a qualitative rather than a quantitative nature. In the special examinations and tests of organ and system function, quantitative measurements were obtained for 17 marijuana users. These subjects were selected for the reason that they had smoked marijuana for the longest period of time. The figures for years of usage and number of cigarettes smoked daily were taken from each subject's statement.

Marijuana users accustomed to daily smoking for a period of from two and a half to sixteen years showed no abnormal system functioning which would differentiate them from the nonusers.

There is definite evidence in this study that the marijuana users were not inferior in intelligence to the general population and that they had suffered no mental or physical deterioration as a result of their use of the drug.

ADDICTION AND TOLERANCE

A drug addiction is characterized by a compelling urge to use the drug for the prevention or relief of distressing mental and physical disturbances which occur when the necessary dose is delayed or omitted. A drug habit is also characterized by an urge to use the drug, but this is not compelling. The abstinence symptoms, which are expressions of nervous states, are not particularly distressing and do not occur as long as the person's attention is placed on other matters.

Drug tolerance in the narrower sense used here means that larger doses than those originally used are required to bring about the effects desired by the subject. In the case of morphine, tolerance develops because of addiction, but in other instances tolerance may be present without addiction and addiction without tolerance. When both are present the matter takes on greater importance because of the extremes to which the addict goes to obtain the drug constantly and in increasing quantities.

As our group of subjects included 48 users of marijuana, opportunity was afforded for some conclusions concerning marijuana addiction and tolerance. Practically all of our group of users stated that they could and often did voluntarily stop the smoking for a time without any undue disturbance from the deprivation. In the sociologic study reported by Dr. Schoenfeld it was found that smokers had no compelling urge for marijuana. If "reefers" were not readily available there was no special effort made to obtain them from known sources of supply. Dr. Walter Bromberg, Psychiatrist-in-Charge, Psychiatric Clinic, Court of General Sessions in New York, states: "The fact that offenders brought up on marijuana charges do not request medical treatment on their incarceration (with its cessation of drug supply) argues for the absence of withdrawal symptoms."[5] From interviews with several hundred marijuana users he concludes that true addiction was absent.

The evidence submitted here warrants the conclusion that as far as New York City is concerned true addiction to marijuana does not occur.

The evidence concerning acquired tolerance is less clear cut.

195

Tolerance develops during the periods when the drug is being taken and accounts for the necessity of increasing the dosage to bring about the desired effects. How long the tolerance persists after the drug administration is stopped has not been definitely established in any instance.

The statements of marijuana usage and time since stoppage given by eight of our subjects are summarized in Table 5-2.

TABLE 5-2

History of marijuana use among eight subjects

Subjects	Years of Usage	Number of Cigarettes Smoked Daily	Period of Deprivation
J.B.	5	5	2 weeks
W.C.	5	8	4 weeks
J.P.	14	10	7 weeks
A.B.	5	5	2 months
J.H.	4	7	2 months
F.G.	8	10	2½ months
O.D.	10	2	7 months
C.B.	8	6	2 years

On one or more of the numerous occasions on which marijuana was administered each of these subjects received what was considered a minimal effective dose. One (J.B.) was given 1 cc., another (A.B.) 3 cc., the others 2 cc. In all instances the customary physical effects, conjunctival injection, dilated and sluggishly reacting pupils, tremors, and ataxia, were observed. With these doses the subjects also experienced the sensation described as "high." The only conclusion warranted here is that if acquired tolerance does occur it persists for a limited period only.

Further evidence, though indirect, was brought out by Dr. Shoenfeld's investigation and by personal interviews with our 48 users. There is agreement in the statements that among users the smoking of one or two cigarettes is sufficient to bring on the effect known as "high." When this state is reached the user will not continue smoking for fear of becoming "too high." When the desired effects have passed off and the smoker has "come down," smoking one cigarette brings the "high" effect on again. This could not be the case had a steadily increasing tolerance developed.

The evidence available then—the absence of any compelling

urge to use the drug, the absence of any distressing abstinence symptoms, the statements that no increase in dosage is required to repeat the desired effect in users—justifies the conclusion that neither true addiction nor tolerance is found in marijuana users. The continuation and the frequency of usage of marijuana, as in the case of many other habit-forming substances, depend on the easily controlled desires for its pleasurable effects.

POSSIBLE THERAPEUTIC APPLICATIONS

If a drug has well-marked pharmacological actions and low toxicity, as appears to be the case with marijuana, a consideration of special interest is its possible therapeutic application. In the older clinical literature marijuana was recommended for use in a wide variety of disorders, but in recent years it has almost disappeared from the materia medica and it was dropped from the United States Pharmacopeia twenty years ago.

In view of the laboratory and clinical findings obtained in this study the question of the therapeutic possibilities of the drug was considered. Marijuana possesses two qualities which suggest that it might have useful actions in man. The first is the typical euphoria-producing action which might be applicable in the treatment of various types of mental depression; the second is the rather unique property which results in the stimulation of appetite. In the light of this evidence and in view of the fact that there is a lack of any substantial indication of dependence on the drug, it was reasoned that marijuana might be useful in alleviating the withdrawal symptoms in drug addicts.

At the Riker's Island Penitentiary observations were made on 56 inmates who were addicted to morphine or heroin. Two groups were selected, the addicts in each being matched with those in the other group as to age, physical condition, duration and intensity of habit, and number of previous attempts at cure. The subjects in one group received no treatment or were given Magendie's solution according to the usual hospital regimen, while those in the other group were treated with 15 mg. of tetrahydrocannabinol three times daily with or without placebo (subcutaneous water injection). An attempt was made to evaluate the severity of the withdrawal signs and symptoms. The impression was gained that those who received tetrahydrocannabinol had less severe withdrawal symptoms and left the

197

hospital at the end of the treatment period in better condition than those who received no treatment or who were treated with Magendie's solution. The ones in the former group maintained their appetite and in some cases actually gained weight during the withdrawal period.

Since psychological factors play a large part in the withdrawal symptoms of at least a certain proportion of morphine addicts, there are grounds for the assumption that a drug having the properties of marijuana might be of aid in alleviating mental distress during the withdrawal period. However, the studies here described were not sufficiently complete to establish the value of such treatment, and before conclusions can be drawn the problem must be investigated under completely controlled conditions.

PHARMACOLOGICAL STUDY[6]

S. Loewe, MD[7]

SUMMARY

1. This review of the pharmacology of marijuana is centered around the chemical and pharmacological identification of the active principles of hemp. Coordination of chemical and pharmacological investigations as a prerequisite to success in the search for unknown principles and of the analysis of the structure-activity relationship of these compounds is discussed.

2. In a survey of the sources of preparations with marijuana activity, hemp seeds are disclosed as a heretofore unknown source of active substances.

3. Varieties of hemp can be distinguished according to genotypic differences of the content of active principles which persist over generations independently of soil and climate.

4. The pharmacological actions of marijuana are analyzed with regard to their specificity and their usefulness as indicators of specific components.

5. Sixty-five substances from the new class of cannabinols and related classes are reviewed, among which are the essential components of the marijuana-active hemp oils. The discovery of this class, the synthesis of these representatives, and their structural elucidation led the way to the discovery of the active substances.

6. Quantitative assay procedures are described for the most important marijuana effects that are observed in the animal experiment. The assay of the ataxia effect in the dog and of the synergistic hypnotic effect in the mouse with refined procedures are shown to be reliable expedients for measuring these two marijuana actions, whereas the areflevia effect in rabbits failed to show the reproducibility required for quantitative purposes.

7. With the aid of these methods the natural tetrahydrocannabinols are shown to be active principles responsible for ataxia in dogs and psychic action in man. They are intermediate products between the two ineffective substances which compose the bulk of hemp oil: a labile excretion product of the plant, cannabidol, and a stable end-product, cannabinol. The conversion of cannabidol into active tetrahydrocannabinol by a natural environmental influence has been paralleled by ultraviolet irradiation *in vitro*.

8. Numerous isomers, homologs and analogs of tetra- and hexahydrocannabinol are shown to possess the specific marijuana action. The potency varies enormously and is highest in natural, optically active—laevogyrous—tetrahydrocannabinols.

9. The significance of many of the structural details of the tetrahydrocannabinol molecule for marijuana activity is elucidated by quantitative determinations of relative potency. Special attention was devoted to a study of the importance of variations in the length of the 3-alkyl side chain of tetrahydrocannabinols. In studying methyl to nonyl homologs of the original amyl derivative occurring in nature, it was found that the maximum potency is not at the amyl, but at the hexyl homolog, and in two out of four homologous series at the representatives with still longer side chains.

10. In addition to the ataxia and the psychic action, other pharmacological attributes of the tetrahydrocannabinols are a decrease in the respiratory and an increase in the pulse rates in the nonnarcotized dog.

11. The synergistic hypnotic action of marijuana in the mouse is to be attributed to the otherwise inert cannabidiol.

12. The corneal areflexia action in the rabbit was much stronger in impure distillate oils than in pure tetrahydrocannabinols, which leads to the conclusion that this action is either poorly reproducible or must be attributed to a different, as yet unknown, principle.

13. Only one among the numerous cannabinol derivatives, 7-methyltetrahydrocannabinol, was found to produce a motor stimu-

lant—convulsant—action concomitant with ataxia action. A cannabidiol derivative, tetrahydrocannabidiol, was found to have specific convulsant action in the dog.

14. A central stimulant (benzedrine) considerably increased the ataxia action of marijuana, whereas a hypnotic (amytal) had no influence.

Bibliography

1. Adams: Science, 92, 115, 1940.
2. Adams, Hunt and Clark: Jour. Amer. Chem. Soc., 62, 196, 1940.
3. Adams, Cain and Wolff: Jour. Amer. Chem. Soc., 62, 732, 1940.
4. Adams, Hunt and Clark: Jour. Amer. Chem. Soc., 62, 735, 1940.
5. Adams, Wolff, Cain and Clark: Jour. Amer. Chem. Soc., 62, 1770, 1940.
6. Adams, Pease and Clark: Jour. Amer. Chem. Soc., 62, 2194, 1940.
7. Adams, Pease, Clark and Baker: Jour. Amer. Chem. Soc., 62, 2197, 1940.
8. Adams, Cain and Baker: Jour. Amer. Chem. Soc., 62, 2201, 1940.
9. Adams, Baker and Wearn: Jour. Amer. Chem. Soc., 62, 2204, 1940.
10. Adams and Baker: Jour. Amer. Chem. Soc., 62, 2208, 1940.
11. Adams, Wolff, Cain and Clark: Jour. Amer. Chem. Soc., 62, 2215, 1940.
12. Adams, Pease, Cain, Baker, Clark, Wolff, Wearn and Loewe: Jour. Amer. Chem. Soc., 62, 2245, 1940.
13. Adams, Pease, Cain and Clark: Jour. Amer. Chem. Soc., 62, 2402, 1940.
14. Adams and Baker: Jour. Amer. Chem. Soc., 62, 2405, 1940.
15. Adams, Loewe, Pease, Cain, Wearn, Baker and Wolff: Jour. Amer. Chem. Soc., 62, 2566, 1940.
16. Adams, Loewe, Jellinek and Wolff: Jour. Amer. Chem. Soc., 63, 1971, 1941.
17. Adams, Smith and Loewe: Jour. Amer. Chem. Soc., 63, 1973, 1941.
19. Adams, Cain, McPhee and Wearn: Jour. Amer. Chem. Soc., 63, 2209, 1941.
20. Adams, Loewe, Smith and McPhee: Jour. Amer. Chem. Soc., 64, 694, 1942.
21. Balozet: League of Nations, O.C./Cannabis/1542, 1937.
22. Bergel and Wagner: Annalen d. Chem., 482, 55, 1930.

23. Bergel, Todd and Work: Chem. Industry, *86*, 1938.
24. Bembry and Powell: Jour. Amer. Chem. Soc., *63*, 2766, 1941.
25. Blatt: Jour. Wash. Acad. Sci., *28*, 465, 1938.
26. Bouquet: League of Nations, O.C./Cannabis/14, 1939.
27. Bouquet: League of Nations, O.C., 1545 (c), 1937.
28. Buergi: Deutsch. Med. Wochenschr., 1924, No. 45.
29. Cahn: Jour. Chem. Soc., 1342, 1932.
30. Cahn: Jour. Chem. Soc., 1400, 1933.
31. Casparis and Baur: Pharm. Acta Helv., *2*, 107, 1927.
32. Chopra and Chopra: Indian Jour. Med. Research Mem. (Mem. No. 31), p. 1, 1939.
33. Fraenkel: Arch. exp. Path. u. Pharmakol., *49*, 266, 1903.
34. Ghosh, Todd, Pascell and Wilkinson: Jour. Chem. Soc., *118*, 1940.
35. Ghosh, Todd and Wilkinson: Jour. Chem. Soc., *118*, 1940.
36. Ghosh, Todd and Wilkinson: Jour. Chem. Soc., 1393, 1940.
37. Ghosh, Todd and Wright: Jour. Chem. Soc., 137, 1941.
38. Gayer: Arch, exp. Path. u. Pharmakol., *129*, 312, 1928.
39. Goodall: Pharm. Jour., *84*, 112, 1910.
40. Haagen-Smit, Wawre, Koepfli, Alles, et al.: Science, *91*, 602, 1940.
41. Hare: Therap. Gazette, *11*, 225, 1887.
42. Houghton and Hamilton: Amer. Jour. Pharm., *80*, 16, 1908.
43. Jacob and Todd: Nature, *145*, 350, 1940; Jour. Chem. Soc., 649, 1940.
44. Joel: Pflügers Arch., *209*, 526, 1925.
45. Loewe: Jour. Pharmacol. and Exper. Therap., *66*, 23, 1939.
46. Loewe: Jour. Amer. Pharm. Assoc., *28*, 427, 1939.
47. Loewe: Jour. Amer. Pharm. Assoc., *29*, 162, 1940.
48. Loewe and Modell: Jour. Pharmacol. and Exper. Therap., *72*, 27, 1941.
49. Liautaud: Ac. Sc., 149, 1844.
50. Macdonald: Nature, *147*, 167, 1941.
51. Marx and Eckhardt: Arch. exp. Path. u. Pharmakol., *170*, 395. 1933.
52. Matchett, Levine, Benjamin, Robinson and Pope: Jour. Amer. Pharm. Assoc., *29*, 399, 1940.
53. Matchett and Loewe: Jour. Amer. Pharm. Assoc., *30*, 130, 1941.
54. Merz and Bergner: Arch. der Pharmaz., *278*, 49, 1940.
55. Powell, Salmon, Bembry and Walton: Science, *93*, 522, 1941.
56. Robinson: Jour. Amer. Pharm. Assoc., *30*, 616, 1941.
57. Robinson and Matchett: Jour. Amer. Pharm. Assoc., *29*, 448, 1940.

58. Russell, Todd, Wilkinson, Macdonald and Woolfe: (a) Jour. Chem. Soc., 169, 1941; (b) ibid. 826, 1941.
59. See: Deutsch, Med. Wochenschr, 679, 1890.
60. Todd: Nature, 829, 1940.
61. U. S. Treasury Dept.: Review of Progress on Marijuana Investigation during 1938.
62. U. S. Treasury Dept.: Marijuana: Its Identification, Washington, 1938.
63. U. S. Treasury Dept., Bureau of Narcotics: Report of the Marijuana Investigation, Summer 1937.
64. Viehoever: Amer. Jour. Pharmacy, *109*, No. 12, 1937.
65. Walton: Marijuana, Philadelphia-London, 1938.
66. Walton, Martin and Keller: Jour. Pharmacol. and Exper. Therap., *62*, 239, 1938.
67. Wiechowski: Arch. exp. Path. u. Pharmakol., *119*, 59, 1927.
68. Wollner, Matchett, Levine and Loewe: Jour. Amer. Chem. Soc., *64*, 26, 1942.
69. Wood, Barlow, Spivey and Easterfield: Jour. Chem. Soc., *69*, 539, 1896.
70. Wood, Barlow, Spivey and Easterfield: Jour. Chem. Soc., *75*, 20, 1899.
71. Work, Bergel and Todd: Biochem. Jour., *33*, 124, 1939.

Addendum to Bibliography:

72. Adams: Harvey Lectures, Ser. XXXVII, 1941–1942, p. 168.
73. Adams, Smith and Loewe: Jour. Amer. Chem. Soc., *64*, 2087, 1942.
74. Alles, Haagen-Smit, Feigen and Dendliker: Jour. Pharm. and Exp. Ther., *76*, 21, 1942.
75. Alles, Icke and Feigen: Jour. Amer. Chem. Soc., *64*, 2031, 1942.
76. Bergel, Morrison, Rinderknecht, Todd, Macdonald and Woolfe: Jour. Chem. Soc., 286, 1943.
77. Fulton: Indus. & Engin. Chem., *14*, 407, 1942.
78. Hitzemann: Arch. der Pharmazie, *276*, 353, 1941.
79. Leaf, Todd and Wilkinson: Jour. Chem. Soc., 185, 1942.
80. Madinaveitia, Russel and Todd: Jour. Chem. Soc., 628, 1942.
81. Russell, Todd, Wilkinson, Macdonald and Woolfe: Jour. Chem. Soc., 826, 1941.
82. Simonsen and Todd: Jour. Chem. Soc., 188, 1942.

Narcotics and Drug Abuse

In 1962 a White House Conference on Narcotic and Drug Abuse was convened in recognition of the fact that drug traffic and abuse were growing and critical national concerns. Large quantities of drugs were moving in illicit traffic despite the best efforts of law enforcement agencies. Addiction to the familiar opiates, especially in big-city ghettos, was widespread. New stimulant, depressant, and hallucinogenic drugs, many of them under loose legal controls, were coming into wide misuse, often by students. The informed public was becoming increasingly aware of the social and economic damage of illicit drug taking.

Organized criminals engaged in drug traffic were making high profits. Drug addicts, to support their habits, were stealing millions of dollars worth of property every year and contributing to the public's fear of robbery and burglary. The police, the courts, the jails and prisons, and social-service agencies of all kinds were devoting great amounts of time, money, and manpower to attempt to control drug abuse. Worst of all, thousands of human lives were being wasted.

Some methods of medical treatment, at least for opiate-dependent persons, were being tried, but the results were generally impermanent; relapse was more frequent than cure. The established cycle for such persons was arrest, confinement with or without treatment, release, and then arrest again. And the cause of all of this, the drug-prone personality and the drug-taking urge, lay hidden somewhere in the conditions of modern urban life and in the complexities of mental disorder.

Responsibility for the drug abuse problem was not at all clear. Was it a Federal or a State matter? Was it a police problem or a medical one? If, as seemed evident, it was a combination of all of these, which agencies or people should be doing what? The Conference did not answer these questions, but it did bring to them a sense of national importance and commitment.[8]

From The President's Commission on Law Enforcement and Administration of Justice, *Task Force Report: Narcotics and Drug Abuse* (Washington: U.S. Government Printing Office, 1967), pp. 1–5, 11–14.

The President's Advisory Commission on Narcotic and Drug Abuse was created in 1963 to translate this commitment into a program of action. The Commission's final report, issued in November of that year, set forth a strategy designed to improve the control of drug traffic and the treatment of drug users.[9] The 25 recommendations of that report have been the basis for most of the subsequent Federal activity in this field. Many of them, notably those pertaining to civil commitment for narcotic addicts and the need for Federal controls on the distribution of nonnarcotic drugs,[10] have been or are in the process of being implemented.

This Commission has not and could not have undertaken to duplicate the comprehensive study and report on drug abuse so recently completed by another Presidential Commission. Yet any study of law enforcement and the administration of criminal justice must of necessity include some reference to drug abuse and its associated problems.

❊   ❊   ❊

THE DRUGS AND THEIR REGULATION

The drugs liable to abuse are usually put into the two classifications of "narcotics" and "dangerous drugs," and the people who abuse them are usually called "addicts" and "users." The terms have been used carelessly and have gathered around them many subjective associations. Some precision is necessary if they are to be used as instruments of analysis.

Addiction

There is no settled definition of addiction. Sociologists speak of "assimilation into a special life style of drug taking." Doctors speak of "physical dependence," an alteration in the central nervous system that results in painful sickness when use of the drug is abruptly discontinued; of "psychological or psychic dependence," an emotional desire, craving or compulsion to obtain and experience the drug; and of "tolerance," a physical adjustment to the drug that results in successive doses producing smaller effects and, therefore, in a tendency to increase doses. Statutes speak of habitual use; of loss of the power of self-control respecting the drug; and of effects detrimental to the individual or potentially harmful to the public morals, safety, health or welfare.[11]

Some drugs are addicting, and some persons are addicted, by one definition but not by another. The World Health Organization Expert Committee on Addiction-Producing Drugs, has recommended that the term "drug dependence," with a modifying phrase linking it to a particular type of drug, be used in place of the term "addiction."[12] But "addiction" seems too deeply imbedded in the popular vocabulary to be expunged. Most frequently, it connotes physical dependence, resulting from excessive use of certain drugs. However, it should be noted that one can become physically dependent on substances, notably alcohol, that are not considered part of the drug abuse problem. It should be noted also that psychic or emotional dependence can develop to any substances, not only drugs, that affect consciousness and that people use for escape, adjustment or simple pleasure.

Narcotics

The dictionary defines a "narcotic" as a substance that induces sleep, dulls the senses, or relieves pain. In law, however, it has been given an artificial meaning. It does not refer, as might be expected, to one class of drugs, each having similar chemical properties or pharmacological effects. It is applied rather to a number of different classes of drugs that have been grouped together for purposes of legal control. Under the federal laws, narcotics include the opiates and cocaine.[13] Under most state statutes, marijuana is also a narcotic.[14]

THE OPIATES

These drugs have a highly technical legal definition,[15] but for purposes of this chapter they may be taken to include opium, morphine, their derivatives and compounds and their synthetic equivalents. The opiates have great medical value. They differ widely in their uses, effects, and addiction potential. The most common are morphine and codeine.[16] The former is a principal drug in the relief of pain, the latter in the treatment of cough. Many opiates are prescribed for use in approved medical settings. While the misuse or illicit use (drug "abuse" includes both) of some of these drugs has presented serious problems for state and federal enforcement agencies, public concern as to the opiates is focused primarily on heroin, a morphine derivative. This is the chief drug of addiction in the United States.[17]

The effect of any drug depends on many variables, not the least of which are the mood and expectation of the taker.[18] Drug effects are therefore best expressed in terms of probable outcomes. The discussion here is selective rather than exhaustive. With these provisos, it may be said that heroin is a depressant. It relieves anxiety and tension and diminishes the sex, hunger, and other primary drives. It may also produce drowsiness and cause inability to concentrate, apathy, and lessened physical activity. It can impair mental and physical performance. Repeated and prolonged administration will certainly lead to tolerance and physical dependence.

This process is set in motion by the first dose. An overdose may lead to respiratory failure, coma, and death. With dosages to which a person is tolerant, permanent organic damage does not occur. However, secondary effects, arising from the preoccupation of a person with the drug, may include personal neglect and malnutrition. The ritual of the American addict is to inject the drug intravenously with a needle, and infections and abscesses may be caused by the use of unsterile equipment. Euphoria is an effect often associated with heroin, often reflecting the relief a particular individual gets from chronic anxiety. Among the symptoms of the withdrawal sickness, which reaches peak intensity in 24 to 48 hours, are muscle aches, cramps, and nausea.[19]

The Bureau of Narcotics maintains a name file of active opiate addicts. As of December 31, 1965, there were 52,793 heroin addicts (out of a total of 57,199 opiate addicts) listed.[20] Most of the names in the file are of persons arrested by state and local police agencies and reported voluntarily to the Bureau on a form the Bureau provides for this purpose. Thus the inclusion of a person's name in the file depends in large measure on his coming to the attention of the police, being recognized and classified as an addict, and being reported. There is some uncertainty at each step. Moreover, some police agencies and many health and medical agencies do not participate in the voluntary reporting system. There is also no place in the system for persons who use opiates without becoming addicted. For these reasons many people feel that the Bureau's file does not present a complete statistical picture of opiate use in this country.[21]

Indeed the Bureau makes no claims of infallibility for the reporting system. It is intended as a device for arriving at a workable estimate of the extent and conception of opiate addiction. The Commissioner of Narcotics has testified numerous times that the Bureau's figures are only approximations.[22] The state of California is another source for statistics on drug addiction; it maintains a file of addicts-users in the state.

It should also be noted that other estimates of the present addict population, some of which cite figures as high as 200,000, are without a solid statistical foundation.[23]

More than one-half the known heroin addicts are in New York. Most of the others are in California, Illinois, Michigan, New Jersey, Maryland, Pennsylvania, Texas, and the District of Columbia.[24] In the states where heroin addiction exists on a large scale, it is an urban problem. Within the cities it is largely found in areas with low average incomes, poor housing, and high delinquency. The addict himself is likely to be male, between the ages of 21 and 30, poorly educated and unskilled, and a member of a disadvantaged ethnic minority group.[25]

The cost of heroin to the addict fluctuates over time and from place to place. So does the quality of the drug. Five dollars is a commonly reported price for a single "bag" or packet of heroin. The substance purchased ranges in purity from 1 to about 30 percent, the remainder consisting of natural impurities, and adulterants such as lactose and mannitol.[26] Usually the addict does not know the strength of the doses he buys. Today, however, the drug available on the street is generally so far diluted that the typical addict does not develop profound physical dependence, and therefore does not suffer serious withdrawal symptoms.[27]

The basic Federal control law, the Harrison Narcotic Act of 1914, is a tax statute.[28] It is administered by the Bureau of Narcotics, an agency of the Treasury Department. The statute imposes a tax upon the manufacture or importation of all narcotic drugs. Payment of the tax is evidenced by stamps affixed to the drug containers. The statute authorizes transfers of narcotics in the original containers by and to persons who have registered with the Treasury Department and paid certain occupational taxes ranging from $1 to $24 a year. Official order forms must be used in completing these transactions. There is an exception for the physician acting in the course of his professional practice. Unauthorized possession under the statute is a criminal offense, whether or not the drug is intended for personal use. Unauthorized sale or purchase is a criminal offense. Unauthorized importation is made punishable by a separate Federal statute.[29] Unauthorized possession and sale are also criminal acts under the Uniform Narcotic Drug Act, the control statute in effect in most states.[30]

Heroin occupies a special place in the narcotic laws. It is an illegal drug in the sense that it may not be lawfully imported or manufactured under any circumstances,[31] and it is not available for use in medical practice. All the heroin that reaches the American user is smuggled into the country from abroad, the Middle East being the reputed primary point of origin. All heroin transactions, and any possession of heroin, are therefore criminal. This is not because heroin has evil properties not shared by other opiates. Indeed, while it is more potent and somewhat more rapid in its action, heroin does not differ in any significant pharmacological effect from morphine.[32] It would appear that heroin is outlawed because of its special attractiveness to addicts and because it serves no known medical purpose not served as well or better by other drugs.

COCAINE

This drug is included as a narcotic under federal and other laws but, unlike the opiates, it is a powerful stimulant and does not create tolerance or physical dependence. It is derived from the leaves of the coca plant cultivated extensively in parts of South America. At present it is not the major drug of abuse that it once was.[33]

MARIJUANA

This is a preparation made from the flowering tops of the female hemp plant. This plant often is found growing wild, or it can be cultivated, in any temperature or semitropical climate, including the United States. Most of the marjuana that reaches American users comes from Mexico. There it is cut, dried, and pulverized and then smuggled across the border, either loose or compressed in brick form. It is commonly converted into cigarettes and consumed by smoking. Other derivatives of the hemp plant, such as hashish, which are more potent than marijuana, are rarely found in the United States.[34]

Marijuana has no established and certainly no indispensable medical use. Its effects are rather complicated, combining both stimulation and depression. Much of its effect depends on the personality of the user. The drug may induce exaltation, joyousness and hilarity, and disconnected ideas; or it may induce quietude or reveries. In the inexperienced taker it may induce panic. Or one state may follow the other. Confused perceptions of space and time and hallucinations in sharp color may occur; the person's complex intellectual and motor functions may be impaired. These effects may follow within minutes of the time the drug is taken. The influence usually wears off within a few hours but may last much longer in the case of a toxic dose. The immediate physiological effects may include nausea and vomiting, but there are no lasting physical effects, and fatalities have not been noted. Tolerance is very slight if it develops at all. Physical dependence does not develop.[35]

There is no reliable estimate of the prevalence of marijuana use. To the limited extent that police activity is an accurate measure, use appears to be increasing. Bulk seizures of marijuana by federal enforcement authorities totaled 5,641 kilograms in 1965 as against 1,890 kilograms in 1960.[36] Bureau of Narcotics arrests for marijuana offenses about doubled over the same period of time.[37] So did the number of arrests by California authorities.[38]

Marijuana use apparently cuts across a larger segment of the general population than does opiate use, but again adequate studies are lacking. An impressionistic view, based on scattered reports, is that use is both frequent and increasing in depressed urban areas, academic and artistic communities, and among young professional persons. There are many reports of widespread use on campuses, but estimates that 20 percent or more of certain college populations have used the drug cannot be verified or refuted.[39]

Marijuana is much cheaper than heroin. The director of the Vice Control Division, Chicago Police Department, testified in 1966 that the price of marijuana in Chicago was roughly 50 to 75 cents for a single cigarette, roughly $25 for a can the size of a tobacco tin, and from $85 to $125 a pound.[40] Prices tend to be lower nearer the Mexican source.

The federal law controlling marijuana is a tax statute, enacted in 1937 and enforced by the Bureau of Narcotics.[41] On its face the statute authorizes marijuana transactions between persons, such as importers, wholesalers, physicians, and others, who have paid certain occupational and transfer taxes. But, in fact, since there is no accepted medical use of marijuana, only a handful of people are registered under the law, and for all practical purposes the drug is illegal. Unauthorized possession, which in this context means possession under almost any circumstance, is a criminal act under federal tax law. Sale or purchase of marijuana are also criminal offenses under this statute. Importation is made punishable by a separate statute.[42] Possession and sale are also offenses under the Uniform Narcotic Drug Act, which controls marijuana in most states.

Dangerous Drugs

The term "dangerous drugs" commonly refers to three classes of nonnarcotic drugs that are habit-forming or have a potential for abuse because of their stimulant, depressant, or hallucinogenic effect. Central nervous system stimulants and depressents are widely used in medical practice and are not considered dangerous when taken in ordinary therapeutic doses under medical direction. They are available on prescription. Drugs in the hallucinogenic class have not yet been proven safe for medical purposes and are not legally available in drugstores. Their sole legitimate use at present is by qualified researchers in connection with investigations reported to and authorized by the Food and Drug Administration.[43] There is an exception in the case of peyote, the use of which is authorized in connection with religious ceremonies of the Native American Church.[44]

The Stimulants

The most widely used and abused of the stimulants are the amphetamines, which are known generally as "pep pills." They bear chemical names such as amphetamine sulfate or dextroamphetamine sulfate and particular nicknames such as "bennies" or "dexies" (after trade names of the two drugs.) There are dozens of amphetamine preparations in the market. They are prescribed and apparently are medically effective for relief of fatigue, for control of overweight, and in the treatment of mental disorder.

The amphetamines cause wakefulness and have the capacity to elevate mood and to induce a state of well-being and elation. This is probably the basis of their medical value. It is also the likely reason for their abuse.

Tolerance develops with the use of amphetamines. This permits gradual and progressive increases in dosage. Too large a dose or too sudden an increase in dose, however, may produce bizarre mental effects such as delusions or hallucinations. These effects are more likely if the drug is injected intravenously in diluted powder form than if it is taken orally in tablet form. Nervousness and insomnia are milder symptoms of abuse. Physical dependence does not develop.[45]

The Depressants

The most widely used and abused of the depressant drugs are the barbiturates. These are known generally as "goofballs." They have chemical names, such as pentobarbital sodium and secobarbital sodium, and particular nicknames, such as "nimbies" and "seccy" (after trade names of the two drugs). There are more than 25 barbiturates marketed for clinical use. They are apparently useful because of their sedative, hypnotic, or anesthetic actions and are most commonly prescribed to produce sleep and to relieve tension and anxiety.

A person can develop tolerance to barbiturates, enabling him to ingest increasing quantities of the drug up to a limit that varies with the individual. Chronic administration of amounts in excess of the ordinary daily dose will lead to physical dependence, resulting, upon withdrawal of the drug, in a sickness marked at peak intensity by convulsions and a delirium, resembling alcoholic delirium tremens or a major psychotic episode. Excessive doses may also result in impairment of judgment, loss of emotional control, staggering, slurred speech, tremor, and occasionally coma and death. Barbiturates are a major suicidal agent. They are also reported, like amphetamines, to be implicated in assaultive acts and automobile accidents.[46]

Among the other depressants involved in the drug abuse problem are a number of sedative and tranquilizing drugs, introduced since 1950, that are chemically unrelated to the barbiturates, but similar in effect. The best known of these are meprobamate (Miltown, Equanil), glutethimide (Doriden), ethinamate (Valmid), etchlorvynol (Placidyl), methyprylon (Noludar), and chlordiazepoxide (Librium). There is a strong evidence that abuse of these agents may lead to drug intoxication and physical dependence. Suicide by overdose, and deaths during withdrawal from some of the drugs, have also been reported.[47]

The Hallucinogens

Hallucinogenic, or psychedelic, drugs and the controversy that surrounds them have recently aroused the attention of the mass media and the public. This is certainly due in part to the increasing incidence of their use on college campuses. It may also be due to the emergence of new substances, such as LSD, many times more potent than such older hallucinogens as peyote and mescaline. All these drugs have the capacity to produce altered states of consciousness. Generally they are taken orally.

LSD, the most potent of the hallucinogens, is a synthetic drug made by a chemical process; lysergic acid is the main component in the chemical conversion. Minute amounts of the drug are capable of producing extreme effects. It is usually deposited on sugar cubes in liquid form, although recently it has been found frequently in pill form.[48] Swallowing such a cube or pill is called "taking a trip." A recent publication of the Medical Society of the County of New York ... cited as dangers of LSD: (1) prolonged psychosis; (2) acting out of character disorders and homosexual impulses; (3) suicidal inclinations; (4) activation of previously latent psychosis; and (5) reappearance of the drug's effects weeks or even months after use. It was reported that between March and December of 1965 a total of 65 persons suffering from acute psychosis induced by LSD were admitted to Bellevue Hospital in New York.[49]

The only legal producer of LSD ceased manufacture in April 1966, and turned over its entire supply of the drug to the federal government. A few closely monitored experimental projects involving LSD are still in progress.[50]

Peyote is the hallucinogenic substance obtained from the button-shaped growths of a cactus plant found growing wild in the arid regions of Mexico. Mescaline is a natural alkaloid, which occurs in the same plant. These drugs have appeared in capsule and liquid form and as a powder that can be dissolved in water.[51]

Psilocybin is a substance extracted from a mushroom fungus. It appears in liquid and powder form.[52]

Different degrees of tolerance to the hallucinogens are reported. Physical dependence apparently does not develop.[53]

There is no reliable statistical information on the prevalence of dangerous drug abuse. However, there are indications of widespread and increasing abuse. The former Commissioner of the Food and

Drug Administration, for example, has testified that enough raw material was produced in 1962 to make over 9 billion doses of barbiturates and amphetamines combined, and he estimated that one-half of these ended up in the bootleg market.[54] There is no similar estimate of the proportion of the more than 1 million pounds of tranquilizer drugs produced each year that fall into the hands of drug abusers, but the figure certainly is high. A spreading use of the hallucinogens has undoubtedly been caused in part by the activities and advertising of groups formed for the very purpose of promoting experience in these drugs. These groups, or cults, have made broad and appealing claims in regard to the capacity of the hallucinogens to expand the power of the mind to understand self, love, God, and the universe.[55] They are likely to understate the dangers that line the route to such mystical experiences. Whatever the other causes, cases of dangerous drug abuse coming to the attention of school and medical authorities and police officials have been steadily increasing in number.[56] The prices of illicit dangerous drugs vary sharply in time and place. Some approximate ranges of reported price are from $0.10 to $1 for an amphetamine or barbiturate tablet, from $1 to $10 for a sugar cube saturated with LSD, and from $0.01 to $0.50 for a peyote button.[57] All of these prices represent significant profits to the seller.

A series of federal enactments that proved inadequate to deal with the traffic in dangerous drugs has given way to the Drug Abuse Control Amendments of 1965. The statute became effective February 1, 1966, and is now the principal federal law in the field. It limits manufacture, sale, and distribution of any controlled drug to certain designated classes of persons, such as registered wholesale druggists and licensed physicians. It requires that inventories be taken and records of receipts and dispositions be maintained. It places restrictions on the refilling of prescriptions. Criminal penalties are provided for violations, including manufacture, sale, or distribution by unauthorized persons. The first offense is a misdemeanor; the second, a felony. Possession of drugs for personal use is not an offense under this statute.

All of the amphetamines and the barbiturates are controlled by specific language in the statute. In addition, any other drug with potential for abuse because of its depressant, stimulant, or hallucinogenic effect may be placed under control by designation. Some 22 other drugs have been so designated, including all the hallucinogens and three of the tranquilizers discussed above. The statute is enforced by the Bureau of Drug Abuse Control, is a newly created agency within the Food and Drug Administration.

Almost all states have some statutory scheme for controlling at least some of the dangerous drugs, but there is complete lack of uniformity in this legislation.

It is obvious that the increasing use of drugs, including particularly those like LSD with great potential for harm, presents a serious challenge to the nation.

❊   ❊   ❊

PENALTIES

Since early in the century we have built our drug control policies around the twin judgments that drug abuse was an evil to be suppressed and that this could most effectively be done by the application of criminal enforcement and penal sanctions. Since then, one traditional response to an increase in drug abuse has been to increase the penalties for drug offenses. The premise has been that the more certain and severe the punishment, the more it would serve as a deterrent. Typically this response has taken the form of mandatory minimum terms of imprisonment, increasing in severity with repeated offenses, and provisions making the drug offender ineligible for suspension of sentence, probation, and parole.

Federal law was changed twice during the last decade. In 1951, following the post-World War II upsurge in reported addiction, mandatory minimum sentences were introduced for all narcotic and marijuana offenses, two years for the first offense, five years for the second, and ten years for third and subsequent offenses. At the same time, suspension of sentence and probation were prohibited for second offenders.[58] In 1956 the mandatory minimum sentences were raised to five years for the first and ten years for the second and subsequent offenses of unlawful sale or importation. They remained at two, five, and ten years for the offense of unlawful possession. Suspension of sentence, probation, and parole were prohibited for all but the first offense of unlawful possession.[59] Many state criminal codes contain comparable, though not identical, penalty provisions.

In support of existing mandatory minimum sentences for narcotics violations, it has been suggested that the high price and low quality of the heroin available on the street and the fact that serious physical dependence on the drug has become a rarity are evidence that there are fewer people willing to face the risk of more severe penalties. On the other hand, with respect to heroin, these trends may have preceded the pattern of mandatory minimum sentence provisions, and enforcement officials have also credited direct enforcement efforts against the international flow of heroin for the changes.[60] And despite the application of such sanctions to marijuana, the use of and traffic in that drug appear to be increasing.[61]

Since the evidence as to the effects of mandatory minimum sentences is inconclusive, the Commission believes that the arguments against such provisions . . . are a firmer basis upon which to rest its judgment in this case.

Within any classification of offenses, differences exist in both the circumstances and nature of the illegal conduct and in the offenders. Mandatory provisions deprive judges and correctional authorities of the ability to base their judgments on the seriousness of the violations and the particular characteristics and potential for rehabilitation of the offender.

There is a broad consensus among judges and correctional authorities that discretion should be restored. A 1964 policy statement of the Advisory Council of Judges[62] and repeated testimony by officials of the Bureau of Prisons and Board of Parole are expressions of this consensus.[63]

Application of the mandatory minimums has had some measurable results. The first of these has been a substantial increase in the percentage of the Federal prison population serving sentences for narcotic and marijuana offenses. At the close of fiscal 1965 there were 3,998 drug-law violators confined in all federal institutions. This number represented 17.9 percent of all persons confined. The average sentence being served by the drug-law violators was 87.6 months, and 75.5 percent of them were ineligible for parole. These figures compare with the 2,017 drug-law violators confined at the close of fiscal 1950, comprising 11.2 percent of all persons confined at that time. The 1950 violators were all eligible for parole, and while average sentence data is not available for that year, it would be safe to estimate that sentences averaged much less than one-half of 87.6 months.[64]

Some differential handling of narcotic addicts after conviction is permitted by the civil commitment laws discussed below, which bypass the penalty provisions. Other devices in the present law also permit some distinctions to be made among drug offenders. First offenders charged with unlawful possession under federal law are eligible for suspended sentence, probation, and parole.[65] Persons under the age of 22 are eligible for indeterminate sentencing under the Federal Youth Correction Act.[66] Some state laws distinguish mere possession from possession with intent to sell and provide separate penalties for the two offenses.[67] Informal practices also are common, such as reduction of charge by the prosecutor (whose discretion is not circumscribed by the law) to avoid the mandatory minimum sentence provided for the greater offense.[68]

In its recommendations on mandatory minimums, the president's 1963 Advisory Commission sought to avoid the evils of treating all narcotics and marijuana offenders alike by dividing offenses into four groups:[69]

> the smuggling or sale of large quantities of narcotics or the possession of large quantities for sale. This would subject the offender to mandatory minimum sentences. Probation, suspension of sentence, and parole would be denied.
>
> The smuggling or sale of small quantities of narcotics, or the possession of small quantities for sale. This would subject the offender to some measure of imprisonment but not to any mandatory minimum terms. Suspension of sentence would not be available but parole would.
>
> The possession of narcotics without intent to sell. The sentencing judge would have full discretion as to these offenses.
>
> All marijuana offenses. The sentencing judge would have full discretion.

MARIJUANA

The basic federal control statute, the Marijuana Tax Act, was enacted in 1937 with the stated objectives of making marijuana dealings visible to public scrutiny, raising revenue, and rendering difficult the acquisition of marijuana for nonmedical purposes (the drug has no recognized medical value) and noncommercial use (the plant from which the drug comes has some commercial value in the production of seed and hemp).[70] At the heart of the act are provisions requiring that all persons with a legitimate reason for handling marijuana register and pay an occupational tax, requiring that all marijuana transactions be recorded on official forms provided by the Treasury Department, subjecting transfers to a registered person to a tax of $1 an ounce, and subjecting transfers to an unregistered person to a prohibitive tax of $100 an ounce.[71] Under the Uniform Narcotic Drug Act in force in most states, marijuana is defined and controlled as a narcotic drug.[72]

The act raises an insignificant amount of revenue[73] and exposes an insignificant number of marijuana transactions to public view, since only a handful of people are registered under the act. It has become, in effect, solely a criminal law imposing sanctions upon persons who sell, acquire, or possess marijuana.

Marijuana was placed under a prohibition scheme of control because of its harmful effects and its claimed association with violent behavior and crime.[74] Another reason now advanced in support of the marijuana regulations is that the drug is a steppingstone or forerunner to the use of addicting drugs, particularly heroin.[75]

The law has come under attack on all counts, and the points made against it deserve a hearing.

The Effects

Marijuana is equated in law with the opiates, but the abuse characteristics of the two have almost nothing in common. The opiates produce physical dependence. Marijuana does not. A withdrawal sickness appears when use of the opiates is discontinued. No such symptoms are associated with marijuana. The desired dose of opiates tend to increase over time, but this is not true of marijuana. Both can lead to psychic dependence, but so can almost any substance that alters the state of consciousness.[76]

The Medical Society of the County of New York has classified marijuana as a mild hallucinogen[77] and this is probably as good a description as any, although hallucinations are only one of many effects the drug can produce. It can impair judgment and memory; it can cause anxiety, confusion, or disorientation; and it can induce temporary psychotic episodes in predisposed people. Any hallucinogenic drug, and many of the other dangerous drugs, can do the same. Marijuana is probably less likely to produce these effects than such moderately potent hallucinogens as peyote, mescaline, and hashish (another derivative of the plant from which marijuana comes), and much less likely to do so than the potent hallucinogen LSD.[78]

Marijuana, Crime, and Violence

Here differences of opinion are absolute and the claims are beyond reconciliation. One view is that marijuana is a major cause of crime and violence. Another is that marijuana has no association with crime and only a marginal relation to violence.

Proponents of the first view rely in part on reports connecting marijuana users with crime. One such report by the district attorney of New Orleans was referred to in the hearings on the 1937 act.[79] It found that 125 of 450 men convicted of major crimes in 1930 were regular marijuana users. Approximately one-half the murders (an unstated number) and a fifth of those tried for larceny, robbery, and assault (again an unstated number) were regular users.[80] However, the main reliance is on case files of enforcement agencies. Excerpts from these files have been used to demonstrate a marijuana-crime causal relation.[81] The validity of such a demonstration involves three assumptions which are questioned by opponents of the present law: (1) The defendant was a marijuana user. Usually this can be determined only by the defendant's own statement or by his possession of the drug at the time of arrest. (2) He was under the influence of marijuana when he committed the criminal act. Again a statement, perhaps a self-serving one, is most often the source of the information. Chemical tests of blood, urine, and the like will not detect marijuana.[82] (3) The influence of the marijuana caused the crime in the sense that it would not have been committed otherwise.

Those who hold the opposite view cannot prove their case, either. They can only point to the prevailing lack of evidence. Many have done so. The Medical Society of the County of New York has stated flatly that there is no evidence that marijuana use is associated with crimes of violence in this country.[83] There are many similar statements by other responsible authorities. The 1962 report of the President's Ad Hoc Panel on Drug Abuse found the evidence inadequate to substantiate the reputation of marijuana for inciting people to antisocial acts.[84] The famous Mayor's Committee on Marijuana, appointed by Mayor La Guardia to study the marijuana situation in New York City, did not observe any aggression in subjects to whom marijuana was given.[85] In addition there are several studies of persons who were both confessed marijuana users and convicted criminals, and these reach the conclusion that a positive relation between use and crime cannot be established.[86]

One likely hypothesis is that, given the accepted tendency of marijuana to release inhibitions, the effect of the drug will depend on the individual and the circumstances. It might, but certainly will not necessarily or inevitably, lead to aggressive behavior or crime. The response will depend more on the individual than the drug. This hypothesis is consistent with the evidence that marijuana does not alter the basic personality structure.[87]

Marijuana as a Prelude to Addicting Drugs

The charge that marijuana "leads" to the use of addicting drugs needs to be critically examined. There is evidence that a majority of the heroin users who come to the attention of public authorities have, in fact, had some prior experience with marijuana.[88] But this does not mean that one leads to the other in the sense that marijuana has an intrinsic quality that creates a heroin liability. There are too many marijuana users who do not graduate to heroin, and too many heroin addicts with no known prior marijuana use, to support such a theory. Moreover there is no scientific basis for such a theory. The basic text on pharmacology, Goodman and Gilman, *The Pharmacological Basis of Therapeutics* (Macmillan 1960) states quite explicitly that marijuana habituation does not lead to the use of heroin.[89]

The most reasonable hypothesis here is that some people who are predisposed to marijuana are also predisposed to heroin use. It may also be the case that through the use of marijuana a person forms the personal associations that later expose him to heroin.[90]

The amount of literature on marijuana is massive. It runs to several thousand articles in medical journals and other publications. Many of these are in foreign languages and reflect the experience of other countries with the use of the drug and with other substances derived from the hemp plant. The relevance of this material to our own problem has never been determined. Indeed, with the possible exception of the 1944 LaGuardia report, no careful and detailed analysis of the American experience seems to have been attempted. Basic research has been almost nonexistent, probably because the principal active ingredient in marijuana has only recently been isolated and synthesized.[91] Yet the Commission believes that enough information exists to warrant careful study of our present marijuana laws and the propositions on which they are based.

six

THE ALCOHOL MINORITY

We have seen from our Bogardus Social Distance Scale (Introduction) that alcoholics are subject to prejudicial treatment, and that prejudiced people are more likely than nonprejudiced people to downgrade alcoholics. Alcohol offenders are a large minority; roughly one-third of the people in jail are there for being drunk in public. Alcoholism is sometimes recognized as a disease, but this recognition does not protect an alcoholic from criminal prosecution. People are not generally born as drunks, but once a person has the habit he is almost as addicted as a heroin user. Once a person has the stigma of being a drunk it may become almost impossible to separate himself from it. It influences his work and social life, and it increases his likelihood of going to jail. The question of the relevancy of treatment—by wives, friends, employers and police—is just now receiving considerable attention. There is no doubt that being drunk interferes with a wide variety of performances, but many contend that current treatments for drunkenness do more harm than good. The inadequacy of the current system of treatment is lucidly analyzed in the following selection from the report of The President's Commission on Law Enforcement and Administration of Justice.

Drunkenness

Two million arrests in 1965—one of every three arrests in America—were for the offense of public drunkenness.[1] The great volume of these arrests places an extremely heavy load on the operations of the criminal justice system. It burdens police, clogs lower criminal courts, and crowds penal institutions throughout the United States.

Because of the sheer size of the problem and because of doubts that have recently been raised about the efficacy of handling drunkenness within the system of criminal justice, the Commission sought to reexamine present methods of treating drunkenness offenders and to explore promising alternatives. It was not in a position to undertake a comprehensive study of the complex medical, social, and public health problems of drunkenness.

THE EXISTING SYSTEM

Drunkenness Laws

Drunkenness is punishable under a variety of laws, generally describing the offense as being "drunk in a public place," often without providing a precise definition of drunkenness itself.[2] Some laws include as a condition that the offender is "unable to care for his own safety."[3]

In some jurisdictions there are no laws prohibiting drunkenness, but any drunkenness that causes a breach of the peace is punishable. In Georgia and Alabama, for example, drunkenness that is manifested by boisterous or indecent conduct, or loud and profane discourse, is a crime.[4] Other jurisdictions apply disorderly conduct statutes to those who are drunk in public. In Chicago, for example, the police, having no drunkenness law to enforce, use a disorderly conduct statute to arrest nondisorderly inebriates.[5] Some jurisdictions permit police to make public drunkenness arrests under both State laws and local ordinances.[6]

From The President's Commission on Law Enforcement and Administration of Justice, *Task Force Report: Drunkenness* (Washington: U.S. Government Printing Office, 1967), pp. 1–4.

The laws provide maximum jail sentences ranging from five days to six months; the most common maximum sentence is 30 days. In some States an offender convicted of "habitual drunkenness" may be punished by a two-year sentence of imprisonment.[7]

The Offenders

The two million arrests for drunkenness each year involve both sporadic and regular drinkers. Among the number are a wide variety of offenders—the rowdy college boy; the weekend inebriate; the homeless, often unemployed single man. How many offenders fall into these and other categories is not known. Neither is it known how many of the offenders are alcoholics in the medical sense of being dependent on alcohol. There is strong evidence, however, that a large number of those who are arrested have a lengthy history of prior drunkenness arrests, and that a disproportionate number involve poor persons who live in slums. In 1964 in the city of Los Angeles about one-fifth of all persons arrested for drunkenness accounted for two-thirds of the total number of arrests for that offense. Some of the repeaters were arrested as many as 18 times in that year.[8]

A review of chronic offender cases reveals that a large number of persons have, in short installments, spent many years of their lives in jail. In 1957 the Committee on Prisons, Probation, and Parole in the District of Columbia studied six chronic offenders and found that they had been arrested for drunkenness a total of 1409 times and had served a total of 125 years in penal institutions.[9]

The great majority of repeaters live on "skid row"—a dilapidated area found in most large and medium-size cities in the United States. On skid row substandard hotels and rooming houses are intermingled with numerous taverns, pawn shops, cheap cafeterias, employment agencies that specialize in jobs for the unskilled, and religious missions that provide free meals after a service. Many of the residents—including the chronic drunkenness offenders—are homeless, penniless, and beset with acute personal problems.[10]

The Arrest of the Drunkenness Offender

The police do not arrest everyone who is under the influence of alcohol.[11] Sometimes they will help an inebriate home. It is when he appears to have no home or family ties that he is most likely to be arrested and taken to the local jail.[12]. . .

Drunkenness arrest practices vary from place to place. Some police departments strictly enforce drunkenness statutes, while other departments are known to be more tolerant. In fact, the number of arrests in a city may be related less to the amount of public drunkenness than to police policy. . . .

In some large and medium-size cities, police departments have "bum squads" that cruise skid rows and border areas to apprehend inebriates who appear unable to care for their own safety, or who are likely to annoy others.[13] Such wholesale arrests sometimes include homeless people who are not intoxicated.[14]

Operation of the Criminal System After Arrest

Following arrest, the drunk is usually placed in a barren cell called a "tank," where he is detained for at least a few hours. The tanks in some cities can hold as many as 200 people, while others hold only one or two. One report described the conditions found in a tank in this way:

> Although he may have been picked up for his own protection, the offender is placed in a cell, which may frequently hold as many as 40–50 men where there is no room to sit or lie down, where sanitary facilities and ventilation are inadequate and a stench of vomit and urine is prevalent.
>
> The drunken behavior of some of the inmates is an added hazard. It is questionable whether greater safety is achieved for the individual who is arrested for his safekeeping.[15]

The chronic alcoholic offender generally suffers from a variety of ailments and is often in danger of serious medical complications,[16] but medical care is rarely provided in the tank; and it is difficult to detect or to diagnose serious illness since it often resembles intoxication.[17] Occasionally, chronic offenders become ill during pretrial detention and die without having received adequate medical attention.[18]. . .

If the offender can afford bail, he usually obtains release after he sobers up.[19] In many jurisdictions an offender is permitted to forfeit bail routinely by not appearing in court.[20] Thus, if the arrested person has the few dollars required, he can avoid prosecution;[21] if he has no money, as is usually the case, he must appear in court.

Drunkenness offenders are generally brought before a judge the morning after their arrest, sometimes appearing in groups of 15 or 20. Rarely are the normal procedural or due process safeguards applied to these cases.[22] Usually defendants are processed through the court system with haste and either released or sentenced to several days or weeks in jail.[23] In some cities only those offenders who request it are jailed.[24] In others chronic offenders, who are likely to be alcoholics, are generally sent to jail.[25]

After serving a brief sentence, the chronic offender is released, more likely than not to return to his former haunts on skid row, with no money, no job, and no plans.[26] Often he is arrested within a matter of hours or days.

In a memorandum of law submitted in a recent case of a homeless alcoholic, defense counsel noted that his client had been arrested 31 times in a period of four months and six days. Counsel maintained that "it is fair to conclude [in view of three commitments during that period of time] that he must have been arrested one out of every two days that he appeared on the public streets of the District of Columbia."[27]

EVALUATION OF THE EXISTING SYSTEM

Effect on the Offender

The criminal justice system appears ineffective to deter drunkenness or to meet the problems of the chronic alcoholic offender. What the system usually does accomplish is to remove the drunk from public view, detoxify him, and provide him with food, shelter, emergency medical service, and a brief period of forced sobriety. As presently constituted, the system is not in a position to meet his underlying medical and social problems.

Effect on the System of Criminal Justice

Including drunkenness within the system of criminal justice seriously burdens and distorts its operations. Because the police often do not arrest the intoxicated person who has a home, there is in arrest practices an inherent discrimination against the homeless and the poor. Due process safeguards are often considered unnecessary or futile. The defendant may not be warned of his rights or permitted to make a telephone call.[28] And although coordination, breath, or blood tests to determine intoxication are common practice in "driving-while-intoxicated" cases, they are virtually nonexistent in common drunk cases. Yet, without the use of such chemical tests, it is often difficult to determine whether the individual is intoxicated or suffering from a serious illness that has symptoms similar to intoxication.[29]

> Authorities in this field recognize that the most skilled physician would have difficulty in arriving at an accurate diagnosis of alcoholic influence or intoxication simply by observing outward indications—clinical or objective symptoms. Ordinarily, a lengthy and detailed clinical examination is required to rule out absolutely many of the pathological conditions which are known to produce the same symptoms.

The handling of drunkenness cases in court hardly reflects the standards of fairness that are the basis of our system of criminal justice.[30] One major reason is that counsel is rarely present.[31] Drunkenness cases often involve complex factual and medical issues. Cross-examination could be conducted on "observations" of the arresting officer such as "bloodshot" and "glassy" eyes, "staggering gait," "odor" of alcohol on the defendant's breath. The testimony of an expert medical witness on behalf of the defendant could be elicited.[32]

The extent of police time allotted to handling drunkenness offenders varies from city to city and from precinct to precinct. In most cities a great deal of time is spent.[33] The inebriate must be taken into custody, transported to jail, booked, detained, clothed, fed, sheltered, and transported to court. In some jurisdictions, police officers must wait, often for hours, to testify in court.

There is a commensurate burden on the urban courts. Notwithstanding the fact that an overwhelming caseload often leads judges to dispose of scores of drunkenness cases in minutes, they represent a significant drain on court time which is needed for felony and serious misdemeanor cases. More subtly, drunkenness cases impair the dignity of the criminal process in lower courts, which are forced to handle defendants so casually and to apply criminal sanctions with so little apparent effect.

In correctional systems, too, resources are diverted from serious offenders. After court appearance, some offenders are sent to short-term penal institutions, many of which are already overcrowded. Correctional authorities estimate that one-half the entire misdemeanant population is comprised of drunkenness offenders.[34] In one city it was reported that 95 percent of short-term prisoners were drunkenness offenders.[35]

seven

PROSTITUTION AND PORNOGRAPHY

We turn once again to *The Wolfenden Report: Report of the Committee on Homosexual Offenses and Prostitution.* As in its view of homosexuality, *The Wolfenden Report* presents us with an authoritative if unconventional view of the phenomenon of prostitution. In England it is not illegal for a woman to "offer her body to indiscriminate lewdness for hire." The report contains recommendations for making the law more strict in the case of public solicitation and procuring, but argues that prostitution by itself is an act of private immorality that should not be the subject of criminal sanctions.

The deviant minority perspective is as revealing on the subject of prostitution as it is in the other forms of deviancy described in this book. Prostitution in the literature is often viewed as a form of pathology that results from negative environmental or social conditions such as poverty, a disorganized family life, seduction in childhood, the absence of a father, conflict with one or both parents, and the like. *The Wolfenden Report* acknowledges that these conditions often do occur in the backgrounds of prostitutes, but that they do not really serve as explanation because many who do *not* turn to prostitution come from the same circumstances, and because many prostitutes come from very favorable backgrounds. In accord with the minority group perspective, the Wolfenden Committee views prostitution as a preferred style of life, "easier, freer, and more profitable. . . . a way of life." Its practitioners are not sociopaths but members of a subculture with an alternative world view different from other people in the society. This suggests a different, more tolerant treatment of prostitutes both in "therapy" and in contact with the law, and even legalization of private acts of prostitution, perhaps subject to government regulation and recognition as a bona fide occupation. Legalization might reduce venereal disease and drug addiction, the main social ills that now accompany prostitution. Prostitutes not subject to government medical examination and certification do much to contribute to the problem of venereal disease. When prostitution is illegal, a prostitute must work in an illegal marketplace that includes drugs as a parallel inducement, in order to ply her trade. Thus does the law exacerbate the problems that accompany an existing form of behavior.

The second part of this chapter contains selections drawn from the report of the recent Commission on Obscenity and Pornography. Here again the matter of alternative perspective arises. The Commission, in examining the current court decisions concerning what is obscene, finds vaguely defined terms such as "prurient," "patently offensive," "redeeming social value," and "contemporary community standards" are used to define obscenity, and points out how different people apply these words to erotic material differently. For this reason the Commission took the stand that as a body they could not recommend a standard operational definition of obscenity because the word was difficult if not impossible to define.

The prevailing official view is reflected in movie ratings—G (General Admission), GP (Parental Discretion Advised), R (Restricted), and X (Adults Only). Films with scenes showing the nude human body receive R or X ratings because they are judged in some degree "obscene," while films with scenes depicting bloody killing, torture, or mutilation may receive G or GP ratings. According to the Commission report, there is a deviant minority of people who do not regard explicit nudity as obscene, but who feel that violence *is* obscene.

As in other types of deviancy discussed in this book, there are numerous public misconceptions about sexually explicit or erotic materials: that such materials precipitate moral breakdown, that they lead to an increase in sex crime, or that they foster an interest in bizarre sex practices. The evidence examined by the Commission shatters these beliefs and indicates that they are held primarily by people who have had little contact with erotic materials, who are generally less well educated, and who attach guilt feelings to anything having to do with sex. Based on its findings, the Commission recommends that "federal, state, and local legislation prohibiting the sale, exhibition, or distribution of sexual materials to consenting adults should be repealed."

Prostitution as a Way of Life

The Wolfenden Report

222. By our terms of reference we are required to consider—"the
     law and practice relating to offenses against the criminal law
     in connection with prostitution and solicitation for immoral pur-
     poses."

So far as our terms of reference relate to offenses in streets and
public places, the problems were examined by an earlier Committee
(the Street Offenses Committee) set up in 1927 under the chairman-
ship of the late Lord Macmillan (then Mr. Hough Macmillan, K.C.);
and we have studied the report of that Committee[1] in coming to
our own conclusions.

223. It would have taken us beyond our terms of reference to
investigate in detail the prevalence of prostitution of the reasons
which lead women to adopt this matter of life. On the former point
we have something to say below[2] in connection with street offenses.
On the latter point, we believe that whatever may have been the
case in the past, in these days, in this country at any rate, economic
factors cannot account for it to any large or decisive extent. Economic pressure is no doubt a factor in some individual cases. So, in
others, is a bad upbringing, seduction at an early age, or a broken
marriage. But many women surmount such disasters without turning to a life of prostitution. It seems to us more likely that these are
precipitating factors rather than determining causes, and that there
must be some additional psychological element in the personality of
the individual woman who becomes a prostitute. Our impression is
that the great majority of prostitutes are women whose psychological make-up is such that they choose this life because they find in
it a style of living which is to them easier, freer, and more profitable

From the Committee on Homosexual Offenses and Prostitution, *The Wolfenden
Report* (London: Her Majesty's Printing Office, 1957), pp. 75–78, 93–96 in
1962 edition.

than would be provided by any other occupation. As one of our women witnesses put it:

Prostitution is a way of life consciously chosen because it suits a woman's personality in particular circumstances.

224. Prostitution in itself is not, in this country, an offense against the criminal law. Some of the activities of prostitutes are, and so are the activities of some others who are concerned in the activities of prostitutes. But it is not illegal for a woman to "offer her body to indiscriminate lewdness for hire," provided that she does not, in the course of doing so, commit any one of the specific acts which would bring her within the ambit of the law. Nor, it seems to us, can any case be sustained for attempting to make prostitution in itself illegal. We recognize that we are here, again, on the difficult borderline between law and morals, and that this is debatable ground. But, for the general reasons . . . we are agreed that private immorality should not be the concern of the criminal law except in the special circumstances therein mentioned.

225. Prostitution is a social fact deplorable in the eyes of moralists, sociologists, and, we believe, the great majority of ordinary people. But it has persisted in many civilizations throughout many centuries, and the failure of attempts to stamp it out by repressive legislation shows that it cannot be eradicated through the agency of the criminal law. It remains true that without a demand for her services the prostitute could not exist, and that there are enough men who avail themselves of prostitutes to keep the trade alive. It also remains true that there are women who, even when there is no economic need to do so, choose this form of livelihood. For so long as these propositions continue to be true there will be prostitution, and no amount of legislation directed towards its abolition will abolish it.

226. It follows that there are limits to the degree of discouragement which the criminal law can properly exercise towards a woman who has deliberately decided to live her life in this way, or a man who has deliberately chosen to use her services. The criminal law, as the Street Offenses Committee plainly pointed out, "is not concerned with private morals or with ethical sanctions." This does not mean that society itself can be indifferent to these matters, for prostitution is an evil of which any society which claims to be civilized

should seek to rid itself; but this end could be achieved only through measures directed to a better understanding of the nature and obligation of sexual relationships and to a raising of the social and moral outlook of society as a whole. In these matters, the work of the churches and of organizations concerned with mental health, moral welfare, family welfare, child and marriage guidance and similar matters should be given all possible encouragement. But until education and the moral sense of the community bring about a change of attitude towards the fact of prostitution, the law by itself cannot do so.

227. At the same time; the law has its place and function in this matter. We cannot do better than quote the words of the Street Offenses Committee:

> As a general proposition it will be universally accepted that the law is not concerned with private morals or with ethical sanctions. On the other hand, the law is plainly concerned with the outward conduct of citizens in so far as that conduct injuriously affects the rights of other citizens. Certain forms of conduct it has always been thought right to bring within the scope of the criminal law on account of the injury which they occasion to the public in general. It is within this category of offenses, if anywhere, that public solicitation for immoral purposes finds an appropriate place.

The statement very clearly represents our own approach and attitude to this part of our inquiry. We are concerned not with prostitution itself but with the manner in which the activities of prostitutes and those associated with them offend against public order and decency, expose the ordinary citizen to what is offensive or injurious, or involve the exploitation of others.

✿   ✿   ✿

STREET OFFENSES

The Extent of the Problem

229. From the evidence we have received there is no doubt that the aspect of prostitution which causes the greatest public concern

at the present time is the presence, and the visible and obvious presence, of prostitutes in considerable numbers in the public streets of some parts of London and of a few provincial towns. It has indeed been suggested to us that in this respect some of the streets of London are without parallel in the capital cities of other civilized countries.

230. Whether or not this particular problem is more serious at the present time than it has been in the past, and if so how much more serious it is, we have no exact means of knowing. The first and obvious place to look for evidence on this point is the statistics of prosecutions of prostitutes for street offenses . . . But if the figures of prosecutions are read without regard to their background they may easily produce an erroneous impression. In the first place, the figures relate to the number of prosecutions, and not to the number of individual prostitutes dealt with during the course of a particular year. For instance, while the number of prosecutions in the West End Central Division of the Metropolitan Police District in 1953 was 6829, the number of prostitutes involved was 808. Secondly, the number of prosecutions must depend to some degree on the number of police available for work of this kind and on the vigor of their activity; and this in turn may well depend on public opinion. At any given moment there may be a state of affairs in the streets which arouses public resentment; this may result in increased police activity and in an increased number of prosecutions. But this increased number of prosecutions does not necessarily represent an increase in the number of offenses committed; it may be no more than an increase in the proportion brought to court of the existing number of offenders. Further it may then happen that, for one reason or another, police activity dies down, with the consequence that the number of prosecutions decreases without any decrease in the number of offenses actually committed.

231. A striking example of this last possibility will be found in a comparison of the English figures for the years 1922 and 1923. In 1922, the number of prosecutions for street offenses by prostitutes in the Metropolitan Police District was 2231. In 1923, it fell to 595, the lowest figure ever recorded, and an equally significant drop was discernible in the figures for the rest of the country. The drop in the metropolis was directly attributed by the then Commissioner of Police to the severe criticism passed on the police, in the Press and elsewhere, as the result of a case in which the London Quarter Ses-

sions found, on appeal, insufficient evidence to show that a person alleged to have been accosted had been "annoyed." The effect of this criticism, according to the Commissioner was to reduce police action to a minimum, and a year later he reported that the conditions existing in the parks and in some of the West End and other thoroughfares were much less satisfactory than they had been a year or two earlier. A similar drop for a similar reason took place in 1929. These examples show that it is dangerous to assume a direct correlation between the number of prosecutions and the number of offenses actually being committed. Equally, it is possible that the substantial increase in the number of prosecutions in England and Wales over the past ten years reflects a conscientious attempt on the part of the police to answer the demand of public opinion that "the streets must be cleaned up."

232. However this may be, it is evident that the problem is no new one. A senior officer of the Metropolitan Police in his evidence to the Select Committee of the House of Lords on the law relating to the Protection of Young Girls said in 1881:

> . . . the state of affairs which exists in this capital is such that from four o'clock, or one may say from three o'clock in the afternoon, it is impossible for any respectable woman to walk from the top of the Haymarket to Wellington Street, Strand. From three or four o'clock in the afternoon Villiers Street and Charing Cross Station and the Strand are crowded with prostitutes, who are there openly soliciting prostitution in broad daylight. At half-past twelve at night a calculation was made a short time ago that there were 500 prostitutes between Piccadilly Circus and the bottom of Waterloo Place . . .

And from representations made to the Home Office by voluntary organizations concerned with public morality some forty years later it appeared that prostitutes then solicited in substantial numbers in the areas of Tottenham Court Road, King's Cross, and Charing Cross.

We have, in short, no reliable evidence whether the number of prostitutes plying their trade in the streets of London has changed significantly in recent years. What has probably happened is that they have shifted the scene of their activities to other and more residential areas and thereby have given ground for complaints from those ordinary citizens who live in these areas and from those who cannot, in going about their daily business, avoid the sight of a state of affairs which seems to them to be an affront to public order and decency.

✿   ✿   ✿

LIVING ON THE EARNINGS OF PROSTITION

298. It is an offense for a male person knowingly to live wholly or in part on the earnings of prostitution. For this purpose, a man who lives with or is habitually in the company of a prostitute, or who exercises control, direction or influence over a prostitute's movements in a way which shows he is aiding, abetting or compelling her prostitution with others, is presumed to be knowingly living on the earnings of prostitution unless he proves the contrary.[3] And it is an offense for a female for purposes of gain to exercise control, direction or influence over a prostitute's movements in a way which shows she is aiding, abetting or compelling her prostitution.[4] The maximum penalty in either case is six months' imprisonment on conviction before a court of summary jurisdiction and two years' imprisonment on conviction on indictment.

299. Where it appears to a justice of the peace (in Scotland, a court of summary jurisdiction) from information on oath that there is reasonable cause to suspect that any house or part of a house is used by a woman for purposes of prostitution, and that a male person residing in or frequenting the house is living wholly or in part on her earnings, the justice (in Scotland, the court) may issue a warrant authorizing a constable to enter and search the house and to arrest the man.[5]

300. There are no reliable figures relating to males dealt with by the courts prior to 1954 for living on the earnings of prostitution. [U]p to that year the offense was combined in the English criminal statistics with the offense of importuning by male persons. In 1954, in England and Wales, 114 men were found guilty of the offense as magistrates' courts and 11 at the higher courts. In 1955, the figures were 113 and 14 respectively. . . . The number of women convicted of exercising control, direction, or influence over a prostitute's movements is negligible, and has not exceeded five in any recent year. No figures relating to either offense are available in respect to Scot-

land, since the figures for these offenses cannot be identified separately from the list of crimes and offenses used for statistical purposes.

301. In its simplest and most usual form, "living on the earnings of prostitution" consists of an arrangement by which a man lives with a prostitute and is wholly or mainly kept by her. Such a man is commonly known as a "ponce" or *souteneur*. Detection of this offense is not without its difficulties, and calls for prolonged observation, usually covering several days and nights, in which the attention of the police is directed to such questions as the following:

(i) whether the man and woman are living together: this is difficult to establish when the couple live in flats or parts of houses;
(ii) whether the woman is, in fact, carrying on prostitution;
(iii) whether the man is doing any work;
(iv) whether the man watches the woman soliciting;
(v) whether the woman is seen to hand the man any money;
(vi) whether they go home together after the woman has finished accommodating her customers.

The difficulties are increased by the fact that many prostitutes—particularly those operating in the West End of London—live with their ponces at some distance from the area in which they carry on their trade.

There is little doubt that the number of prosecutions could be appreciably increased if sufficient manpower were available to undertake the prolonged observation necessary to obtain satisfactory evidence, but we are satisfied that within the resources available to them the police do all they can to deal with this particular offense.

302. Such evidence as we have been able to obtain on this matter suggests that the arrangement between the prostitute and the man she lives with is usually brought about at the instance of the woman, and it seems to stem from a need on the part of the prostitute for some element of stability in the background of her life. As one writer has put it: —

This man may be literally the "bully," which is another of his titles; he may have forced her into the mode of life and be compelling her continuance in it. But he may also be, whether

her legal husband or not, the equivalent of a husband to the promiscuous woman; he is frequently the only person in the world towards whom she feels affection and sense of possession; he is usually her champion in disputes and her protector in a skirmish. He is deeply despised by the police and by the public outside his trade; but he may be nevertheless the one humanizing element in the life of the woman on whom he lives.[6]

It may be the case that once the arrangement is established the "ponce" makes more and more financial demands on the prostitute. It may also be the case that he sometimes is "literally 'the bully.'" But in the main the association between prostitute and "ponce" is voluntary and operates to mutual advantage. To say this is not to condone exploitation; the "ponce" or "bully" has rightly been the subject of universal and unreserved reprobation, and we have already expressed the view that the law should deal with the exploitation of others.

303. We have no doubt that behind the trade of prostitution there lies a variety of commercial interests, to some of which we refer below. The evidence submitted to us, however, has disclosed nothing in the nature of "organized vice" in which the prostitute is an unwilling victim, coerced by a vile exploiter. This does not mean that there is not "organization," in the sense of encouragement to willing girls and women to enter or continue upon a life of prostitution.

304. The present law seems to be based on the desire to protect the prostitute from coercion and exploitation. When it was framed, the prostitute may have been in some danger of coercion; but today, either through the effectiveness of the law or through changes which have removed some of the economic and social factors likely to result in a life of prostitution, she is in less danger of coercion or exploitation against her will.

305. The popular impression of vast organizations in which women are virtually enslaved is perhaps in part due to the indiscriminate use of words which suggest an entirely passive role for the women concerned. We have, for example, learned of an arrangement between several prostitutes and a car-hire firm whereby the firm made large sums of money out of the use of their cars by the prostitutes. The firm was said to "run" a group of prostitutes, with the implication that they organized the women's activities. Another

group of prostitutes lived in rooms, at various addresses, of which one particular man was landlord. This man, who had several convictions for brothel keeping and living on the earnings of prostitution, was said to be "running several girls." In both cases, however much unpleasant exploitation there might appear to the outsider to be, and might indeed actually be, the association between the prostitute and the "exploiter" was entirely voluntary and operated to mutual advantage.

306. It is in our view an oversimplification to think that those who live on the earnings of prostitution are exploiting the prostitute as such. What they are really exploiting is the whole complex of the relationship between prostitute and customer; they are, in effect, exploiting the human weaknesses which cause the customer to seek the prostitute and the prostitute to meet the demand. The more direct methods with which we have dealt above are not the only means by which the trade is exploited; that it continues to thrive is due in no small measure to efforts deliberately made to excite the demand on which its prosperity depends. Abraham Flexner, in his work on "Prostitution in Europe," to which the Street Offenses Committee made reference, says (page 41) "A very large constituent in what has been called the irresistible demand of natural instinct is nothing but suggestion and stimulation associated with alcohol, late hours and sensuous amusements." At the present time, entertainments of a suggestive character, dubious advertisements, the sale of pornographic literature, contraceptives and "aphrodisiac" drugs (sometimes all in one shop), and the sale of alcoholic liquor in premises frequented by prostitutes, all sustain the trade, and in turn themselves profit from it. With most of these evils the law attempts to deal so far as it can without unduly trespassing on the liberty of the individual; and, as in the case of prostitution itself, it is educative measures rather than to amendment of the law that society must look for a remedy.

307. It has been suggested to us that the present penalties provided by the law for living on the earnings of prostitution are inadequate and should be increased. We feel that the maximum of two years' imprisonment for which the law provides is adequate for this offense.

Pornography: Overview of Findings

Report of the Commission on Obscenity and Pornography

I. THE VOLUME OF TRAFFIC AND PATTERNS OF DISTRIBUTION OF SEXUALLY ORIENTED MATERIALS[7]

A. The Industries

When the Commission undertook its work, it could find no satisfactory estimates of the volume of traffic in obscene and pornographic materials. Documented estimates describing the content of materials included therein were not available. The first task was to determine the scope of the subject matter of investigation. The very ambiguity of the terms "obscene" and "pornographic" makes a meaningful single overall estimate of the volume of traffic an impossibility. It is clear that public concern applies to a broad range of materials. Therefore, the Commission determined to report on the commercial traffic and distribution of sexually oriented materials in motion picture films, books, and periodicals. The Commission's examination included these materials, whether publicly or privately exhibited or sold in retail outlets, by individual sales, or through the United States mails.

Two overall findings may appropriately be stated at the outset. Articles appearing in newspapers, magazines, and in other reports have variously estimated the traffic in the "pornography" or "smut" industry to be between $500 million and $2.5 billion per year, almost always without supporting data or definitions which would make such estimates meaningful.

The Commission can state with complete confidence that an estimate of $2.5 billion sales grossly exaggerates the size of the

From the Commission on Obscenity and Pornography, *Report of the Commission on Obscenity and Pornography* (Washington: U.S. Government Printing Office, 1970), pp. 7–27, 37–44.

"smut" industry in the United States under any reasonable definition of the term. In addition, a monolithic "smut" industry does not exist; rather, there are several distinct markets and submarkets which distribute a variety of erotic materials. Some of these industries are fairly well organized, while others are extremely chaotic. These industries vary in terms of media, content, and manner of distribution. Some of the industries are susceptible to fairly precise estimates of the volume of materials, others are not.

We will describe briefly, and provide estimates of dollar and unit volume for most of the industries involved in the production and distribution of broadly defined sexually oriented material.

MOTION PICTURES

Movies have long been one of the primary recreational outlets for Americans. Box office receipts from nearly 14,000 theaters were estimated at $1.065 billion for 1969, and approximately 20 million persons attended motion pictures weekly.

Until the past year or two, motion pictures distributed in the United States fell rather neatly into three categories: general release, art, and exploitation films. By far the most important and familiar are general release films produced and distributed by well-known companies, starring well-known actors, and exhibited in 90 percent or more of the theaters across the country. These account for the vast majority of theater attendance in the United States. Art films are an undefined, amorphous group of films which appeal to a limited audience. Exploitation films, usually known in the industry as "skin flicks," are low-budget sex-oriented movies which have a rather limited exhibition market.

In addition to these well-defined types of films recognized by the industry for many years, in the past year or two quite a number of highly sexually oriented hybrid films (which combine elements of all three traditional types) and films of a totally new genre have appeared. Another group of films, known in the trade as "16mm" films, which are generally among the most sexually explicit available, have also come onto the market.

The Rating System. The recent acceleration in sexual content of films has been approximately coincident in time with the initiation of a movie-rating system for the guidance of viewers. The rating system represents an industry judgment of the appropriateness of the content for children, and reflects to some degree the explicitness of the sexual content of a rated movie. The rating system contains four classifications, two that are not age restricted and two that are age restricted: G, all ages admitted; GP, all ages admitted, parental guidance suggested; R, restricted because ot theme, content, or treatment to persons under 17 unless accompanied by a parent or adult guardian; and X, no one under 17 admitted.

The rating system provides rough guidelines for judging the sexual content of rated films. G-rated films contain little in the way of sexual matter or vulgar language. Although the G rating of a few films has been criticized in the past, the application of this rating has probably become more strict in the past year or so. Little beyond conventional embracing and kissing is allowed. Films with an "anti-social" theme are not rated G.

GP-rated films are rated with the "maturing adolescent" in mind. Some degree of sexual implication is allowed, flashes of nudity from a distance are sometimes shown, and some vulgar language is permitted. If discussion of sexual topics becomes "too candid" or if approval is expressed for such activities as premarital sex or adultery, the film will be rated R or X.

R-rated films can contain virtually any theme. Considerable partial nudity is allowed as is a good deal of sexual foreplay. Several R films have contained scenes of full female nudity (genitalia). The chief difference between R- and X-rated films is the quantity and quality of the erotic theme, conduct or nudity contained in the film rather than a set of absolutes which automatically classify a film as R or X.

X rated films are those which, in the judgment of the industry organization charged with rating, cannot be given any other classification. Films which concentrate almost exclusively on eroticism are placed in this category. An X rating may be self-applied by producers who do not submit their product to the Code and Rating Administration (the only classification which can be so applied).

General Release Films. Since the beginning of the motion picture industry, the sexual content and themes of movies have been the target of criticism. In recent years, general release films have become more sexually explicit. They are the target of the most public criticism because of their nationwide distribution to large diversified audiences. This criticism is magnified because of the large volume of newspaper advertising, gossip columns, and stories, articles, and pictures appearing in periodicals.

The trend towards increased sexual content of general release films has accelerated in the past two years. The candid treatment of sexual subjects has affected all aspects of films, i.e., theme, activity depicted, and degree of nudity. At present, there are few areas of sexual conduct which have not been the central subject of widely distributed general release films, including adultery, promiscuity, abortion, perversion, spouse-swapping, orgies, male and female homosexuality, etc. These themes, which were sometimes dealt with discretely in an earlier era, are now presented quite explicitly. Further, the requirement of an earlier day for "just retribution" for sexual misdeeds is no longer a requirement.

Sexual activity depicted on the screen has also become much more graphic. Scenes of simulated intercourse are increasing. Other sexual acts, including masturbation, fellatio, and cunnilingus, are sometimes suggested and occasionally simulated.

Partial nudity (female breasts and buttocks and male buttocks) may be seen in many general release films. The depiction of full female nudity (pubic area) has been increasing, and a few general release films have shown both sexes totally nude (genitalia).

Art Films. During the 1950s, "art films" treated sexual matters with a degree of explicitness not found in general release films of the same era. Today only the "foreignness" or limited audience appeal sets such films apart from many general release movies.

Exploitation Motion Pictures. Exploitation films (usually known as "skin flicks"), are low-budget films which concentrate on the erotic. Ordinarily, these films are shown only in a limited circuit of theaters and the film titles, though advertised, are not familiar to most people for lack of publicity. Until one or two years ago, the lines of demarcation between these films and general release movies were quite clear. However, the increase of sexually related themes and the incidence of nudity in the latter have blurred many of the former distinctions to a point where there is a considerable overlap. Today, perhaps the chief distinction between some sexually oriented general release films and exploitation films is that the latter (a) are much less expensive to produce (an average cost of $20,000 to $40,000); and (b) are ordinarily exhibited in far fewer theaters (about

6 percent of all theaters exhibit such films at least on a part-time basis).

The vast majority of exploitation films are directed at the male heterosexual market. Relatively few films are produced for a male homosexual audience, but the number of these films has apparently increased in the past year or two. Full female nudity has become common in the last year or two, although full male nudity is virtually unknown except in those films directed at the male homosexual market. Sexual activity covering the entire range of heterosexual conduct leaves very little to the imagination. Acts of sexual intercourse and oral-genital contact are not shown, only strongly implied or simulated; sexual foreplay is graphically depicted.

The majority of theaters exhibiting exploitation films are old, run-down, and located in decaying downtown areas. However, there has been a trend toward building new theaters and opening such theaters in suburban areas.

"Hybrid" and "New Genre" Motion Pictures. Within the past two years, there has been a radical increase in sexually oriented motion pictures which receive relatively wide distribution. These "hybrid" films combine the sexual explicitness of exploitation films with the distribution patterns of general release films. In addition, an entirely new genre of highly sex-oriented films has been created. Some of these films graphically depict actual sexual intercourse on the screen, an activity which had previously been shown only in private or semi-private exhibitions.

Exploitation films normally achieve relatively limited exhibitions in an established circuit of theaters (perhaps 500–600 theaters on the average). Popular general release films can expect to be exhibited in 5000 or more theaters. The market for popular hybrid sexually oriented films falls somewhere in between; many have been exhibited in 1000 to 2000 theaters and extended runs are common. In addition, such films are not limited to exhibitions in run-down theaters in decaying downtown areas; many play in first-class theaters in downtown and suburban areas. The most sexually explicit of all motion pictures (herein labeled "new genre" films) as yet have received only limited distribution in major cities.

Sixteen Millimeter Motion Pictures. Recently, an additional form of sexually oriented motion pictures shown in theaters has emerged—known in the industry as "16mm films." As of August,

1970, a majority of the 16mm theaters in the country exhibit silent color films of young females displaying their genitals, but in a few cities 16mm films graphically depict sexual intercourse and oral-genital contact. Usually, 16mm films are the most sexually graphic films shown in the locality.

It is very difficult to estimate the number of 16mm theaters currently in operation, but a figure of 200 seems reasonably accurate.

As yet there are no recognizable film titles moving from city to city, and there is almost no nationwide distribution of such films. However, although 16mm films are in their infancy and as yet are a minor factor in the traffic of sexually oriented materials, the market definitely seems to be expanding.

Box Office Receipts of Motion Pictures.   An analysis of reported box office receipts for films since the rating system has been in effect reveals no dramatic differences in reported grosses among G-, GP-, and R-rated films, although as a group G films tended to have consistently higher grosses.

Total box office receipts are not available for either individual films or for classes of films. Each year, however, a trade journal reports on the movies which returned the greatest film rental fees to their distributors. In 1969, 25 G movies returned $119 million; 28 GP films returned $92 million; 18 R rated films accounted for $57 million; 3 X films returned $14 million; and 16 unrated films (most of which were released before the rating system went into effect) returned $56 million; of these, four were clearly sex-oriented and returned over $11 million in rentals. Box office receipts for these films were probably between 2 and 2.5 times the rental fees.

Final figures for 1970 are not available, but an analysis of the reported 50 top box office films each week in 20-24 cities for the first six months of 1970 (a total of 222 films) can be summarized as follows:

The weekly list of the top 50 box office films undoubtedly distorts the importance of R, X, and unrated films because the survey is limited to metropolitan areas. This provides a disproportionate allocation of the nationwide market for sexually oriented films because theaters in many smaller cities and towns do not exhibit such films at all. Thus, the actual nationwide percentage accounted for by G and GP films is probably significantly greater than the projection, and R, X, and unrated sexually oriented hybrid films probably account for less of the national market than indicated. However, the projection is useful in that it marks the maximum traffic in sexually oriented films.

TABLE 7-1   Breakdown of "Top Fifty" Films,
January-July, 1970

Rating	Number Of Films	Percentage Of Films	1970 Gross Receipts [1] (in millions)	Percentage of Gross Receipts
G	44	19.7 %	$44.4	25.9 %
GP	69	30.9 %	57.3	33.5 %
R	46	20.6 %	44.9	26.2 %
X	15	6.8 %	12.4	7.2 %
Non-Sex Unrated	15	6.8 %	2.7	1.6 %
Sex-Oriented Unrated [2]	33	15.2 %	9.5	5.6 %
TOTAL	222	100.0 %	$171.1	100.0 %

[1] Many of the films listed in the "Top Fifty" during the first six months of 1970 were originally released in 1969. Only 1970 gross receipts for these films were included.

[2] These films are characterized as hybrid or new genre films in this Report. Judgments on the classification were made by the Commission Staff.

If the results of those films which were listed among the weekly top 50 are projected against the estimated box office gross for 1970, the following would result:

TABLE 7-2   Box-Office Receipts, by Classification

Rating	1970 Projected Receipts (in millions) [1]	Percentage of Receipts
G	$ 259	23.5 %
GP	335	30.5 %
R	262	23.8 %
X	72	6.6 %
Non-Sex Unrated	16	1.5 %
Sex-Oriented Unrated [2]	56	5.0 %
Art Films [3]	35	3.2 %
Exploitation Films [4]	65	5.9 %
TOTAL	$1,100	100.0 % [5]

[1] The first six figures in this column are projected from the "Percentage of Gross Receipts" column in Table 1 against an estimated gross of $1 billion for all but art and exploitation films.

[2] These films are characterized as hybrid or new genre films in this Report. Judgments on the classification were made by the Commission Staff.

[3] "Art films" play in between 500 and 600 theaters in an established "art circuit." Few if any of these films reach the Top 50, but the total box-office receipts can be estimated at $30-$40 million simply on the basis of the number of theaters exhibiting such films.

[4] Estimated at $60-$70 million; see succeeding section of this Report.

[5] SOURCE: U.S. Industrial Outlook, 1970.

Exploitation Films. Estimates by the exploitation film industry indicate a $60 million box office business in 1969. Additional studies indicate gross receipts for all exploitation theaters may have been as high as $70 million in 1969. Industry sources have indicated that 1970 receipts are likely to be considerably lower because of increased competition from sexually oriented motion pictures playing outside the exploitation market.

BOOKS AND MAGAZINES

The distribution and sale of sexually oriented publications in the United States can be roughly divided into two categories: (a) those which are a part of the mass market, i.e., books and periodicals available to a general audience; and (b) so-called "adults only" publications, a sub-market of sexually oriented printed matter which receives relatively limited distribution.

The Mass Market. There are several channels by which mass market publications are distributed from the publisher to the consumer: national distributors, national jobbers, book clubs, local wholesale distributors, and retailers. In many cases, publications skip over some of the intermediate steps, and flow directly from publisher to retailer and from publisher to consumer.

The book publishing industry in 1968 (latest figures available) estimated its receipts at almost $2.6 billion. Of that total, material which could conceivably be within the areas of study by the Commission would be found only in "Adult Trade Books" ($179 million), "Paperback Books" ($167 million) and "Book Club" ($204 million)— a total of $550 million, or some 21 percent of the entire book industry.

The periodical industry in the latest official consensus of business (1967) reported total receipts of approximately $2.6 billion. Of this, only general periodicals such as comics, women and home service magazines, news, business, and entertainment magazines could possibly be of interest to the Commission. These produced receipts of $1.445 billion, of which $560 million came from single copy and subscription sales (25 percent of total receipts) and $885 million from advertising.

The Commerce Department estimates that during 1970 publishers' receipts will reach approximately $5.6 billion (both books and periodicals) but the proportion of the market of interest to the Commission will probably remain about the same as before.

The book and periodical publishing industry in the United States is the largest and most diversified in the world. For example, over 10,000 periodicals are published per year and their sales per issue range from a few thousand copies to over 17.5 million. The total average sales, per issue, for all mass market magazines is almost 250 million copies and the total number of magazines sold in 1969 has been estimated at more than 2.5 billion. Approximately 30,000 new book titles have been published each year for the past several years.

Although there are no official estimates of the total number of copies of mass market paperbacks distributed yearly, industry sources estimate that over 700 million paperback books are distributed each year and that over 330 million of these are sold. The retail sales volume of mass market paperback books exceeded $340 million in 1968.

Mass market paperback and hard-cover books and periodicals which might be classified as sexually oriented are distributed in basically the same manner as other mass publications. Such materials are usually not the most sexually explicit available in most localities and certainly not in any of the larger population centers. These publications are the most widely available sexually oriented printed material, however. There are approximately 110,000 retail outlets for general magazines, 80,000 of which display and sell paperback books; 10,000 sell mass market hard-cover books. Even more copies of both books and periodicals are sold through the mails by subscription and book clubs.

Sexually Oriented Mass Market Periodicals. Although the wide range of periodicals makes it difficult to distinguish which publications should be classified as sexually oriented, the mass market industry recognizes certain types of magazines as such.

"Confession" or "romance" magazines emphasize fictional accounts of the sexual problems of young women. These magazines do not explicitly describe sex organs or sexual activity and always resolve sexual problems in a moral context. In 1969, 38 confession magazines had total sales of 104.4 million copies and total retail sales of nearly $40 million. These magazines accounted for the vast bulk of the market.

"Barber shop" magazines, aimed at a male readership, primarily feature "action" stories, some of which are sex-oriented. Pictorial content primarily consists of "glamour" or "pin-up" photographs, but recently there has been an increase in photos of partially nude females. During 1969, sales of 20 such magazines (which make up almost the entire market) were approximately 30 million copies and retail sales totaled approximately $12 million.

The mass market magazines with the highest degree of sexual orientation are known in the industry as "men's sophisticates." These magazines generally have a standardized formula which devotes a substantial portion to photographs of partially nude females (with breast and buttock exposure) in modeling poses. Total 1969 sales figures for 62 "sophisticate" magazines were approximately 41 million copies, and the total retail sales were at least $31 million. Almost all the market was included. Publishers and distributors agree that during 1969 and into 1970, the market for men's sophisticates has declined.

There is a special group of sex-oriented mass market magazines which do not adequately fit any of the above classifications. Preeminent among these is *Playboy*, unique in the periodical industry. Each issue of *Playboy* contains no less than three, and sometimes four or five, pictorial layouts which feature partially nude females. In most cases, there is only breast and buttock exposure, although on occasion very discrete photographs of feminine pubic hair have been printed. Some of the articles and fiction contain a significant degree of sexual orientation, but many articles on other topics are written by well-known authors and distinguished persons. During 1969, just under 64 million copies were sold, and retail dollar sales were over $65 million.

There are a few other mass market magazines which contain a substantial amount of sexual orientation, but are not easily categorized. Total combined copy sales of these magazines are less than 20 million copies, and retail dollar sales are less than $15 million.

Sexually Oriented Mass Market Books.   Most major paperback publishers produce titles which might be classified as sexually oriented. For example, *Bestsellers,* a trade journal for magazine and paperback wholesalers and retailers, lists the 20 best-selling paperback books each month. Between January 1969 and July 1970, eighteen paperbacks which could easily be considered to be sexually oriented appeared on the *Bestsellers* list for more than one month.

Three of these reached the number one position, and five ranked as high as second. Almost all of the major book lines were represented.

Although it is impossible to arrive at total sales figures, tens of millions of paperback books with some degree of sexual orientation are sold each year.

An indication of the interest in sexually oriented hard-cover books can be projected from the fact that two of the top ten best-selling fiction titles of 1968 were regarded as "sexy books." In 1969, six of the top ten hard-cover fiction "best sellers" and eight of the top 20 were regarded as sexually oriented. During 1968 and 1969, none of the top ten nonfiction best sellers were related to sex. As of June 1970, three of the top four nonfiction best sellers relate to sex.

Newspapers. The sexual content of daily newspapers was not investigated. Most newspapers, however, reflect a somewhat increased candor in articles and news stories relating to sexual matters.

The sexual content of one genre of newspaper, the so-called "underground press," has been the subject of considerable comment, although these are primarily political in nature. It has been estimated that there are 200 such newspapers in the United States with a readership of 6,000,000. The accuracy of such claims, however, is open to question. Sales figures for five of the best known newspapers indicated average weekly sales of over 200,000 and yearly sales of 10,500,000 in 1969.

The Secondary or "Adults Only" Market. Self-labeled "adults only" printed materials are of far less economic importance than are mass market publications. Separate or "secondary" channels of national and local wholesale distribution and of local retail sales have been created for this "adult" market. However, there is an overlap of sexually oriented materials between the mass and the "adult" markets; some publishers produce materials for both, and many other publishers constantly seek to expand distribution of their "secondary" product into the mass market.

Twenty or 30 of approximately 100 publishers producing primarily for the secondary market are important market-place factors. Most are located either in California or the New York City area.

Sexual Content of "Adults Only" Paperback Books. The sexual content of paperback books published for the "adults only" market has become progressively "stronger" in the past decade. Today, the content of "adults only" paperback books runs the gamut from traditional "sex pulp" books (stories consisting of a series of sexual adventures tied together by minimal plot, in which the mechanics of the sex act are not described, euphemistic language is substituted for common or clinical terms, and much of the sexual content is left to the reader), through modern "sex pulp" (common terms for sexual activity and detailed descriptions of the mechanics of sex act are used), "classic" erotic literature, "pseudo-medical" (alleged case-study analysis of sexual activity), illustrated marriage manuals, and illustrated novels (with photographs in which young females pose with the focus of the camera directly on their genitalia), to "documentary" studies of censorship and pornography containing illustrations depicting genital intercourse and oral sex. Insofar as the textual portions of many of these books are concerned, it is probably not possible to exceed the candor, graphic descriptions of sexual activity, and use of vulgar language in some currently distributed "adults only" paperback books. The pictorial content of some illustrated paperback books similarly cannot be exceeded in explicit depictions of sexual activity.

The vast majority of "adults only" books are written for heterosexual males, although about 10 percent are aimed at the male homosexual market and a small percentage (less than 5 percent) at fetishists. Virtually none of these books is intended for a female audience.

Sexual Content of "Adults Only" Magazines. "Adults only" magazines of today contain little textual material and are devoted principally to photographic depictions of female and male nudity with emphasis on the genitalia. Some of these depictions contain two or three models together and some pose both males and females in the same photograph. The posing of more than one model in a single photograph has resulted in a considerable amount of implied sexual activity, either intercourse or oral-genital contact, but neither actual sexual activity nor physical arousal of males is depicted at the present time. Nearly 90 percent are intended for a male heterosexual audience. About 10 percent are directed to male homosexuals and feature male nudes. Fetish and sadomasochistic magazines featuring bondage, chains, whips, spanking, rubber or leather wearing apparel, high-heeled boots, etc., are a rather insignificant part of the total production (less than 5 percent).

Production Costs. The cost of producing "adults only" paperback books and magazines is usually greater than the cost of these items for a mass general audience. Press runs for mass market paperback books seldom are below 100,000; only a very few "adults only" publishers had press runs as high as 40,000 in 1969 and 1970, and the typical press run of these publishers did not exceed 15,000 or 20,000 Since the fixed costs are apportioned to a much smaller number of copies, the unit cost is significantly higher for the "adults only" publications. "Adults only" paperback books usually cost between $.10 and $.20 to produce although some are considerably higher; "adults only" magazines are considerably more expensive to produce, in the $.45 to $.60 range, because of higher printing and preparation costs.

Distribution Channels. Many publishers of "adults only" materials act as their own distributors directly to retail outlets. However, there are now approximately 60 local wholesale distributors of "adults only" materials almost all of whom are located in large metropolitan areas.

There are approximately 850 self-labeled retail "adult" bookstores and 1400 retail outlets which provide a restricted access section for "adult" material in addition to selling other products in a nonrestricted access area. Most of these are located in metropolitan areas of 500,000 or more population. Many of these stores have estimated average gross sales of $200 to $300 a day and gross yearly sales of nearly $100,000. Average yearly retail sales are probably closer to $60,000 to $70,000. Net profits sometimes are in excess of $20,000 per store per year.

Retail outlets displaying and selling "adults only" material tend to be located in downtown or central city areas; a few are found in suburban shopping centers or in local neighborhoods. The stores range in appearance from seedy to respectable with the majority in the former category. The primary product of these retail "adult" bookstores are paperback books and magazines, although some sell sexual devices and some operate arcade type movie machines. A store may display as few as 200 or as many as 1000 or more titles of paperback books and from 100 to 500 or more separate titles of magazines.

Total Sales of "Adults Only" Publications. The total volume of "adults only" materials sold at retail in the U.S. was estimated by several different means. The most useful of these was an industry-wide analysis conducted by the Internal Revenue Service which disclosed that 20 of the largest "adult" publishers had gross receipts of approximately $21 million and an aggregate profit of $450,000 in tax year 1968. Combining all sources of information, the Commission estimates that 25 to 30 million "adults only" paperback books were sold in 1969 for a total retail value of $45 to $55 million; "adults only" magazine sales were approximately $25 to $35 million for 14 to 18 million copies. The best estimate is that "adults only" materials in the U.S. accounted for between $70 and $90 million in retail sales in 1969.

MAIL ORDER

Method of Doing Business. The American public is inundated annually by over 21 billion pieces of mail which advertise products and solicit purchases. A small percentage of this volume (less than 0.25 percent), attempts to sell sexually oriented materials. The number of businesses advertising sexually oriented materials through the mails varies greatly over time because the market offers easy and inexpensive entry and is in a constant state of flux. There are probably several hundred individuals or firms dealing in mail-order erotica at present, most of whom are located in the New York City and Los Angeles metropolitan areas. Of these, fewer than 20 are major factors and only about five generate a substantial volume of complaints from the public.

Mail-order operators offer a wide variety of sexually oriented materials for sale and cater to almost every conceivable taste. The most popular items are heterosexually oriented magazines, books, 8mm movies, sexual devices, and advertisements for "swingers" clubs. There are also materials designed for male homosexuals (10 percent) and a small amount for fetishists.

There are three types of advertising in this industry: solicited, semi-unsolicited, and unsolicited. Solicited advertising is that received by an individual who has made a request to be put on a specific mailing list. Semi-unsolicited advertising is usually received after a purchase or inquiry, or from a mailer who has obtained the individual's name and address from another mailer in the same business. Unsolicited advertising is received by an individual who has never made a purchase from, or inquiry of any dealer in sexually oriented materials. Most mail-order dealers in sexually oriented materials mail only to solicited or semi-unsolicited names. However, a few mail a large volume of advertising to unsolicited names. These are responsible for the majority of public complaints about erotica in the mails.

The business of advertising and selling sexually oriented materials through mail order is subject to the same rules of economics as any mail order operation. Mail-order selling can be profitable, but it is an expensive way of doing business. The cost to reach the potential customers with an advertising message is high and responses to sexually oriented mail advertising do not greatly differ from responses to mail advertising of any other products. The mail-order erotica business is very tenuous and stories that vast fortunes have been made overnight are apocryphal for the most part. Even the giants of the industry (fewer than ten) are relatively small-time operators and the profit of the largest probably does not exceed $200,000 before taxes per year.

Public Complaints. In April 1968 the federal Anti-Pandering Act went into effect and allowed recipients of unsolicited sexually provocative advertisements to request the Postmaster General to issue an order to the mailer to refrain from further mailings to the addressee. During the first two years of operation, the Post Office received over 450,000 requests for prohibitory orders and issued over 370,000. Prohibitory orders have been issued against hundreds of separate business firm names. However, two mailers accounted for nearly 40 percent of the total prohibitory orders and three others accounted for another 20 percent. Approximately 5 percent of prohibitory orders were issued on behalf of minors under the age of 19. Although the number of prohibitory orders issued since the law went into effect is substantial, less than one-half of 1 percent of all sexually oriented advertising results in a complaint to the Post Office. Post Office figures show a decline of approximately 50 percent in requests for prohibitory orders during the first six months of fiscal 1970 as compared with the same period in fiscal 1969.

Volume of Mail and Sales. Twenty-eight major mailers and three mailing services specializing in processing sexually oriented advertising spent over $2 million on postage during fiscal 1969. This was enough to mail approximately 36 million letters. It is estimated that these dealers accounted for approximately 75 to 80 percent of the total mail volume. Therefore, the total volume of sexually oriented mail was approximately 45 to 48 million letters during fiscal year 1969. Retail sales value of the sexually oriented materials bought through mail order probably did not exceed $12 to $14 million in fiscal 1969. (The Internal Revenue Service analyzed the receipts and income of most of the volume mailers for the tax year of 1968. These

255

mailers had gross sales of $5.5 million and reported an aggregate loss of $3000 for that year. However, the majority of the mailers did make a profit for the year).

"Under-The-Counter" or *"Hard-Core"* *Materials.* In 1970, a very limited amount of sexual material is being sold "under the counter." Such materials, which the market defines as "hard-core pornography," generally are limited to photographic reproductions of sexual intercourse depicting vaginal, anal, or oral penetration. These photographic materials are generally available in three forms: motion pictures (popularly called "stag films"), photo sets, and picture magazines. It has been estimated that between 3000 and 7000 stag films have been produced in the last 55 years, but an accurate estimate of the number on the market is virtually impossible to make. The stag film production is primarily a localized business with no national distribution and is extremely disorganized. There are no great fortunes to be made in stag film production. It is estimated that there are fewer than half a dozen individuals who net more than $10,000 per year in the business.

The traffic in picture magazines of sexual intercourse is apparently increasing. Today, the source of these materials appears to be principally Scandinavia or domestic copies of foreign publications. Photos or photo sets depicting sexual activity are a very minor part of the market at present.

Traffic and distribution of under-the-counter materials appears to be a very minor part of the total traffic in erotic materials. Imports of such materials from Scandinavia, however, appear to be increasing. Although the retail sales of these imports is almost certainly less than $5 million per year, this market appears to be growing. The total market in under-the-counter materials is estimated to be between $5 and $10 million.

Organized Crime. Law enforcement officers differ among themselves on the question of whether "organized crime" is involved in the pornography business. Some believe very strongly that it is; others believe just as strongly that it is not.

There is some evidence that the retail "adult bookstore" business, which purveys materials that are not only at the periphery of legitimacy but also at the margin of legality, tends to involve individuals who have had considerable experience with being arrested. The business does involve some risk of arrest and, therefore, would be avoided by persons with more concern for legitimacy and general reputation. There is a greater likelihood that persons with some back-ground of conflict with the legal system will be found among "adult" bookstore proprietors. This is not the same, however, as being an adjunct or subsidiary of "organized crime." At present there is insuf-ficent data to warrant any conclusion in this regard.

B. The Consumers

ADULT EXPERIENCE WITH SEXUALLY EXPLICIT MATERIALS

Approximately 85 percent of adult men and 70 percent of adult women in the U.S. have been exposed at sometime during their lives to depictions of explicit sexual material in either visual or textual form. Most of this exposure has apparently been voluntary, and pic-torial and textual depictions are seen about equally often. Recent ex-perience with erotic materials is not as extensive as total experience, e.g., only about 40 percent of adult males and 26 percent of adult females report having seen pictorial depictions of sexual intercourse during the past two years.

Experience with explicit sexual materials varies according to the content of the depictions; depictions of nudity with sex organs ex-posed and of heterosexual intercourse are most common; depictions of homosexual activities and oral sex are less common; and depic-tions of sadomasochistic sexual activity are least common in Ameri-cans' experience. Thus portrayals of sex that conform to general cul-tural norms are more likely to be seen than are portrayals of sexual activity that deviate from these norms.

Experience with explicit sexual materials also varies according to the characteristics of the potential viewer. Men are more likely to be exposed to erotic materials than are women. Younger adults are more likely to be exposed than are older adults. People with more education are more likely to have experience with erotic materials. People who read general books, magazines, and newspapers more, and see general movies more also see more erotic materials. People who are more socially and politically active are more exposed to erotic materials. People who attend religious services more often are less likely to be exposed to erotica.

Although most males in our society have been exposed to explicit sexual materials at some time in their lives, a smaller proportion has had relatively extensive experience with erotica. From one-fifth to one-quarter of the male population in the U.S. has somewhat regular experience with sexual materials as explicit as depictions of heterosexual intercourse.

Few people report that they buy erotic materials. Between one-quarter and one-half of people who have ever seen explicit sexual materials have ever purchased such materials. A major proportion of the acquisition of erotic materials occurs by obtaining it from a friend or acquaintance at no cost. Unsolicited mail accounts for a very small proportion of the exposure to erotic materials. Thus, most exposure to erotica occurs outside the commercial context and is a social or quasi-social activity. Erotica is a durable commodity for which there are several consumers for each purchase.

The informal distribution of erotica among friends and acquaintances is asymmetrical. Many more people have had sexual materials shown or given to them than report showing or giving these materials to others. Sharing is predominantly with friends of the same sex or with spouses. Only 31 percent of men and 18 percent of women report knowing of a shop which specializes in sexual materials.

Although the percentage of the population purchasing erotic materials is relatively small, the total number constitutes a sizeable market.

The patterns of experience of adults in Denmark and Sweden with erotic materials are similar to that described for American adults.

YOUNG PEOPLE'S EXPERIENCE WITH SEXUALLY EXPLICIT MATERIALS

First experience with explicit sexual materials usually occurs in adolescence for Americans. Roughly three quarters of adult American males report having been exposed to such materials before age 21. Retrospective reporting on adolescent experience by adult males indicates that the experience with erotica during adolescence was not isolated but rather both extensive and intensive.

Several recent studies of high school and college age youth are quite consistent in finding that there is also considerable exposure to explicit sexual materials on the part of minors today. Roughly 80 percent of boys and 70 percent of girls have seen visual depictions or read textual descriptions of sexual intercourse by the time they reach age 18. Substantial proportions of adolescents have had more

258

than an isolated exposure or two, although the rates of exposure do not indicate an obsession with erotic materials. A great deal of this exposure occurs in pre-adolescent and early adolescent years. More than half of boys have had some exposure to explicit sexual materials by age 15. Exposure on the part of girls lags behind that of boys by a year or two. Exposure of adolescents to depictions of genitals and heterosexual intercourse occurs earlier and more often than does exposure to oral-genital and homosexual materials. Experience with depictions of sadomasochistic material is much rarer, although it does occur.

Young people below the age of 21 rarely purchase sexually explicit books, magazines, and pictures; the mails and underground newspapers are negligible sources of exposure to erotica. By far the most common source of exposure to sexually explicit books, magazines, and pictures is a friend about the same age, and this exposure occurs in a social situation where materials are freely passed around. There is some suggestion that young people who are less active socially are less likely to be acquainted with sexual materials.

Thus, exposure to explicit sexual materials in adolescence is widespread and occurs primarily in a group of peers of the same sex or in a group involving several members of each sex. The experience seems to be more a social than a sexual one.

PATRONS OF ADULT BOOKSTORES AND ADULT MOVIE THEATERS

Patrons of adult bookstores and adult movie theaters may be characterized as predominantly white, middle class, middle aged, married males, dressed in business suit or neat casual attire, shopping or attending the movie alone. Almost no one under 21 was observed in these places, even where it was legal for them to enter.

The average patron of adult bookstores and movie houses appears to have had fewer sexually related experiences in adolescence than the average male in our society, but to be more sexually oriented as an adult. The buyers of erotica report frequencies of intercourse fairly similar to those of nonconsumers, and report a similar degree of enjoyment of intercourse. Their high degree of sexual orientation in adulthood encompasses, in addition to pictorial and textual erotica, a variety of sexual partners and of sexual activities within a consensual framework. Activities most frowned upon by our society, such

259

as sadomasochism, pedophilia, bestiality, and nonconsensual sex, are also outside the scope of the interests of the average patron of adult bookstores and movie houses.

II. THE EFFECTS OF EXPLICIT SEXUAL MATERIALS[8]

The Effects Panel of the Commission undertook to develop a program of research designed to provide information on the kinds of effects which result from exposure to sexually explicit materials, and the conditions under which these effects occur. The research program embraced both inquiries into public and professional belief regarding the effects of such materials, and empirical research bearing on the actual occurrence and condition of the effects. The areas of potential effect to which the research was addressed included sexual arousal, emotions, attitudes, overt sexual behavior, moral character, and criminal and other antisocial behavior related to sex.

Research procedures included (1) surveys employing national probability samples of adults and young persons; (2) quasi-experimental studies of selected populations; (3) controlled experimental studies; and (4) studies of rates and incidence of sex offenses and illegitimacy at the national level. A major study, which is cited frequently in these pages, was a national survey of American adults and youth which involved face-to-face interviews with a random probability sample of 2486 adults and 769 young persons between the ages of 15 and 20 in the continental United States.[9]

The strengths and weaknesses of the various research methods utilized are discussed in Section A of the Report of the Effects Panel of the Commission.[10] That report is based upon the many technical studies which generated the data from which the panel's conclusions were derived.

A. Opinion Concerning Effects of Sexual Materials

There is no consensus among Americans regarding what they consider to be the effects of viewing or reading explicit sexual materials. A diverse and perhaps inconsistent set of beliefs concerning the effects of sexual materials is held by large and necessarily overlapping portions of American men and women. Between 40 and 60 percent believe that sexual materials provide information about sex, provide entertainment, lead to moral breakdown, improve sexual relationships of married couples, lead people to commit rape, produce boredom with sexual materials, encourage innovation in marital sexual technique and lead people to lose respect for women. Some of these presumed effects are obviously socially undesirable while others may be regarded as socially neutral or desirable. When questioned about effects, persons were more likely to report having personally experienced desirsable than undesirable ones. Among those who believed undesirable effects had occurred, there was a greater likelihood of attributing their occurrences to others than to self. But mostly, the undesirable effects were just believed to have happened without reference to self or personal acquaintances.

Surveys of psychiatrists, psychologists, sex educators, social workers, counselors and similar professional workers reveal that large majorities of such groups believe that sexual materials do not have harmful effects on either adults or adolescents. On the other hand, a survey of police chiefs found that 58 percent believed that "obscene" books played a significant role in causing juvenile delinquency.

B. Empirical Evidence Concerning Effects

A number of empirical studies conducted recently by psychiatrists, psychologists, and sociologists attempted to assess the effects of exposure to explicit sexual materials. This body of research includes several study designs, a wide range of subjects and respondents, and a variety of effect indicators. Some questions in this area are not answered by the existing research, some are answered more fully than others, and many questions have yet to be asked. Continued research efforts which embrace both replicative studies and inquiries into areas not yet investigated are needed to extend and clarify existing findings and to specify more concretely the conditions under which specific effects occur. The findings of available research are summarized below.

PSYCHOSEXUAL STIMULATION

Experimental and survey studies show that exposure to erotic stimuli produces sexual arousal in substantial portions of both males and females. Arousal is dependent on both characteristics of the stimulus and characteristics of the viewer or user.

Recent research casts doubt on the common belief that women

are vastly less aroused by erotic stimuli than are men. The supposed lack of female response may well be due to social and cultural inhibitions against reporting such arousal and to the fact that erotic material is generally oriented to a male audience. When viewing erotic stimuli, more women report the physiological sensations that are associated with sexual arousal than directly report being sexually aroused.

Research also shows that young persons are more likely to be aroused by erotica than are older persons. Persons who are college educated, religiously inactive, and sexually experienced are more likely to report arousal than persons who are less educated, religiously active, and sexually inexperienced.

Several studies show that depictions of conventional sexual behavior are generally regarded as more stimulating than depictions of less conventional activity. Heterosexual themes elicit more frequent and stronger arousal responses than depictions of homosexual activity; petting and coitus themes elicit greater arousal than oral sexuality, which in turn elicits more than sadomasochistic themes.

SATIATION

The only experimental study on the subject to date found that continued or repeated exposure to erotic stimuli over 15 days resulted in satiation (marked diminution) of sexual arousal and interest in such material. In this experiment, the introduction of novel sex stimuli partially rejuvenated satiated interest, but only briefly. There was also partial recovery of interest after two months of nonexposure.

EFFECTS UPON SEXUAL BEHAVIOR

When people are exposed to erotic materials, some persons increase masturbatory or coital behavior, a smaller proportion decrease it, but the majority of persons report no change in these behaviors. Increases in either of these behaviors are short lived and generally disappear within 48 hours. When masturbation follows exposure, it tends to occur among individuals with established masturbatory patterns or among persons with established but unavailable sexual partners. When coital frequencies increase following exposure to sex stimuli, such activation generally occurs among sexually experienced persons with established and available sexual partners. In one study, middle-aged married couples reported increases in both the frequency and variety of coital performance during the 24 hours after the couples viewed erotic films.

In general, established patterns of sexual behavior were found to be very stable and not altered substantially by exposure to erotica. When sexual activity occurred following the viewing or reading of these materials, it constituted a temporary activation of individuals' preexisting patterns of sexual behavior.

Other common consequences of exposure to erotic stimuli are increased frequencies of erotic dreams, sexual fantasy, and conversation about sexual matters. These responses occur among both male and females. Sexual dreaming and fantasy occur as a result of exposure more often among unmarried than married persons, but conversation about sex occurs among both married and unmarried persons. Two studies found that a substantial number of married couples reported more agreeable and enhanced marital communication and an increased willingness to discuss sexual matters with each other after exposure to erotic stimuli.

ATTITUDINAL RESPONSES

Exposure to erotic stimuli appears to have little or no effect on already established attitudinal commitments regarding either sexuality or sexual morality. A series of four studies employing a large array of indicators found practically no significant differences in such attitudes before and after single or repeated exposures to erotica. One study did find that after exposure persons became more tolerant in reference to other persons' sexual activities although their own sexual standards did not change. One study reported that some persons' attitudes toward premarital intercourse became more liberal after exposure, while other persons' attitudes became more conservative, but another study found no changes in this regard. The overall picture is almost completely a tableau of no significant change.

Several surveys suggest that there is a correlation between experience with erotic materials and general attitudes about sex: Those who have more tolerant or liberal sexual attitudes tend also to have greater experience with sexual materials. Taken together, experimental and survey studies suggest that persons who are more sexually tolerant are also less rejecting of sexual material. Several studies show that after experience with erotic material, persons become less fearful of possible detrimental effects of exposure.

EMOTIONAL AND JUDGMENTAL RESPONSES

Several studies show that persons who are unfamiliar with erotic materials may experience strong and conflicting emotional reactions when first exposed to sexual stimuli. Multiple responses, such as attraction and repulsion to an unfamiliar object, are commonly observed in the research literature on psychosensory stimulation from a variety of nonsexual as well as sexual stimuli. These emotional responses are short-lived and, as with psychosexual stimulation, do not persist long after removal of the stimulus.

Extremely varied responses to erotic stimuli occur in the judgmental realm, as, for example, in the labeling of material as obscene or pornographic. Characteristics of both the viewer and the stimulus influence the response: For any given stimulus, some persons are more likely to judge it "obscene" than are others; and for persons of a given psychological or social type, some erotic themes are more likely to be judged "obscene" than are others. In general, persons who are older, less educated, religiously active, less experienced with erotic materials, or feel sexually guilty are most likely to judge a given erotic stimulus "obscene." There is some indication that stimuli may have to evoke both positive responses (interesting or stimulating), and negative responses (offensive or unpleasant) before they are judged obscene or pornographic.

CRIMINAL AND DELINQUENT BEHAVIOR

Delinquent and nondelinquent youth report generally similar experiences with explicit sexual materials. Exposure to sexual materials is widespread among both groups. The age of first exposure, the kinds of materials to which they are exposed, the amount of their exposure, the circumstances of exposure, and their reactions to erotic stimuli are essentially the same, particularly when family and neighborhood backgrounds are held constant. There is some evidence that peer group pressure accounts for both sexual experience and exposure to erotic materials among youth. A study of a heterogeneous group of young people found that exposure to erotica had no impact upon moral character over and above that of a generally deviant background.

Statistical studies of the relationship between availability of erotic materials and the rates of sex crimes in Denmark indicate that the increased availability of explicit sexual materials has been accompanied by a decrease in the incidence of sexual crime. Analysis of police records of the same types of sex crimes in Copenhagen during the past 12 years revealed that a dramatic decrease in reported sex crimes occurred during this period and that the decrease coincided with changes in Danish law which permitted wider availability of explicit sexual materials. Other research showed that the decrease in reported sexual offenses cannot be attributed to concurrent changes in the social and legal definitions of sex crimes or in public attitudes toward reporting such crimes to the police, or in police reporting procedures.

Statistical studies of the relationship between the availability of erotic material and the rates of sex crimes in the United States presents a more complex picture. During the period in which there has been a marked increase in the availability of erotic materials, some specific rates of arrest for sex crimes have increased (e.g., forcible rape) and others have declined (e.g., overall juvenile rates). For juveniles, the overall rate of arrests for sex crimes decreased even though arrests for nonsexual crimes increased by more than 100 percent. For adults, arrests for sex offenses increased slightly more than did arrests for nonsex offenses. The conclusion is that, for America, the relationship between the availability of erotica and changes in sex crime rates neither proves nor disproves the possibility that availability of erotica leads to crime, but the massive overall increases in sex crimes that have been alleged do not seem to have occurred.

Available research indicates that sex offenders have had less adolescent experience with erotica than other adults. They do not differ significantly from other adults in relation to adult experience with erotica, in relation to reported arousal or in relation to the likelihood of engaging in sexual behavior during or following exposure. Available evidence suggests that sex offenders' early inexperience with erotic material is a reflection of their more generally deprived sexual environment. The relative absence of experience appears to constitute another indicator of atypical and inadequate sexual socialization.

In sum, empirical research designed to clarify the question has found no evidence to date that exposure to explicit sexual materials plays a significant role in the causation of delinquent or criminal behavior among youth or adults.[11] The Commission cannot conclude that exposure to erotic materials is a factor in the causation of sex crime or sex delinquency.

❖   ❖   ❖

III. Law and Law Enforcement[12]

A. Existing Obscenity Legislation and Cost of Enforcement[13]

FEDERAL STATUTES

There are presently five federal laws which prohibit distributions of "obscene" materials in the United States. One prohibits any mailing of such material (18 U.S.C. section 1461); another prohibits the importation of obscene materials into the United States (19 U.S.C. section 1305); another prohibits the broadcast of obscenity (18 U.S.C. section 1464); and two laws prohibit the interstate transportation of obscene materials or the use of common carriers to transport such materials (18 U.S.C. sections 1462 and 1465).[14] In addition, the 1968 federal Anti-Pandering Act (39 U.S.C. section 3008)[15] authorizes postal patrons to request no further mailings of unsolicited advertisements which they deem sexually offensive in their sole judgment, and it further prohibits mailers from ignoring such requests. There is no present federal statute specifically regulating the distribution of sexual materials to young persons.

Five federal agencies are responsible for the enforcement of the foregoing statutes. The Post Office Department, the Customs Bureau, and the Federal Communications Commission investigate violations within their jurisdictions. The F.B.I. investigates violations of the statutes dealing with transportation and common carriers. The Department of Justice is responsible for prosecution or other judicial enforcement.

The cost to the federal government of enforcing the five federal statutes generally prohibiting the distribution of obscene materials appears to be at least $3 to $5 million per year. Enforcement of the Anti-Pandering Act has cost the Post Office about an additional $1 million per year.[16]

STATE STATUTES

Forty-eight of the states have statutes which generally prohibit the distributions[17] of "obscene" materials. In addition, the statutes of 41 states contain some type of special prohibition regarding the distribution of sexual materials to minors. The cost of enforcing these statutes cannot be determined with any precision. The total of all state and local enforcement activity, however, far exceeds federal enforcement in terms of number of arrests and prosecutions, so that the aggregate cost of state law enforcement for all jurisdiction is, conservatively, $5 to $10 million per year. More than 90 percent of all state and local prosecutions recently have involved distribution to adults rather than enforcement of juvenile statutes.

FEDERAL AND STATE STATUTORY DEFINITIONS OF "OBSCENITY"

None of the federal statutes generally prohibiting the distribution of "obscene" material defines that term. State statutes generally prohibiting the distribution of "obscene" material either do not define the term or verbally incorporate the constitutional standard established by the Supreme Court and discussed below. State juvenile statutes frequently incorporate relatively specific descriptive definitions of material prohibited for minors, qualified by subjective standards adapted from the constitutional standard for adults.

B. The Constitutional Basis for Prohibitions upon the Dissemination of Explicit Sexual Materials

For many years the Supreme Court assumed, without deciding, that laws generally prohibiting dissemination of obscenity were consistent with the free speech guarantees of the Constitution. In 1957, in the case of Roth v. United States, the Court held that such laws were constitutional, but it required that they utilize a narrowly restrictive standard of what is "obscene."

In upholding the constitutionality of obscenity prohibitions, the Roth decision did not rely upon findings or conclusions regarding the effect of sexual materials upon persons who are exposed to them. Rather, the fundamental premise of Roth was that "obscene" materials are not entitled to the protections accorded to "speech" by the

267

First and Fourteenth Amendments to the Constitution. The Court based this conclusion upon its findings (1) that the Framers of the Bill of Rights did not intend the free speech guarantee of the First Amendment to apply to all utterances and writings, (2) that "obscene" speech—like libel, profanity and blasphemy—was not intended to be protected by the Amendment, and (3) that a universal c sensus had existed for many years that the distribution of obscenity should be legally prohibited.

In 1969, in Stanley v. Georgia, the Supreme Court modified the premise of the Roth decision to some extent by holding that the constitutional guarantee of free speech protects the right of the individual to read or view concededly "obscene" material in his own home. Some lower federal courts have held that the Stanley decision gives constitutional protection to some distributions of obscenity, as well as to its private possession. Specifically, courts have held unconstitutional the federal importation prohibition as applied to the importation of obscene material for private use, the federal mail prohibition as applied to the mailing of obscene material to persons who request it, and a state prohibition applied to films exhibited to adults at theaters to which minors were not admitted. These courts have held that the constitutional right to possess obscene materials established in Stanley implies a correlative right for adults to acquire such materials for their own use or to view them without forcing them upon others. Other lower federal courts have not applied the Stanley decision to these situations. The Supreme Court has not yet explicitly passed upon these questions, but has set for argument in the 1970 term three cases raising these issues.

C. Constitutional Limitations upon the Definition of "Obscene"

ADULT OBSCENITY STATUTES

Although upholding the constitutionality of broad prohibitions upon the dissemination of obscene materials, the Roth decision imposed a narrow standard for defining what is "obscene" under such prohibitions. Subsequent decisions have narrowed the permissible test even further.

The prevailing view today in the Supreme Court of the United States, the lower federal courts and the courts of the States is that three criteria must all be met before the distribution of material may be generally prohibited for all persons, including adults, on the ground that it is "obscene." These criteria are: (1) the dominant theme of the material, taken as a whole, must appeal to a "prurient" interest in sex; (2) the material must be "patently offensive" because it affronts "contemporary community standards" regarding the depiction of sexual matters; and (3) the material must lack "redeeming social value." All three criteria must coalesce before material may be deemed "obscene" for adults.

The requirement that the material appeal to a "prurient" interest in sex is not clear in meaning but appears to refer primarily to material which is sexually arousing in dominant part. Material must appeal to the prurient interest of the "average" person, unless it is designed for and distributed to a particular group, in which case it is the interests of the members of that group which are relevant. The Supreme Court has never settled the question whether the "community" by whose standards "offensiveness" is to be determined is a "national" community or whether it is the State or locality where the distribution occurs. Whatever the relevant community, a substantial consensus that particular material is offensive is apparently required to violate the community's "standard." There is some disagreement in the Supreme Court over the precise role played by the "social value" criterion. All the Justices have agreed that social value is relevant to obscenity determinations. A plurality (not a majority) has held that unless material is "utterly" without redeeming social value it may not be held to be obscene; a minority of Justices would permit a small degree of social value to be outweighed by prurience and offensiveness. Nor has the Court authoritatively defined what values are redeeming "social" values, although it has suggested that these may include entertainment values as well as the more firmly established scientific, literary, artistic and educational values. Finally, the Court permits the manner of distribution of material to be taken into account in determining the application of the three criteria, at least where the material itself is close to the line of legality.

The application of these three Roth criteria to specific materials requires a great deal of subjective judgment because the criteria refer to emotional, aesthetic and intellectual responses to the material rather than to descriptions of its content. As noted above, the precise meaning of the criteria is also unclear. This subjectivity and vagueness produces enormous uncertainty about what is "obscene" among law enforcement officials, courts, juries and the general public. It is impossible for a publisher, distributor, retailer or exhibitor to know in advance whether he will be charged with a criminal offense for distributing a particular work, since his understanding of the three tests and their application to his work may differ from that of the police, prosecutor, court or jury. This uncertainty and consequent fear of prosecution may strongly influence persons not to distribute new works which are entitled to constitutional protection and thus have a damaging effect upon free speech. These definitional problems are also cited by law enforcement officials at all levels as their chief difficulty in enforcing existing obscenity laws. There is, therefore, almost universal dissatisfaction with present law.

A series of decisions of the Supreme Court, generally rendered without opinion, has given an exceedingly narrow scope of actual application to the constitutionally required three-part standard for adult legislation. These decisions leave it questionable whether any verbal or textual materials whatever may presently be deemed "obscene" for adults under the constitutional standard and suggest that only the most graphic pictorial depictions of actual sexual activity may fall within it. Present law for adults is therefore largely ineffective.

The results of empirical research regarding the application of the three constitutional criteria confirm the difficulties of application as well as their exceedingly narrow scope. Several studies have found that "arousingness" and "offensiveness" are independent dimensions when applied to sexual materials; that is, material that is offensive may or may not be arousing, and material that is arousing may or may not be offensive. Only a very restricted range of material seems to be capable of meeting both of these criteria for most people. Further, there is very little consensus among people regarding either the "arousingness" or the "offensiveness" of a given sexual depiction. A wide distribution of judgments in these two areas occurs, for example, for depictions of female nudity with genitals exposed, for explicit depictions of heterosexual sexual intercourse, and for graphic depictions of oral-genital intercourse. In addition, judgments differ among different groups: Males as a group differ from females as a group in their judgments of both "offensiveness" and "arousingness"; the young differ from the old; the college-educated differ from those with only a high school education; frequent church attenders differ from less frequent church attenders.

An additional and very significant limiting factor is introduced by the criterion of social value. In the national survey of American public opinion sponsored by the Commission, substantial portions of the population reported effects which might be deemed socially valuable from even the most explicit sexual materials. For example, about 60 percent of a representative sample of adult American men felt that looking or reading such materials would provide information about sex and about 40 percent of the sample reported that such an effect had occurred for himself or someone he personally knew. About 60 percent of these men felt that looking at or reading explicit sexual materials provided entertainment and almost 50 percent reported this effect upon himself or someone he personally knew. Half of these men felt that looking at or reading explicit sexual materials can improve sex relations of some married couples, and about a quarter of the sample reported such an effect on themselves or on someone they knew personally. Fewer women reported such effects, but 35 percent, 24 percent, and 21 percent reported, respectively, information, entertainment, and improved sexual relations in themselves or someone they personally knew as a result of looking at or reading very explicit sexual materials. As previously indicated, two experimental studies found that a substantial number of married couples reported more agreeable and enhanced marital communication and an increased willingness to discuss sexual matters with each other after exposure to erotic stimuli.

In pursuit of its mandate from Congress to recommend definitions of obscenity which are consistent with constitutional rights, the Commission considered drafting a more satisfactory definition of "obscene" for inclusion in adult obscenity prohibitions, should such prohibitions appear socially warranted. To be satisfactory from the point of view of its enforcement and application, such a definition would have to describe the material to be proscribed with a high degree of objectivity and specificity, so that those subject to the law could know in advance what materials were prohibited and so that judicial decisions would not be based upon the subjective reactions of particular judges or jurors. In light of the empirical data, described above, showing both the lack of consensus among adults as to what is both arousing and offensive and the values attributed by substantial numbers of adults to even the most explicit sexual materials, the construction of such a definition for adults within constitutional limits would be extremely difficult. In any event, the Commission, as developed in its legislative recommendations set forth later in this Report, does not believe that a sufficient social justification exists for the retention or enactment of broad legislation prohibiting the consensual distribution of sexual materials to adults. We, therefore, do not recommend any definition of what is "obscene" for adults.

SPECIFIC OBSCENITY STATUTES

The extreme definitional problems which occur for adult obscenity under the Roth case do not apply to statutes which do not seek to interfere with the right of adults to read or see material of their own choice. In 1967, in Redrup v. New York the Supreme Court noted that, in contrast with general obscenity laws prohibiting sale to adults, legislatures have much wider latitude when formulating prohibitions which restrict themselves to impeding only certain types of distributional conduct—such as distribution of explicit sexual materials to minors and the thrusting of explicit sexual materials upon unwilling recipients through unsolicited mail and public display. Definitions in these areas need only be rationally related to the problem which the legislation seeks to address and no particular definitional formulation is constitutionally required.

Specific prohibitions incorporating broader definitions than are permissible in adult legislation must be restricted in their application to the specific area of their concern. Thus, statutes designed to protect minors from exposure to material which may not be deemed obscene for adults may only prohibit distributions to minors; prohibitions may not be placed upon all adults in order to protect minors. Public display and unsolicited mail prohibitions which restrict material which may not constitutionally be deemed obscene for adults must also be carefully drafted to avoid interference with consensual adult distribution or exhibition.

The areas of latitude for greater control overlap the areas of greatest public concern. Prosecuting attorneys who reported a serious community concern about obscenity to the Commission attributed this concern primarily to the thrusting of offensive materials upon unwilling recipients and to fear that materials would be distributed to minors. It is in these areas that effective legislative prohibitions may be formulated and enforced.

Although greater latitude is allowed constitutionally in restricting explicit sexual materials in the areas of public display, unsolicited mailings and direct disseminations to minors, satisfactory definitions again require the use of explicit objective provisions specifically describing the material to be restricted. Concern about rigidly codifying in law definitions which may soon be outmoded by changing social custom can be alleviated by building into laws a periodic review of their content.

D. Public Opinion Concerning Restrictions on the Availability of Explicit Sexual Materials

A national survey of American public opinion sponsored by the Commission shows that a majority of American adults believe that adults should be allowed to read or see any sexual materials they wish. On the other hand, a substantial consensus of American adults favors prohibiting young persons access to some sexual materials. Almost half the population believes that laws against sexual materials are impossible to enforce. Americans also seem to have an inaccurate view of the opinions of others in their communities; the tendency is to believe that others in the community are more restrictive in outlook than they actually are.

Public opinion regarding restrictions on the availability of explicit sexual materials is, however, quite divided in several ways. Principally this split of opinion is related to the characteristics of the person expressing the attitude and the issue of potential harmfulness of the material.

CHARACTERISTICS OF PERSONS EXPRESSING THE ATTITUDE

Advocacy of restrictions on the availability of explicit sexual materials is more likely to be found accompanying an orientation against freedom of expression generally. In addition, females tend to be more restrictive than males, older people more restrictive than younger people, those with a grade school education more restrictive than the high-school-educated, who in turn tend to be more restrictive than the college educated, and people who attend church regularly tend to be more restrictive than those who attend less often.

THE POTENTIALITY OF HARMFUL EFFECTS

When questioned as to whether they favored access of adults or young persons to sexually explicit materials, about 40 percent of all the respondents on the national survey made their responses contingent on the issue of whether or not such materials cause harm. About two thirds of the persons who favor no legal restrictions said their views would be changed if it were clearly demonstrated that certain materials have harmful effects. On the other hand, about one-third of the persons who favor some restrictions or extensive restrictions would change their views if it were clearly demonstrated that sexual materials have no harmful effects.

E. Obscenity Laws in Other Countries

Countries other than the United States differ widely in the terms of and extent of their legal restrictions regarding the distribution of explicit sexual materials. A summary of existing legal provisions in fifteen other countries is contained in the Report of the Legal Panel of the Commission.

A trend has appeared in recent years toward substantial reevaluation and revision of obscenity laws, often through the use of commissions similar to this Commission. Such an official commission report in Denmark has resulted in the repeal of that country's adult obscenity legislation (with juvenile and nonconsensual exposure restrictions being retained). A similar recommendation has been made in Sweden and final enactment of the repeal of adult legislation in that country will apparently take place in the fall of 1970. Advisory commissions in Israel and the United Kingdom have also recently recommended elimination of prohibitions upon distribution of sexual materials to consenting adults. The constitutional court of West Germany presently has under consideration the question of the constitutionality of that country's adult legislation in view of free speech guarantees. Advisory commissions in countries other than the United States have, like this Commission, all concluded that consensual exposure of adults to explicit sexual materials causes no demonstrable damaging individual or social effects.

eight

THE CONVICTED MINORITY

At Attica State Prison in New York, eleven hostages and 32 inmates died in the fall of 1971 in an assault by state troopers to put down a prison rebellion there. Not long before that, at the Tombs, medieval, body-jammed jail in Manhattan, riots left ten guards injured and $313,000 damage as prisoners, armed with no more than bare hands and rage, ripped up iron table legs bolted to the floor, smashed through steel locking devices, tore holes in foot-thick walls of brick and concrete.

In California, violence has erupted at three prisons for medium and maximum security custody: Soledad, Folsom, and San Quentin. At San Quentin, three correctional officers and three inmates, including revolutionary George Jackson, were killed. Fourteen were killed at Soledad between February 1970 and February 1971. Three were killed at Folsom in September, 1971.

Prison officials have traditionally attributed such incidents to "outside agitators," "revolutionaries," and "ring leaders." No one has used the old saw "communist conspiracy" yet, but perhaps this is implicit. Such explanations tend to suggest that the solution to prison ferment is to "increase the security"—to isolate (and sometimes exterminate) the rebel leaders and to close off the prisons from outside influences, but because these violent incidents have typically taken place in maximum security prisons, it seems doubtful that more security is really the solution, or even a possibility.

In the "correctional community"—jails and prisons—the oppression of deviant and ethnic minorities becomes extreme. The forms of oppression are common knowledge: Inmates may be beaten, maimed, or killed by guards or "correctional" officers, who are not charged with any crime since there are no credible witnesses and since inmates ordinarily are unable to seek court redress. Guards can inflict punishment simply by looking the other way whenever aggressive inmates sexually assault, beat, stab, or torture other inmates. And these shocking excesses are in addition to the repressive conditions—physical deprivation of freedom, good food, and sex; overcrowding; the torment of isolation and loneliness; and the expectation of lifelong stigma—that all inmates must experience.

The minority group perspective contains a simple explanation of violent crime: Most "criminals" start out as victimless offenders: juvenile delinquents charged with truancy, runaway, incorrigibility, curfew; drug abusers; prostitutes; homosexuals; drunks. When these offenders are apprehended and incarcerated, they are subjected—often even before they have been tried and found guilty—to the conditions described above and thus alienated not just from the prison or jail staff but from the very society that put them there in the first place and that permits such brutality. They return to the free world filled with alienation and rage, where as an all too visible minority (it is not difficult to find out that a person has a prison record) they are subject to discrimination in employment, housing, courts, voting, etc. The conventional world is closed off, so most of them have little choice except to turn to violent or predatory crime as a means of livelihood, and most of them are emotionally outraged enough to do so.

The minority group perspective also helps to explain the rash of jail and prison uprisings that have taken place in the last few years. Inmates, in and through the act of asserting their rights, have emerged as a self-aware minority group—aware that minorities out-side of prison have succeeded in gaining redress through the courts and through protest and desperately eager for a piece of the action. There has been a striking increase in recent years in the number of inmates who have become "jailhouse lawyers," have learned the laws and sought redress for abuse and denial of rights in courts that are increasingly willing to hear their cases. Inmates are also using other tried and true means of protests—sit-ins, strikes, boycotts, non-compliance, and riots. The violence in prison is a consequence of the general trend among prisoners to join together in a solidarity group. In Colorado State Penitentiary blacks and Chicanos have organized their own groups to bring in outside speakers and discuss racial and political issues. In Jackson State Prison, Michigan, prisoners staged a three-day strike to support demands for a minimum wage of one dollar an hour. At Sing Sing in New York prisoners staged a protest of lock-step discipline and inadequate rehabilitation programs. In Lansing, Kansas, twelve prisoners cut their Achilles tendons to pro-test conditions there.

These recent protests within prisons are paralleled by develop-ment of quasi-civil rights organizations for ex-cons like the Seven Step Foundation, Jobs Opportunity Vocational Training (JOVE), and Community Achievement and Improvement Group (CAIG), or-ganized and operated by ex-cons for their mutual welfare. They hold weekly rap sessions and encounters, facilitate jobs and other eco-nomic resources, and fight against discrimination in the courts and through political action.

Indirectly, the violence in prisons can be seen as the inmates' attempt to solve the crime problem by bringing about change in the areas where society's criminogenic conditions are most concen-trated—its jails and prisons.

The readings in this chapter, from the report of the President's Commission on Law Enforcement and Administration of Justice, are a chronicle of these conditions and abuses. This report was pub-lished in 1967, but the conditions it describes still exist today. In it we can trace the "career" of the inmate from juvenile to adult years.

We have seen that a juvenile may be denied probation, not be-cause he is felt to be a danger to the community, but solely because probation service is not available in his jurisdiction. Once he is tried, he may be incarcerated in a state reform school or local institution, many of which still use corporal punishment and are characterized by the lax staff attitude about inmate aggression that is common in jails. Afterward he may leave the institution without any arrangements for appropriate aftercare. A good many juveniles have started criminal careers at this point.

The first entry into the adult judicial system may be as a misdemeanant. The majority of people in the nation's jails are charged with victimless crimes, mainly drunkenness and drug offenses. Rehabilitation, as the readings have shown, is practically nonexistent in such county or city programs, in fact, more money is spent for rehabilitation of the hardened criminal in state prisons than upon the beginner in crime. Eventually the person may be convicted of a felony, at which point he enters a state prison, where he will be exposed to the most abusive treatment of the entire criminal justice system. In prison his only shelter is an alternative "inmate subculture." Initiation into this subculture is frequently what determines his later inclinations and skills as a professional or violent criminal. The last section of the chapter deals with the ways that convicts are deprived almost totally of their rights, a deprivation that permits abuse and makes redress very difficult to seek. Prison inmates are without the constitutional guarantees of due process in disciplinary hearings and parole hearings. Once out of prison, they can be returned without due process simply by violating any of their parole conditions, which themselves may violate such constitutional rights as freedom of speech. Even after the parole term has ended, they are still denied the right to vote, to hold office, to serve as jurors, to testify in court, to be bonded, to obtain many business or professional licenses, and as ex-cons they are also excluded from most civil service jobs and many other occupations.

This report shows how convicts are abused and clearly deprived of constitutional rights. This corresponds to our finding of public stereotyping of the ex-con described in the Introduction. They are a minority created by society. Prison riots are protests of that minority status, protests against society's "overkill" of what at the outset were victimless criminals or simply participants in a minority way of life. In California, prison inmates have banded together to form the Prisoners' Union, an organization led by John Irwin, a former inmate and author of the book *The Felon*. The emergence of convicts as a self-aware minority, can not only lead to humane treatment of convicts, but can also, for reasons stated above, help to reduce the incidence of violent and predatory crime.

Juvenile Detention

Corrections

At one time, detaining an accused person was based on the fear that, if left at liberty, he would fail to appear for trial or might commit other violations. Times have changed. Pretrial release on bond or recognizance is now commonplace for adults, especially those with money or influence. Not so for children, who may be detained —no matter how inadequate the place of detention or the type of care given—by exercise of the *parens patriae* doctrine upon which juvenile courts were established.

INTRODUCTION

Juvenile detention is the practice of holding children of juvenile court age in secure custody for court disposition. The most common reason for its misuse and overuse is that it is allowed to function as a substitute for probation and other community services and facilities.

Unlike statutes pertaining to adults, juvenile court law permits a child to be taken into custody for his protection from situations that endanger his health and welfare. This purpose can be served by two distinctly different types of temporary care:

1. *Detention.* Temporary care of a child who has committed a delinquent act and requires secure custody, in a physically restricting facility pending court disposition or the child's return to another jurisdiction or agency. Any place for temporary care with locked outer doors, a high fence or wall, and screens, bars, detention sash, or other window obstruction designed to deter escape is a detention facility. If a substantial part of a building is used for detention as defined above, it is a detention facility no matter how flimsy the restricting features may be.[1]

2. *Shelter.* Temporary care in a physically unrestricting fa-

From the President's Commission on Law Enforcement and Administration of Justice, *Task Force Report: Corrections* (Washington: U.S. Government Printing Office, 1967) Appendix A, pp. 119–22, 129, 133–34, 142–43, 150–54.

cility pending the child's return to his own home or placement for longer term care. Shelter care is generally used for dependent and neglected children in boarding homes, group homes, and, in the larger cities, temporary care institutions; it is also used for children apprehended for delinquency whose homes are not fit for their return but who, with proper handling, are not likely to run away and therefore do not need secure custody.

Juvenile detention, properly used, serves the juvenile court exclusively; shelter care is a broader child-welfare service not only for the court but also for child and family agencies, both public and private.

❖   ❖   ❖

SURVEY FINDINGS

The average daily population of delinquent children in places of detention is more than 13,000. In 1965, the total number admitted to detention facilities was more than 409,000, or approximately two-thirds of all juveniles apprehended. . . . These youngsters were held in detention homes and jails for an estimated national average stay of 12 days at a total cost of more than $53,000,000—an average cost of $130 per child. (The average length of stay of children detained in the sample counties is 18 days.)

These estimates do not include children held in police lockups; they do include children held, prior to any official court disposition, in 242 juvenile detention homes, four training schools, and an unknown number of county jails and jail-like facilities in 2766[2] jurisdictions.

Jails and Police Lockups

The standard declares that no child should be admitted to a jail or a jail-like place of detention.

The survey found that 93 percent of the country's juvenile court jurisdictions, covering about 2800 counties and cities comprising 44 percent of the population (*a*) have no place of detention other than a county jail or police lockup and (*b*) detain too few children to justify establishing a detention home.

If we add to the 87,951 children of juvenile court age held in county jails . . . the number who are held in police lockups, the total number admitted to jails and jail-like facilities in the United States would exceed 100,000.

The claim that jails are never used for children is made by only Connecticut, Puerto Rico, and Vermont. Several states have successfully reduced their jailing of delinquent children by using shelter care in special boarding homes when secure custody is not essential.

Less than 20 percent of the jails in which children are held have been rated as suitable for adult federal offenders.[3] Nine states forbid placing children in jail, but this prohibition is not always enforced. In 19 states the law permits juveniles to be jailed if they are segregated from adults, but this provision also is not always adhered to.

When children are segregated from adults, lack of supervision (even by adult prisoners) has resulted in physical and sexual aggression, suicide, and even murder by other children held in the jail.

In Arizona in January 1965, four teenage boys, jailed on suspicion of stealing beer, died of asphyxiation from a defective gas heater when they were left alone for 11 hours in a jail.

In Indiana, a 13-year-old boy, who had been in five foster homes, drove the car belonging to the last of his foster fathers to a county jail, considered one of the finest in the state, and asked the sheriff to lock him up. The boy was well segregated from adults pending a hearing for auto theft. When he had been detained for about a week, his body was found hanging from one of the bars of his cell. Next to it was a penciled note: "I don't belong anywhere."

Incidents such as these, which have occurred from time to time in all parts of the country, graphically illustrate not only the lack of proper facilities, but also the lack of child welfare and court personnel to implement the intent of juvenile court law so that when a child is removed from his home and his parents the court shall secure for him care as nearly as possible equivalent to that which they should have given him. The jailing of children is condemned not only by the law in most states and by the standard, but also by psychologists, psychiatrists, sociologists, penologists, the International Association of Chiefs of Police, the National Sheriff's Association, the U.S. Children's Bureau, and the National Council on Crime and Delinquency.[4]

Although 13 states have taken some responsibility for juvenile detention, only 9 states have taken responsibility for providing regional detention centers for counties with too few children to detain to justify constructing local facilities.

Children under seven years of age have been held in substandard county jails for lack of shelter care in foster homes. Some of the youngsters had committed delinquent acts; some were merely dependent or neglected. On the same day that the Arizona tragedy was reported, a police chief in New Jersey took two teenage runaway larceny suspects to his own home for lack of any suitable place of detention pending hearing and commitment.

Jail detention is characterized by enforced idleness, no supervision, and rejection. It is a demoralizing experience for a youngster at a time when his belief in himself is shattered or distorted. Repeated jailing of youth has no salutary effect on the more sophisticated youngster; on the contrary, it reenforces his delinquency status with his peers and his self-identification as a criminal. Enforced idleness in a jail gives the sophisticated juvenile ample time and reason for striking back at society.

Juvenile detention is frequently misused as an immediate punishment for delinquent acts. If punishment is the court's only disposition, it ought to be administered only after all the facts are in— not as an immediate reaction to the charge.

CONFUSED OBJECTIVES: A SUMMARY

Confusion and misuse pervade detention. It has come to be used by police and probation officers as a disposition; judges use it for punishment, protection, storage, and lack of other facilities. More than in any other phase of the correctional process, the use of detention is colored by rationalization, duplicity, and double talk, generally unchallenged because the law is either defective or not enforced, and because it is always easy to make a case for detaining on the grounds of the child's offenses or the demands of the public as interpreted by the police or the press.

Detention too often serves as storage, a means of delaying action. It protects the police, the probation officer, and the judge from criticism in the event that a released child commits another law violation while awaiting court hearing. It removes from the probation officer his obligation to help parents assume responsibility for supervising their child in his own home and to help the child assume responsibility for his own behavior in the community. In short, it serves as a substitute for the casework so urgently needed by both parent and child to begin unraveling the problem of which the delinquent act is but a symptom. What are some of the "delinquent acts" for which many children are detained? Truancy, for one; the child is detained because the school has failed to deal with the causes of his truancy. Incorrigibility, for another; often it is the parents that need help as much as the child. Or he may be a runaway, frequently with good reason for running. These youngsters and their parents need assistance, which is frequently delayed by the detaining process; sometimes, they never get it.

The child, the parent, and the public are led to believe that the youngster's detention was, in fact, his correctional treatment and that, after a lecture from the judge and possibly a postcard type of probation, he is supposed to straighten out. Little wonder that many law enforcement officers object to the leniency of the juvenile court. They reason that if they detain, at least they have played their part in punishing the child and safeguarding the community, even though the court may dismiss the case. (The statistics show 409,218 children detained but only 242,275 children placed on probation or committed to an institution.)

Many judges, realizing that prolonged detentions are unsatisfactory and bending to community pressures for prompt action, are quick to commit delinquent children to training schools already crowded with youngsters who failed to receive effective probation services in the community.[5] The result of a high commitment rate is a backlog of children in jails and detention homes awaiting transfer—and so the vicious circle continues.

If the evils of detention are to be corrected, it is necessary first to strengthen probation and other correctional treatment services; second, to develop community resources for shelter care; third, to use detention only for its proper functions.

❖　　❖　　❖

JUVENILE PROBATION, SURVEY FINDINGS

Probation Coverage

Juvenile probation service is authorized by statute in each of the 50 states and the Commonwealth of Puerto Rico. The study conducted in conjunction with the preparation of this report shows that in one recent year some 192,000 written social studies were made on behalf of children referred to our courts and that some 189,000 children were placed under probation supervision. At the time of the survey, approximately 223,800 children were under such supervision. Supervision usually extends over significant periods of the child's life. Among the agencies included in the sample, the average period of supervision ranged from three months to three years, with a median of 13 months. In the sample of 250 counties, 233 had probation services.

Fundamental to any definition of desirable probation practice is the availability of paid, full-time probation service to all courts and all children needing such service.

The survey reveals that, though every state makes statutory provision for juvenile probation, in many states probation service is not uniformly available in all counties and localities. The data on this point may be summarized as follows:

1. In 31 states all counties have probation staff service.

2. A total of 2306 counties (74 percent of all counties in the United States) theoretically have such service. In some of these the service may be only a token.

3. In 16 states that do not have probation staff coverage in every county, at least some services are available to courts in some counties from persons other than paid, full-time probation officers. The sources of such services include volunteers (in six states), child welfare departments (in five states), and a combination of child welfare, sheriff, and other departments (in five states).

4. In 165 counties in 4 states, no juvenile probation services at all are available.

Generally, the country's more populous jurisdictions are included among the counties served by probation staff. However, in the smaller counties service may be expected to be spotty. Comments such as the following occur in the observations of the experienced practitioners gathering the survey data:

> The . . . State Department of Public Welfare does provide, upon request, probation and aftercare services to the courts and to institutions. These services are part of the child welfare program, and no differentiation is made as to specific caseloads. A general impression is that . . . there is not an acceptance of this service, and it is not used in many counties.

Many of the state agencies that are theoretically responsible for providing services are not prepared to do so. However, some child welfare departments acknowledge the provision of probation services as a major responsibility, assign capable staff to the function, and provide services of good caliber. . . . [Yet] the development of practitioners in the court setting who have specialized knowledge of the diagnosis and treatment of acting-out, behavior-problem children remains a challenge to probation practice. This task is doubly difficult when the staff is not oriented specifically to these problems. It is particularly inappropriate to expect specialists in law enforcement (sheriffs, police, etc.) to become skilled in probation diagnosis and treatment as well as in their own specialized functions. And rare is the volunteer who has the time, energy, and resources to so equip himself (though the volunteer often plays a valuable role when working upon carefully defined problems in cooperation with a trained and experienced member of the probation staff).

Whether a child subjected to the truly awesome powers of the juvenile court will be dealt with on the basis of knowledge and understanding, usually the product of a good probation social study, is determined by chance—the accident of his place of residence. The same accident determines whether the community treatment resource of probation as an alternative to incarceration will be available to him. The following observation about one State was made by a member of the survey team:

> In the entire state, only two counties have probation services. The other counties have no service. A child placed on probation in these counties is presumed to be adjusting satisfactorily until

he is brought back to the court with a new charge. . . . The Department of Welfare will not accept referrals of delinquent children from the courts.

❖   ❖   ❖

JUVENILE INSTITUTIONS, SURVEY FINDINGS

The survey findings are organized around three factors that significantly affect the operation of juvenile training facilities—(1) the presence of working philosophies that are consistent with what makes change possible; (2) a use of juvenile institutions by the courts and related groups that allows a program focused on change to operate; and (3) the presence of personnel, physical facilities, administrative controls, and other resources tailored to the job of producing change.

Working Philosophy

A good working philosophy clearly relates the institution's activities to its purpose and to the problems it must meet in serving this purpose.

Such a relationship between purpose and program is clearly outlined in the operations of some facilities. As a general matter, however, the absence of a clear working philosophy that ties programs to the achievement of more responsible attitudes is a significant weakness crucial to the problem of improving services.

Lack of understanding concerning the practicality of newer philosophies is a major problem. The difficulty of securing their acceptance is clearly illustrated by developments in the issue of discipline. For some years standards have declared that "corporal punishment should not be tolerated in any form in a training school program." The misbehaving youngster should see, to the greatest degree possible, the reason for a rule and its meaning for the particular brand of difficulty he encounters on the "outs." In this way discipline can become an avenue to new behavior having the force of personal meaning. The use of force shifts the emphasis away from the youngster and onto the smooth running of the institution. For someone with antagonistic attitudes, hitching behavior to the good of something he dislikes can be expected to have little lasting effect.

Thus, apart from the issue of whether physical abuse results, use of corporal punishment can reasonably be taken as a rough statistical indicator of the degree to which treatment viewpoints are actually operating. The survey found that corporal punishment is authorized in juvenile institutions in ten states.

Another indicator of working philosophy is found in an institution's answer to the question, "How much security?" The institution's need to develop the youngsters' self-control often collides with the public's concern over escapes. Caught between the two, the administrator may set up a system of tight management which, he rationalizes, is for the youngsters' "own good." Thus the juvenile is used to serve the institution instead of the other way around.

A solution can be achieved by public and professional education. Though public expectations toward training facilities are often unrealistic, they must be met by the administrator if he wants to hold his job. Therefore, maximum efficiency—doing the best that current knowledge will allow—cannot be reached until this blurring effect is looked at honestly. If training facilities are to change youngsters, they must be allowed to operate out of philosophies consistent with this purpose. The public needs to learn that treatment approaches which allow "breathing room" are not naive but are, on the contrary, extremely practical. Properly conceived, they are directed at getting the trainee to assume more responsibility for his life rather than assigning it later to the police.

Uses Being Made of Training Schools

In theory, training schools are specialized facilities for changing children relatively hardened in delinquency. In practice, as the survey shows, they house a nonselective population and are primarily used in ways which make the serving of their theoretical best purpose, that of "change," beside the point.

This is not to say that other purposes being served by the typical training facility are not important in themselves. Rather, the point is whether they can best be served by a training facility, and, if they cannot, the effect of this extraneousness on the facility's prime reason for existence, the basic job for which it is intended. The extent to which its ability to do this job is diminished becomes clear from the following list of its "other" expedient purposes:

Use as a detention or holding facility for youngsters awaiting completion of other plans for placement.

Providing basic housing for youngsters whose primary need is a foster home or residential housing.

Housing large numbers of youngsters whose involvement in trouble is primarily situational rather than deep-seated and who could be handled more efficiently under community supervision.

Caring for mentally retarded youngsters committed to the training school because there is no room in a mental retardation facility or because no such institution exists.

Providing care for youngsters with severe psychiatric problems who are committed to the training school because of no juvenile residential treatment program.

Use of girls' facilities to provide maternity services.

The problem of varied intake is further complicated by differences in court commitment philosophies, each of which is a working view of "the best purpose a training facility should ideally serve." In summary, the effects of the diverse elements cited contribute to training facilities wherein no one is best served and most are served in default.

Variations in use of training schools are found among the states as a whole, as well as among the counties of a single state, and further show that many reference points other than "change" are the determiners of practice. If juvenile institutions were actually working in allegiance to a common "best use," statistics which reflect practice would have some uniformity of meaning. That this is not true is revealed by some of the statistical sketches below. For example, length-of-stay statistics do not now reflect differences in time needed to effect "change." If they did, one system's length of stay could be compared with another's, as a guideline for the efficacy of a given program. Rather, the data show that length of stay reflects some extraneous factor such as "overcrowding," or a population whose primary need is "housing," or children awaiting unavailable placements, or children who, though better suited to a probation program, must be held "long enough" to avoid court or community problems.

* * *

JUVENILE AFTERCARE, SURVEY FINDINGS

An Overview of Aftercare Today

The major items in this survey include data from the 40 state-operated special aftercare programs,[6] but not from programs administered by city and county correctional systems, private institutions, and noncorrectional services of child and public welfare departments, since full information could not be obtained from them.

The 40 states reported a total of about 48,000 youth under aftercare supervision. Estimates for the other states, based on a projection of that figure, indicate that about 59,000 are under aftercare supervision in the United States. The number of juveniles in state programs ranges from 110 to 13,000.

Any study of aftercare today at the national level is plagued by inadequate statistics coming from the 50 states and Puerto Rico. As long as this situation persists, attempting a thorough study of juvenile aftercare can be described only as an exercise in futility. The gaps in vital information are so great that the reliability and validity of the few national statistics that can be gathered must be viewed with extreme caution. Efforts are being made to change this condition, but extensive organizational programing for statewide data collection is needed.

State operating costs range from $7,000 to over $4 million a year. Together the states are spending about $18 million a year. Average per capita cost is $320 a year.

This expenditure is small in comparison with the cost of state-operated juvenile institutions, which spend over $144 million a year to care for an average daily population of slightly over 42,000 at an average per capita cost of about $3400 a year.

The fact that aftercare costs less than one-tenth as much as institutional care is nothing to be proud of. As reported by the 40 states, its relative cheapness reflects the inadequacy of the programs at least as much as it demonstrates inherent economy. It is not uncommon for 250 adolescents to be assigned to a program staffed by only two or three aftercare counselors located at the state capital or training school, which may be hundreds of miles from the communities where the juveniles are supposedly under supervision. Aside from the excessiveness of the supervisors' caseloads, sheer distance reduces the effectiveness of the program.

Thus, aftercare programs should not be judged solely by their relative economy of operation. Rather, the question should be asked: How much should be spent to make aftercare truly effective? For it should be remembered that effective aftercare is one of the best methods of preventing recidivism.

The Misdemeanant in the Correctional System

The focus of corrections generally is on felons and juvenile offenders. But misdemeanants form a far larger group than both of the others combined in terms of the number of cases handled by the criminal justice system.

A 12-state study revealed that 93.5 percent of persons arraigned in 1962 in these States for offenses other than traffic violations were charged with misdemeanors.[7] The ratio of misdemeanants to felons showed wide variation from state to state. Iowa had four times as many misdemeanants as felons; New Hampshire had 30 times as many. (See Table 8-1)

TABLE 8-1.   Misdemeanor and Felony Defendants in
12 States, 1962[7]

	Misdemeanor defendants		Felony defendants	
	Number	Percent of total	Number	Percent of total
Alaska..........................	8,098	93.2	587	6.8
California.......................	505,521	93.6	34,767	6.4
Connecticut.....................	53,009	96.8	1,769	3.2
Iowa............................	26,985	79.1	7,113	20.9
Kansas.........................	66,516	95.0	3,502	5.0
Massachusetts..................	126,365	93.7	8,498	6.3
New Hampshire.................	31,348	97.0	955	3.0
New Jersey.....................	122,398	91.4	11,566	8.6
New York.......................	[2]412,330	95.8	18,027	4.2
North Carolina.................	[2]122,153	90.4	[3]13,000	9.6
Oregon.........................	62,111	94.4	3,676	5.6
Wisconsin......................	27,061	83.5	5,352	16.5
Total..................	1,563,895	93.5	108,812	6.5

[1] Motor vehicle offenses excluded.
[2] Inferior courts only.
[3] Estimated.

SOURCE: Lee Silverstein, "In Defense of the Poor" (Chicago: American Bar Foundation, 1965), p. 124.

From the President's Commission on Law Enforcement and Administration of Justice, *Task Force Report: Corrections* (Washington: U.S. Government Printing Office, 1967) Appendix A, pp. 72–76.

Determination of the total number of misdemeanant offenders in the United States can only be approximated because of the variations in definition, the lack of record-keeping, and the large number of felony arrests which are subsequently reduced to misdemeanors.

The definition of a misdemeanor varies from jurisdiction to jurisdiction. Typically a misdemeanor is an offense carrying a maximum sentence of up to one year, usually in the local jail rather than the State prison. Some criminal codes specifically identify offenses as misdemeanors or felonies. Other statutes stipulate that all offenses not specifically enumerated as felonies are misdemeanors. Still other jurisdictions distinguish between "high" and "low" misdemeanors—with a "high" misdemeanor carrying a sentence in excess of one year. In some cases, a single act may be either a felony or a misdemeanor, depending upon prosecutorial or judicial discretion. Finally, some statutes add an additional category of crimes called "summary offenses" or more simply "offenses," among them disorderly conduct, vagrancy, and public drunkenness.

In its Uniform Crime Reports, the Federal Bureau of Investigation does not distinguish between felonies and misdemeanors but employs instead various offense categories such as gambling, homicide, burglary, rape, and vandalism. When arrests for offenses commonly identified as misdemeanors are totaled, the number of arrests for misdemeanors reaches almost 5 million a year. The large bulk of these cases are disposed of by fines or suspended sentences.

Misdemeanants who are committed to correctional programs are characteristically handled in institutions or probation departments administered locally by city or county officials. High population turnover is one of the chief features of these programs. Of the nearly 2 million commitments to all correctional facilities and programs in 1965, over two-thirds were based on a misdemeanant conviction. However, because of the misdemeanants' generally shorter sentences, the average daily population in misdemeanant corrections was only 342,688 in 1965, as compared with 591,494 felons and 348,204 juveniles.

About 41 percent of the misdemeanants were in institutions, the rest on probation. These figures do not include facilities receiving persons committed for less than 30 days. Such inclusion would undoubtedly raise the proportion of institutionalized offenders significantly.

DIVERSITY OF MISDEMEANANT GROUPS

The range and diversity of misdemeanant offenders are far greater than those of the felony and juvenile groups. Some appreciation of this diversity and the problems it poses for corrections is a necessary starting point for any analysis of how improvements could be made.

For one thing, a considerable volume of misdemeanors involve motor vehicle laws. Misdemeanor courts also handle a variety of other regulatory violations in health, housing, safety, and commercial fields. This class of cases seldom reaches corrections, since in most instances such matters are disposed of by fines or license suspensions.

Another very large group consists of drunkenness offenders. The National Survey of Corrections indicated that, excluding traffic offenders, nearly half of all misdemeanants are arrested for public drunkenness or offenses related to drinking. In some jurisdictions, strict enforcement of such laws is the policy; in others, relatively few cases even reach the courts. Many drunkenness offenders, as noted in Chapter 9 of the Commission's General Report, are skid row derelicts who may spend much of their lives in and out of local jails and work farms on short sentences. Much the same pattern holds true of prostitutes and vagrants. In some of these instances, police, prosecutors, or courts refer offenders to various welfare agencies outside the criminal justice system. In most cases, however, they are handled by misdemeanant correctional facilities.

These facilities have generally not attempted much by way of rehabilitation. But neither have they been exclusively concerned with punishment or even custody. In practice, jails and other misdemeanant institutions have become adapted in many such instances to the performance of miscellaneous social tasks for which they are not suited and which they generally do not perform as well as programs specifically aimed at doing such tasks. Jails are used in many cities, for example, to get skid row drunks off the street and dry them out, to give prostitutes medical checkups, to house the homeless. But these have been simply stopgap measures, not solutions to underlying problems, and indeed they may often aggravate the situations they are employed to alleviate. Often these tasks have come to be carried out under deplorable conditions, with little attention to the rights of individual offenders or the dignity of the law.

Another substantial and varied group of misdemeanants have committed offenses generally characteristic of inner-city life, including among others, after-hours liquor offenses, weapons offenses, and gambling. Some of the offenders in this group can easily become involved in the kinds of crimes with which the mainstream of corrections deals. Indeed, weapons offenses, such as "pointing a gun," suggest the ease with which they may happen and the consequent seriousness of such matters. But many of these offenders are also engaging in behavior which their community does not strongly and generally condemn as an offense. "Playing the numbers," for example, is an established part of life in many slum neighborhoods.

In many such instances, extensive correctional programs may not seem warranted. The cost of successfully changing behavior not strongly condemned by the community is, for one thing, extremely high in comparison to the interest of society in being protected against such offenses. Moreover, it is difficult to justify in other terms any very extensive interference with the liberty or values of persons who have not engaged in crimes directly threatening in any substantial way the person or property of another.

The correctional challenge in those personal and property crime misdemeanors that more resemble felonies is not so unique. As a group, these misdemeanants present the same dangers to the community and the same need and potential for rehabilitation. It is with respect to them that the statement of Myrl Alexander, director of the Federal Bureau of Prisons, holds most true: "In distinguishing between a felony and a misdemeanor the laws are directed to the deed rather than the doer."[8] Indeed, even the deed in many of these cases is not very different in the case of misdmeanors and felonies. The distinction is in general one of degree, but the dividing line is necessarily often arbitrary or elusive—$99 thefts are often misdemeanors, $100 thefts are felonies; simple assault is generally a misdemeanor and aggravated assault a felony—but the distinction turns on questions of intent or possession of weapons that do not always make sense within the confines of a single case.

In fact many cases are processed initially as felonies and later reduced to misdemeanors, often as the result of negotiation between prosecutor and defense counsel. A housebreaking felony will, for example, be reduced to a petit larceny misdemeanor, a forgery to a "bad check" violation. In the District of Columbia in 1965 more than half of felony arrests were thus disposed of,[9] and this rate is not uncommon.

The less serious nature of misdemeanor property and personal crimes means, of course, that there are likely to be more "casual" offenders and marginal cases than with felonies. Driving a car without the owner's consent can be a relatively innocent frolic of youth, quite different from habitual auto theft or the abandoning, stripping, or selling of stolen cars. Shoplifting, if not habitual, is usually diverted from the criminal justice process at an early stage. Full-scale correctional intervention, whether aimed at deterrence or rehabilitation, does not appear appropriate in most such cases.

But in many of the more serious misdemeanors against property or persons, correctional intervention clearly is just as necessary as in the case of felonies. It is in these cases that the misdemeanor-felony distinction seems least meaningful from the correctional standpoint. This is particularly true since many misdemeanants subsequently commit felonies. Table 8-2 presents results of a study of a sample of the first felony admissions in California. Of the total, 73.5 percent had a history of previous misdemeanor offenses. These offenses fell preponderantly in the personal and property crime groups, a fact especially significant considering the relatively small absolute volume of such offenses compared to traffic and public order violations. Also although its analysis did not specifically focus on misdemeanants, the Commission's Science and Technology Task Force studies of recidivism patterns in the so-called "Index crimes" of the FBI Uniform Crime Reports indicated that, at least with respect to traditional property and personal offenses, there is some evidence of a tendency for offenders to graduate to more serious crimes. (See Chapter 11 of the Commission's General Report.)

TABLE 8-2.   Sample of First Felony Admissions to State Prison with Previous Misdemeanor History, California, 1964

Previous misdemeanors	Number	Previous misdemeanors	Number
Offenses against property.....	67	Drugs......................	6
Offenses against persons......	27	Other......................	15
Offense against public order...	13		
Drunkeness.................	25	Total................	173
Traffic.....................	20		

SOURCE: California Department of Corrections.

PRESENT MISDEMEANANT SERVICES

The handling of such diverse groups creates perplexing problems for modern corrections. The classic sentencing alternatives for the wide assortment of acts denominated misdemeanors or petty offenses have been a fine and jail, often in the alternative, such as "$30 or 30 days." This sentencing structure provides generally the same alternatives in terms of deterrence and punishment as the felony and juvenile systems; and, as long as the function of corrections centered on these purposes, there was nothing particularly anomalous in the way misdemeanants were treated.

But as the correctional focus has turned with other offenders to rehabilitation, the processes of misdemeanant corrections have become harder to justify. Suspended sentences are widely used in many jurisdictions; but formal probation is much less common, and the supervision offered is rarely more than nominal. Parole is virtually nonexistent. The lack of meaningful rehabilitative intervention in community treatment programs is even more true of jails.

The general inadequacies of misdemeanant corrections are indicated by the fact that its average yearly expenditure per offender is only $142 for community treatment, compared with $198 for felons and $328 for juveniles. Misdemeanant institutions spend on the average $1046 per offender per year, felony institutions $1966, and juvenile institutions $3613.

Moreover, the lack of rehabilitative efforts, with respect to such misdemeanant groups as drunks, has also pointed up the frequent failure of misdemeanant corrections to deter, at least in terms of preventing recidivism. Studies consistently indicate that a large number of misdemeanants are repeatedly convicted of criminal offenses. For example, a survey of five county misdemeanant penitentiaries in New York State found, as shown in Table 8-3, that half of the men committed in 1963 had prior commitments and a fifth had been committed ten times or more.

While it is true that misdemeanants with extensive prior records are most often found among those convicted of a petty offense or for an alcohol-related charge such as disorderly conduct, they do not totally account for all the severely recidivistic groups found in misdemeanant corrections. In a special study, a sample of 1342 persons sentenced to jail in Los Angeles and San Joaquin Counties, Calif., in 1966 was divided into two categories.[10] Group A included

296

more serious offenses such as assault, burglary, and theft. Group B contained violations considered less serious, including gambling, vandalism, and drunkenness; of these, over 50 percent had ten or more prior convictions. While the more serious offenders in group A had on the average fewer prior convictions, 18.4 percent of them had ten or more.

TABLE 8-3.   Number of Times Male Prisoners Committed Have Been Confined, New York County Penitentiaries, 1963

	Counties					Total	
	Albany	Erie	Monroe	Onon-daga	West-chester	Indi-viduals	Percent
1st time............	931	765	715	542	615	3,568	49.62
2nd time............	13	243	82	108	247	693	9.64
3d time............	11	141	56	23	177	408	5.67
4th time............	3	68	37	20	107	235	3.27
5th time............	2	53	40	21	91	207	2.88
6th time............	....	78	28	26	48	180	2.50
7th time............	....	45	30	28	53	156	2.17
8th time............	....	33	29	23	50	135	1.88
9th time............	....	22	25	16	42	105	1.46
10th time and over...	....	342	436	305	421	1,504	20.91
Total..........	960	1,790	1,478	1,112	1,851	7,191	100.0

SOURCE: Adapted from New York State Commission of Correction, "Thirty-Seventh Annual Report, 1963," p. 485.

Misdemeanant corrections is a collection of relatively autonomous and uncoordinated programs and institutions. Probation departments are administered by local courts, county jails by sheriffs, and some other local institutions for adult misdemeanants by corrections personnel. The other institutions differ from jails in that as a rule they handle only sentenced prisoners and not those detained for trial. There are several varieties of these institutions: the workhouse, which is in effect a penitentiary for misdemeanants; and work farms and work camps, where programs (conducted for the most part outdoors) tend to be more flexible than those of workhouses.

By and large, each unit acts independently of both higher governmental authority and similar units at its own level. Minimal coordination of operations is accomplished out of obvious need to service a common offender population, but there is virtually no comprehensive planning or conduct of programs.

Indeed, such planning would be next to impossible at present, if only because of the lack of coordinated statistical reporting. Law enforcement agencies collect statistics on arrests but not on court dispositions. Although court reports commonly show the number of convictions, they do not ordinarily reveal the dispositions which follow. Jail statistics show the number of offenders admitted but do not relate these figures to the total number of offenders processed by police and judicial agencies. The result is that the limited information which is collected does not begin to provide an accurate account of the handling of the misdemeanant offender in the United States.

The National Survey of Corrections estimated that there were about 3500 local institutions for misdemeanants in the Nation in 1965. Three-quarters of the institutions in the 250-county sample were jails, and the remainder were designated as workhouses, camps, farms, or institutions having some of the characteristics of all three. Not only are the great majority of these facilities old, but many do not even meet the minimum standards in sanitation, living space, and segregation of different ages and types of offenders that have obtained generally in the rest of corrections for several decades.

Of one State, a consultant noted:

> This state has nine jails which confine nearly 25,000 people a year. Five are more than 100 years old, and three have been standing for 160 years. In four jails, there were 899 cells without sanitary facilities.

Another consultant concluded after covering the jail system of a western state:

> Most counties and cities persist in operating their own jails, nearly all of which are nothing more than steel cages in which people stay for periods of time up to a year. Most of the jails are custody-oriented and supervised by ill-trained, underpaid personnel. In some cases, the institution is not manned except when a police officer on duty can look in once during his eight-hour shift.

Two-thirds of the sample of 215 local correctional institutions covered by the National Survey reported no type of rehabilitative program at all. If consideration were given to facilities handling those sentenced for 30 days or less, not included in the National

Survey, the proportion of institutions without such programs would undoubtedly be greater. Table 8-4 sets forth the number of institutions having various kinds of programs.

TABLE 8-4.   Rehabilitative Programs in 215 Jails and Other Local Correctional Institutions, 1965

Type of program	Institutions having programs [1]	
	Number	Percent
Group counseling	19	9
Work release	24	11
Alcoholics	15	7
Educational	22	10
Other	44	20
None	140	65
Unknown	3	1

[1] Institutions having more than 1 type of program are counted for each.

SOURCE: National Survey of Corrections.

Over 19,000 persons were employed to staff jails and local correctional institutions in 1965. The distribution of this staff, by type of assignment, is presented in Table 8-5.

This distribution reveals in striking clarity the priority of custody as an objective of jail programs. Only 500 people, less than 3 percent of total staff, perform rehabilitative duties in the country's 3500 jails and other local misdemeanant correctional institutions, and some of these people work only part time. On the average, in the Nation's jails, there is one psychologist for each 4300 inmates and one academic teacher for each 1300 inmates. Most treatment posi-

TABLE 8-5.   Personnel in Jails and Other Local Correctional Institutions, 1965, by Type of Position and Ratio of Staff to Inmates

Position	Number	Ratio of staff to inmates
Social workers	167	1:846
Psychologists	33	1:4,282
Psychiatrists	58	1:2,436
Academic teachers	106	1:1,333
Vocational teachers	137	1:1,031
Custodial officers	14,993	1:9
Other	3,701	1:38

SOURCE: National Survey of Corrections.

tions are concentrated in the larger facilities, leaving the great bulk of institutions without any teachers, psychologists, or social workers.

Community Services

Community treatment program for misdemeanants suffer from the same lack of resources as do programs for felons and juveniles, but in aggravated form due to even higher average caseloads and generally shorter periods of supervision.

Probation. As the study of misdemeanant sentencing in eight jurisdictions presented in Table 8-6 shows, formal probation is used relatively infrequently in most jurisdictions. This appears to be true even in jurisdictions with strong and well administered probation services, such as New York City, where probation is used in less than 2 percent of misdemeanant cases. Apparently, judges in such jurisdictions choose to concentrate probation resources on a small proportion of offenders where they are most needed, using fines or suspended sentences in other cases.

In 11 states there are no probation services for misdemeanants in any county. None of these states encompasses a very large metropolitan area, and most are not highly urbanized. Only two of these 11 jurisdictions were above the median per capita income in 1964, and six were in the bottom quarter.

About one-third of the 250 counties in the National Survey had no probation services for misdemeanants. Eight counties reported having a probation service but no cases; four counties did not report; and 59 counties were unable to report the total cases on probation during their last reporting year.

Over the country, then, probation services to misdemeanants are sparse and spotty. Some exceptions are seen in a few states which have combined services to felons and misdemeanants in large metropolitan areas which have probation departments either exclusively for the misdemeanant or as part of an integrated service for both misdemeanants and felons. Even here caseloads are too high to permit adequate presentence investigations and meaningful supervision of probationers.

In 20 states misdemeanant probation is organized nominally on a statewide basis. Some of these programs, however, provide only minimal services. Comments such as "service provided occasionally" or "as the caseload permits" or "will so provide if asked" typify the

TABLE 8-6.   Disposition of Misdemeanors in Selected
Lower Courts, 1964, 1965

[In percent]

Jurisdiction	Disposition				
	Jail sentence	Probation	Fine	Suspended sentence	Other
Baltimore....................	28.6	2.5	15.7	17.8	35.3
Denver......................	20.6	19.7	31.2	28.5	....
Detroit.....................	26.4	5.7	56.6	8.7	2.6
Los Angeles County...........	32.0	8.9	....	....	¹ 59.1
New York City...............	47.6	1.7	18.9	31.8	....
San Mateo County, Calif.........	66.2	19.6	....	....	¹ 14.2
Washington, D.C................	63.3	10.0	16.7	10.0	....
Westchester County, N.Y........	30.8	2.4	51.3	11.4	10.6

: Includes fine and supended sentence cases.

SOURCES: New York City data from Criminal Court of the City of New York, "Annual Report," 1964; Westchester County data from a special study by the National Council on Crime and Delinquency; San Mateo County data from California Department of Justice; all other data from studios by Commission Consultants.

reports on probation service to misdemeanant offenders in several of these states. In another 20 states, probation services are organized on a city, city-count, county, or court district basis. These states contain slightly over half of the nation's population.

Both the state-level and the local services vary widely in the adequacy of the service provided. In California, for example, a full range of probation service is provided to the lower courts, with misdemeanant cases constituting 57 percent of all offender groups placed on probation. However, the adequacy of this service is seriously handicapped by extremely high caseloads.

As Table 8-7 shows, such high caseloads are the rule in most jurisdictions. A few counties covered by the National Survey reported caseloads in excess of 200, and one county reported 400. Of all misdemeanants on probation, 76 percent were supervised in caseloads of over 100. For the country as a whole, the average caseload was estimated at 114 cases. Added to this workload is an estimated average of 85 percent reports per officer annually.

Field researchers describe the probation process in high-caseload areas as one in which the client comes to the office once a month, sees his probation officer for a few minutes, and then departs. Probation here is a checking rather than counseling function, and even its checking aspect is so limited as to be of very little value. Other surveys of probation services have concluded that, as a result of inadequate staffing, individuals are jailed when they should be placed on probation, and those who are placed on probation often fail because of inadequate supervision.[11]

In the National Survey, 62 percent of the sample counties reported no unusual rehabilitative programs for misdemeanants in operation by probation departments. Given the high workload and limited financial support, this lack of program development is not surprising.

Legal restrictions on the use of probation at the misdemeanant level exist only in nine states. In two states and Puerto Rico, misdemeanants are specifically not eligible for probation. In another state, a variety of qualifications must be met, such as no prior felony convictions or imprisonment within the last five years. Two states prohibit probation for particular misdemeanant offenses.

TABLE 8-7.   Distribution of Misdemeant Probationers, 1965,
by Size of Caseload in Which Supervised

Caseload size	Percentage supervised	Caseload size	Percentage supervised
Under 40	0.7	71–80	2.4
41–50	.2	81–90	1.4
51–60	4.2	91–100	10.9
61–70	3.9	Over 100	76.3

SOURCE: National Survey of Corrections.

Parole for Misdemeanants.   The use of parole for misdemeanants is extremely limited. ... [T]he National Survey found a very small number of misdemeanants on parole in 1965. Short sentences undoubtedly contribute to this low rate of parole. However, more significant is the fact that, in a number of jurisdictions, parole for misdemeanants is not even provided by law. Further, many of those states which have statutory provisions for the parole of misdemeanants have very inadequately staffed programs and parole boards often include local law enforcement officials as ex-officio board members, a procedure rejected as poor practice in the parole of felons.

Considerable attention needs to be focused on the development of parole services for misdemeanants. As the next section will illustrate, such services are vital for effective misdemeanant programs of community reintegration.

Corrections

DISPOSITION PENDING TRIAL

Corrections also has an important role in the nondecisional aspect of intake: the handling of persons pending adjudication. At present this role is almost entirely confined to detention of those not released on bail or on their own recognizance. For adults, local jail facilities used for detention are in fact ... generally operated by law enforcement officials and limited to merely custodial functions. Both for those who are held in custody and for those released in the community pending adjudication, however, there are much wider possibilities for correctional service.

❈ ❈ ❈

While the situation for juveniles in detention is deplorable in many jurisdictions, conditions for adult detainees can only be described as worse. Local jails are commonly used not only for prisoners serving sentences but for detention of suspects awaiting trial and not released on bail or otherwise. The lengthy delays often attendant upon pretrial processes give rise to frequent situations of persons serving weeks or months while legally innocent only to be released or given a shorter term upon conviction.

... [O]ther prosecutorial reforms ... Bail would go far to alleviate this situation by eliminating unnecessary delays and obtaining release pending trial for a greater number of individuals for whom detention is not necessary for community security. Corrections has an important role to play in providing information for the decisions which must be made in these programs. Indeed, over one-third of the 42 bail projects operating in 1965 utilize correctional personnel for screening.[12]

Largely because of the historical development of bail procedures and the shortage of probation staff, there has been very little use of correctional resources to supervise persons released in the

From The President's Commission on Law Enforcement and Administration of Justice, *Task Force Report: Corrections* (Washington: U.S. Government Printing Office, 1967) Appendix A, pp. 23–28, 45–47, 60.

community pending trial. It is quite common for persons released on recognizance to be placed under the responsibility of their families, their lawyers, or other private citizens interested in them. In some jurisdictions, such as St. Louis, persons released on recognizance are required to check in periodically with a probation officer. Such supervision is also authorized by the Federal Bail Reform Act of 1965. With adequate resources, it might be employed to advantage in many cases, at least to ascertain a suspect's presence in the jurisdiction.

❈   ❈   ❈

It is probably true that persons who have not yet been convicted of a crime are subjected to the worst aspects of the American correctional system. Unconvicted persons, as yet legally innocent, are almost inevitably subjected to the tightest security and receive the least attention of any group in jails.

❈   ❈   ❈

This primary concern for security imposes regimentation, repeated searches, and close surveillance on detainees. Most jails also have poor facilities for visiting, thus hampering a detainee's efforts to arrange for his defense and maintain contacts with the community. A detainee's lawyer, family, and friends have little opportunity for privacy. Where extreme security measures are the rule, visiting takes place in rooms where visitors are separated from the prisoner by heavy screens and conversation is carried on by telephone. . . .

Pretrial detention involves substantial numbers of persons each year, although incomplete reporting makes it difficult to estimate precisely the number of persons detained. Some data from various jurisdictions give an indication that the numbers are quite large. A one-day census in California revealed that about 25,000 persons were confined in local jails and camps. Of this number 9000 were unsentenced prisoners.[13] In Multnomah County, Oregon, more than 1700 were confined awaiting trial during the fiscal year 1966.[14] The District of Columbia held 10,520 during a comparable period.[15] According to several surveys, the percentage of persons charged who were subsequently detained awaiting trial ranged from 31 percent in a New Jersey County to 75 percent in Baltimore. Average time served in detention ranged from six weeks to eight months in some jurisdictions.[16]

PROBATION

Slightly more than half of the offenders sentenced to correctional treatment in 1965 were placed on probation—supervision in the community subject to the authority of the court. Table 8-8 sets forth data

TABLE 8-8. Number of Offenders on Probation, and on Parole or in Institutions, 1965; Projections for 1975

Location of offender	1965		1975	
	Number	Percent	Number	Percent
Probation	684, 088	53	1, 071, 000	58
Parole or institution	598, 298	47	770, 000	42
Total	1, 282, 386	100	1, 841, 000	100

SOURCES: 1965 data from National Survey of Corrections and special tabulations provded by the Federal Bureau of Prisons and the Administrative Office of the U.S. Courts; 1975 projections by R. Christensen, of the Commission's Task Force on Science and Technology, as described in Appendix B of this report.

from the National Survey of Corrections and the Federal corrections system on the number of persons under probation on an average day in 1965 and the number in institutions or on parole. Also shown are estimates of what these populations are likely to be in 1975.... As the table indicates, probation is the correctional treatment used for most offenders today and is likely to be used increasingly in the future.[17]

The estimates for probation shown in the above table project a growth in the number of adults on probation almost two and one-half times greater than the growth in institutional and parole populations. The projected growth in juvenile probation is also substantial. ... [T]here are rapidly developing very promising intensive community supervision and residential programs, which could further shift the number of juveniles destined for institutions to community-based treatment. Thus, the projections for juvenile probation might actually be low.

The best data available indicate that probation offers one of the most significant prospects for effective programs in corrections. It is also clear that at least two components are needed to make it operate well. The first is a system that facilitates effective decision-making as to who should receive probation; the second is the existence of good community programs to which offenders can be assigned. Probation services now available in most jurisdictions fall far short of meeting either of these needs.

Present Services and Needs

Current probation practices have their origin in the quasi-probationary measures of an earlier day. The beginnings of probation are usually traced to Boston, where in 1841 a bootmaker bailed a number of defendants in the lower court on a volunteer basis. In 1897, Missouri passed legislation that made it possible to suspend execution of sentence for young and for petty offenders. This statute did not make provision for the supervision of probationers. However, Vermont established such a plan on a county basis in 1898, and Rhode Island established a state-administered system in 1899.[18]

After the turn of the century, the spread of probation was accelerated by the juvenile court movement. Thirty-seven states and the District of Columbia had a children's court act by 1910. Forty of them had also introduced probation for juveniles. By 1925, probation for juveniles was available in every state, but this did not happen in the case of adult probation until 1956.

Within states, probation coverage is still often spotty. Services for juveniles, for example, are available in every county in only 31 states. In one state, a National Survey staff observer noted, only two counties have probation services. A child placed on probation in the other counties is presumed to be adjusting satisfactorily until he is brought back to court with a new charge.

Table 8-9 shows the number of delinquents and adult felons on probation at the end of 1965 and the annual costs of these services. It is quickly apparent in terms of the number of persons served and of total operating costs that the juvenile system has relatively greater resources than the adult. Cost comparisons, however, require qualification. The juvenile total includes the cost of many foster homes and some private and public institutional costs. Furthermore, juvenile probation in some jurisdictions has a substantial responsibility for orphaned or other nondelinquent dependent children.

Probation in the United States is administered by hundreds of independent agencies operating under a different law in each state and under widely varying philosophies, often within the same state. They serve juvenile, misdemeanant, and felony offenders. In one

TABLE 8-9.   Number of Felons and Juveniles on Probation, 1965,
and Annual Costs of Services for Each Group

Type of probation	Number on probation	Annual costs
Felony	257,755	$37,937,808
Juvenile	224,948	75,019,441
Total	482,703	112,957,249

SOURCES: National Survey of Corrections and special tabulations provided by the Federal Bureau of Prisons and the Administrative Office of the U.S. Courts.

city, a single state or local agency might be responsible for handling all three kinds of probation cases; in another, three separate agencies may be operating, each responsible for a different type of probationer. All of these probation programs must contend with similar issues.

*   *   *

CORRECTIONAL INSTITUTIONS

Just as probation and parole fail to recognize their potential, so do prisons, training schools, and other institutions. Incarceration can serve not only as a means of incapacitating offenders for whom considerations of community safety permit no other alternative, and as a deterrent and sanction in a wider range of cases, but also as an aid to treatment and rehabilitation. A period of institutionalization can in some cases help an offender by removing him from the pressures and undesirable influences of his outside life, so that he may be subjected to intensive treatment which will provide a basis for reconstruction of noncriminal community ties.

The present use of institutionalization, however, almost universally falls short of this optimum. Deficiencies in resources, inadequate knowledge, and lack of community support handicap institutions as they do community treatment. Institutional corrections suffers also from long and indiscriminate use simply for punishment and banishment, purposes which inspire in the system little imagination, hope, or effort to improve.

The average daily population handled by all correctional services in the United States in 1965 was about 1.3 million. Of this total, about 5 percent were in juvenile institutions and 28 percent were in prisons or jails. . . .

The number of inmates in state and federal prisons for adults has decreased about 1 percent per year in the past few years, despite increases in the total population of the country and in serious crime.[19] Apparently the courts are making increased use of alternatives to commitment at the adult level. The population projection for the prison system shows the smallest aggregate increase of any of the correctional activities. By 1975 an estimated increment of some 7 percent is expected to bring the state and federal prison load to a total of 237,000 inmates.

* * *

According to the National Survey of Corrections, there were 398 state facilities for adults in 1965 and 220 for juveniles. These included a variety of special facilities such as forestry camps, reception centers, minimum-security prisons, institutions with specialized functions such as trade training, and maximum-custody institutions. Most of the special facilities were found in a relatively few states. The majority of states typically had only a training school for boys, a training school for girls, a penitentiary, and usually a separate facility, such as a reformatory, for younger felons.

* * *

The Traditional Institution

To appreciate the problems and potentials of correctional institutions, one must have an understanding of the kind of regime that developed in the authoritarian, fortress-style prisons . . . and that still persists to a greater or lesser degree in many institutions today.

PREMISES OF THE AUTHORITARIAN REGIME

A major premise of traditional institutions is that, in order to minimize the danger to both the institutional staff and the community, security should be regarded as the dominant goal. Mechanical security measures are instituted, including the building of high walls or fences around prisons, construction of gun-towers, the searching of inmates as they pass through certain check-points, pass systems to account for inmate movement, and counts at regular intervals. The objective of custody is met quite effectively since few prisoners escape and those who do usually are quickly apprehended.

These measures also serve the idea that deterrence requires extremes of deprivation, strict discipline, and punishment, all of which, together with considerations of administrative efficiency, make institutions impersonal, quasi-military places. Mail is censored, visiting is limited and closely supervised, privacy is virtually non-existent, inmates march in groups and are identified by number.

Rules stressing custodial control result in special forms of "etiquette" for maintaining distance between staff and inmates. Staff are discouraged from, or even suspended or dismissed for, calling inmates "mister"; they must address prisoners only by first name, last name, or nickname. But prisoners are required to address staff members as "mister," "officer," "lieutenant," or some other title, together with their surname. Staff are not to "fraternize" with prisoners; they must deal with them in an authoritative and impersonal manner, while inmates may not "act familiar" with staff. If differences of opinion occur, particularly as to how an inmate behaved, the staff version is always to be regarded as correct.

Social distance between staff and inmates is reinforced by the mass handling of prisoners. If inmates are almost always marched in groups—to work, to eat, to play, to the barbershop, to the commissary, to their sleeping quarters—there is little chance for staff to treat them on a personal basis, especially when the groups are large. If staff see most inmates only for brief specialized functions, such as checking them through a gate or issuing them prison clothing, there also is likely to be little opportunity for them to be viewed as individuals.

Actually, in a traditional institution, these differences frequently break down, particularly when the assignment of inmates places them in contact with the staff over an extended period of time. The differences also tend to break down where the staff and inmates cooperate in a common job which they share an interest in completing satisfactorily. But they still give to life in traditional institutions its basic character.

The authoritarian institution often seems to proceed, too, on the premise that it, and it alone, should be responsible for changing the offender. This assumption justifies the isolation of inmates from community contact and results in similar isolation for staffs. Not only are such institutions generally located away from large cities and frequently even from main transportation lines, but they are also generally expected to operate without any disturbance or incident that would attract public attention: escapes resulting from failures of security, crimes committed by parolees, even the appearances of inmates in the community.

An exaggerated concern for security and the belief in autonomous institutional responsibility for handling offenders combine to limit innovation and the development of community ties. Isolated, punitive, and regimented, the traditional prison and many juvenile training schools develop a monolithic society, caste-like and resistive to change.

Inmate Subcultures

Distance between staff and inmates is accentuated by forces that operate unofficially through inmates. Because staff have nearly absolute authority to punish or reward, inmates are especially concerned with keeping many of their activities covert. Accordingly, whenever an inmate communicates with staff, he runs the risk of being accused by his fellows of informing on them and thus of suffering violent reprisals.

In a situation where inmates have minimal recourse to staff, they are also more vulnerable to abuse and exploitation by other inmates. As a consequence, inmates tend to become progressively more wary of each other as well as of staff. "Do your own time" becomes the inmate slogan, signifying aloofness from and indifference to the interests of both staff and other inmates. This selfcenteredness is, in turn, encouraged by staff as a device to inhibit solidarity among inmates.

As a result of this situation, a peculiar social structure develops among both inmates and staff.[20] The elite inmate group, the "politicians" or "big shots," are those inmates who have not only earned respect among their fellows but also have developed rapport with staff. These tend to be persons with extensive institutional experience, who have been tested in interactions with other inmates sufficiently that they are neither readily "pushed around" by their fellows nor distrusted as "stool pigeons."

They have also been tested sufficiently by staff to be assigned jobs in offices or other locations where they can communicate readily with staff and often have access to institutional records. Because of their possession of "inside" information and their access to staff, they can command considerable deference from other inmates. However, they can also convince inmates that they generally work for their interest through manipulating the staff. They are thus the leadership in the inmate caste and the middlemen between the staff and inmates.

Beneath the "politicians" in status are the great mass of inmates, often called "right guys" or "straights." Among them a few may ultimately move to politician status. Most of them, however, are not routinely thrown into very personal contact with staff. Should they have an opportunity for private communication with staff, they are likely to be suspected by inmates.

The lowest stratum of inmate society is occupied by the sex offenders, the physically weak and immature, the mentally disordered and retarded. Aggressive inmates are distrusted by both staff and inmates and do not necessarily occupy a high position in the inmate society. They are feared by inmates and sometimes by the staff. Their tendency toward violence rather than manipulation imperils the stability of the institution and the maintenance of reciprocal relationships between staff and inmates.

In all institutions, but especially in those for juveniles, the achievement or preservation of a reputation for toughness, smartness, and independence from authority can be a primary inmate concern— even an obsession. Such a reputation may be nurtured by conspicuous challenge to staff authority or by evasion of institution rules. In institutions for juveniles and youth, these pursuits are often collective endeavors by cliques or gangs, organized at least partially in groups reflecting lines of affiliation in the large cities from which the inmates come.

In a stable repressive institution, the staff controls inmates largely through other key inmates. A few state prisons still use selected inmates to guard others. In many other prisons there is less blatant but still serious exploitation of inmates by those who are in strategic assignments and on good terms with staff. The resulting system permits extensive rackets, coerced homosexuality, and much violence to occur unknown to the staff.

A prisoner's prime concern in such an institution is to cope with the most aggressive inmates. He comes to have extreme distrust of all persons, but especially of all officials. He sees violence or threat of violence as a practical necessity for preserving self-integrity in even relatively minor conflict situations.

In this kind of institution, custodial staff clearly dominate, and such treatment staff as may be employed—chaplains, teachers, case-workers, physicians—either share the repressive orientation of custodial staff or are relatively isolated and uninfluential. The treatment emphasis of the past century has promoted a very gradual expansion in the number and influence of treatment staff of all types in traditional institutions. They usually affect decisions on institutional programs through such relatively mechanical methods as participating with senior custody staff in a prison's classification committee.

However, in most prisons such a committee's recommendations tend to be advisory only and affect primarily the work and living assignment plans for new inmates. Because custody has traditionally been considered the first function of prison management and because custodial staff are more numerous and have more firsthand knowledge of inmates than do treatment staff, they make most of the day-to-day decisions in innate management.

It is easy to see why deterring offenders from further crime is almost impossible in such a climate. Despite its avowed purpose, the authoritarian regime is deficient in instilling discipline and respect for authority. The maintenance of distance between staff and inmates reinforces the idea of many criminals and delinquents that law and authority are ranged against them; the emphasis on a myriad of rules, unexplained to inmates and often unreasoned in their operation, hardly educates a prisoner in the values of order of society. The existence of an illegitimate subculture of inmate relationships, often founded on violence and corruption, intensifies the criminal's commitment to these values.

The Collaborative Institution

In the past few decades, and increasingly in recent years, the traditional institutional regime has been undergoing modifications along the "collaborative" lines. ... The collaborative institution is structured around the partnership of all inmates and staff members in the process of rehabilitation. It tries to oppose the tendency for an institution to become isolated from the community physically and in terms of values, and instead seeks to assimilate inmates in normal noncriminal ways of life, partly through close identification with staff and partly through increased communication with the outside community.

❋   ❋   ❋

PAROLE AND AFTERCARE

Because probation terms are longer on the average than jail terms, projections assuming a growth in its use yield a larger total population under correctional control at any given time than would have been the case if sentencing trends have been held constant. Thus the estimates of the total correctional population in 1975 . . . would be about 7 percent lower if no allowance were made for an increased use of probation. . . .

However calculated, all evidence indicates that there will be increasing pressure on adult and juvenile probation and on the juvenile system generally in the coming years. Changes in correctional practice must deal simultaneously with these pressures as well as old practices.

❋   ❋   ❋

Reintegration of the Offender into the Community

The general underlying premise for the new directions in corrections is that crime and delinquency are symptoms of failures and disorganization of the community as well as of individual offenders. In particular, these failures are seen as depriving offenders of contact with the institutions that are basically responsible for assuring development of law-abiding conduct: sound family life, good schools, employment, recreational opportunities, and desirable companions, to name only some of the more direct influences. The substitution of deleterious habits, standards, and associates for these strengthening influences contributes to crime and delinquency.

The task of corrections therefore includes building or rebuilding solid ties between offenders and community, integrating or reintegrating the offender into community life—restoring family ties, obtaining employment and education, securing in the larger sense a place for the offender in the routine functioning of society. This requires not only efforts directed toward changing the individual offender, which has been almost the exclusive focus of rehabilitation, but also mobilization and change of the community and its institutions. And these efforts must be undertaken without giving up the important control and deterrent role of corrections, particularly as applied to dangerous offenders.

❖   ❖   ❖

The connection between social factors and crime was first systematically revealed in a series of studies carried on by Shaw and McKay at the University of Chicago during the 1920s.[21] These showed consistently high rates of delinquency in deteriorated areas within large cities, areas characterized by poverty and unemployment, residential mobility, broken homes, and evidence of disrupted social relationships such as mental illness, suicide, alcoholism, and narcotic addiction. Crime became in this perspective one of a wide array of symptoms of urban disorganization.

Other researchers undertook to explain the connection. One key to understanding delinquency in such deteriorated areas is the fact that people acquire the beliefs, values, attitudes, and habits of the groups with whom they are most closely associated. This idea is elaborated in Edwin Sutherland's theory of differential association,[22] which hypothesized that people become delinquent to the extent that they participate in groups and neighborhoods where delinquent ideas and techniques are viewed favorably. The earlier, the longer, the more frequently, and the more intensely people participate in such social settings, the greater is the probability of their becoming delinquent.

An important corollary of this theory is that a person's attitude toward himself is determined by the evidence of support or opposition he sees in the responses of others toward him. If he receives praise, he comes to think of himself in the same light. When praise is associated with violations of society's codes and laws, the individual may accept nonconformity as a pathway of the favorable appraisals of others. The reverse, of course, is also true.

Other modern theories place emphasis on the concepts of "cultural disorganization" and "delinquent subcultures." Culture in this context refers to the system of goals and values that guide the conduct of a society's members. Cultural disorganization occurs when goals are contradictory and values conflicting. The term subculture describes a group that strongly endorses values and goals at odds with those of the dominant culture; a delinquent subculture is a system of values, beliefs, and practices that encourages participation in law violation and awards status on the basis of such participation.

Perhaps the development of these concepts most pertinent to reintegration as a mode of correctional treatment is that of Cloward and Ohlin[23] which built on work by Cohen[24] and others. It asserts that much delinquency is the result of inability to gain access to legitimate opportunities in our society, coupled with availability of illegitimate opportunities that are seized as alternatives by frustrated persons. Corrective action therefore should seek to increase the opportunities of the offender to succeed in law-abiding activities, while reducing his contacts with the criminal world.

Such theories have been formulated mainly in the context of crime by slum dwellers, particularly the young. The experiments and data on which they are based have most concerned this group, and their concentration on economic and social deprivation as the causative background of crime and delinquency reflects this perspective. But in fact these theories are not so exclusive in their implications. They can, for example, be applied to the many instances of middle-class and suburban delinquency in which school failure, family problems, and even the lack of exciting and challenging legitimate opportunities for use of leisure time are precipitating factors.

Nor do they deny that psychological causes operate in many criminal cases, particularly because the social and family disturbances on which they concentrate are also recognized today as important in psychological disturbance. Admittedly, however, further research and experimentation are necessary to develop these theories of social effect to the point where they can be of specific help in correctional treatment of particular offender types.

The Legal Status of Convicted Persons

A variety of rights and privileges are traditionally lost upon conviction of a crime. While before conviction the Government must justify every assertion of authority, after conviction such assertions stand on a different footing. An offender threatened with discipline for misconduct is not provided with the elaborate procedural protections which surround the defendant in a criminal trial. And virtually all of an offender's activities may be subject to regulation by correctional officials, particularly in institutions. He has no absolute right to see friends or relatives or to do any of a multitude of things that the rest of society takes for granted. Moreover, a criminal conviction ordinarily affects the offender's legal status not only during the period of his sentence but for the rest of his life. A felony conviction commonly results, for example, in permanent loss of the right to vote and ineligibility for certain professions and businesses.

A substantial portion of our population is affected by the law in this area. Approximately 1.3 million people are at any one time subject to correctional authority; untold millions have criminal records. There is increasing doubt as to the propriety of treating this large group of persons as, in varying degrees, outcasts from society. And there is increasing recognition that such treatment is not in the ultimate interests of society. Denying offenders any chance to challenge arbitrary assertions of power by correctional officials, and barring them from legitimate opportunities such as employment, are inconsistent with the correctional goal of rehabilitation, which emphasizes the need to instill respect for and willingness to cooperate with society and to help the offender assume the role of a normal citizen.

This chapter does not discuss problems regarding the rights of juvenile offenders as distinguished from adult offenders. While much of what is said in this chapter is, in principle, applicable to the juvenile area, there are significant differences in the two legal systems

From the President's Commission on Law Enforcement and Administration of Justice, *Task Force Report: Corrections* (Washington: U.S. Government Printing Office, 1967) Appendix A, pp. 7–8, 10–11, 82–92.

as they operate today. The juvenile correctional system is, for example, simpler: There is no legislation comparable to the elaborate sentencing, good time, and parole eligibility provisions in the adult area. And juvenile records do not result in nearly so many disabilities and disqualifications as do criminal convictions.

LEGAL NORMS AND THE CORRECTIONAL SYSTEM

Correctional officials have always had enormous power over the lives of imprisoned offenders. But . . . the present range of discretion following conviction is to a great extent the result of developments in penology which emphasize differential treatment and rehabilitation. Formerly conviction of crime led quite automatically to a set penalty. But emphasis on the individual offender and his potential for rehabilitation produced sentencing legislation which allowed judges and correctional authorities to take into account individual characteristics in determining sentence. The new penology has led also to the development of a whole variety of correctional programs. Instead of a simple choice between freedom and imprisonment, sentencing judges and correctional decision-makers in a number of jurisdictions are now faced with a large range of possibilities—maximum versus minimum security institutions, a variety of rehabilitative programs, work-release furloughs, probation, and parole, to name but a few. In addition, decisions as to both length of imprisonment and kind of correctional treatment have increasingly been relegated to correctional authorities. They are thought to be more qualified than the sentencing judge to make judgments about how to treat individual offenders, because of their training and experience and because they are in a position to observe offenders following conviction.

Sentencing, the major correctional decision, is itself generally in need of reforms to regularize it and minimize the chance for unfairness. Chapter 5 of the General Report and Chapter 2 of the Task Force report on courts discuss various methods of guiding and controlling sentencing discretion—improved legislative guidelines, appellate review, and sentencing councils.

There is a similar need to develop means for guiding and controlling the numerous important decisions which must be made following the imposition of sentence: decisions by correctional authorities regarding the treatment of offenders during imprisonment, the date and conditions of release from imprisonment, and the revocation of parole; and decisions by judges regarding the revocation of probation or a suspended sentence.[25]

Legislation ordinarily provides little guidance for these correctional decisions. Correctional administrators have been slow to develop policies and procedures to guide correctional officials and protect the rights of offenders. And trial and appellate courts have been reluctant to review either the merits of such decisions or the procedures by which they are made.

Yet it is inconsistent with our whole system of government to grant such uncontrolled power to any officials, particularly over the lives of persons. The fact that a person has been convicted of a crime should not mean that he has forfeited all rights to demand that he be fairly treated by officials.

A first tenet of our governmental, religious, and ethical tradition is the intrinsic worth of every individual no matter how degenerate. It is a radical departure from that tradition to accept for a defined class of persons, even criminals, a regime in which their right to liberty is determined by officials wholly unaccountable in the exercise of their power and through processes which deprive them of an opportunity to be heard on the matters of fact and policy which are relevant to the decisions made.[26]

There are increasing signs that the courts are ready to abandon their traditional hands-off attitude. They have so far been particularly concerned with the procedures by which parole and probation are revoked. But recent cases suggest that the whole correctional area will be increasingly subject to judicial supervision. The real question is what form this supervision will take. There is some danger that in the absence of legislative and administrative action, the courts will impose inflexible and unrealistic requirements on corrections. Chapter 2 of the Task Force volume on the police discusses the need for and advantages of administrative policymaking in a comparable area—that of police practices. It is important that correctional administrators, who are most knowledgeable about the problems involved, develop policies and procedures which will accommodate the needs of the system as well as the interests of convicted offenders. The more adequate such internal controls are, the less it will be necessary for courts to intervene to define necessary procedures or to review the merits of correctional decisions. This need has been recognized by many in the correctional field and in a number of jurisdictions substantial progress has been made.

But there continues to be strong resistance to the introduction of increased legal controls in the correctional area. Legal controls are often said to be inappropriate because the decisions to be made in this area are professional and diagnostic in character. But expert judgments in the field of corrections are no less fallible than judgments by labor boards or other administrative agencies. There is some concern that introduction of increased legal controls will unduly limit flexibility and experimentation. It has for example been argued that correctional authorities will be more reluctant to release an offender on parole if they know that he cannot be returned to the institution without some kind of inquiry into the justification for his return. But there is no evidence that this has happened in jurisdictions which have expanded the safeguards surrounding parole revocation. And, while these may be valid arguments against infusion of the full requirements of judicial due process into the correctional system, they do not justify complete exemption of the system from legal norms.

> * * * [T]he common demand twenty-five years ago for freedom of the administrator to get on with his job free of the harassment of legal imperatives is the same demand made today by those who administer the new penology. A beginning in the correctional area awaits a general recognition that the correctional agency is not sui generis, but another administrative agency which requires its own administrative law if it is to make its maximum contributions harmoniously with the values of the general social order in which it functions.[27]

There is some danger that if prisoners are conceded certain legal rights they will devote their energies to fighting legal battles, rather than accepting the correctional regimen and devoting themselves to more productive activities, and that, therefore, rehabilitation will be impeded. But the fact that rehabilitation may be one aim of correctional treatment does not remove the need for legal controls. Justice Brandeis warned that "Experience should teach us to be most on our guard to protect liberty when the Government's purposes are beneficent."[28] There is increasing recognition today of the need for legal controls in mental commitments and juvenile court proceedings,[29] despite the fact that the government's primary purpose in such proceedings is assumed to be benevolent.

In any event, it is clear that the purposes of correctional treatment are not limited to rehabilitation. Correctional decision-makers are, for example, concerned with maintaining orderly institutions, restraining dangerous offenders, and, at times, issues of deterrence. Moreover, a system which recognizes that offenders have certain rights is not inconsistent with the goal of rehabilitation. A person who receives what he considers unfair treatment from correctional authorities is likely to become a difficult subject for reformation. And the "collaborative regime" advocated in this volume is one which seeks to maximize the participation of the offender in decisions which concern him, one which seeks to encourage self-respect and independence in preparing offenders for life in the community. It is inconsistent with these goals to treat offenders as if they have no rights, and are subject to the absolute authority of correctional officials.

Some correctional authorities believe that legal controls will make it difficult to maintain security within institutions and to protect the community against dangerous offenders. There is concern, for example, that expanding offenders' rights upon parole revocation will prevent parole boards from removing from the community offenders they consider dangerous but against whom they have no proof of parole violation. The same problem arises throughout the criminal justice system—legal safeguards such as counsel at trial make it more difficult to convict the guilty as well as the innocent. A balance must be struck in the correctional area as elsewhere between protection of the community and fairness towards the individual accused.

An obvious danger in conceding some legal rights to convicted offenders is that courts, as well as correctional authorities, will be flooded with frivolous claims by prisoners who have little better to do with their time. This is no doubt a major reason why courts have for so long treated claims regarding correctional treatment as beyond their jurisdiction. But with respect to similar problems raised by the availability of habeas corpus to challenge the validity of conviction, Chapter 4 of the Administration of Justice Task Force volume points out that there are ways of discouraging frivolous claims, or at least disposing of them quickly, which do not silence offenders with legitimate claims. For example, provision for legal assistance in prisons, discussed in more detail below, would help courts to distinguish between frivolous cases and cases deserving serious consideration. Fuller administrative review would dispose of many cases. The standard of judicial review in most matters would be such as to avoid detailed inquiries or concern for minor grievances.

It is not easy, however, to determine what legal rights offenders should have. The fact of conviction justifies treating the offender, at least for the period of his sentence, differently from the average citizen. The deprivation of a certain measure of right seems a necessary concommitant, and perhaps a desirable instrument, of correctional treatment. Correctional officials must be able to make some decisions quickly. And there are serious practical problems with introducing too many legal controls into the correctional process. Their cost in money and in the time already overburdened defense counsel and correctional personnel would be great. Given scarce resources throughout the criminal justice system, it is obvious that some priorities must be established.

What is needed is to provide offenders under correctional authority certain protections against arbitrary action, not to create for all correctional decisionmaking a mirror image of trial procedures. What sorts of protections are proper will depend upon the importance of the decision. For some kinds of decisions, such as decisions to revoke probation or parole, offenders should be accorded the basic elements of due process, such as notice, representation by counsel, and opportunity to present evidence and to confront and cross-examine opposing witnesses. For other less important decisions it might be enough simply to allow offenders a decent opportunity to hear the basis of an official's proposed decision and to present any relevant opposing facts and arguments.

For certain decisions, providing offenders with legal assistance might be appropriate. But for many decisions, representation by a member of the correctional staff or a nonlawyer might be adequate. Hearings and representation are one way to ensure careful decisionmaking. But for many decisions it may be enough simply to provide for detailed administrative review.

It is too early to attempt to define absolute standards in this area but it is of utmost importance that a beginning be made in considering and experimenting with a variety of methods of safeguarding the rights of offenders.

Imprisonment

Enormous discretion is left to correctional administrators to define the conditions of imprisonment. They determine the way in which the offender will live for the term of imprisonment; how he is fed and clothed; whether he sleeps in a cell or a dormitory; whether he spends his days locked up or in relative freedom; what opportunity he has for work, education, or recreation. They regulate his access to the outside world by defining mailing and visiting privileges. They define rules of conduct and the penalties for violation of such rules. And, increasingly, they make classification decisions—assigning different prisoners to different kinds of correctional programs. This may involve decisions to place prisoners in different institutions or to grant certain prisoners relative freedom in the community, as for example on educational or work-release programs.

Traditionally, few external controls have been imposed on correctional decisions in this area. Present legislation may set certain outside limits. It may, for example, prohibit corporal punishment and define the sorts of institutions and programs to which prisoners can be assigned. But it does not generally provide guidelines for the exercise of the vast discretion which remains, or indicate the procedures by which important decisions should be made. And courts have traditionally denied prisoners' claims on the ground that questions involving treatment during imprisonment are beyond their jurisdiction to consider.

But in recent years courts have been much more ready to intervene.[30] They have been more willing to consider on the merits claims that prison authorities have denied prisoners decent medical care, or have imposed cruel and unusual punishment, or have violated prisoners' First Amendment rights. In addition courts have taken steps to ensure that prisoners have some means of enforcing their legal rights. Thus the writ of habeas corpus has been made increasingly available to those with legitimate grievances against correctional treatment. And the Supreme Court recently broke with tradition to hold that federal prisoners could sue under the Federal Tort Claims Act for injuries caused by the negligence of prison officials.[31]

Courts have also begun to show some concern with practical limits imposed by correctional authorities on prisoners' rights of access to the courts. It has been held that prisoners cannot be disciplined for filing suit against prison officials[32] or for making allegedly false statements in court petitions before the merits of the petitions are decided by the courts.[33] Courts have been increasingly solicitous of prisoners' rights of access to legal advice[34] and material.[35]

But there are practical limits on the extent to which the courts alone can guarantee fair treatment during imprisonment. If, for example, a prisoner is denied the opportunity to prepare legal papers or to send papers to the court, he has no way to raise the problem of access in the court. One solution would be for defender organizations to establish prison legal aid programs. In the last few years such programs have been established at Leavenworth, Lewisburg, and a number of other prisons, by law schools and defender organizations, working in cooperation with correctional authorities. These can serve a number of important functions in addition to guaranteeing access to the courts. They can provide increased visibility for a system that has generally been too isolated, helping to mobilize public opinion and bring political pressure to bear where needed for reform. The mere presence of outsiders would serve to discourage illegal, unfair, or inhumane practices. The potential dangers of leaving the correctional system entirely isolated from the outside world are illustrated by the recent investigation of conditions in the Arkansas prison system, which included widespread corruption and physical abuse. Such programs can, moreover, help indigent inmates with meritorious claims present those claims to correctional authorities as well as to courts, and could be instrumental in helping develop better protective procedures within corrections. There are of course dangers that lawyers will view their role in this area in an unduly narrow and restrictive fashion. Similar problems are raised in expanding the right to counsel in the juvenile justice system, and are discussed in some detail in the Task Force report on juvenile delinquency and youth crime. There is a need to train and educate criminal lawyers in skills other than those suited for trial litigation, and to expand traditional notions of the lawyer's role.

Many of the functions that would be served by introducing lawyers into the correctional process could also be served by nonlawyers. If, for example, a jurisdiction decided to establish some sort of ombudsman to deal generally with problems involving abuse by government officials, it would be appropriate for this official to assume some responsibility for safeguarding the rights of prisoners.

The legal controls needed will depend on the kinds of decisions being made and the importance of the matters at issue. Correctional authorities should, for example, remain free to make most treatment and management decisions without elaborate procedural formality. Decisions as to what employment or educational program a prisoner is assigned to would not ordinarily seem appropriate subjects for extended administrative process, let alone court contests. But some safeguards should be provided to ensure that such decisions are not made arbitrarily. And where such decisions have major impact upon the prisoner's freedom, and turn on adjudicable facts, the offender should be given an opportunity to present facts and arguments relevant to the decisions. Thus, a decision to transfer a prisoner from a halfway house to a high security institution or to expel him from a work-release program, on the grounds of alleged misconduct, should not be made without informing him of the misconduct of which he is accused and allowing him a reasonable opportunity to explain his side of the story.

Haircuts, clothing, personal belongings, reading matter and many minor details of daily routine are in some institutions the subject of official regulations. . . . [T]hese regulations may in many cases be unnecessary or unwise from a correctional standpoint. But it appears that such minor matters should ordinarily remain within the discretion of correctional authorities.

There has so far been little consideration of the procedures appropriate for different kinds of correctional decisions. Correctional administrators should assume responsibility for experimenting in this area, and developing procedures which will accommodate the interests both of prisoners and of the correctional system. Similarly, they should develop guidelines defining prisoners' rights with respect to such issues as access to legal materials, correspondence, visitors, religious practice, medical care, and disciplinary sanctions. Many correctional systems have taken important steps in this direction, but there is a long way to go.

Such action on the part of correctional administrators will enable the courts to act in a reviewing rather than a directly supervisory capacity. Where administrative procedures are adequate, courts are not likely to intervene in the merits of correctional decisions. And where well thought-out policies regarding prisoners' procedural and substantive rights have been established, courts are likely to defer to administrative expertise.

324

Early Release and Conditional Freedom

Probably the most important correctional decisions which are made subsequent to the judge's initial sentencing decision are those governing the release of imprisoned offenders and, conversely, the imprisonment of offenders previously granted conditional freedom.

Date of Release From Imprisonment. Ordinarily, broad power is vested in correctional authorities to determine the length of an offender's term of imprisonment. He generally becomes eligible for parole when some fraction of his maximum term is served—one-third or one-half—or at the end of the minimum, sometimes less good time. In some jurisdictions he may become eligible as soon as he begins to serve his term. In addition, "good time" laws generally provide for the reduction of an offender's term of imprisonment for good behavior.

Legislation usually provides for some type of hearing when parole eligibility is established, but does not further define the prisoner's rights. Parole boards tend to rely primarily on presentence and institutional reports, and parole investigations. They usually give prisoners what can best be described as an interview. Thus prisoners rarely are represented by counsel. No right to appointed counsel is generally recognized; and many parole boards refuse to allow representation by retained counsel either in preparation for the hearing or at the hearing itself.[36]

Claims that parole was wrongfully denied have been uniformly rejected by the courts. Even those courts that have insisted upon procedural safeguards on parole revocation, are reluctant to extend them to the parole granting decision. Courts are even more reluctant to review the merits of such decisions.

The usual answer to all claims regarding release on parole is that parole, like probation, is "an act of grace and clemency," a matter of "privilege" not of "right"— terminology inherited from the era of executive clemency. Probation and parole were originally designated, like executive clemency, to ameliorate the harshness and rigidity of the early criminal law. But today judges and parole boards are expected to exercise their discretion to determine the proper sentence based upon the characteristics of the individual offender— the legal maximum is not considered the norm. Parole and probation should not be considered any more a matter of grace than any sentence which is less than the maximum provided for by statute.

Parole legislation involves essentially a delegation of sentencing power to the parole board. The parole decision involves many of the same kinds of factors that are involved in the original sentencing decision. An offender who is eligible for parole[37] should therefore be provided with safeguards similar to those recommended by the Commission for the defendant who is being sentenced. He should, for example, have an opportunity to present to the board facts and arguments regarding his behavior during imprisonment and his readiness to return to the community, as well as an opportunity to challenge any opposing position taken by correctional authorities.

And there seems no legitimate reason for limiting representation by retained counsel at parole hearings.[38] The role that counsel can play in presenting relevant facts and in preparing plans for release into the community has been recognized at sentencing hearings. Counsel could serve essentially similar functions in parole hearings. Providing indigent offenders with free legal representation would, however, involve a significant additional burden on available legal resources. By contrast, representation at the original sentencing hearing adds only slightly to the obligations of a lawyer who has represented a defendant throughout the trial. The establishment of legal aid services in prisons, discussed above, and enlisting of the help of nonlawyers, might provide an answer.

It will often be of great importance to the offender being considered for parole that he have access to the data on which the parole board will base its decision. The issues involved are directly analogous to those involved in determining the defendant's right to disclosure of the presentence report, and rules similar to those advocated by the Commission in that area should govern. In the absence of compelling reasons for nondisclosure of specific information, the defendant and his lawyer should be permitted access to all such information.[39]

Some record of the proceedings and the reasons for the board's devision should be made so that, where a denial of parole is challenged in court, meaningful review is possible. Courts would presumably be concerned primarily with the adequacy of parole board procedures; experience with appellate review of sentencing decisions indicates that even if courts assumed the power to review parole decisions on the merits, reversals on the ground of an abuse of discretion would be rare.

Decisions regarding the withholding or forfeiture of good time credit generally differ from the parole decision in that they turn solely on the offender's behavior during his period of imprisonment: Good behavior entitles him to early release regardless of anyone's judgment as to his potential for living a law-abiding life in the community. He should therefore have an opportunity to challenge charges of misconduct. Where such charges may lead to a substantial loss of good time and a resultant increase in the actual length of imprisonment,[40] the prisoner should be given reasonable notice of the charges, full opportunity to present evidence and to confront and cross-examine opposing witnesses, and the right to representation by counsel.

Parole Conditions. When offenders are released on parole, parole boards have the power to define the conditions of their release.... [N]umerous restrictions on liberty may be imposed: The offender may, for example, be required to meet with his officer at regular intervals, pursue some program of treatment, avoid certain companions, obtain permission before marrying, or make restitution to a victim.

Legislation gives almost no guidance to the sorts of conditions which should be imposed on parole, and correctional authorities again have done little to work out guidelines in this area. The traditional judicial answer to almost all claims that conditions placed on liberty are illegal has been that the alternative of imprisonment was more onerous and therefore the offender has no legitimate complaint; ordinarily this is joined with the argument that the offender was free to choose imprisonment, but instead consented to the imposition of the conditions.

But if parole is the appropriate disposition the fact that the conditions may be less onerous than imprisonment is irrelevant in determining whether those conditions are proper. Some conditions may be too burdensome or too unrelated to the rehabilitation of the offender or the protection of the community to be justified in the particular case. Conditions may violate other important values of our system without serving any necessary correctional purpose. They may, for example, interfere with freedoms of speech, press and religion, protected by the First Amendment. And conditions may be so vague that the parolee is not adequately warned of the kind of conduct which will justify revocation.

Courts are beginning to assume some responsibility in this area by striking down conditions that are too vague and indefinite, and insisting that rules be reasonable and not against public policy. It is essential that parole boards act to develop adequate policies. They should, for example, ... make sure that conditions are simple and clear, that they are put in writing, and that they are understood by the offender.

Revocation.   Judicial concern for fair procedure in the correctional process has focused primarily upon revocation of probation (or a suspended sentence) and parole. A survey of the reported decisions reveals that there are about as many cases dealing with some aspect of revocation as there are dealing with all other aspects of the correctional process. And there has been a marked increase in the last few years in the volume and variety of issues being presented for decision. Some courts, interpreting statutory guarantees of a revocation hearing, have held that the defendant has a right to be represented by retained counsel, to present evidence, and to hear and controvert the evidence against him.... [T]he Supreme Court has recently accepted two cases involving the right to counsel on probation revocation.[41]

There is an enormous variety of legislation in this area, ranging from express authorization of revocation without a hearing to express guarantees of a hearing. In general legislation is vague and ambiguous in the extreme. Where hearings are required, statutes ordinarily do not elaborate on what the bare right to a hearing entails.[42]

In most jurisdictions offenders threatened with revocation are in fact provided with only minimal procedural safeguards. This is particularly true on parole revocation. About half the states grant hearings as a matter of grace rather than regarding them as an obligation of the parole board. Some states have no hearings at all. Generally, where hearings are held they occur sometime after a parolee's freedom has been terminated and he has been returned to prison for an alleged violation. Hearings are often perfunctory. Almost nowhere does the parolee have a right to appointed counsel. In many places he does not even have the right to be represented by retained counsel at the hearing. Indeed only half of the states responding to a recent survey indicated that the parolee could retain counsel if he chose. In a few jurisdictions the charges are not made known to the parolee until the actual hearing. Parole revocation hearings "are usually limited to an appearance by the parolee before the board at which time he may explain, admit, or deny the charges. Witnesses against the parolee rarely appear before the board, even if the facts are disputed by the parolee. Instead, the board relies on reports submitted by the parole authorities. The reports are generally kept confidential."[43]

Probation revocations are generally characterized by more procedural formalities, presumably because they are conducted by courts rather than parole boards.[44] The trial court has the power to order witnesses produced, and witnesses generally are produced if the facts are disputed by the probationer. But in some jurisdictions the probationer has no right to confront and cross-examine opposing witnesses or to present evidence. In most cases probation revocation is based on a prerevocation report, perhaps in conjunction with informal testimony by the probation officer. Only about one-third of the jurisdictions responding to a recent survey indicated that the report was made available to the probationer or his counsel on request. Although almost all jurisdictions permit probationers to be represented by retained counsel, only about half of the jurisdictions reporting to the survey indicated that the court would assign counsel for indigents.[45]

Claims to greater procedural safeguards are again met with the traditional grace argument. But even if it were conceded that the grant of conditional freedom was a matter of grace it does not follow that that freedom can be arbitrarily withdrawn. A related argument is the freedom was granted, and accepted, on the condition that it might be summarily revoked. But this simply avoids the essential question as to whether such a condition would be appropriate.

It is also argued that revocation of parole requires no elaborate procedural safeguards because the parolee "is legally in custody the same as the prisoner allowed the liberty of the prison yard, or of working on the prison farm. The realm in which he serves has been extended."[46] But, as discussed in the previous section, the fact that an offender is legally in custody does not mean that decisions to transfer him from, for example, a low security institution to a high security institution should be free from all procedural safeguards.

Moreover, there are vital differences between probation or parole and prison custody, including custody in a halfway house or prerelease guidance center. These differences justify requiring more

elaborate procedural safeguards for revocation than for any trans-
ferrals during the term of imprisonment. In the first place the conditions of probation or parole seldom involve restrictions on freedom
that are at all comparable to the restrictions imposed during a term
of imprisonment. The trend is, of course, for the distinction to be
less sharp. And in the future it may be usual to allow offenders
relative freedom in the community before the end of their term of
commitment, or to require as a condition of parole that an offender
reside in an institution comparable to a halfway house. But in any
event there is an enormous difference today in the degree of freedom
accorded prisoners as against persons on probation or parole.

And there are differences beyond the actual restraints on liberty.
The offender whose sentence is suspended, or who is placed on
parole or probation, is given a guarantee by law that unless he
violates certain defined conditions he will not be placed under more
severe restrictions. Correctional authorities are not authorized to
imprison him solely because they have reason to believe prison
would be more appropriate correctional treatment; they can intervene only if he violates the conditions of his release. Prisoners who
are assigned to some particularly desirable program or institution
are given no such guarantee—they may be returned to regular
custody if they are not adjusting, or if for some other reason it is
considered appropriate. In addition, a probationer or parolee, or a
person whose sentence is suspended, ordinarily has no right to credit
for "street time," but upon revocation may be imprisoned for whatever part of his full sentence he has not served.[47] For these purposes
he is not considered to be in custody. Revocation, therefore, may
mean an increase in the total period during which he is subject to
correctional authority. In a very practical sense, therefore, the decision is not comparable to, for example, a decision to transfer an
offender from a low-security institution to a regular prison. Thus if
an offender with four years of his original sentence remaining, serves
three years in such an institution, he would have only one year to
serve if transferred. If, however, he spent those three years on parole,
he might have the full four years to serve upon revocation.

The offender threatened with revocation should therefore be
entitled to a hearing comparable to the nature and importance of
the issue being decided. Where there is some dispute as to whether
he violated the conditions of his release, the hearing should contain
the basic elements of due process—those elements which are designed

to ensure accurate factfinding. It may not be appropriate to require the heavy burden of proof required for criminal conviction, or to provide for jury trials. But the hearing should include such essential rights as reasonable notice of the charges, the right to present evidence and witnesses, the right to representation by counsel—including the right to appointed counsel[48]—and the right to confront and cross-examine opposing witnesses. Parole boards should have the power to issue subpoenas; and subpoenas should be issued by boards and courts upon a satisfactory showing of need.

Where the basic facts as to the alleged misconduct are undisputed, a decision must still be made regarding disposition. This, like the parole granting decision, ordinarily deserves the kinds of safeguards which the Commission recommends for the sentencing decision.

Of course, the procedures required might vary according to such questions as whether the offender receives credit for street time, or how long a term of imprisonment he is subject to upon revocation.

❀ ❀ ❀

It is not possible at this time to establish definitely what rights offenders should have while they are under correctional authority. This is an essentially uncharted area—little consideration has been given to the issues involved. But this does not justify deferring action. Moreover, there is unprecedented opportunity in this area for experimentation and flexibility. Compared for example, to the police, the correctional system is relatively free from restrictions imposed by constitutional provisions and court rulings. Legislatures and, especially, correctional administrators must begin now to explore the area—to define offenders' rights and to establish procedures which will protect those rights.

COLLATERAL CONSEQUENCES OF A CRIMINAL CONVICTION

Convicted persons are subjected to numerous disabilities and disqualifications quite apart from the sanction imposed in their sentence, and though their sentence may eventually be served, these may never be removed. The inhumanity and irrationality of much

331

of the law in this area has received severe criticism from those who have considered it, but reform has been slow.[49]

Persons convicted of felonies and certain serious misdemeanors have traditionally lost a number of "civil rights"—rights possessed by most citizens, such as the right to vote and hold public office, to serve as a juror, or testify in court. In addition a convicted person may be prohibited from participating in numerous activities regulated by the government for the protection of society. He may, for example, be barred from obtaining professional, occupational, and business licenses and from certain kinds of employment.

Rights may be suspended for some period of time such as the period of imprisonment or of sentence, or they may be forfeited permanently. Most states have some procedure for the restoration of rights which have been forfeited. Generally restoration statutes have the effect of restoring only certain rights, namely the "civil rights," but they may also remove legal barriers to the restoration of licenses and such, enabling the respective regulating agencies to act as they see fit.

The loss and restoration of rights raise confusing jurisdictional problems. Each jurisdiction generally determines the extent to which convicted persons can exercise various rights and privileges in that jurisdiction, relying as it sees fit on convictions in other jurisdictions. One jurisdiction may remove disabilities and disqualifications result- ing from convictions in other jurisdictions through its own pro- cedures. It may on the other hand demand that the convicted person obtain a restoration certificate or pardon in the convicting jurisdic- tion.

The problem with much of present-day law in this area is not inherent in the concept of imposing various disabilities and disquali- fications as consequences of a conviction of crime, but rather results from the misuse of that concept. Many deprivations during imprison- ment can be justified on the grounds of administrative convenience or on the grounds that they are appropriate to punitive aims of im- prisonment—thus rights to hold public office or to serve as a juror or to carry on one's business, may properly be considered incom- patible with the purpose and nature of imprisonment. Further, it is clear that certain deprivations may be useful as independent sanc- tions for criminal behavior. Thus suspending or revoking a driver's license for a conviction involving dangerous driving might be a far more appropriate sanction than a fine or term of imprisonment. It is likely to be a highly effective deterrent. It protects society from the particular kind of danger this persons poses, thus providing almost as effective incapacitation as imprisonment without its costs or harmful side effects.

But little of the present law in this area can be so justified. As a general matter it has simply not been rationally designed to accommodate the varied interests of society and the individual convicted person. There has been little effort to evaluate the whole system of disabilities and disqualifications that has grown up. Little consideration has been given to the need for particular deprivations in particular cases. It is quite common to provide for the blanket loss or suspension of "civil rights" or "civil liberties." And even where rights or privileges are dealt with specifically, it is common to provide that conviction of any felony, or any misdemeanor involving moral turpitude, justifies forfeiture. As a result, convicted persons are generally subjected to numerous disabilities and disqualifications which have little relation to the crime committed, the person committing it or, consequently, the protection of society. They are often harsh out of all proportion to the crime committed. And by cutting the offender off from society, including, perhaps, his chosen occupation, they may impede efforts at rehabilitation.

The law in this area is inordinately complex and confusing. The relevant statutes are hard to locate, even within one jurisdiction. Enacted for various reasons at various times, they are spread throughout the legislative code. Statutes providing for the blanket loss or suspension of civil rights produce great uncertainty as to exactly what rights are lost and for what period of time. Similarly, where provision is made for the restoration of rights, it is often unclear what rights are restored and what disabilities and disqualifications remain.

The legal situation, confusing even to the trained lawyer, is generally quite beyond the understanding of the convicted offender who ordinarily is not advised as to the disabilities and disqualifications accompanying his conviction, nor as to any procedures which may be available for their removal. Such complexity and confusion would seem to detract from whatever deterrent function disabilities might serve. Similarly, restoration procedures cannot accomplish their purpose if convicted offenders are unaware of their availability.

There is a general need to clarify legislation so that offenders are adequately informed of rights lost and of restoration procedures available. But it is of even more basic importance to reevaluate all disabilities and disqualifications to design a system more responsive to the various interests of society as a whole, including the interests of convicted persons themselves. To do this it is necessary to consider each right or privilege individually to determine whether its forfeiture would be appropriate as a deterrent or means of protecting society, and if so what particular crimes should call for forfeiture, and for what period of time. Where practical, cases should be considered individually to determine whether the various applicable disabilities and disqualifications are necessary and appropriate.

Section 306.1[1] of the American Law Institute's Model Penal Code is an example of legislation that would insure that careful consideration be given to the need for particular disqualifications and disabilities:

> No person shall suffer any legal disqualification or disability because of his conviction of a crime or his sentence on such conviction, unless the disqualification or disability involves the deprivation of a right or privilege which is:
> (a) necessarily incident to execution of the sentence of the Court; or
> (b) provided by the Constitution or the Code; or
> (c) provided by a statute other than the Code, when the conviction is of a crime defined by such statute; or
> (d) provided by the judgment, order or regulation of a court, agency or official exercising a jurisdiction conferred by law, or by the statute defining such jurisdiction, when the commission of the crime or the conviction or the stentence is reasonably related to the competency of the individual to exercise the right or privilege of which he is deprived.

Civil Rights

To a large extent the law in this area represents an archaic holdover from the past. At common law, conviction of a felony generally meant death and forfeiture of property. In the United States early statutes provided for "civil death" where the sentence was for death or life imprisonment. Present laws regarding the loss of civil rights, inherited from this era, are simply not appropriate today, when the death penalty is nearly extinct and most offenders given life sentences are eventually released. Similarly, many laws suspending civil rights during sentence date from times when sentence for a period of years meant imprisonment for that full term; the result today is that persons released on probation or parole are subjected to deprivations appropriate only for prisoners. Efforts to improve the situation have generally been piecemeal—elaborate procedures are established to restore rights which should have been removed either not at all or only temporarily.

To give a brief description of the law in this area is difficult because there is such variation between different jurisdictions, and often complexity and confusion within particular jurisdictions.[50] Most of the rights and privileges in this area derive from the states, and it is primarily state statutes and constitutions which provide for their deprivation. Federal law provides for the loss of certain rights such as the right to sit on a federal jury, the right to hold federal offices, and to hold union offices. The state statutes which provide for the blanket loss or suspension of "civil rights" are variously interpreted to include rights to sue; to contract; to transfer, devise or inherit property; to vote; to hold public office; to testify; and to serve as a juror.[51] States may, in addition, provide specifically for the loss of other rights. Many states have no such blanket statutes; each deprivation is specified. A few states provide that no civil rights are lost.

State statutes generally do not refer to specific convictions. Ordinarily any felony results in forfeiture; sometimes any misdemeanor involving moral turpitude has the same effect.

Forfeiture of rights may depend on whether conviction results in imprisonment, probation or suspension of sentence—even on whether it was the imposition or the execution of sentence that was suspended. Rights may be merely suspended until discharge from the period of imprisonment or supervision, or until satisfaction of the sentence, or for some other period of time. (This may be termed "automatic restoration.") Often, however, they are forfeited permanently unless restoration is obtained through some formal procedure.

Without attempting to be all-inclusive it is worth discussing some of the more significant disabilities in some detail.

Voting. There may be some justification for suspending the right to vote during imprisonment, on the grounds that prisoners as a class have an insufficient interest in the outcome of elections.[52] But there seems no justification for permenently depriving all convicted

335

felons of the vote, as the laws in most states provide. The convicted person may have no strong personal interest in voting, but to be deprived of the right to representation in a democratic society is an important symbol. Moreover, rehabilitation might be furthered by encouraging convicted persons to participate in society by exercising the vote.

Holding Public Office and Positions of Private Trust. Many states deprive convicted felons permanently of the right to hold public office, presumably appointive as well as elective. In some states, provision is merely made for forfeiture of offices held at the time of conviction or suspension of the right to hold office during some period such as the term of imprisonment.

Although certain offenses are clearly related to fitness to hold such positions, it is rarely necessary to provide for automatic disqualification in order to protect society. Instead, where there is someone with authority to appoint or remove, or where the public has such authority through its power to elect, it seems generally preferable to rely on their judgment. The relevance of particular convictions or terms of imprisonment to fitness for the particular position can then be considered.[53] It may however, be necessary to provide for forfeiture of elective office and any appointive office for a term, since there may be no other feasible means of removing an unfit officer.[54]

Jury Service. Suspension of the privilege of serving as a juror may be necessary during imprisonment. But there seems little justification for the laws which exist in a number of states permanently disqualifying all convicted felons from serving as jurors.[55] Reliance should instead be placed primarily on the powers given both parties to challenge jurors, since they and the judge are in a position to consider the relevance of a particular case. The legislature might prescribe certain convictions as grounds for challenges for cause; the judge could allow other convictions to constitute such grounds according to their relevance to the case. In addition, it might be appropriate for the legislature to provide for disqualification in certain cases at least for some period of years.

Testimonial Capacity. The right to testify is commonly suspended during imprisonment. In a few states, persons convicted of perjury are permanently disqualified from being a witness. Such

336

provisions often harm unnecessarily not only the convicted person but others interested in obtaining his testimony.

Certain limits on prisoners' ability to testify in court may be justified during imprisonment but provision should be made for prisoners to give testimony by deposition or in response to interrogatories; and where necessary in the interests of justice to appear in court.[56] No conviction should make a person incompetent to testify. Instead, any convictions particularly relevant to credibility should be admissible to impeach the witness, permitting the finder of fact to weigh the value of the testimony.

Property and Contract Rights; Right to Court Process.   In a few states, convicted felons may lose or have suspended during imprisonment, rights to contract and to take or transfer property. Similarly, the right to sue civilly may be lost or suspended during imprisonment.

Since such rights may be essential in order to live a normal life in the community, it is inconsistent with the correctional goal of rehabilitation to impose such restrictions on any persons not actually imprisoned. Moreover, while certain limitations on these rights may be necessary incidents of imprisonment, absolute suspension during imprisonment is inappropriate. Thus it may be proper to restrict prisoners' rights to conduct personal business from within prison or to appear in court to conduct law suits. But if the prisoner is allowed to retain his rights to possess property he should be allowed to inherit property. And rights to transfer property and to contract may be necessary to preserve assets and to support dependents.

Similarly, the right to sue may be necessary to protect assets against third parties and to attack illegal treatment by correctional officials. Allowing suit upon release by tolling the statute of limitations during imprisonment, as many jurisdictions do, is not an adequate substitute for granting the immediate right to sue. Irreparable damage may be done in the meanwhile; and proof may be made impossible by the passage of years. Suit would not necessitate absence from prison. Conduct of the suit could be put in the hands of an attorney; the prisoner's testimony, if needed, could be taken in prison.

Some jurisdictions provide for the appointment of a committee or trustee to manage the affairs of prisoners deprived variously of

337

rights to convey and transfer property, to contract, and to sue in court. But such legislation often is designed primarily to protect rights of creditors and dependents. There seems no reason not to permit the prisoner simply to act through his own agent, when it is impracticable for him to act directly.[57]

Rights to Participate in Activities Regulated by the State

Primarily because of the potential danger—actual or ostensible —to the public welfare posed by a number of private activities, state and local governments frequently limit participation in such activities to those considered qualified. Criminal convictions often result in disqualification either as a direct result of legislation, or because of action taken by a court or, more frequently, an administrative agency entrusted with regulation of the particular activity.

[In many places] private employment activities are [also] regulated in this way. . . . Numerous activities not necessarily involving employment are similarly regulated. Persons may be unable to drive a car, possess a gun, or fish without a license. . . . [T]here are legitimate uses of such disqualifications. Thus it seems appropriate to suspend or revoke licenses for offenses involving dangerous driving, both to remove the unfit driver from the road and to deter such behavior. But to ban convicted persons from numerous activities without regard to the particular conviction's relevance to the particular activity can be expected seriously to impede efforts to rehabilitate offenders by encouraging their participation in society, without any compensating benefit to society.

Most of the law in this area is overly broad. Thus, good character is often made a prerequisite for activities where it is of no particular relevance. It is, for example, a common requirement for obtaining a barber's license. Yet it is doubtful whether good character is of any more importance to exercise of one's duties as a barber than to most other occupations. And regulatory legislation generally makes no effort to define the kind of character, and thus the kind of convictions, relevant to fitness. Instead, where legislatures provide for automatic disqualification, all felonies and sometimes all serious misdemeanors are likely to result in such disqualification. Thus in several jurisdictions any felony will bar a person from the practice of

338

law or medicine. Similarly, where discretionary power is given to regulatory agencies to disqualify on the basis of criminal convictions, there is generally no attempt by the legislature to ensure that only those convictions relevant to fitness for the particular activity be considered. Thus, the California Business and Professions Code makes conviction of any felony or any offense involving moral turpitude grounds for disciplinary action in approximately 40 occupations and professions, including those of physical therapy, nursing, barbering, and guide dog training.[58] Often discretionary power is given to disqualify simply on the basis of lack of good moral character. Most convictions would reflect on one's character, and could thus constitute bars to qualification. Of course, an agency can exercise its discretion and refuse to disqualify on the basis of a conviction it considers irrelevant to fitness. But such general statutes do not invite discrimination among convictions, and the agency's decision to disqualify would be virtually unreviewable.

Most of the disabilities and disqualifications in this area result from the actions of various administrative agencies, rather than directly from the conviction. In the area of individual licenses, professional and occupational groups are often given the power to determine who is initially qualified to receive a license, and to regulate the standards of those licensed by defining rules of conduct and revoking or suspending licenses for breach of those rules.[59] Such groups tend to be primarily concerned with advancing the interests of their own members. Thus, when faced with the problem of whether to license persons with criminal records, they may be unduly concerned with the effect on the status of their professions. Further, to the extent they try to consider the public interest, they are likely to have an unrealistic view of the importance of their own profession or occupation and the potential harm to the public that might be done by unfit persons. They tend to give inadequate weight to the interests of the convicted person, and to those of society as a whole in having the contributions of this person and in not forcing him back into a life of crime.

The need for a thorough overhaul of licensing and regulatory restrictions on exoffenders has been noted . . . Criminal convictions should be considered only to the extent actually relevant to fitness to participate in activities posing particular dangers to society. The legislature might specify particular convictions as grounds for disqualification, leaving it to a court or agency to determine the merits of each case. The legislature might mandate disqualification on the basis of selected, particularly relevant convictions. But it would ordinarily be best to provide for discretion so that the relevance of particular convictions could be weighed in light of, for example, the period of time since the criminal offense, the behavior of the individual during that time, and the hardship that disqualification might cause.

The power of excluding offenders from certain activities could be given to the sentencing judge and the correctional system. They could be given the responsibility for deciding the extent to which disqualification is justified for the purposes of public protection and deterrence. This is frequently done today with respect to loss or suspension of drivers' licenses for driving offenses.

But where a licensing or other regulatory agency is entrusted with power to determine fitness to pursue a particular activity, that agency would ordinarily be the appropriate body to determine whether an offender should be disqualified. Wherever discretion is confided to a licensing agency, however, and particularly where that agency is associated with the occupation or interests it licenses, care must be taken to guard against the tendency to discriminate against offenders without rational basis that such bodies have commonly exhibited. This should be done by providing explicit legislative guidelines where possible and perhaps by requiring that the agency justify any license denial in terms of a specific danger in an individual case. But irrational discrimination against offenders by regulatory agencies may be inevitable, particularly where such agencies are quasi-private in nature.[60] It may therefore be necessary to provide some procedure whereby decisions regarding the qualification of offenders can be made by a court or an independent board. This is discussed in more detail in the following section.

Assuming that regulatory agencies are given the power to decide, within limits set by the legislature, on the qualifications required for participation in certain activities, there should be some procedure whereby they can obtain relevant information from correctional authorities. Such information would be valuable in deciding whether to license someone with a criminal record, or whether to suspend for some definite or indefinite period of time or to disqualify permanently someone previously licensed, or whether to reinstate someone whose license had been withdrawn.

Restoration of Rights

If rights are "permanently" forfeited, partial or total restoration will often be possible through a variety of procedures,[61] the most common of which is some form of clemency procedure, ordinarily gubernatorial pardon: since this power is generally designed primarily to remedy wrongful convictions and unduly harsh sentences, the result is an erratic and irrational pattern of restoration.[62] In a few states, offenders can apply for restoration to an administrative board or to the warden of their institution. Such procedures ordinarily have the effect only of restoring such civil rights as have been lost. They may, in addition, remove legislative barriers to participation in regulated activities. But where the power of disqualification has been vested in licensing or other agencies, pardons or restoration certificates ordinarily cannot erase the effects of convictions, although agencies will presumably consider their relevance along with that of convictions.

In general, restoration procedures are, for practical reasons, not very effective solutions to the disabilities problem. Offenders often lack the funds, knowledge, or ability to pursue such procedures. And those who have established themselves in a new life are understandably reluctant to request restoration since this usually involves an investigation with all the risks that the past will be brought to light again. Rights should therefore be removed only where there is clear justification and only for the period of time necessary, eliminating the need wherever possible for offenders to pursue formal restoration procedures.[63]

But some restoration procedures will probably nevertheless be necessary. Thus where the legislature considers it necessary for the protection of society to provide for the automatic loss or suspension of certain rights, there should ordinarily be some procedure whereby the offender can obtain relief from the legislative mandate. Such rights could be considered individually,[64] but where many rights are automatically lost by operation of law, the convicted person should probably be able to obtain a general certificate of rehabilitation or restoration. Such procedures may be necessary simply because the offender's rights in other jurisdictions may be unjustly restricted unless he is able to obtain such a certificate in the convicting jurisdiction.[65]

Some such procedure may also be necessary to restore rights to offenders disqualified by licensing or other regulatory agencies. Where authority is vested in such an agency to determine fitness to participate in a particular occupation, it would in general seem irrational to give to the court or another agency power to determine whether convicted offenders should or should not be disqualified.[66] But this may be the only practical way of dealing with the problem of discrimination against offenders by such agencies.

Some authorities have proposed establishment of an annulment procedure, whereby the offender's records would be expunged or sealed, and he would be entitled to say he had never been convicted, or, alternatively, private individuals and official agencies would be prohibited from asking about such convictions.[67] Somewhat the same dilemma is presented in this area. Logically, annulment procedures seem unnecessary to deal with problems of State-imposed disabilities and disqualifications. The convicting jurisdiction can accomplish the same result by simply not depriving the offender of the rights or by restoring them in some appropriate fashion. Actually to expunge records removes all discretion from those legitimately concerned with previous convictions. Thus, while it may not be justifiable to deprive convicted felons of the right to hold public office, those in the position of electing or appointing should presumably know of such convictions. And it would be nearly impossible to determine in one annulment procedure that particular convictions had no relevance for any future decision. In addition to these practical problems, some would question the propriety of government telling an offender that he has a right to deny a prior conviction, and of removing from private individuals or other jurisdictions the right to consider for themselves the relevance of a prior criminal record. But some annulment procedure may be necessary to deal with problems of irrational discrimination against past offenders by licensing agencies, private employers, and society generally.

nine

TOWARD PLURALISM: THE EMERGENCE OF DEVIANT MINORITIES

A central theme in this book—that the law and criminal justice system should not be used to enforce private morality—has come to be widely shared among those who study and deal with deviance and social problems. When we attempt to regulate private behavior, be it sex practices, drug use, alcohol, or gambling, we come very close to regulating life styles, the ways people are; and when we pass laws against certain ways of life, we create deviant minorities. As minorities they will tend toward the extremes of behavior that minority status brings: crime as a means of livelihood, retaliatory violence, mental disorder, disease, and suicide. When we penalize certain ways of life, we drive the practitioners of these ways to extremes.

There are now two parallel trends away from this repressive treatment of deviant minorities. One in government, particularly at the national level, in the direction of liberalizing laws regulating the deviant minorities. The reports in this volume are the products of this trend. The other trend is the "coming out" of deviant minorities. More and more the minorities we have talked about in this volume are coming out into the open, asserting their right to exist and to full citizenship.

On the government side of liberalization are the civil rights laws—the Supreme Court decisions on school desegregation (Brown v. Board of Education of Topeka), on the right of due process for juveniles (In re Gault), and on the right to read or view concededly "obscene" material in one's own home (Stanley v. Georgia)—and of course the numerous commissions whose central theme has been the need for tolerance of both ethnic and deviant minorities. The trend has been in the direction of legal protection for minorities, which perhaps is the first step toward pluralism, the state of mutual toleration and respect among minorities and in relation to the majority group.

The other trend may be seen in the development of civil rights, self-help, and solidarity organizations. The black community has been the paradigm for all the others, what with the NAACP and Urban League, followed by more activist protest organizations like SCLC and CORE, and finally the militant organizations like the Black Panthers and US. The young—especially the radical young—have developed similar militant organizations—SNCC, SDS, the Weathermen, the Yippies, and the like. Self-help organizations for the drug user in almost every metropolitan area have provided hot lines, free clinics, detoxification centers, crash pads, and runaway centers. Such organizations often try to help the offender avoid police bust, gain employment, and generally function in the society, rather than to "cure" the drug or other delinquency problem. Similarly, homophile organizations—the Mattachine Society, SIR, GULF, the Daughters of Bilitis—modelled in part after the black power movement, assert the right to be "gay," claim oppression from the police, and vie for constitutional rights and the right to maintain their way of life. The emergence of pornography is seen in the liberalization of censorship laws and regulations. Sexually explicit movies are coming out of backrooms and stag parties and into neighborhood theatres. Prostitution has been legalized in Nevada. Abortion has been legalized in Colorado, Hawaii, and New York. Off-track betting has been legalized in New York.

These emergences are beautifully described in the article by Becker and Horowitz that concludes this volume. The article describes the treatment of ethnic and deviant minorities in San Francisco, a city animated by a "culture of civility"—a low-key approach to deviance, a common attitude of tolerance not only of undigested ethnic minorities but also of deviant minorities that "create enclaves whose differences add to the pleasure of city life." When deviants live openly, the stereotypes we have break down and our tolerance of them increases. In exchange for this new freedom, the deviants refrain from extremes of violence, aggression and crime.

Deviance and Democracy in "The City"

The Culture of Civility

Deviants of many kinds live well in San Francisco—natives and tourists alike make that observation. The city's apparently casual and easygoing response to "sex, dope, and cheap thrills" (to crib the suppressed full title of Janis Joplin's famous album—itself a San Francisco product) astounds visitors from other parts of the country who can scarcely credit either what they see happening or the way natives stroll by those same events unconcerned.

> Walking in the Tenderloin on a summer evening, a block from the Hilton, you hear a black whore cursing at a policeman: "I wasn't either blocking the sidewalk! Why don't you motherfucking fuzz mind your own goddamn business!" The visiting New Yorker expects to see her arrested, if not shot, but the cop smiles goodnaturedly and moves on, having got her back into the doorway where she is supposed to be.
>
> You enter one of the famous rock ballrooms and, as you stand getting used to the noise and lights, someone puts a lit joint of marijuana in your hand. The tourist looks for someplace to hide, not wishing to be caught in the mass arrest he expects to follow. No need to worry. The police will not come in, knowing that if they do they will have to arrest people and create disorder.
>
> Candidates for the city's Board of Supervisors make their pitch for the homosexual vote, estimated by some at 90,000. They will not be run out of town; the candidates' remarks are dutifully reported in the daily paper, as are the evaluations of them by representatives of SIR, the Society for Individual Rights.

From Howard S. Becker and Irving Louis Horowitz, "The Culture of Civility," in *Transaction*, 7:6 (April 1970), pp. 12–19. Reprinted by permission of the authors.

The media report (tongue in cheek) the annual Halloween Drag Ball, for which hundreds of homosexuals turn out at one of the city's major hotels in full regalia, unharassed by police.

One sees long-haired, bearded hippies all over the city, not just in a few preserves set aside for them. Straight citizens do not remark their presence, either by gawking, hostility or flight.

Nudie movies, frank enough to satisfy anyone's curiosity, are exhibited in what must be the largest number of specialty movie houses per capita in the country. Periodic police attempts to close them down (one of the few occasions when repression has been attempted) fail.

The items can be multiplied indefinitely, and their multiplicity demands explanation. Most cities in the United States refuse to let deviants indulge themselves publicly, let alone tolerate candidates who seek their bloc votes. Quite the contrary. Other cities, New York and Chicago being good examples, would see events like these as signs of serious trouble, omens of a real breakdown in law enforcement and deviance control, the forerunner of saturnalia and barbarian take-over. Because its politicians and police allow and can live with activities that would freak out their opposite numbers elsewhere, San Francisco is a natural experiment in the consequences of tolerating deviance. We can see from its example what results when we ignore the warnings of the custodians of conventional morality. We can see too what lessons can be learned about the conditions under which problems that perhaps lie deeper than matters of morals or life style can be solved to the satisfaction of all the parties to them.

A CULTURE OF CIVILITY

We can summarize this low-key approach to deviance in the phrase "a culture of civility." What are its components, and how does it maintain itself?

San Francisco prides itself on its sophistication, on being the most European of American cities, on its picturesque cosmopolitanism. The picturesque quality, indeed the quaintness, rests in part on physical beauty. As the filling of the Bay and the destruction of the skyline by high-rise buildings proceeds to destroy that beauty,

347

the city has come to depend even more on the presence of undigested ethnic minorities. It is as though San Francisco did not wish its Italians, Chinese, or Russians to assimilate and become standard Americans, preferring instead to maintain a panoply of ethnic differences: religious, cultural and culinary (especially culinary). A sophisticated, livable city, on this view, contains people, colonies and societies of all kinds. Their differences create a mosaic of life styles, the very difference of whose sight and smell give pleasure.

Like ethnic minorities, deviant minorities create enclaves whose differences add to the pleasure of city life. Natives enjoy the presence of hippies and take tourists to see their areas, just as they take them to see the gay area of Polk Street. Deviance, like difference, is a civic resource, enjoyed by tourist and resident alike.

To enjoy deviance instead of fearing it requires a surrender of some common sense notions about the world. Most people assume, when they see someone engaging in proscribed activity, that there is worse to come. "Anyone who would do that [take dope, dress in women's clothes, sell his body or whatever] would do anything" is the major premise of the syllogism. "If you break one law or convention, who knows where you'll stop." Common sense ignores the contrary cases around us everywhere: professional criminals often flourish a legionnaire's patriotism: housewives who are in every other respect conventional sometimes shoplift; homosexuals may be good family providers; some people, who habitually use the rings from poptop cans to work the parking meter, would not dream of taking dope, and vice versa. "Deviance," like conforming behavior, is highly selective. San Francisco's culture of civility, accepting that premise, assumes that if I know that you steal or take dope or peddle your ass, that is all I *know*. There may be more to know; then again, there may be nothing. The deviant may be perfectly decent in every other respect. We are often enjoined, in a generalization of therapeutic doctrine, to treat other people as individuals; that prescription comes nearer to being filled in San Francisco than in most places in the United States.

Because of that tolerance, deviants find it possible to live somewhat more openly in San Francisco than elsewhere. People do not try so hard to catch them at their deviant activities and are less likely to punish them when caught. Because they live more openly, what they do is more visible to straight members of the community. An established canon of social psychology tells us that we find it harder to maintain negative stereotypes when our personal experience belies them. We see more clearly and believe more deeply that hippies or homosexuals are not dangerous when we confront them on the street day after day or live alongside them and realize that beard plus long hair does not equal a drug-crazed maniac, that limp wrist plus lisp does not equal child-molester.

When such notions become embodied in a culture of civility, the citizenry begins to sense that "everyone" feels that way. We cannot say at what critical point a population senses that sophistication about deviance is the norm, rather than a liberal fad. But San Francisco clearly has that critical mass. To come on as an anti-deviant, in a way that would probably win friends and influence voters in more parochial areas, risks being greeted by laughter and ridicule in San Francisco. Conservatives who believe in law and order are thus inclined to keep their beliefs to themselves. The more people keep moralistic notions to themselves, the more everyone believes that tolerance is widespread. The culture maintains itself by convincing the populace that it is indeed the culture.

It gets help from public pronouncements of civic officials, who enunciate what will be taken as the collective sentiment of the city. San Francisco officials occasionally angle for the conservative vote that disapproves licentiousness. But they more frequently take the side of liberty, if not license. When the police, several years ago, felt compelled to close the first of the "topless joints," the judge threw the case out. He reasoned that Supreme Court decisions required him to take into account contemporary community standards. In his judgment San Francisco was not a prudish community; the case was dismissed. The city's major paper, the *Chronicle*, approved. Few protested.

Similarly, when California's leading Yahoo, Superintendent of Public Instruction Max Rafferty, threatened to revoke the teaching credentials of any San Francisco teacher who used the obscene materials listed in the standard high school curriculum (Eldridge Cleaver's *Soul on Ice* and LeRoi Jones' *Dutchman*), the City did not remove the offending books from its curriculum. Instead, it successfully sued to have Rafferty enjoined from interfering in its operation.

In short, San Franciscans know that they are supposed to be sophisticated and let that knowledge guide their public actions, whatever their private feelings. According to another well-known law of social psychology, their private feelings often come to resemble their public actions, and they learn to delight in what frightens citizens of less civil cities.

We do not suggest that all kinds of deviation are tolerated endlessly. The police try, in San Francisco as elsewhere, to stamp out some vices and keep a ceiling on others. Some deviance frightens San Franciscans too, because it seems to portend worse to come (most recently, users and purveyors of methedrine—"speed merchants" and "speed freaks"—whose drug use is popularly thought to result in violence and crime). But the line is drawn much farther over the side of "toleration" in San Francisco than elsewhere. A vastly wider range of activities is publicly acceptable. Despite the wide range of visible freakiness, the citizenry takes it all in stride, without the fear and madness that permeates the conventional sectors of cities like Detroit, Chicago, New York, Washington, D.C., and similar centers of undaunted virtue.

MADAMS AND UNIONISTS

How does a culture of civility arise? Here we can only speculate, and then fragmentarily, since so few cities in the United States have one that we cannot make the comparisons that might uncover the crucial conditions. San Francisco's history suggests a number of possibilities.

It has, for one thing, a Latin heritage. Always a major seaport, it has long tolerated the vice that caters to sailors typical of such ports. It grew at the time of the gold rush in an explosive way that burst through conventional social controls. It ceded to its ethnic minorities, particularly the Chinese, the right to engage in prostitution, gambling, and other activities. Wickedness and high living form part of the prized past every "tourist" city constructs for itself: some minor downtown streets in San Francisco, for instance, are named for famous madams of the gold rush era.

Perhaps more important, a major potential source of repressive action—the working class—is in San Francisco more libertarian and politically sophisticated than one might expect. Harry Bridges' longshoremen act as bellwethers. It should be remembered that San Francisco is one of the few major American cities ever to experience a general strike. The event still reverberates, and working people who might support repression of others know by personal experience that the policeman may not be their friend. Trade unionism has a

left-wing, honest base which gives the city a working-class democracy and even eccentricity, rather than the customary pattern of
authoritarianism.

Finally, San Francisco is a town of single people. Whatever actual proportion of the adult population is married, the city's culture
is oriented toward and organized for single people. As a consequence, citizens worry less about what public deviance will do to
their children, for they don't have any and don't intend to, or they
move from the city when the do. (Since there are, of course, plenty
of families in the city, it may be more accurate to say that there are
fewer white middle-class families, that being the stratum that would,
if family-based, provide the greatest number of complaints about
deviance. Black, Chicano, and Oriental populations ordinarily have
enough to worry about without becoming guardians of public
morality.)

THE PLACE TO LIVE

San Francisco is known across the country as a haven for deviants. Good homosexuals hope to go to San Francisco to stay when
they die, if not before. Indeed, one of the problems of deviant communities in San Francisco is coping with the periodic influx of a new
generation of bohemians who have heard that it is the place to be:
the beatnik migration of the late fifties and the hippie hordes of
1967. But those problems should not obscure what is more important:
that there are stable communities of some size there to be disrupted.
It is the stable homosexual community that promises politicians
90,000 votes and the stable bohemian communities of several vin-
tages that provide both personnel and customers for some important
local industries (developing, recording, and distributing rock music
is now a business of sizeable proportions).

Stable communities are stable because their members have
found enough of what they want to stay where they are for a while.
If where they were proved totally unsatisfying, they presumably
would move elsewhere, unless restrained. But no one forces deviants
to live in San Francisco. They stay there because it offers them, via
the culture of civility, a place to live where they are not shunned as
fearsome or disgusting, where agents of control (police and others)
do not regard them as unfortunate excrescences to be excised at the
first opportunity. Because they have a place to stay that does not

harass them, they sink roots like more conventional citizens: find jobs, buy houses, make friends, vote, and take part in political activities and all the other things that solid citizens do.

Sinking roots stabilizes deviants' lives, as it does the lives of conventional citizens. They find less need to act in the erratic ways deviants often behave elsewhere, less need to fulfill the prophecy that because they are deviant in one respect they will be deviant in other, more dangerous ways. San Francisco employers know that homosexuals make good employees. Why not? They are not likely to be blackmailed by enterprising hustlers. The police seldom haul them off to jail for little reason or beat them because they feel like pushing some "queers" around. Homosexuals fear none of this in San Francisco, or fear it much less than in most places, and so are less given to the overcompensatory "camping" that gets their fellows into trouble elsewhere.

Police and others do not harass deviants because they have found, though they may deny it for public relations purposes, that looking the other way is sometimes a good policy. It is easier, when a Be-In is going on, to turn your back on the sight of open marijuana smoking than it is to charge into the crowd and try to arrest people who will destroy the evidence before you get there, give you a hard time, make a fool of you, and earn you a bad press—and have no conviction to show for it. At the same time, when you turn your back, nothing worse is likely to happen: no muggings, no thefts, no rapes, no riots. Police, more calculating than they seem, often choose to reach just this kind of accommodation with stable deviant communities.

The accommodation works in circular fashion. When deviants can live decent lives, they find it possible to behave decently. Furthermore, they acquire the kind of stake they are often denied elsewhere in the present and future structure of the community. That stake constrains them to behave in ways that will not outrage nondeviants, for they do not want to lose what they have. They thus curb their activities according to what they think the community will stand for.

The community in turn, and especially the police, will put up with more than they might otherwise, because they understand that nothing else is forthcoming, and because they find that what they are confronted with is not so bad after all. If homosexuals have a Halloween Drag Ball, the community discovers it can treat it as a good-natured joke; those who are offended discover that they needn't go near the Hilton while it is happening.

No doubt neither party to such a bargain gets quite what he would like. Straight members of the community presumably would prefer not to have whores walking the downtown streets, would prefer not have gay bars operating openly. Deviants of all kinds presumably would prefer not to have to make any concessions to straight sensibilities. Each gives up something and gets something, and to that degree the arrangement becomes stable, the stability itself something both prize.

DEVIANCE AND DEMOCRACY

What we have just described verges on the idyllic, Peace and Harmony in Camelot forever. Such a dream of perfection does not exist in San Francisco, though more deviants there have more of the advantages of such a bargain, perhaps, than in any other city in the United States. Nor is it clear that the system we described, even in its perfect form, would be such an idyll.

In San Francisco, as everywhere, the forces of decency and respectability draw the line somewhere and can be every bit as forceful and ruthless the other side of that line as the forces of decency and respectability anywhere else. When the Haight-Ashbury got "out of hand" with the overcrowded transiency of 1967, the city moved in the police Tactical Squad, the City Health Department, and all the other bureaucratic weapons usually used to roust deviants. They did it again with the growth of violence in that area associated with the use and sale of methedrine. In general, the city has responded with great toughness to those deviants it believes will not be satisfied with something "reasonable." In particular, political dissent has sometimes been met with force, though San Francisco police have never indulged themselves on any large scale such as that which made Chicago police internationally detested.

The system has beauty only for those deviants who do not mind giving up some portion of their liberty, and then only if the portion they are willing to give up is the same as what the community wants given up. This no doubt is the reason an accommodative system works well with those whose deviant desires are narrowly circumscribed, and may have less utility with those whose wants can be accommodated only at the expense of others who will not easily

353

give up their privileges. In fact, current political difficulties clearly result from the breakdown of accommodation.

These considerations indicate the more general importance of San Francisco's experiment in tolerating and accommodating to the minor forms of deviance encompassed in sex, dope, and cheap thrills. How can a complex and differentiated society deal with variety and dissent and simultaneously with its own urges for centralized control? An accommodative relationship to difference, in which it is allowed to persist while it pays some minimal dues to the whole, is what San Francisco recommends to us, suggesting that the amount of the dues and the breadth of the license be set where both parties will, for the time being, stand still for it. The resulting working arrangement will be at least temporarily stable and provide for all concerned a tranquility that permits one to go about his business unharmed that many will find attractive.

But is this no more than a clever trick, a way of buying off deviant populations with minor freedoms while still keeping them enslaved? Beneath the rhetoric, the analysis is the same. The more radical statement adds only that the people who accept such a bargain ought not to, presumably because they have, if they only knew it, deeper and more important interests and desires which remain unsatisfied in the accommodative arrangement. So, of course, do those who hold them in check. Perhaps that is the ultimate lesson of San Francisco: the price of civilization, civility, and living together peacefully is not getting everything you want.

LIMITS OF ACCOMMODATION

It is tempting to think that an accommodation based on civility and mutual interest provides a model for settling the conflicts now wracking our urban areas. Our analysis suggests that this is a possibility, but no more than that. Peace can occur through accommodation, the example of the potheads and pimps tells us, only under certain not so easily attained conditions. Those conditions may not be present in the ethnic and political problems our major cities, San Francisco among them, are now experiencing.

Accommodation requires, as a first condition, that the parties involved prize peace and stability enough to give up some of what they want so that others may have their desires satisfied as well. But people take that point of view only when the accommodation leaves them enough of a share to want no more. Some urban groups no longer believe that they are getting that necessary minimum, either because they have learned to interpret their situation in a new light or because they have lost some advantages they once had.

Members of black communities may be no worse off than ever, but they are considerably worse off than whites and know it. For a variety of historical reasons, and as a matter of simple justice, some of them no longer regard the little they have as sufficient reason to keep the peace. All the discussion about how many blacks feel this way (is it 10 percent or 50 percent?) and how strongly they feel it (are they willing to fight?) is irrelevant to the main point: enough feel strongly enough to make a lot of trouble for the white community, thus changing the balance of costs to the whites and insisting on a new division of rights as the price of stability.

Some members of white communities probably are objectively worse off and may resent it sufficiently to give up peace and stability in an effort to raise the costs to others and thus minimize their losses. Many whites in civil service positions, in the skilled trades, and in similar protected occupational positions have lost or are in danger of losing competitive job advantages as governments act to do something about the injustice that afflicts black communities. Without a general expansion of the economy, which is *not* what blacks demand, injustices inflicted on blacks can be remedied only by taking something away from more favorably situated whites. It may be possible to improve the education of poor black children, for instance, only by taking away some of the privileges of white teachers. It may be possible to give black youths a chance at apprenticeships in skilled trades only by removing the privileged access to those positions of the sons of present white union members. When whites lose those privileges, they may feel strongly enough to fracture the consensus of civility.

The deviant communities of San Francisco show us cases in which the parties involved agree in a way that leaves each enough. But that may only be possible when the interests to be accommodated involve morals and life styles. When those interests include substantial economic prizes, major forms of privileges, and real political power, it may be that nothing less than a real-life assessment of relative intensities of desire and ability to inflict costs on others will suffice. That assessment takes place in the marketplace of conflict.

This suggests a second, more procedural condition for the achievement of urban peace through accommodation and civility.

355

Mechanisms and procedures must exist by which the conflicting desires and resources for bargaining can be brought together to produce a temporarily stable working arrangement. The accommodations of enforcement officials and deviants typically occur in a host of minor bargaining situations. Hassles are settled by the people immediately involved, and settled "on their own merits"—which is to say, in a way that respects the strength of everyone's feelings and the amount of trouble each is prepared to make to have his way. The culture of civility works well because the myriad of separate local bargains respect and reflect what most of the involved parties want or are willing to settle for.

We do not allow ourselves this extreme degree of decentralized decision-making with respect to many important problems (though many critics have suggested we should). Instead, we allow federal, state or city bureaucracies to make general policies that inhibit local accommodation. While government might well intervene when circumstances make bargaining positions unequal, we know now that it is not ordinarily well equipped to reach accommodative agreements that will work at the grass roots. Unable to know what the people who inhabit local areas will want and settle for, officials turn to technocrats for solutions.

Thus, when we confront the problem of slums and urban renewal, we send for the planner and the bulldozer. But the lives of urban residents are not determined by the number or newness of buildings. The character of their relationships with one another and with the outside world does that. Planners and technocrats typically ignore those relationships, and their influence in shaping what people want, in constructing solutions. They define "slums" impersonally, using such impersonal criteria as density or deterioration, and fail to see how awakened group consciousness can turn a "slum" into a "ghetto," and a rise in moral repute turn a "ghetto" into a "neighborhood."

Too often, the search for "model cities" implies not so much a model as an ideology—a rationalistic vision of human interaction that implies a people whose consistency of behavior can nowhere be found. We already have "model cities": Brasilia at the bureaucratic end and Levittown at the residential end. And in both instances, the force of human impulses had to break through the web of formal models to make these places inhabitable. In Brasilia the rise of shantytown dwellings outside the federal buildings made the place "a city," whereas the Levittowners had to break the middle-class mode and pass through a generation of conformity before they could produce a decent living arrangement. To design a city in conformity to "community standards"—which turn out to be little more than the prejudices of building inspectors, housing designers and absentee landlords—only reinforces patterns of frustration, violence and antagonism that now characterize so many of America's large cities. To think that the dismal failure of large housing projects will be resolved by their dismal replacement of small housing projects is nonsense. Minibuildings are no more of a solution than maxibuildings are the problem.

In any event, centralized planning operating in this way does not produce a mechanism through which the mutual desires, claims and threats of interested groups can sort themselves out and allow a *modus vivendi*, if one exists, to uncover itself. The centralized body makes bargains for everyone under its influence, without knowing their circumstances or wants, and so makes it impossible for the people involved to reach a stable accommodation. But centralized planning still remains a major solution proffered for urban problems of every kind.

Accommodations reached through the mechanism of old-fashioned city political machines work little better, for contemporary machines typically fail to encompass all the people whose interests are at stake. Richard Daley demonstrated that when the Chicago ghetto, supposedly solidly under his control, exploded and revealed some people his famed consensus had not included. Lyndon Johnson made the same discovery with respect to opponents of the Vietnam war. Insofar as centralized decision-making does not work, and interested parties are not allowed to make bargains at the local level, accommodative stability cannot occur.

So the example of San Francisco's handling of moral deviance may not provide the blueprint one would like for settling urban problems generally. Its requirements include a day-to-day working agreement among parties on the value of compromise and a procedure by which their immediate interests can be openly communicated and effectively adjusted. Those requirements are difficult to meet. Yet it may be that they are capable of being met in more places than we think, that even some of the knottier racial and political problems contain possibilities of accommodation, no more visible to us than the casual tolerance of deviance in San Francisco was thinkable to some of our prudish forebearers.

Notes

Chapter 1: Introduction

[1] Louis Wirth, in *The Science of Man in the World Crisis*, ed. Ralph Linton (New York: Columbia University Press, 1945), p. 347 as cited in George Simpson and J. Milton Yinger, *Racial and Cultural Minorities* (New York: Harper and Brothers, 1958), p. 22.

[2] J. L. Simmons, *Deviants* (Berkeley: The Glendessary Press, 1969), pp. 32–33.

[3] Simmons, *Deviants*, pp. 27–30.

[4] Bruce Hartley, *Problems in Prejudice* (King's Crown, 1946), p. 26, as cited in Simpson and Yinger, *op. cit.*, p. 92.

[5] Simmons, *Deviants*, p. 32.

Chapter 1: Racism in American Society

[1] The term "ghetto" as used in this report refers to an area within a city characterized by poverty and acute social disorganization, and inhabited by members of a racial or ethnic group under conditions of involuntary segregation.

[2] A "central city" is the largest city of a standard metropolitan statistical area, that is, a metropolitan area containing at least one city of 50,000 or more inhabitants.

[3] E. Franklin Frazier, *Black Bourgeoisie* (New York: Collier Books, 1962).

[4] Robert O. Blood, Jr., and Donald M. Wolfe, *Husbands and Wives: The Dynamics of Married Living* (Illinois: The Free Press of Glencoe, 1960), p. 34.

[5] *Ibid.*, p. 35.

[6] *Ibid.*

[7] Based on preliminary draft of a report by the President's Committee on Equal Employment Opportunity.

[8] Whitney Young, *To Be Equal* (New York: McGraw Hill Book Company, 1964), p. 25.

[9] *Ibid.*, p. 175.

[10] Thomas F. Pettigrew, *op. cit.*, p. 16.

[11] Deton Brooks, quoted in *The New Improved American* by Bernard Asbell (New York: McGraw Hill Book Company, 1965), p. 76.

[12] Dorothy Height, in the Report of Consultation of Problems of Negro Women, President's Commission on the Status of Women, April 19, 1963, p. 35.

[13] Duncan M. MacIntyre, *Public Assistance: Too Much or Too Little?* (New York: New York State School of Industrial Relations, Cornell University, Bulletin 53–1, December 1964), pp. 73–74.

[14] Robin M. Williams, Jr., *Strangers Next Door* (Englewood Cliffs, New Jersey, Prentice-Hall, Inc., 1964), p. 240.

[15] *Youth in the Ghetto, op. cit.*, p. 195.

[16] Martin Deutch and Bert Brown, 'Social Influences in Negro-White Intelligence Differences," *Social Issues*, April 1964, p. 27.

[17] *Ibid.*, p. 29.

[18] *Ibid.*

[19] *Ibid.*, p. 31.

[20] *Ibid.*

[21] "Negroes in Apprenticeship, New York State," *Monthly Labor Review*, September 1960, p. 955.

[22] Mary H. Diggs, "Some Problems and Needs of Negro Children as Revealed by Comparative Delinquency and Crime Statistics," *Journal of Negro Education*, 1950, 19, pp. 290–97.

[23] Maude M. Craig and Thelma J. Glick, 'Ten Years Experience with the Glueck Social Prediction Table," *Journal of Crime and Delinquency*, July 1963, p. 256.

[24] F. R. Scarpitti, Ellen Murray, S. Dinitz, and W. C. Reckless, "The 'Good' Boy in a High Delinquency Area: Four Years Later," *American Sociological Review*, 1960, 25, pp. 555–58.

[25] W. Mischel, "Father-Absence and Delay of Gratification: Cross-Cultural Comparisons," *Journal of Abnormal and Social Psychology*, 1961, 63, pp. 116–24.

[26] W. Mischel, "Preference for Delayed Reinforcement and Social Responsibility," *Journal of Social and Abnormal Psychology*, 1961, 62, pp. 1–7.
"Delay of Gratification, Need for Achievement, and Acquiescense in Another Culture," *Journal of Abnormal and Social Psychology*, 1961, 62, pp. 543–52.

[27] O. H. Mowrer and A. D. Ullman, "Ttime as a Determinant in Integrative Learning," *Psychological Review*, 1945, 52, pp. 61–90.

[28] Thomas F. Pettigrew, *op. cit.*, p. 22.

[29] Erdman Palmore, "Factors Associated with School Dropouts on Juvenile Delinquency Among Lower Class Children," *Social Security Bulletin*, October 1963, p. 6.

[30] Thomas P. Monahan, "Family Status and the Delinquent Child," *Social Forces*, March 1957, p. 254.

[31] See Shaw and McKay, *Juvenile Delinquency in Urban Areas, supra* note 13; also see McKay and Kobrin, *supra* note 12.

[32] Shaw and McKay, *id.* at p. 149.

[33] *Id.* at pp. 151–52.

[34] *Id.* at p. 152.

[35] *Id.* at pp. 152–53.

[36] McKay and Kobrin, *supra* note 12.

[37] *Id.* at table 57.

[38] *Id.* at p. 125.

[39] Earl R. Moses, "Differentials in Crime Rates Between Negroes and Whites," *American Sociological Review*, August 1947, 12:411–20.

[40] *Id.* at p. 417.

[41] *Id.* at table V, p. 418.

[42] *Id.* at p. 418.

[43] Christen T. Jonassen, "A Re-evaluation and Critique of the Logic and Some Methods of Shaw and McKay," *American Sociological Review*, October 1949, 14:608–14. Also see rejoinder by Shaw and McKay, pp. 614–17.

[44] Sophia M. Robison, *Can Delinquency be Measured?* (New York: Columbia University Press, 1936), pp. 187 and 122.

[45] Shaw and McKay, *supra* note 50, p. 615.

[46] *Ibid.*

[47] Norman S. Hayner, "Delinquency Areas in the Puget Sound Region," *American Journal of Sociology*, November 1933, 39:319.

[48] *Ibid.*

[49] *Ibid.*

[50] Helen G. MacGill, "The Oriental Delinquent in the Vancouver, B.C., Juvenile Court," *Sociology and Social Research*, May–June 1938, 22:430.

[51] *Ibid.*

[52] *Id.* at pp. 432–38.

[53] Pauline V. Young, "Urbanization as a Factor in Juvenile Delinquency," *Publications of the American Sociological Society*, 1930, 24:162–66.

[54] Lind, *supra* note 5, p. 217.

[55] Erdman B. Palmore and Phillip E. Hammond, "Interacting Factors in Juvenile Delinquency," *American Sociological Review*, December 1964, 29:848–54.

[56] *Id.* at p. 849.

[57] *Id.* at table 1, p. 850.

[58] *Id.* at p. 850.

[59] *Id.* at table 3, p. 851.

[60] *Id.* at p. 851.

[61] *Id.* at table 4, p. 851.

[62] *Id.* at table 5, p. 851.

Chapter 2: Youth as a Minority

[1] Gerald Farber, *The Student as Nigger* (North Hollywood: Contact Books, 1969), pp. 114–15, 118, 125.

[2] For a summary of the evidence, see Empey, "Peer Group Influences in Correctional Programs" (Consultant's Paper submitted to President's Commission on Law Enforcement and Administration of Justice, 1966).

[3] See Wolfgang, *op. cit. supra* note 26.

[4] See Goodman, *Growing Up Absurd* (1956); Matza, *op. cit. supra* note 32.

[5] See Block and Niederhoffer, *op. cit. supra* note 32, for discussion of gang behavior in connection with transitions of adolescence.

[6] See generally Cohen, *op. cit. supra* note 24; Whyte, *Street Corner Society* (1955); Yablonsky, *op. cit. supra* note 32.

[7] Among the growing number of studies of the effects of labeling on the development of delinquent behavior patterns, see Werthman, *supra* note 32; Becker, *Outsiders: Studies in the Sociology of Deviance* (1963); Kitsuse, "Societal Reaction to Deviant Behavior," in Becker, ed., *The Other Side, Perspectives on Deviance* (1964); Cicourel, *The Social Organization of Juvenile Justice* (in press); Chwast, "Value Conflicts in Law Enforcement," *American Sociological Review*, 1965, 30:1; Vinter and Sarri, "Malperformance in the Public School: A Group Work Approach," *Social Work*, 1965, 10:3; Piliavin and Briar, *op. cit. supra* note 32.

[8] See Spergel, *Street Gang Work* (1960); Shaw, *The Jack Roller* (1930); Sutherland and Cressy, *Principles of Criminology* (4th ed., 1955), pp. 76–80.

[9] Yablonsky, *op. cit. supra* note 32; Klein and Meyerhoff, eds., *Juvenile Gangs in Context, Theory, Research and Action* (1964); Miller, "Violent Crimes in City Gangs," *The Annals* 364:96 (Wolfgang, ed., 1966); Short and Strodtbeck, "Why Gang Fights," *Trans-Action* Sept.–Oct. 1964, pp. 25–29.

[10] This was the experience, for example, of street workers with the New York City Youth Board during the gang wars of the 1950's.

[11] Gordon, Short, Cartwright, and Strodtbeck, "Values and Gang Delinquency: A Study of Street-Corner Groups," *American Journal of Sociology*, 1963, 69:109–28; Karacki and Toby, The Uncommitted Adolescent: Candidate for Gang Delinquency and Anomie," in Clinard, ed., *Anomie and Deviant Behavior* (1964).

[12] See Office of Education, U.S. Department of Health, Education and Welfare, *Delinquency and the Schools*, published as an appendix to the President's Commission on Law Enforcement and Administration of Justice, *Task Force Report: Juvenile Delinquency and Youth Crime* (Washington: U.S. Government

Printing Office, 1967). And see Schafer and Polk, *Delinquency and the Schools,* also appended to the same report.

[13] For an annotated bibliography of the literature on cultural deprivation in children, see Silverman, "Bibliography," in Bloom, Davis, and Hess, *Compensatory Education for Cultural Deprivation* (1965).

[14] Coleman, *op. cit. supra* note 30; Cloward and Jones, *supra* note 30 at p. 60.

[15] See Sloward and Jones, *supra* note 30; Vinter and Sarri, *supra* note 63.

[16] Among the studies that document this situation are Eddy, *Urban Education and the Child of the Slum* (Hunter College Project TRUE, 1965); Havighurst, *The Public Schools of Chicago* (1963); Sexton, *Education and Income* (1960); *Education in Deprived Areas, op. cit. supra* note 30; Riessman and Hannah, "Teachers of the Poor," *PTA Magazine,* November 1964.

[17] This is the major finding of the Coleman report. This factor accounted for more variation in student achievement than any other school. condition. See also Reiss and Rhodes, *A Sociopsychological Study of Adolescent Conformity and Deviation* (U.S. Office of Education Cooperative Research Porject No. 507, 1959), relating school segregation and student performances to delinquency rates.

[18] See Davidson and Lang, "Children's Perceptions of Their Teacher's Feelings Toward Them Related to Self-Perception, School Achievement and Behavior," *Journal of Experimental Education,* 1960, p. 114; "Harlem Youth Opportunities Unlimited," *Youth in the Ghetto* (1964), p. 227; Ravitz, "The Role of the School in the Urban Setting," in *Education in Depressed Areas, op. cit. supra* note 30; Gottlieb, "Teaching and Students: The Views of Negro and White Students," *Sociology of Education,* 1964, p. 345; Clark, *Dark Ghetto* (1965), p. 139.

[19] See, e.g., Eels, "Some Implications for School Practices of the Chicago Studies of Cultural Bias in Intelligence Tests," 1963, *Harvard Educational Review* 223:284. Vernon, "Coaching for All Advised," *The London Times Education Supplement,* Feb. 1, 1952 and Dec. 12, 1952, on changing IQ scores by intense coaching.

[20] See, e.g., Conant, *Slums and Suburbs* (1961); Harrington, *The Other America* (1962); House Commission on Education and Labor, *A Task Force Study of the Public Schools in the District of Columbia as it Relates to the War on Poverty* (1966); Sexton, *op. cit. supra* note 72, at p. 43; Schafer, "High School Curriculum Placement: A Study of Educational Selection," paper before Annual Meeting of the Pacific Sociological Association, Vancouver, B.C., April 1966.

[21] See, e.g., Klineberg, "Life Is Fun in a Smiling, Fair-Skinned World," *The Saturday Review,* 1965, 46:75; Bullock and Singleton, "The Minority Child and the Schools," in Gowan and Demos, eds., *The Disadvantaged and Potential Dropout* (1956).

[22] Interview by Commission staff members with members of Rebels With a Cause, youth group in Washington, D.C.

[23] *Ibid.*

[24] See Stinchcombe, *Rebellion in a High School* (1965), relating to perceived irrelevancy of education and delinquency. See also Elliot, "Delinquency and Perceived Opportunity," *Sociological Inquiry,* 1962, pp. 216–22.

[25] U.S. Department of Labor, *The Negro in the Economy* (1961).

[26] Sexton, *op. cit. supra* note 72.

[27] See Vinter and Sarri, *op. cit. supra* note 63, on how different schools define and emphasize behavior problems in children and how the school's response, as well as the child's personality, play a part in adjustment to school. See also Polk and Richmond, *Those Who Fail* (Lane County Youth Project, Eugene,

Oregon, 1966); Wilkerson, "Prevailing and Needed Emphasis in Research on the Education of Disadvantaged Children and Youth," *Journal of Negro Educational Yearbook*, 1964, 33.

[28] See Werthman, *supra* note 44; Bertrand and Smith, "Environmental Factors and School Attendance," *Louisiana State University Bulletin* No. 533 (1960).

[29] Polk and Richmond, *supra* note 83. Also see Gold, *Status Forces in Delinquent Boys* (Inter-City Program on Children, Youth, and Family Life, Institute for Social Research, University of Michigan, 1963), pp. 154, 161; and Short, "Gang Delinquency and Anomie" in *Anomie and Deviant Behavior, op. cit. supra* note 67.

[30] See Werthman, *The Function of Social Definitions in the Development of Delinquent Careers*, published as an appendix to President's Commission on Law Enforcement and Administration of Justice, *Task Force Report: Juvenile Delinquency and Youth Crime* (Washington: U.S. Government Printing Office, 1967); Reissman and Hannah, *supra* note 72.

[31] See, on the formation of a negative identity during adolescence, the writings of Erik Erikson, e.g., "Identity and the Life Cycle," *Psychological Issues*, 1959, 1:1.

[32] The statistics in this section are from *Profile of Youth*, a report prepared for the Subcommittee on Employment, Manpower, and Poverty of the Commission of Labor and Public Welfare, U.S. Senate, 1966.

[33] See *Getting Hired and Getting Fired*, a report prepared by the National Committee on Employment of Youth (U.S. Department of Health, Education and Welfare, 1965), describing the importance of information systems and work experience in finding employment. See also Boodish, "Automation and School Dropouts," *Social Studies*, 1964, 55:67–70; Ellington, "Unemployment and Unfilled Jobs: A Dropout Paradox," *Minnesota Journal of Education*, 1963, 44:9–10.

[34] Sparer, *Employability and the Juvenile Arrest Rate* (New York University Center for the Study of Unemployed Youth, 1966).

[35] Cloward and Ohlin, *Delinquency and Opportunity*, argue that delinquent behavior is a response to the availability or paucity of opportunities. Also see Fleisher, *The Economics of Delinquency* (1966) (data linking school dropout status, unemployment, and delinquency).

Chapter 3: The Poor as a Minority

[1] See especially Coleman, *Equality of Educational Opportunity* (1966); see also Cloward and Jones, "Social Class: Educational Attitudes and Participation," in Passow, ed., *Education in Depressed Areas* (1963). Concerning the effects of conflicting values on young people in the slums, see Muller, "Lower Class Culture as a Generating Milieu of Gang Delinquency," *Journal of Social Issues* 1958, 11:5–19; Kobrin, "The Conflict of Values in Delinquency Areas," *American Sociological Review* (1951), p. 653–61.

[2] See, e.g., President's Commission on Crime in the District of Columbia, *Report* 120 (1966).

[3] See Block and Neiderhoffer, *The Gang* (1958); Matza, *Delinquency and Drift* (1964); Short and Strodtbeck, *Group Process and Gang Delinquency* (1965); Yablonsky, *The Violent Gang* (1962). See also Werthman, "The Function of Social Definitions in the Development of Delinquent Careers," published as an appendix to President's Commission on Law Enforcement and Administration of Justice, *Task Force Report: Juvenile Delinquency and Youth Crime* (Washington: U.S. Government Printing Office, 1967); Cicourel, *Social Class*,

Family Structure and the Administration of Juvenile Justice (Office of Juvenile Delinquency and Youth Development, U.S. Department of Health, Education and Welfare, Grant No. 62224, 1963); Piliavin and Briar, *Police Encounters with Juveniles* (Office of Juvenile Delinquency and Youth Development, U.S. Department of Health, Education and Welfare, Grant No. 62224, 1968).

[4] Among recent writings arguing against the idea of the hard-core single-track delinquent are Matza, *op. cit. supra* note 32, and Lerman, "Issues in Subcultural Delinquency" (unpublished thesis, Columbia University School of Social Work).

[5] See Toby, "Affluence and Adolescent Crime," published as an appendix to President's Commission on Law Enforcement and Administration of Justice, *Task Force Report: Juvenile Delinquency and Youth Crime.*

[6] For a discussion of the effects of slum conditions on behavior, see Schorr, *Slums and Social Security* (1963).

[7] This and the following quotations from inner-city children are from Fine, *Neighbors of the President,* President's Commission on Juvenile and Youth Crime, 1963.

[8] Gold, *Status Forces in Delinquent Boys* (1963), pp. 107–122.

Chapter 4: The Gay Minority

[1] Barbara Wootton, "Sickness or Sin," in *The Twentieth Century* (May 1956).

[2] There are reasons for supposing that paedophilia differs from other manifestations of homosexuality. For example, it would seem that in some cases the propensity is for partners of a particular age rather than for partners of a particular sex. An examination of the records of the offenses covered by the Cambridge survey reveals that 8 percent of the men convicted of sexual offenses against children had previous convictions for both heterosexual and homosexual offenses.

Chapter 5: The Drug Minority

[1] Walton, R. P. *Marihuana: America's New Drug Problem.* J. B. Lippincott Co., Philadelphia, 1938.

[2] W. Bromberg, "Marijuana: A Psychiatric Study," in *J.A.M.A.* 113: 4, 1939.

[3] Now named the Goldwater Memorial Hospital.

[4] While sufficient experimentation has not been made to validate the finding, it should be noted that the personality changes produced by 2 cc. or marijuana cigarettes are almost always in agreement in contrast to the changes resulting from the ingestion of 5 cc. The 2 cc. dosage apparently more nearly approximates the amount a person would take if left to his own devices.

[5] W. Bromberg, "Marijuana: A Psychiatric Study," in *J.A.M.A.* 113: 4, 1939.

[6] From the Department of Pharmacology, Cornell University Medical College.

[7] Part of the experimental work here reported was conducted in collaboration with W. Modell.

[8] *Proceedings, White House Conference on Narcotic and Drug Abuse* (Washington, September 27, 1962), pp. 27–28 (hereinafter cited as *Proceedings*).

[9] President's Advisory Commission on Narcotics and Drug Abuse, *Final Report,* 1963.

[10] *Id.* at pp. 70–73, 43–44.

[11] On the general problem of defining addiction, see Lindesmith, "Basic Problems in the Social Psychology of Addiction and a Theory," in O'Donnell & Hall, eds., *Narcotics Addiction* (1966), pp. 91, 92–95.

[12] Eddy, Halbach, Isbell, and Seevers, "Drug Dependence: Its Significance and Characteristics," *Bulletin of World Health*, 1965, 32:721, 722.

[13] *Internal Revenue Code of 1954*, Sec. 4731(a).

[14] *Uniform Narcotic Drug Act*, Sec. 1(14).

[15] *Internal Revenue Code of 1954*, Sec. 4731(g)(1).

[16] See generally U.S. Treasury Department, *Traffic in Opium and Other Dangerous Drugs*, 1965, pp. 54–55; Permanent Central Narcotics Board, *Report to the Economic and Social Council* on the work of the Board, 1965, pp. 15–43.

[17] American Medical Association Council on Mental Health, "Report on Narcotics Addiction," in AMA *Narcotics Addiction—Official Actions of the American Medical Association*, 1963, p. 11. See also *Proceedings*, pp. 280–81 (Report of an Ad Hoc Panel on Drug Abuse).

[18] *Id.* at p. 275. See also Blum, assisted by Funkhouser-Balkaby, *Mind-Altering Drugs and Dangerous Behavior: Dangerous Drugs* (hereinafter cited as Blum, *Dangerous Drugs*), published as appendix A-1, President's Commission on Law Enforcement and Administration of Justice, *Task Force Report: Crime and Its Impact—An Assessment* (Washington: U.S. Government Printing Office, 1967); also Blum, assisted by Lauraine Braunstein, *Mind-Altering Drugs and Dangerous Behavior: Narcotics* (hereinafter cited as Blum, *Narcotics*), published as appendix A-2 in President's Commission on Law Enforcement and Administration of Justice, *Task Force Report: Crime and Its Impact—An Assessment* (Washington: U.S. Government Printing Office, 1967).

[19] For a discussion of the effects of heroin, see *id.* at pp. 280–81; Eddy, Halbach, Isbell, and Seevers, *supra* note 5 at pp. 724–25; Isbell, "Medical Aspects of Opiate Addiction," in *Narcotics Addiction, op, cit. supra* note 4 at p. 62 (1966); Maurer and Vogel, *Narcotics and Narcotic Addiction* (2nd ed., 1962); AMA Council on Mental Health, *supra* note 10 at pp. 11–13.

[20] U.S. Treasury Department, *Traffic in Opium and Other Dangerous Drugs*, 1965, pp. 37–46.

[21] Eldridge, *Narcotics and the Law* (1962) pp. 68–78; Lindesmith, *The Addict and the Law* (1965), pp. 99–134; Winick, "Epidemiology of Narcotics Use," in Wilner and Kasselbau, eds., *Narcotics* (1965), pp. 3–6; Chein, "The Use of Narcotics as a Personal and Social Problem," *id.* at pp. 103–108.

[22] E.g., *Hearings on S. 2113, S. 2114, S. 2152 Before a Special Subcommittee of the Senate Judiciary Committee*, 89th Congress, 2nd Session, 1966, pp. 455–56; *Hearings on Organized Crime and Illicit Traffic in Narcotics Before the Permanent Subcommittee on Investigations of the Senate Governmental Operations Committee*, 88th Congress, 1st and 2nd Sessions, 1964, part 3 at p. 670.

[23] *Proceedings* (Report of Ad Hoc Panel on Drug Abuse), pp. 290–91.

[24] U.S. Treasury Department, *Traffic in Opium and Other Dangerous Drugs*, 1966, pp. 37, 43.

[25] *Id.* at p. 41; "Epidemiology of Narcotics Use," in *Narcotics, op. cit. supra* note 14; California Narcotics Rehabilitation Advisory Council, *Second Annual Report* (1966); Public Health Service, *Division of Hospitals Annual Statistical Summary for Fiscal Year 1965*, part 2, at pp. 207–223. See also Blum, *Narcotics*.

[26] See, e.g., testimony of Henry L. Giordano, Commissioner, Federal Bureau of Narcotics, in *Hearings on S. 2113, S. 2114, S. 2152, supra* note 15 at p. 453; testimony of Patrick J. McCormack, Deputy Chief Inspector and Commanding Officer, Narcotics Bureau, New York City Police Department, in *Hearings on Organized Crime and Illicit Traffic in Narcotics, supra* note 15, at p. 733.

[27] *Proceedings* (Report of an Ad Hoc Panel on Drug Abuse), p. 281.

[28] *Internal Revenue Code of 1954*, Secs. 4701–4736.

[29] U.S.C., 1964, Sec. 171–185.

[30] *Uniform Narcotic Drug Act*, Sec. 2.

[31] 21 U.S.C., 1964, Secs. 173, 502, 505.

[32] *Proceedings*, pp. 280–81 (Report of an Ad Hoc Panel on Drug Abuse); AMA Council on Mental Health, *supra* note 10 at p. 11.

[33] *Proceedings*, pp. 285–86.

[34] See generally Maurer and Vogel, *supra* note 12, at pp. 103–108; Winick, "Marijuana Use by Young People," in *Harms, ed., Drug Addiction in Youth* (1965).

[35] Eddy, Halbach, Isbell and Seever, *supra* note 5, at pp. 728–29; Winick, "Marijuana Use by Young People," in Harms, ed., *Drug Addiction in Youth* (1965); *Proceedings*, p. 286; Blum, *Dangerous Drugs.*

[36] Compare U.S. Treasury Department, *Traffic in Opium and Other Dangerous Drugs* (1965), p. 51, with U.S. Treasury Department, *Traffic in Opium and Other Dangerous Drugs* (1960), p. 72.

[37] Compare U.S. Treasury Department, *Traffic in Opium and Other Dangerous Drugs* (1965), p. 47, with U.S. Treasury Department, *Traffic in Opium and Other Dangerous Drugs* (1960), p. 69.

[38] California Department of Justice, "1965 Drug Arrests in California: A Preliminary Survey" (an unpublished draft), p. 4.

[39] *New York Medicine*, May 5, 1966, p. 3. See also Blum, *Dangerous Drugs.*

[40] *Hearings on S. 2113, S. 2114, S. 2152, supra* note 15, at p. 185 (testimony of John J. Neurater).

[41] *Internal Revenue Code of 1954*, Secs. 4741–4776.

[42] U.S.C., Sec. 176a, 1964.

[43] Goddard, "The Menace of Drug Abuse," *American Education*, May 1966.

[44] The controlling regulation may be found in 21 C.R.R. Sec. 166.3.

[45] For a discussion of the effects of amphetamine abuse, see Eddy, Halbach, Isbell, and Seevers, *supra* note 5, at pp. 729–30; AMA Committee on Alcoholism and Addiction and Council on Mental Health, "Dependence on Amphetamines and Other Stimulant Drugs," *Journal of American Medical Association,* 1966, 197:1023; *Proceedings*, pp. 286–88; Blum, *Dangerous Drugs.*

[46] For a discussion of the effects of barbiturate abuse, see Eddy, Halbach, Isbell, and Seevers, *supra* note 5, at pp. 725–27; AMA Committee on Alcoholism and Addiction and Council on Mental Health, "Dependence on Barbiturates and Other Sedative Drugs," Journal of American Medical Association, 1965, 193:673; *Proceedings*, pp. 283–285; Fort, "The Problem of Barbiturates in the United States of America," *Bulletin on Narcotics*, January–March 1964, 16:17, reprinted in *Hearings on H.R. 2 Before the House Interstate and Foreign Commerce Committee*, 89th Congress, 1st Session, 1965, p. 66; Blum, *Dangerous Drugs.*

[47] For discussion of the effects of these drugs when abused, see AMA Committee on Alcoholism and Addiction and Council on Mental Health, "Dependence on Barbiturates and Other Sedative Drugs," *Journal of American Medical Association*, 1965, 193:673; Essig, "Addiction to Nonbarbiturate Sedative and Tranquilizing Drugs," *Clinical Pharmacology and Therapeutics*, May–June 1964, 5:334, reprinted in *Hearings on H.R. 2, supra* note 39 at p. 33. see also Blum, *Dangerous Drugs.*

[48] See generally the testimony of James L. Goddard, Commissioner, Food and Drug Administration, in *Hearings on S. 2113, S. 2114, S. 2152, supra* note 15, at p. 320.

[49] *New York Medicine*, May 5, 1966, pp. 5–7.

[50] *Hearings on S. 2113, S. 2114, S. 2152, supra* note 15, at p. 330 (testimony of Commissioner Goddard).

[51] See Ludwig and Levine, "Patterns of Hallucinogenic Drug Abuse" *Journal of American Medical Association*, 1965, 191:92.

[52] *Id.* at p. 93.

[53] *Id.* at pp. 95–96; Eddy, Halbach, Isbell, and Seevers, *supra* note 5, at p. 731.

[54] *Hearings on H.R. 2, supra* note 39 at p. 23 (statement of George Larrick). See also Goddard, *supra* note 36.

[55] See, e.g., the testimony of Arthur Kleps, Director, Neo-American Church, in *Hearings on S. 2113, S. 2114, S. 2152, supra* note 15 at p. 413. There are also books and magazines (such as *Psychedelic Review*) which describe and promote experiences with hallucinogenic drugs.

[56] E.g., statement of John J. Neurater, Director, Vice Control Division, Chicago Police Department, in *Hearings on S. 2113, S. 2114, S. 2152, supra* note 15 at pp. 181, 186–87.

[57] Ludwig and Levine, *supra* note 44 at p. 93; *New York Medicine*, May 5, 1966, pp. 1–5; Blum, *Dangerous Drugs*.

[58] Act of November 2, 1951, known as the *Boggs Act*.

[59] The present penalty provisions are contained in *Internal Revenue Code of 1954*, Sec. 7237.

[60] See testimony of Harry J. Anslinger, former Commissioner of Narcotics, *Hearings on Illicit Narcotics Traffic Before the Subcommittee on Improvements in the Federal Criminal Code of the Senate Judiciary Committee*, 84th Congress, 1st Session, 1955, p. 42; cf. Lindesmith, *supra* note 14 at p. 57.

[61] See Blum, *Dangerous Drugs*. See also *Hearings on S. 2113, S. 2114, supra* note 66, at p. 185 (statement of John L. Neurater of Chicago Police Department) and p. 224 (exhibit 46). And see references cited in notes 29–31 *supra*.

[62] Advisory Council of Judges of the National Council on Crime and Delinquency, *Narcotics Law Violations: A Policy Statement*, 1964, pp. 15–16.

[63] *Hearings on Civil Commitment and Treatment of Narcotic Addicts Before Subcommittee No. 2 of the House Judiciary Committee*, 89th Congress, 1st and 2nd Sessions, 1966, pp. 370, 376 (testimony of Myrl E. Alexander); *Proceedings,* p. 255 (statement of James V. Bennett) and p. 264 (statement of Richard A. Chappell). See also *id.* at p. 228 (statement of Senator Thomas J. Dodd), discussing a joint project of the Senate Subcommittee on Juvenile Delinquency and the Subcommittee on National Penitentiaries. In the course of that project, a questionnaire was sent to Federal district judges, Federal chief probation officers, Federal prison authorities, and U.S. Attorneys, inquiring about the effects of the mandatory minimum sentence provisions, and the elimination of probation and parole in the handling of narcotic offenders. Of the Federal prison wardens who responded, 92 percent were opposed to the mandatory minimum sentence provisions, and 97 percent were opposed to the prohibition of probation or parole. Of the responding probation officers, 83 percent were opposed to the first, and 86 percent were opposed to the second. Of the Federal judges who responded, 73 percent were opposed to the first, and 86 percent were opposed to the second. *Ibid.*

[64] The information in this paragraph was derived from unpublished statistical reports prepared by the Research and Statistics Branch of the Bureau of Prisons in 1965 and 1966.

[65] *Internal Revenue Code of 1954*, Sec. 7237(d).

[66] 18 U.S.C. Secs. 5005–5026 (1964).

[67] *New York Penal Law* Sec. 220 (effective September 1967).

[68] Cf. Eldridge, *op. cit. supra* note 66, at pp. 88–89.

[69] President's Advisory Commission on Narcotic and Drug Abuse, *Final Report*, 1963, pp. 40–42.

[70] *Senate Report No. 900,* 75th Congress, 1st Session, 1937; *House of Representatives Report No. 792,* 75th Congress, 1st Session, 1937, p. 1.

[71] *Internal Revenue Code of 1954,* Secs. 4741, 4744, 4751, 4753.

[72] *Uniform Narcotic Drug Act,* Sec. 1(14).

[73] The revenues attributable to Federal marihuana taxes (occupational tax, transfer tax, and charges for order forms) for the 5 fiscal years 1962–1966 total $418,000. By contrast, the revenues attributable to the Federal narcotic taxes (occupational tax, commodity tax, and charges for order forms) for the same period total $5,813,000. Staff interview with officials in the Reports Division, Internal Revenue Service.

[74] *Senate Report No. 900, supra* note 84 at p. 3; *House of Representatives Report No. 792, supra* note 84, at pp. 1–2.

[75] See references cited in note 28, *supra.* See also Bromberg, "Marihuana: A Psychiatric Study," *Journal of American Medical Association,* 1939, 113:4 Reichard, "Some Myths About Marihuana," *Federal Probation,* October–December 1946, 10:15; Murphy, "The Cannabis Habit: A Review of Recent Psychiatric Literature," *Bulletin on Narcotics,* January–March 1943, 15:15. And see *Hearings on S. 2113, S. 2114, S. 2152, supra* note 64, at p. 449 (testimony of Henry L. Giordano); Blum, *Dangerous Drugs.*

[76] See references cited in note 89 *supra.*

[77] *New York Medicine,* May 5, 1966, pp. 3–4.

[78] See references cited in note 89 *supra.*

[79] *Hearings on Taxation of Marihuana Before the House Ways and Means Committee,* 75th Congress, 1st Session, 1937.

[80] The New Orleans report has also been mentioned in Bromberg, "Marihuana: A Psychiatric Study," *Journal of American Medical Association,* 1939, 113:4; and Winick, "Marihuana Use by Young People," in Harms, ed., *Drug Addiction in Youth* (1965).

[81] See, e.g., Anslinger and Tompkins, *The Traffic in Narcotics* (1953), pp. 20–25; Munch, "Marihuana and Crime," *Bulletin on Narcotics,* April–June, 1966, 18:15.

[82] Murphy, *supra* note 89, at p. 15.

[83] *New York Medicine,* May 5, 1966, p. 3.

[84] *Proceedings,* p. 286.

[85] Mayor's Committee on Marihuana, *The Marihuana Problem in the City of New York: Sociological, Medical, Psychological and Pharmacological Studies* (1944).

[86] See, e.g., Anrade, "The Criminogenic Action of Cannabis (Marihuana) and Narcotics," *Bulletin on Narcotics,* October–December, 1964, 16:23; Bromberg, "Marihuana: A Psychiatric Study," *Journal of American Medical Association,* 1939, 113:4; Bromberg, "Marihuana Intoxication," *American Journal of Psychiatry,* 1934, 91:302; Bromberg and Rogers, "Marihuana and Aggressive Crime," *American Journal of Psychiatry,* 1946, 102:825; Reichard, "Some Myths about Marihuana," *supra* note 89 at pp. 17–18; Blum, *Dangerous Drugs.*

[87] Blum, *Dangerous Drugs.*

[88] *New York Medicine,* May 5, 1966, p. 4. California Narcotics Rehabilitation Advisory Council, *Second Annual Report,* 1966, p. 9.

[89] Pp. 173–174.

[90] Eddy, Halbach, Isbell, and Seevers, "Drug Dependence: Its Significance and Characteristics," *Bulletin of World Health Organization,* 1966, 32:721, 729.

[91] Goodman and Gilman, *The Pharmacological Basis of Therapeutics* (1960), p. 171; staff interview with Dr. Roger E. Mayer, Research Psychiatrist, Center for Studies of Narcotics and Drug Abuse, NIMH.

Notes

Chapter 6: The Alcohol Minority

[1] 1965 FBI *Uniform Crime Reports,* p. 117 (table 25). In 1965, 1,516,548 drunkenness arrests were reported by 4,043 agencies, embracing a total population of 125,139,000. Projections based upon these figures indicate that there were over 2 million arrests in the entire country during 1965. An undetermined number of additional arrests for drunkenness are made under disorderly conduct, vagrancy, loitering, and related statutes. See, e.g., Foote, "Vagrancy-Type Law and Its Administration," *University of Pennsylvania Law Review,* 1956, 104:603 (discussion of interchanging of statutes for like purposes); Murtagh, "Arrests for Public Intoxication," *Fordham Law Review,* 1966, 35:1–7 (description of the prior New York City practice of using a disorderly conduct statute to arrest nondisorderly inebriates.)

[2] E.g., *D. C. Code Annotated* Secs. 25–128 (1961). The D. C. statute also prohibits drinking an alcoholic beverage in public.

[3] E.g., *Wisconsin Statutes* Sec. 947.03 (1955).

[4] *Alabama Criminal Code* Secs. 14–120 (1958); *Georgia Code Ann.* Secs. 58–608 (1965).

[5] See note, "The Law on Skid Row," *Chicago-Kent Law Review,* CR:22,42 (1964) ("they are detained, whether or not their actions fit the legal criteria of 'disorderly conduct.'") *Chicago Police Department Bulletin No. 9,* March 4, 1963.

[6] *New York Penal Law* Sec. 1221 (McKinney 1944); Syracuse, New York, *Review of Ordinances,* chapter 16, sec. 5, 1961.

[7] *North Carolina General Statutes,* Secs. 14–335 (1953). See *Driver v. Hinnant,* 356 F. 2d 761 (4th Circuit, 1966) for reversal of conviction and 2-year sentence under the North Carolina statute.

[8] Statistics gathered by the Los Angeles Police Department. During 1964 there were 71,494 drunkenness arrests—47,401, of which involved 13,048 offenders. In 1955, 45,748 of the drunkenness arrests in Los Angeles involved 6,665 offenders. In 1961, 12,000 individuals accounted for approximately 30,000 of the 49,000 arrests in Atlanta, Georgia. Department of Psychiatry, Emory University School of Medicine, Alcohol Study Project 5 (unpublished 1963) (hereinafter cited as *Emory Department of Psychiatry*).

[9] *D.C. Commission on Prisons, Probation, and Parole Report* (1957), pp. 114–119.

[10] Bogue, *Skid Row in American Cities* (1963), pp. 1–4.

[11] It is often the express policy of a police department to refrain from arresting a person for drunkenness in cases in which he may be placed in a taxicab or he is with friends who are able to escort him home. See, e.g., Columbus, Ohio, *Police Department Training Bulletin,* rev. August 1958, unit 6, 1:2; President's Commission on Crime in the District of Columbia, *Report 475,* 1966, citing letter from District of Columbia Police Chief John B. Layton to President's Commission on Crime in the District of Columbia, April 1, 1966.

[12] The police make this determination by observing, *inter alia,* the apparent affluence of the inebriate. Moreover, the lack of funds for transporting will influence the determination to arrest. The result is that the poor are more likely to be arrested than the well-to-do. See President's Commission on Crime in the District of Columbia, *Report 475,* 1966. See also *Washington Daily News,* December 21, 1965, p. 5 at p. 35 (interview with precinct commanding officer: "We do tend to enforce the laws more rigidly on 14th Street than in, say, Crestwood, a better part of the precinct.")

[13] Lafave, *Arrest: The Decision to Take a Suspect into Custody* (1965), p. 441 note 13.

[14] The Atlanta Alcohol Study Project found that there are a "significant number of individuals who are arrested for public intoxication and who are not drunk at the time of arrest." *Emory Department of Psychiatry,* p. 18. Similar findings were reported in other cities: see, for example, reports by Klein, "The Criminal Law Process vs. the Public Drunkenness Offender in San Francisco," 1964 (unpublished, on file at Stanford University Institute for the Study of Human Problems), and by Nash, "Habitats of Homeless Men in Manhattan," November 1964 (unpublished, on file at Columbia University Bureau of Applied Social Research).

[15] Committee on Alcoholism Community Welfare Council of the Greater Sacramento Area, Inc., "The Alcoholic Law Offender," p. 4 (unpublished 1965). Another tank was described in a 1966 newspaper article:

"There are at least two men in each 4 x 8 cell and three in some. . . . The stench of cheap alcohol, dried blood, urine and excrement covers the cell blocks. . . . There are no lights in the cells. . . . There are no mattresses. Mattresses wouldn't last the night, a policeman explains. And with prisoners urinating all over them, they wouldn't be any good if they did last. . . ."

Hoagland, "Cell Blocks' Common Denominator: A Stench of Alcohol and Dried Blood," *Washington Post,* March 29, 1966, p. A–1, col. 3.

[16] University of Minnesota and Minneapolis Housing and Redevelopment Authority, "A General Report on the Problem of Relocating the Population of the Lower Loop Redevelopment Area," p. 170 (unpublished 1958) ("health conditions in this area are catastrophically bad"). The report provided a detailed description of illnesses which exist in skid row areas and states that the "tuberculosis rate in the lower loop is 320 times as high as the rate for the rest of the city." *Id.* at p. 170. See also Department of Psychiatry, Temple University School of Medicine, "The Men of Skid Row: A Study of Philadelphia's Homeless Man Population," p. 88 (unpublished 1960) (57% of the men reported one or more serious conditions). Bogue's study, *op. cit. supra* note 10, at pp. 222–223, depicted the great need for medical care and observed that "among the heavy drinkers, alcoholism is complicated by chronic sickness in a substantial portion of cases."

[17] One of the biggest obstacles in handling a case of drunkenness is that it is often difficult to distinguish between effects produced by alcohol or drugs and those produced by injury or illness. For instance, a person may smell of alcohol, and he may stagger and seem drunk . . . or lie unconscious in an apparent drunken stupor. Yet he may have had only a drink or two—or none at all! . . . Correctional Association of New York and International Association of Chiefs of Police, *Alcohol and Alcoholism, A Police Handbook* (1965), p. 22.

[18] "Man, 52, Dies in Court Lockup," *Washington Post,* September 5, 1965, p. A–3; "Man Detained as Drunk Dies from Pneumonia," *id.,* December 15, 1965, p. D–21, cols. 1–2; "Man, 63, Found Dead in Alexandria Jail Cell," *id.,* November 22, 1966, p. B–4, cols. 1–2. In the President's Commission on Crime in the District of Columbia, *Report 476* (1966), it was reported that "16 persons arrested for intoxication died while in police custody in 1964–1965."

[19] Stationhouse bail permits the release of defendants pending a subsequent court appearance. See generally Freed and Wald, *Bail in the United States* (1964). Outright release—with no obligation to return to court—is sometimes permitted by the police. See Lafave, *op. cit. supra* note 16, at pp. 440–442, for a variety of release systems ranging from outright police discretion to a payment

to the city of $4.35. In Detroit the police have a "golden rule" procedure which resulted in 1965 in the release of 2,383 offenders out of a total of 8,715 drunkenness arrests. In Omaha, Nebraska, the majority of offenders are released after a few hours of detention. The Omaha system includes referral to community agencies following release, in appropriate cases. The police bring some offenders to the agencies where shelter and food are provided.

[20] Bail or collateral forfeiture is common in some jurisdictions. The defendant pays $10 to $20, depending upon the stipulated amount in the jurisdiction, and he is not penalized for failing to return to court. See President's Commission on Crime in the District of Columbia, *Report 477* (1966); *Emory Department of Psychiatry*, p. 11.

[21] In Washington, D.C., for example, approximately 20,000 of the 44,218 people arrested during 1965 obtained release by forfeiting $10 collateral. President's Commission on Crime in the District of Columbia, *Report 475* (1966). In Atlanta, Georgia, approximately 20,000 of 49,805 arrests during 1961 resulted in ($15) collateral forfeitures. *Emory Department of Psychiatry*, p. 11. Those who post and forfeit collateral avoid the risk of a jail sentence.

[22] See generally Foote, *supra* note 1; Labovitz, "Some Legal Problems of Skid Row Residents," draft of report to be issued by the Diagnostic and Relocation Center, Philadelphia, Pennsylvania. These conclusions are supported by observation made in court during the early part of 1966 by Commission staff attorneys. The right of cross-examination, confrontation of the accuser, and the privilege against self-incrimination were repeatedly disregarded. In the absence of counsel the courts and prosecutors sometimes act sua sponte to assure that all defenses are asserted on behalf of the defendant. Chief Judge Green of the District of Columbia Court of General Sessions has concluded that "the court has the obligation to inject this issue [alcoholism] on its own motion when it appears likely from the evidence that the defense may be available." *District of Columbia* v. *Walters, Congressional Record*, 112:22716 (daily ed., September 22, 1966). See also *Whalem v. United States*, U.S. App. D.C. 331, 346 F.2d 812 (D.C. Cir. 1965) (en banc); *Overholser* v. *Lynch*, 109 U.S. App. D.C. 404, 288 F.2d 388 (D.C. 1961), *rev'd in part on other grounds*, 369 U.S. 705 (1962); *Pate v. Robinson*, 383 U.S. 375 (1966). With respect to the importance of prosecutors bringing potential defenses to the attention of the court, see Canon 5 of the *Canons of Professional Ethics of the American Bar Association, United States v. Ragen*, 86 F. Supp. 382, 387 (N.D., Ill., 1949) (holding the "suppression of vital evidence [to be] . . . a denial of due process"); Jackson, "The Federal Prosecutor," *Journal of American Judicial Society*, 1940, 24:18. See generally address by Peter Barton Hutt, attorney, *The Recent Court Decisions on Alcoholism: A Challenge to the North American Judges Association and Its Members*, NAJA annual meeting, Colorado Springs, Colorado, November 3, 1966, published as appendix H of President's Commission on Law Enforcement and Administration of Justice, *Task Force Report: Drunkenness* (Washington: U.S. Government Printing Office, 1967).

[23] In Portland, Oregon, for example, the first offense receives a suspended sentence, the second offense brings a 2-day jail sentence, and the fifth offense within a 12-month period brings a 6-month sentence. *The Sunday Oregonian*, April 17, 1966, p. F–4, col. 4; Oregon Mental Health Division, *Proceedings: the Alcoholic and the Court* (1963), p. 39. In Atlanta, Georgia, the fourth conviction within a 12-month period brings a fine, and the fifth conviction results in a 30-day jail sentence. *Emory Department of Psychiatry*, p. 28. A 1957 study showed that 13,146 sentences out of 15,111 in Washington, D.C., were for 30

days or less. D.C. Commission on Prisons, Probation, and Parole, *Report 106* 1957.

[24] Labovitz, *supra* note 22. This procedure was observed by the Commission staff.

[25] See Pittman and Gordon, *Revolving Door: A Study of the Chronic Police Case Inebriate* (1958), pp. 30, 125; *supra* note 11.

[26] "He is merely transported from the workhouse to the city of Washington, dumped on the streets at 14th and Independence Avenue S.W., with only the clothes on his back. He has no place to stay, no food to eat, and no job. It is ridiculous, under such circumstances, to expect any improvement in the problem of the 'skid row' alcoholic." D.C. Commission on Prisons, Probation, and Parole, *Report 110* (1957).

[27] *District of Columbia v. Strother,* Motion to Reopen Proceedings, No. 25861–66, D.C. Court of General Sessions, September 14, 1966.

[28] Some police officials told staff members of the President's Commission on Law Enforcement and Administration of Justice that the defendant charged with drunkenness is not permitted to place a telephone call upon request until a 4-hour "sobering-up" period following arrest has elapsed. Such policy would deny the use of the telephone to some innocent people and to others who would be physically able to confer with counsel. A Commission staff attorney observed the right denied to a person charged with drunkenness who was physically able to call counsel. In another case a 17-year-old youth with no prior criminal record was arrested at 10 P.M. and denied the right to telephone his parents until the end of the "sobering-up" period. Since the call had to be placed to a neighbor's home (his parents were unable to afford a telephone), he chose not to exercise his right at what he considered an unreasonable hour. He appeared in court the following morning without counsel, pleaded guilty to public intoxication, and was sentenced to 3 months in jail. His parents were not notified of his whereabouts until he arrived in the county penitentiary. They contacted an attorney who secured the youth's release pending appeal of the conviction. Transcript of proceedings, *People v. Jones,* Syracuse, New York, Police Court, September 13, 1965.

[29] See *People v. Butts,* 21 Misc. 2d 799, 804–05, 201 New York S. 2d 926, 932–33 (1960); Donigan, *Chemical Tests and the Law* (Northeastern University Traffic Institute, 1957), p. 4:

[30] See generally Foote, *supra* note 1. Observations made in court by Commission staff attorneys support this thesis. One case observed in the early part of 1966 involved an obviously indigent defendant charged with "drinking in public." The police officer testified that a bottle containing an alcoholic beverage was in the defendant's pocket. The trial judge asked the officer whether the defendant was drinking from the bottle. The officer replied that "he must have been" since the bottle was "half empty." The defendant was found guilty and fined $30. He lacked the funds to pay the fine and was compelled to serve 30 days in jail.

[31] The assignment of counsel to skid row inebriates had a profound effect on the handling of such cases in New York City. More than 95% of the defendants were acquitted after trial on disorderly conduct charges. See Murtagh, "Comments," *Inventory* 16:13,14 (North Carolina Rehabilitation Program, July–September 1966), for a discussion of the background and reasons for the program. In March 1966 there were 1,326 defendants arraigned in Social Court in New York City, of whom 1,280 were acquitted. In March 1965, in the absence of defense counsel, there were 1,590 arraignments, 1,259 guilty pleas and only 325

acquittals." Address by Hon. Bernard Botein, Presiding Justice, Appeals Division, 1st Department Superior Court, April 22, 1966, in Governor Rockefeller's Conference on Crime (1966), p. 149; *New York Times,* April 23, 1966, p. 14, col. 4. Court records show that in April and May 1966, 1,838 of 2,103 defendants in New York City's Social Court were acquitted. As a result of the high acquittal rate Chief Judge John M. Murtagh directed court clerks not to draw complaints on nondisorderly drunkenness. From June 1, 1966, through September 30, 1966, a total of 189 cases was brought to Social Court, of which 161 resulted in convictions.

The effect of the assignment of counsel was to reduce the number of arrests in New York City's skid row. The appearance of many more inebriated people on skid row seemed to make the underlying public health problem more visible, and the establishment of alternate facilities became more urgent. See "Derelicts Dislike Non-Arrest Policy," *New York Times,* July 29, 1966, p. 27, col. 8.

[32] See President's Commission on Crime in the District of Columbia, *Report 500* (1966), in which the following recommendation was made: "As long as drunkenness offenders remain subject to penal sanctions, the Commission believes that they should be provided with counsel."

[33] The extent to which drunkenness offenses interfere with other police activity is illustrated in Washington, D.C., where the uniformed tactical police force, a special unit used "to combat serious crime," devotes a substantial amount of time to the handling of drunks. *The Washington Daily News,* December 1, 1965, p. 5. During one 9-month sample period, the tactical force made 14,542 arrests, of which 6,363 were for drunkenness. Statistics supplied by Washington, D.C., Police Department to President's Commission on Crime in the District of Columbia.

[34] One study showed that in August 1962, 63% of all inmates in the Monroe County Penitentiary (Rochester, New York) were committed for drunkenness. Rochester Bureau of Municipal Research, *Man on the Periphery, Report on the Monroe County Penitentiary,* 1964, p. 29.

[35] See *Emory Department of Psychiatry,* p. 51.

Chapter 7: Prostitution and Pornography

[1] Comd. 3231 (1928).

[2] See paragraph 230.

[3] England and Wales: Sexual Offenses Act, 1956, Section 30. Scotland: Immoral Traffic (Scotland) Act, 1902, Section 1 (1) and (3).

[4] England and Wales: Sexual Offenses Act, 1956, Section 31. Scotland: Criminal Law Amendment Act, 1913, Section 7 (4).

[5] England and Wales: Sexual Offenses Act, 1956, Section 42. Scotland: Immoral Traffic (Scotland) Act, 1902, Section 1(2).

[6] Hall, "Prostitution: A Survey and a Challenge," in Williams and Norgate (1933), p. 40.

[7] The Report of the Traffic and Distribution Panel of the Commission provides a more thorough discussion and documentation of this overview.

[8] The Report of the Effects Panel of the Commission provides a more thorough discussion and documentation of this overview.

[9] The study was conducted by Response Analysis Corporation of Princeton, New Jersey, and the Institute of Survey Research of Temple University, Philadelphia, Pennsylvania.

[10] See also the Preface of the Commission's Report.

[11] Commissioners G. William Jones, Joseph T. Klapper, and Morris A. Lipton

believe "that in the interest of precision a distinction should be made between two types of statements which occur in this Report. One type, to which we subscribe, is that research to date does not indicate that a causal relationship exists between exposure to erotica and the various social ills to which the research has been addressed. There are, however, also statements to the effect that 'no evidence' exists, and we believe these should more accurately read 'no reliable evidence.' Occasional aberrant findings, some of very doubtful validity, are noted and discussed in the Report of the Effects Panel. In our opinion, none of these, either individually or in sum, are of sufficient merit to constitute reliable evidence or to alter the summary conclusion that the research to date does not indicate a causal relationship."

[12] The Report of the Legal Panel of the Commission provides a more thorough discussion and documentation of this overview.

[13] A description of the history of obscenity prohibitions is set forth in the Legal Panel Report.

[14] Two other statutes impose supplementary regulations. 39 U.S.C. section 3006 (Numbered 39 U.S.C. section 4006 prior to the 1970 Postal Reorganization Act.) authorizes the Postmaster General to block incoming mail to persons using the mails to solicit remittances for obscene matter. 47 U.S.C. section 503(b)(E) imposes civil penalties upon prohibited broadcasts of obscene matter.

[15] This Act was numbered 39 U.S.C. section 4009 prior to the 1970 Postal Reorganization Act.

[16] The cost to the Post Office Department in fiscal 1968 is estimated by the department as approximately $1 million—$.75 million allocated to the Postal Inspection Service, which attempts to detect violations, and $.25 million allocated to the General Counsel's Office. The cost to the Customs Bureau in fiscal 1968 is estimated by that bureau at approximately $1 million. Neither the F.B.I. nor the Justice Department supplied cost figures to the Commission. Other data supplied by the Justice Department indicate significant enforcement activity on the part of the F.B.I., Justice and several United States Attorneys' offices throughout the country of the statutes within their jurisdictions. The Commission believes that these costs would aggregate at least $1 million per year.

To the foregoing total of about $3 million must be added the costs to federal courts and the cost to the Federal Communications Commission. In addition, obscenity enforcement activities on the part of at least two of the Departments—Post Office and Justice—have increased substantially since fiscal 1968.

[17] Several of these statutes contain narrowly drawn exemption provisions such as exemptions for persons distributing materials in the course of scientific or artistic pursuits.

Chapter 8: The Convicted Minority

[1] NCCD. *Standards and Guides for the Detention of Children and Youth.* 2nd ed., 1961.

[2] This figure includes 5 jurisdictions, each of which has more than 1 detention home, and a number of small jurisdictions in which no children are detained; it does not include 63 jurisdictions known to use detention homes in other counties.

[3] *Report of Attorney General's Committee on Poverty and the Administration of Criminal Justice,* p. 69.

[4] See "Children in Jail," a careful onsite documentation, in *Parade* magazine, Nov. 17, 1963.

Notes

[5] NCCD surveys show that in approximately half the commitments to State training schools, probation had not been attempted at all or had been only nominal. That is, there was no recorded attempt to work with the child and parents around the problems which resulted in his delinquency. In many instances there was failure to investigate other more appropriate placement possibilities.

[6] States which do not operate centralized juvenile aftercare programs are Alabama, Arkansas, Kansas, Maryland, Mississippi, New Mexico, North Carolina, North Dakota, Pennsylvania, and Virginia.

[7] Lee Silverstein, "In Defense of the Poor" (Chicago: American Bar Foundation, 1965), p. 123.

[8] Myrl E. Alexander, "Current Concepts in Corrections" (Tacoma, Wash.: Pacific Lutheran University, 1960), p. 7.

[9] Harry Subin, "Criminal Justice in a Metropolitan Court" (Washington: U.S. Government Printing Office, 1966), pp. 33–36.

[10] Data taken from reports submitted by Malcolm Matheson, a task force consultant who conducted the study and developed other materials for this chapter.

[11] Robert L. Smith, "Probation Study" (Sacramento: California Board of Corrections, Sept. 1965).

[12] "Bail and Summons: 1965," *Institute on the Operation of Pretrial Release Projects*, New York, October 14–15, and *Justice Conference on Bail and Remands in Custody, London, November 27, 1965* (Washington: U.S. Department of Justice and Vera Foundation, Inc., 1966), foldout sheet.

[13] *Crime and Delinquency in California, 1965* (Sacramento: California Department of Justice, 1966), p. 131.

[14] Data supplied by the Sheriff's Office, Multnomah County, Oregon.

[15] Data supplied by the District of Columbia Department of Corrections.

[16] Freed and Wald, *op. cit.*, pp. 40–41.

[17] These projections are drawn from the special study completed by R. Christensen, of the *Commission's Task Force on Science and Technology*, which is described in appendix B of this report. The projections, together with the 1965 data supplied by the National Survey of Corrections and special tabulations provided by the Federal Bureau of Prisons and the Administrative Office of the U.S. Courts, indicate the following: the number of adults in jails and prisons and on parole in 1965 was 475,042; for 1975 it is projected as 560,000. There were 459,140 adults on probation in 1965; for 1975 the number is projected as 693,000. The population of juvenile training schools and parole programs in 1965 was 123,256; for 1975 it is projected as 210,000. The number of juveniles on probation in 1965 was 224,948, and for 1975 the number is projected as 378,000.

[18] Paul W. Tappan, *Crime, Justice, and Correction* (New York: McGraw-Hill Book Co., 1960), pp. 546–549.

[19] U.S. Department of Justice, Bureau of Prisons, *National Prisoner Statistics: Prisoners in State and Federal Institutions for Adult Felons, 1965* (Washington: The Bureau, 1966), table 1.

[20] See chapter 8 by Clarence Schrag and chapters 4 and 7 by Richard H. McCleery in Donald R. Cressey, ed., *The Prison: Studies in Institutional Organization and Change* (New York: Holt, Rinehart and Winston, 1961). See also John Irwin and Donald R. Cressey, "Thieves, Convicts and the Inmate Culture" in Howard S. Becker, ed., *The Other Side: Perspective on Deviance* (New York: Free Press, 1964), pp. 225–245.

[21] See, for example, Clifford R. Shaw, Henry D. McKay, and others, *Delinquency Areas, a Study of the Distribution of School Truants, Juvenile Delin-*

quents, and Adult Offenders in Chicago (Chicago: University of Chicago Press, 1929).

[22] Edwin H. Sutherland and Donald R. Cressey, *Principles of Criminology* (7th ed., Philadelphia: J. B. Lippincott Co., 1966), pp. 77–100.

[23] Richard A. Cloward and Lloyd E. Ohlin, *Delinquency and Opportunity* (Glencoe, Ill., Free Press, 1960).

[24] See Albert K. Cohen, *Delinquent Boys: The Culture of the Gang* (Glencoe, Ill.: Free Press, 1955).

[25] See generally Cohen, "Legal Norms in Corrections" (paper prepared for the President's Commission on Law Enforcement and Administration of Justice). Much of the material in this chapter is drawn from this paper.

[26] Kadish, "Legal Norm and Discretion in the Police and Sentencing Processes," 75 Harv. L. Rev. 904, 923 (1962).

[27] *Id* at 930–931.

[28] *Olmstead v. United States*, 277 U.S. 438, 479 (1928) (dissenting opinion).

[29] See the discussion of the juvenile justice system in chapter 3 of the Commission's General Report.

[30] See generally Barkin, "The Emergence of Correctional Law and the Awareness of the Rights of the Convicted," 45 Neb. L. Rev. 669 (1966); Note, "Constitutional Rights of Prisoners: The Developing Law," 110 U. Pa. L. Rev. 985 (1962); Note, "Beyond the Ken of the Courts: A Critique of Judicial Refusal to Review the Complaints of Convicts," 72 Yale L.J. 506 (1963).

[31] *United States* v. *Muniz*, 374 U.S. 150 (1963).

[32] *Cleggett v. Pate*, 229 F. Supp. 818, 821–22 (N.D. Ill. 1964).

[33] In re Riddle, 22 Cal. Rptr. 472, 478, 372 P. 2d 304, 308–09 (1962).

[34] *Brabson* v. *Wilkins*, 45 Misc. 2d 286, 256 N.Y.S. 2d 693 (Sup. Ct. 1965) (involving correspondence with counsel); *Johnson* v. *Avery*, 252 F. Supp. 783 (M.D. Tenn. 1966) (appeal taken) (involving prison rule prohibiting one inmate from drafting legal pleadings for another).

[35] *Bailleaux* v. *Holmes*, 177 F. Supp. 361 (D. Ore. 1959), *rev'd sub nom. Hatfield* v. *Bailleaux*, 290 F. 632 (9th Cir.) *cert. denied.* 368 U.S. 862 (1961).

[36] See Sklar, "Law and Practice in Probation and Parole Revocation Hearings," 55 J. Crim. L., C. & P.S. 175, 176, 177 (1964); Kadish, "The Advocate and the Expert—Counsel in the Peno-Correctional Process," 45 Minn. L. Rev. 803, 813–14 (1961).

[37] Obviously the legislative scheme will determine such questions as when the offender has a right to a hearing and whether he has a right to more than one. The discussion here is focused on the typical situation in which, after serving a portion of his sentence, the offender becomes eligible for parole.

[38] The American Law Institute's Model Penal Code provides that the prisoner is entitled to the assistance of counsel in preparing for the parole hearing, but apparently the board need not permit counsel to appear at the hearing. An earlier draft expressly permitted counsel to appear at the hearing. Model Penal Code § 305.7, comments (Proposed Official Draft, 1962).

[39] The Commission's recommendation regarding the disclosure of presentence reports is discussed in Chapter 5 of the General Report, pp. 144–145. The issues are discussed in more detail in Chapter 2 of the Administration of Justice Task Force volume.

[40] The Bureau of Prisons' policy statement on the withholding, forfeiture, and restoration of good time (No. 7400.6, issued December 1, 1966), provides fairly elaborate procedures for the forfeiture of good time, but permits the withholding of good time creditable for the single month during which the violation occurs without such procedures.

Notes

[41] *Memphis* v. *Rhay, Walking* v. *Rhay*, Nos. 424, 734, 1966 term.

[42] See Sklar, "Law and Practice in Probation and Parole Revocation Hearings," 55 J. Crim. L., C. & P.S. 175, 176–77 (1964).

[43] *Id.* at 191–92.

[44] Offenders on suspended sentence are generally dealt with in the same manner as probationers where revocation is threatened. Their rights—like the probationer's—may turn on whether the imposition or the execution of sentence has been suspended. If sentence has not yet been imposed, they are ordinarily granted a fuller hearing.

[45] Sklar, *supra* note 18 at 193.

[46] *McCoy* v. *Harris*, 108 Utah 407, 410, 160 P. 2d 721, 722 (1945).

[47] Of course, where statutes do not give the offender a right to credit, it is often possible for the judge or the parole board to exercise their discretion to give credit. This is always true where the judge has suspended imposition of sentence.

[48] The Model Penal Code (Proposed Official Draft, 1962) is more solicitous of the probationer than the parolee. For example, on probation revocation the defendant has a right to be represented by counsel, while on parole revocation he is only allowed to advise with retained counsel. Compare § 301.4 with § 305.15.

[49] See generally Note, "Civil Disabilities of Felons," 53 Va. L. Rev. 403 (1967).

This chapter discusses civil disabilities and disqualifications imposed through legislative, judicial or administrative action. Chapter 3 discusses limitations, both private and official, on offenders ability to secure employment.

[50] See generally Federal Probation Officers Association, "A Compilation of State and Federal Statutes Relating to Civil Rights of Persons Convicted of Crime" (1960); Cozart, "Civil Rights and the Criminal Offender," 80 Fed. Prob. 3 (1966); Tappan, "The Legal Rights of Prisoners," 293 Annals 99 (1954); Note, "The Effect of State Statutes on the Civil Rights of Convicts," 47 Minn. L. Rev. 835 (1963); Comment, "The Rights of Prisoners While Incarcerated," 15 Buffalo L. Rev. 397 (1965).

[51] Under civil death statutes the life prisoner, in addition to the above disabilities, lost the right to hold property (it was distributed as if he were dead), his marriage might be automatically dissolved, and his children adopted without need for his consent. Such statutes are, happily, almost extinct today and are therefore not discussed here.

[52] The American Law Institute's Model Penal Code provides that "a person who is convicted of a crime shall be disqualified * * * from voting in a primary or election if and only so long as he is committed under a sentence of imprisonment * * *." Model Penal Code § 306.3 (Proposed Official Draft, 1962) [hereinafter cited as Model Penal Code].

[53] If it is found necessary to provide for some mandatory disqualifications, then the kinds of convictions and sentences resulting in such disqualifications should be narrowly defined and disqualification should ordinarily be limited to relatively short periods of time. Thus only certain relevant convictions will bar a person from holding Federal office. Similarly, Federal law provides that certain felony convictions bar a person from holding certain union offices within 5 years from the date of conviction. Labor Management Reporting and Disclosure Act of 1959, 29 U.S.C. § 504(a), 73 Stat. 519, 536–37.

[54] See Model Penal Code § 306.2; ALI Proceedings 299–300, 305 (1961).

[55] Compare Model Penal Code § 306.3(2), providing that a person convicted

of "a crime" be "disqualified * * * from serving as a juror until he has *satisfied his sentence.*" [Emphasis added.]

[56] The Model Penal Code's provisions seem appropriate. See, *e.g.,* § 306.4(2): *"Upon the order of the Court to Warden or other administrative head of an institution* in which a prisoner is confined *shall arrange for the production of the prisoner to testify* at the place designated in the order. Such order shall be issued whenever the Court is satisfied that the testimony of the prisoner is required in a judicial or administrative proceeding and that the ends of justice can not be satisfied by taking his deposition at the institution where he is confined." [Emphasis added.]

[57] See Model Penal Code § 306.5, Appointment of Agent, Attorney-in-Fact or Trustee for Prisoner: (1) *"A person confined* under a sentence of imprisonment *shall have the same right to appoint an agent, attorney-in-fact or trustee to act in his behalf with respect to his property or economic interests as if he were not so confined.* (2) *Upon the application of a person confined* or about to be confined under a sentence of imprisonment, *the Court* [insert appropriate court of record] of the county where the prisoner resided at the time of sentence or where the sentence was imposed *may appoint a trustee to safeguard his property and economic interests* during the period of his confinement." [Emphasis added.]

[58] Calif. Bus. and Prof. Code §§ 2685(d), 2761(f), 6576, 7211.9(d); see Note, 14 Stan L. Rev. 533, 541 (1962).

[59] Barron, "Business and Professional Licensing—California, as a Representative Example," 18 Stan. L. Rev. 640, 654–57 (1966).

[60] See *id.* at 664, suggesting that licensing power be removed from quasi-private agencies and entrusted to official agencies. Compare suggestion in Note, 15 Hastings L.J. 355, 359 (1964), that the solution to the problem of narrowly oriented professional boards might be to remove the power of reinstatement from them and place it with the court having power to grant certificates of rehabilitation.

[61] See, *e.g.,* Amer. Correctional Assoc., "Manual of Correctional Standards" 272 (1966); Tappan, "Crime, Justice and Correction" 428–29 (1960).

[62] See Tappan, "The Legal Rights of Prisoners," 293 Annals 99, 102–05 (1954); Tappan, "Crime, Justice and Correction" 428 (1960).

[63] Compare the position of the National Council on Crime and Delinquency in its Standard Probation and Parole Act:

"Dispositions other than commitment to an institution, and such commitments which are revoked within sixty days, shall not entail the loss by the defendant of any civil rights" (§ 12); "Such discharge [discharge from parole], and the discharge of a prisoner who has served his term of imprisonment, shall have the effect of restoring all civil rights lost by operation of law upon commitment, and the certification of discharge shall so state" (§ 27).

[64] Thus the Labor Management Reporting and Disclosure Act of 1959 prohibits persons convicted of certain crimes from being eligible for certain union offices for a period of 5 years from the date of conviction, but provides that this prohibition is terminated if the Governor grants a certificate of restoration, or the U.S. Board of Parole certifies eligibility to hold office. 29 U.S.C. § 504(a)(2) (A) & (B), 73 Stat. 519, 536–37.

[65] See Model Penal Code § 306.6(2); A.L.I. Proceedings 312 (1961).

[66] See Model Penal Code § 306.6 (1); (3)(a), (d)—Order Removing Disqualifications or Disabilities; Vacation of conviction; Effect of Order of Removal or Vacation.

"(1) In the cases specified in this subsection *the Court may order that* so long as the defendant is not convicted of another crime, *the judgment shall not there-after constitute a conviction for the purpose of any disqualification or disability imposed by law* because of the conviction of a crime."

"(3) An order entered under subsection (1) or (2) of this section: (a) 1 as only prospective operation *and does not require the restoration of the defendant to any office, employment or position forfeited or lost* in accordance with this article. . . . (d) *Does not preclude proof of the conviction as evidence of the commission of the crime, whenever the fact of its commission is relevant to the exercise of the discretion of a court, agency or official authorized to pass upon the competency* of the defendant to perform a function or to exercise a right or privilege which such court, agency or official is empowered to deny, *except that in such case the court, agency or official shall also give due weight to the is-suance of the order."* [Emphasis added.]

[67] See Nussbaum, "First Offenders—A Second Chance" 26–27 (1956) (propos-ing that 5 years after the date of discharge by probation or suspended sentence, or after the date of release from incarceration, first offenders receive total absolu-tion—"in very aspect of his activities and interests of a noncriminal nature, he shall have the absolute right to affirm that he has never been arrested or con-victed of any past crime or offense").

See also N.C.C.D. Model Act (1962) (in 8 Crime and Delinquency 97, 100 (1962), providing for discretionary power in judge to expunge records:

"In any application for employment, license, or other civil right or privilege, or any appearance as a witness, a person may be questioned about previous original record only in language such as the following: 'Have you ever been arrested for or convicted of a crime which has not been canceled by a court?'"

Compare Model Penal Code § 306.6(3)(f):

"An order entered under subsection (1) or (2) of this section, does not justify a defendant in stating that he has not been convicted of a crime, unless he also calls attention to the order."

Under Nussbaum's scheme, even after a first offender's record has been "totally expunged," licensing boards would retain the right to consider such convictions in determining fitness for reinstatement. Nussbaum, "First Offenders—A Second Chance" 26–27 (1956).